THE BLACKWELL ENCYCLOPEDIA OF MANAGEMENT

ENTREPRENEURSHIP

THE BLACKWELL ENCYCLOPEDIA OF MANAGEMENT

SECOND EDITION

Encyclopedia Editor: **Cary L. Cooper**
Advisory Editors: **Chris Argyris and William H. Starbuck**

THE BLACKWELL ENCYCLOPEDIA OF MANAGEMENT

SECOND EDITION

ENTREPRENEURSHIP

Edited by
Michael A. Hitt and
R. Duane Ireland
Texas A&M University

Blackwell
Publishing

BLACKWELL PUBLISHING
350 Main Street, Malden, MA 02148-5020, USA
108 Cowley Road, Oxford OX4 1JF, UK
550 Swanston Street, Carlton, Victoria 3053, Australia

The Blackwell Encyclopedia of Management
First published 1997 by Blackwell Publishers Ltd
Published in paperback in 1999 by Blackwell Publishers Ltd
This volume published with the Second Edition in 2005 by Blackwell Publishing Ltd

Library of Congress Cataloging-in-Publication Data

The Blackwell encyclopedia of management. Entrepreneurship /
edited by Michael A. Hitt and R. Duane Ireland.
p. cm.—(The Blackwell encyclopedia of management ; v. 3)
Includes bibliographical references and index.
ISBN 1-4051-1650-1 (hardcover : alk. paper)
1. Entrepreneurship—Dictionaries. 2. Management—Dictionaries.
I. Hitt, Michael A. II. Ireland, R. Duane. III. Blackwell Publishing
Ltd. IV. Title: Entrepreneurship. V. Series.
HD30.15.B455 2005 vol. 3
[HB615]
658′.003 s—dc22
[338′.04′03]
2004004342

ISBN for the 12-volume set 0-631-23317-2

A catalogue record for this title is available from the British Library.

Set in 9.5 on 11pt Ehrhardt
by Kolam Information Services Pvt. Ltd, Pondicherry, India
Printed and bound in the United Kingdom
by TJ International, Padstow, Cornwall

The publisher's policy is to use permanent paper from mills that operate a sustainable forestry policy, and which has been
manufactured from pulp processed using acid-free and elementary chlorine-free practices. Furthermore, the publisher
ensures that the text paper and cover board used have met acceptable environmental accreditation standards.

For further information on
Blackwell Publishing, visit our website:
www.blackwellpublishing.com

Contents

Preface

This volume focuses on the young but maturing field of entrepreneurship, which in recent years has grown in interest for academics, students, and practitioners. The number of universities offering entrepreneurship courses and majors continues to increase, partly because of the interest among students. Likewise, scholars are engaging in a greater amount of research to address significant questions in the field of entrepreneurship. Because of the importance of entrepreneurship to economic development and job creation, politicians and governments are showing an enhanced interest in the topic.

Thus, the development of this volume is timely. Top international scholars, who examined critical research questions in the field, have prepared explanations of 90 important entrepreneurship concepts. Importantly, each scholar's work is grounded in the theory and research of entrepreneurship and related disciplines. Varying in their length, each explanation is concise, yet comprehensive. The results should be valuable for students, researchers, teachers, and practitioners.

A total of 110 people wrote these presentations, each of which was carefully developed and reviewed for scholarly accuracy. We are indebted to the fine scholars who lent their expertise to produce these high quality discussions. The volume is robust with these rich descriptions. They should facilitate learning about the entrepreneurship field and serve as a catalyst and support for research. We are pleased to present this volume to you and hope that it facilitates your work and provides a support base for the continuing development of entrepreneurship teaching, research, and practice.

Michael A. Hitt
R. Duane Ireland

About the Editors

Contributors

Allan Afuah
University of Michigan

David Ahlstrom
Chinese University of Hong Kong

Gautam Ahuja
University of Michigan

Matthew Allen
Cornell University

Stephen A. Allen
Babson College

Sharon A. Alvarez
Ohio State University

Raphael Amit
University of Pennsylvania

Anjali Bakhru
City University

Charles E. Bamford
University of Richmond

Jay B. Barney
Ohio State University

Robert A. Baron
Rensselaer Polytechnic Institute

William C. Bogner
Georgia State University

Candida G. Brush
Boston University

Garry D. Bruton
Texas Christian University

Andrew Burrows
University of Nottingham

S. Michael Camp
Ohio State University

Nancy M. Carter
University of St. Thomas

S. Trevis Certo
Texas A&M University

Ming-Jer Chen
University of Virginia

James J. Chrisman
Mississippi State University

Jess H. Chua
University of Calgary

Russell Coff
Emory University

Christopher J. Collins
Cornell University

Joseph E. Coombs
University of Richmond

Arnold C. Cooper
Purdue University

Jeffrey G. Covin
Indiana University

Catherine M. Daily
Indiana University

Dan R. Dalton
Indiana University

Richard D'Aveni
Dartmouth College

Per Davidsson
Jonkping University

Thomas J. Dean
University of Colorado at Boulder

Julio De Castro
Instituto De Empresa

David L. Deeds
Case Western Reserve University

Gregory G. Dess
University of Texas at Dallas

Timothy B. Folta
Purdue University

Robert C. Ford
University of Central Florida

Vance H. Fried
Oklahoma State University

Gerard George
University of Wisconsin-Madison

K. Matthew Gilley
Oklahoma State University

Javier Gimeno
INSEAD

Mary Ann Glynn
Emory University

Robert M. Grant
Georgetown University

Patricia G. Greene
Babson College

Anil K. Gupta
University of Maryland

Jeffrey S. Harrison
University of Richmond

Troy Harting
University of Virginia

Robert L. Heneman
Ohio State University

Kurt A. Heppard
United States Air Force Academy

Michael A. Hitt
Texas A&M University

Ha Hoang
INSEAD

Frank Hoy
University of Texas at El Paso

George P. Huber
University of Texas at Austin

Andrew C. Inkpen
Thunderbird, Garvin School of International
Management

R. Duane Ireland
Texas A&M University

Franz Kellermanns
Mississippi State University

Donald F. Kuratko
Ball State University

David Lei
Southern Methodist University

Andy Lockett
University of Nottingham

Michael Lounsbury
Cornell University

G. T. Lumpkin
University of Illinois at Chicago

Patricia P. McDougall
Indiana University

Rita Gunther McGrath
Columbia University

Patrick G. Maggitti
University of Maryland

Jeffrey A. Martin
University of Texas at Austin

G. Dale Meyer
University of Colorado at Boulder

Steven C. Michael
University of Illinois

Morgan P. Miles
Georgia Southern University

C. Chet Miller
Wake Forest University

Danny Miller
HEC Montreal

Michael Morris
Syracuse University

Donald O. Neubaum
University of Central Florida

Benjamin M. Oviatt
Georgia State University

Antoaneta Petkova
University of Maryland

J. William Petty
Baylor University

Michael D. Pfarrer
University of Maryland

Roberto Ragozzino
Ohio State University

Abdul A. Rasheed
University of Texas at Arlington

Stuart Reed
University of Washington

Jeffrey J. Reuer
University of North Carolina at Chapel Hill

Violina Rindova
University of Maryland

Frank T. Rothaermel
Georgia Tech

Michael D. Santoro
Lehigh University

Saras D. Sarasvathy
University of Maryland

Paul J. H. Schoemaker
University of Pennsylvania

Claudia Bird Schoonhoven
University of California-Irvine

Matthew Semadeni
University of South Carolina

Pramodita Sharma
Wilfrid Laurier University

Dean A. Shepherd
University of Colorado at Boulder

Donald Siegel
Rensselaer Polytechnic Institute

Mark Simon
Oakland University

Dennis P. Slevin
University of Pittsburgh

Ken G. Smith
University of Maryland

Scott Snell
Cornell University

Lloyd P. Steier
University of Alberta

Judith W. Tansky
Ohio State University

PuayKhoon Toh
University of Michigan

Deniz Ucbasaran
University of Nottingham

Sankaran Venkataraman
University of Virginia

K. Mark Weaver
Rowan University

Paul Westhead
University of Nottingham

Johan Wiklund
Stockholm School of Economics

Robert Wiltbank
University of Washington

Mike Wright
University of Nottingham

Xaoli Yin
Purdue University

JiFeng Yu
Georgia State University

Andrew Zacharakis
Babson College

Shaker A. Zahra
Babson College

Zhe Zhang
University of Central Florida

Jing Zhou
Rice University

Christoph Zott
INSEAD

A

absorptive capacity and entrepreneurship

Shaker A. Zahra and Gerard George

Ideas for entrepreneurial activities do not necessarily reside within a firm's boundaries. Firms source their ideas and opportunities for entrepreneurial businesses from their competitors or from related industries. Organizations seeking to nurture entrepreneurial activities need to learn about new ideas at their formative stages, understand the strategic implications for their businesses, and creatively assimilate these ideas into their operations. The infusion of new ideas stimulates employee thinking, especially the possibility of combining them with the firm's resources, knowledge, and capabilities. Infusion of knowledge may fuel discordant opinions on strategy, but may also form the basis for the creation of combinative knowledge, which is at the core of innovation and venture creation.

KNOWLEDGE AND ENTREPRENEURSHIP

Entrepreneurial firms use different approaches to acquire knowledge. Many firms invest in environmental scanning activities, carefully monitoring and analyzing trends in their industry and elsewhere. Environmental scanning allows companies to identify changing technological, social, political, and economic trends that could affect their businesses. This information is also useful in defining a firm's business and its strategy. The information gleaned from scanning activities, however, is rarely sufficient to develop specific capabilities in a competitive niche. Firms invest in research and development (R&D) activities to build these capabilities to enhance innovation. Organizations also invest in start-up firms inside and outside their industries, hoping to learn more about technological trends and how to build the skills necessary to

compete. Firms join strategic alliances and technology consortia, with the intent of learning from their competitors and partners. Some firms use acquisitions as a mechanism to access competencies from other companies in order to renew their existing operations or venture into new arenas.

DEFINITION AND DIMENSIONS OF ABSORPTIVE CAPACITY

Firms are not assured of significant benefits from their investments in alliances, acquisitions, or other activities aimed at bringing new knowledge into their operations. Structural and cultural factors act as barriers to ideas developed elsewhere; ideas that are often viewed with skepticism and hostility and therefore resisted. Organizations may lack the requisite absorptive capacity, defined as the ability to identify and exploit knowledge within organizational boundaries (Cohen and Levinthal, 1990). Zahra and George (2002) suggested that absorptive capacity is a set of capabilities, composed of routines and resources, to acquire, assimilate, transform, and exploit knowledge. It is important to understand how this multiplicity of capabilities underlying a firm's absorptive capacity may influence entrepreneurial behavior.

Identification. Entrepreneurial activities require breadth and depth of knowledge content pertinent to markets, competitors, customers, and technologies. Organizations promoting entrepreneurial activities have to identify the most useful knowledge for their operations. Identifying this knowledge is a difficult task because competitors attempt to isolate their intellectual property from imitation. Even though competitive intelligence can help in this process, closeness to other companies is crucial to learning and spotting new knowledge, which tends to be tacit in nature. Tacit knowledge is difficult to articulate or share with others. Even when knowledge is explicit, it is embedded in competitor operations and systems, making it difficult for outsiders to identify and imitate. Consequently, entrepreneurial companies actively join alliances and research consortia hoping to gain a first-hand understanding of emerging and possibly radical technologies.

Comprehension. Knowledge is difficult to observe and understand. This is particularly true in the case of tacit knowledge that people acquire by doing or developing as they explore new ways of doing things. Tacit knowledge is difficult to verbalize and those who possess it are often unaware of its existence. This tacitness poses major challenges for entrepreneurial firms that seek to internalize new knowledge from the outside. These firms cannot comprehend easily externally generated knowledge, because it might embody unique characteristics and codes that cannot be deciphered or understood. Organizations combine their knowledge in unique ways, thereby constraining others' ability to unbundle their products and technologies. Alternatively, the recipient firm may not have the knowledge or skills to comprehend the information it has received. Cohen and Levinthal (1990) point out that those companies with even modest amounts of knowledge in a given field are better adept at comprehending incoming knowledge in that area. This is why some entrepreneurial companies devote resources to acquire this knowledge. For example, they send their technical and managerial personnel to professional conferences and encourage them to read new publications inside and outside their field. Firms may also create systems that diffuse knowledge about changing paradigms (e.g., new research findings) and share such information with their employees.

Assimilation. Understanding and comprehending incoming knowledge sets the stage for assimilating this knowledge into the firm's operations. Assimilation means that incoming knowledge becomes an integral part of the firm's knowledge base through routinization and codification. Assimilation of incoming knowledge is difficult

because of the structural, cognitive, and political barriers that might exist in the recipient firm. The firm's formal structure often limits its search for new knowledge, keeping focused on knowledge that is consistent with what the firm already knows. Incoming knowledge may disrupt the existing frames of reference and mental models that prevail within the firm about the industry and competition. If incoming knowledge has the potential to change the firm's strategy, it could alter the patterns of resource allocations and corresponding power bases in the organization. Managers, therefore, may discard threatening knowledge or that which does not conform to their expectations. Entrepreneurial firms create task forces to identify best practices by competitors (or even from other industries) and share them with employees. They also integrate different types of knowledge to glean insights that could be leveraged to develop new products, systems, business models, and even businesses. Knowledge sharing and integration (Zahra, Ireland, and Hitt, 2000) help firms to assimilate incoming knowledge.

Exploitation. Entrepreneurial firms excel in harvesting the knowledge embedded in their operations to capture and exploit new knowledge by building new products, goods, and services. These firms also use this knowledge in building dynamic capabilities that serve as the foundation for their competitive advantage. Dynamic capabilities refer to the set of integrated capabilities for organizational change and renewal that a firm can deploy to achieve differentiation from its rivals. Keeping these capabilities current requires the firm to learn new skills. This type of exploratory learning expands the firm's cognitive map and exposes it to new ideas that may not produce immediate financial gains (McGrath, 2001). Yet this exploratory learning is important for successful long-term performance.

Zahra and George (2002) suggest that companies often fail to exploit their absorptive capacity to the fullest. One reason is the tendency among some companies to emphasize certain types of skills over others in their pursuit of a competitive advantage. As a result, some skills are overused while others are underutilized or even overlooked. This might happen because managers become comfortable and familiar with certain types of knowledge and not others. Further, because absorptive capacity usually embodies multiple types of knowledge at different levels of currency and efficacy, managers cannot always synchronize the use of all knowledge they possess.

NURTURING AND UPGRADING ABSORPTIVE CAPACITY

Managers define and invest in the development and deployment of capabilities to ensure the continued survival and performance of firms. Such investments require a thorough understanding of industry and market reality, as well as a vision of growth by leveraging the firm's technology. Effectively developing and deploying the routines to acquire, assimilate, transform, and exploit knowledge to create value is at the core of a superior absorptive capacity. Entrepreneurial firms generate value by entering new business niches, creating technological breakthroughs, and by reinvigorating their operations. They do so by investing in building and strengthening their absorptive capacity to keep it current, efficient, and dynamic.

Bibliography

Cohen, W. M. and Levinthal, D. A. (1990). Absorptive capacity: A new perspective on learning and innovation. *Administrative Science Quarterly*, 35: 128–52.

McGrath, R. G. (2001). Exploratory learning, innovative capacity, and managerial oversight. *Academy of Management Journal*, 44: 118–31.

Zahra, S. A. and George, G. (2002). Absorptive capacity: A review, reconceptualization and extension. *Academy of Management Review*, 27: 185–203.

Zahra, S. A., Ireland, R. D., and Hitt, M. A. (2000). International expansion by new venture firms: International diversity, mode of market entry, technological learning, and performance. *Academy of Management Journal*, 43: 925–50.

Austrian economics

Sharon A. Alvarez

Traditional Austrian economics represented a subdiscipline in the field that departed from traditional neoclassic economics about the time of the introduction of the Walrasian general equilibrium model. Traditional Austrian economists do not believe that it is legitimate for markets to begin in equilibrium and even less plausible that once markets are in disequilibrium that they can achieve equilibrium. Between the 1930s and early 1950s there was a shift from the traditional view to what is referred to as the modern view of Austrian economics, led primarily by Ludwig von Mises and Friedrich Hayek. Modern Austrian theorists argue that competition for "pure profit" is the source of the market's equilibrative properties. In this view, equilibrium is seen as the outcome of the competitive process (certainly, there are still many Austrian economists that are not modernists and continue to believe in the traditional view of Austrian economics in which equilibrium is not attainable).

Mises and Hayek's fundamental contributions to modern Austrian economics can be found in their treatment of discovery and knowledge in the market process, which differ from traditional neoclassical economics. Mises (1948) suggested that markets are entrepreneurially driven rather than consumer driven. Hayek (1949) suggested that knowledge was enhanced through market interaction and therefore deviated significantly from neoclassical assumptions of perfect information.

In mainstream economics, the term *imperfect information* suggests that there are search costs associated with acquiring and analyzing information. While modern microeconomics has evolved thereby, altering some of its original assumptions of perfect information (Stiglitz was the pioneer in this area), imperfect information now is assumed to refer to known and available information which is costly to produce. In microeconomics, imperfect information is a matter of informational inefficiency.

In the modern Austrian view, imperfect information is termed "previously unthought-of knowledge" (Thomsen, 1992: 61). In this approach, imperfect information is not necessarily related to searching, but instead results from random events that are accompanied by unexpected events. These assumptions form the basis

of entrepreneurial alertness (*see* ENTREPRE-
NEURIAL ALERTNESS) and entrepreneurial
discovery (*see* ENTREPRENEURIAL DISCOV-
ERY). Entrepreneurial discovery is gradually
and systematically revealed to the market participants, resulting in competition and driving
up prices toward values consistent with
equilibrium – which the modern Austrians
assume to be consistent with perfect information.

In the Austrian view, imperfect information is
information that is yet to be known and is unknowable (one cannot buy this information).
This condition of "unrecognized information"
enables individuals to be entrepreneurially alert.
The differences are summarized by Hayek
(1949: 42):

> The concept of equilibrium merely means that
> the foresight of the different members of the
> society is...correct...in the sense that every
> person's plan is based on the expectation of
> just those actions of other people which those
> other people intend to perform and that all these
> plans are based on the expectation of the same
> set of external facts...Correct foresight is
> then...the defining characteristic of a state of
> equilibrium.

From the neoclassic view, Arrow (1959: 43)
notes: "Each individual participant in the economy is supposed to take prices as given and
determine his choices as to purchases and sales
accordingly, there is no one left over whose job it
is to make a decision on price."

If information asymmetries cannot be cor-
rected through search processes, a potential
research question is what processes can help
entrepreneurs to exploit information asymmetries.

Bibliography

Arrow, K. J. (1959). Toward a theory of price adjustment.
In M. Abramowitz et al. (eds.), *The Allocation of Eco-
nomic Resources*. Stanford, CA: Stanford University
Press.
Hayek, F. A. von (1949). *Individualism and Economic
Order*. London: Routledge and Kegan Paul.
Mises, L. von. (1948). *Human Action*. New Haven, CT:
Yale University Press.
Thomsen, E. F. (1992). *Prices and Knowledge: A Market
Process Perspective*. New York: Routledge.

autonomous business unit

Anil K. Gupta

This article reviews the historical origins of the
concept of "business unit" and present a synop-
sis of what theoretical and empirical research
tells us about the implications of granting higher
vs. lower levels of autonomy to a business unit.

ORIGINS OF THE CONCEPT OF BUSINESS UNIT

The concept of "business unit" – more specifically, "strategic business unit" (SBU)[1]– is generally believed to have been invented at General
Electric (GE) in 1957, although the company
waited until a 1969 consulting study by McKinsey and Co. to implement it. At that time, for
strategic planning and control purposes, GE was
organized into 10 groups, 46 divisions, and over
190 departments. Fred Borch, GE's CEO from
1963 to 1972, made the following observations
on the McKinsey study (Aguilar and Hamermesh, 1981: 3):

> One [of their recommendations] was that we re-
> cognize that our departments were not really busi-
> nesses. We had been saying that they were the
> basic building blocks of the company for many
> years, but they weren't. They were fractionated
> and they were parts of larger businesses. The
> thrust of the recommendation was that we re-
> organize the company...and create...Strategic
> Business Units – the terminology stolen from a
> study we made back in 1957. They gave certain
> criteria for these and in brief what this amounted
> to were reasonably self-sufficient businesses that
> did not meet head-on with other strategic business
> units in making the major management decisions
> necessary. They also recommended as part of this
> that the 33 or 35 or 40 strategic business units
> report directly to the CEO regardless of the size of
> the business or the present level in the organiza-
> tion.

Following GE's creation of strategic business
units and then treating these as the building
blocks for strategic planning and control, this
concept has been adopted by other organizations
and is now used widely by most medium- to
large-sized enterprises across the world. In the
early 1990s, even the US Central Intelligence
Agency was reported to have reorganized itself

along clearly defined "business units"! The literature and business experience suggest that there are multiple advantages that can potentially accrue from organizing any enterprise along distinct but reasonably self-sufficient business units: superior strategies, reduced intra-corporate conflicts, reduced organizational barriers to acquiring or adding new businesses as well as divesting or spinning off existing ones, increased ability to pursue distinctly different strategies across SBUs, increased ability to adopt different but tailored control mechanisms for each SBU, and so forth (Gupta and Govindarajan, 1984; Gupta, 1987).

How Autonomous Should A Business Unit Be?

Considerable research has been devoted to the question of how much autonomy should be granted to individual business units. In general, the theoretical arguments as well as empirical findings have been that the greater the autonomy granted to a business unit, the more innovative and entrepreneurial it tends to be (Govindarajan, 1986). At first glance, this might lead to the conclusion that the more autonomy, the better. In fact, the very notion of defining business units in terms of self-sufficient businesses suggests that all business units should have a high degree of decision-making autonomy in virtually all key functions.

The reality, however, is that, in most companies, it is either infeasible or uneconomical to make every business unit completely self-sufficient in terms of needed resources such as production facilities, research centers, sales and distribution networks, technologies, and other types of know-how. Consider the case of Procter and Gamble (P&G). The disposable diapers business constitutes one of P&G's largest global business units. Yet many raw materials are common to disposable diapers as well as other paper businesses of P&G, such as paper towels, toilet paper, feminine hygiene products, etc.; thus, there potentially exist large economies of scale in coordinated raw material sourcing. Also, research in absorbency is fungible across many of these business units, thereby suggesting potential scale economies from partly centralized R&D. Finally, large and powerful customers such as Wal-Mart demand that, when deciding what and how much to buy from P&G and at what prices, they negotiate with the entire company as one entity, rather than separately with each of P&G's many business units.

In short, given an increasingly competitive environment, companies are realizing that the internal and external imperatives to facilitate sharing of valuable and fungible resources across different business units are simply too strong to ignore. As Porter (1985) argued two decades ago, the competitive advantage of any individual SBU may well depend crucially, although not exclusively, on its ability to leverage complementary resources of peer SBUs. A recent but perhaps controversial example of this argument would be the overthrow by Microsoft's Internet Explorer of Netscape Navigator in the web-browser segment; most analysts have attributed Explorer's success to its ability to leverage the established dominance of Microsoft Windows, a peer business unit. At the corporate level, the salience of resource sharing among SBUs is demonstrated persuasively by the large number of studies that have reported that "related" diversified firms generally outperform "unrelated" diversified firms (see Ramanujam and Varadarajan, 1989, for a review). Even at GE, the original incubator of the SBU concept, creating a "boundary-less corporation" where SBUs would be eager to share ideas and resources with each other was one of the central ideas to stimulate innovation and productivity that was pushed by Jack Welch, who served as the company's highly successful CEO for nearly two decades from 1981 onwards.

In summary, in deciding how much decision-making autonomy they should grant to an individual SBU, corporate executives find themselves sitting on the proverbial horns of a dilemma. Greater autonomy has the potential to foster innovation and entrepreneurship at the business unit level, while dramatically cutting down on the costs of corporate bureaucracy. However, what if these benefits are more than negated by the opportunity costs of large but unrealized cross-business synergies? In other words, might an intermediate level of autonomy be the optimal solution for most business units? As we argue next, not necessarily so.

Current thinking in both academic as well as corporate circles is to search for organizational mechanisms that would induce vigorous and self-directed pursuit of cross-business synergies by business units that generally operate with a high degree of decision-making autonomy. If such mechanisms can be identified and implemented, then one can eliminate the need for suboptimal compromises. Two key mechanisms that many corporations are utilizing or experimenting with are: (1) the use of high powered incentives that are tied partly to the success of the entire corporation rather than solely to that of the focal business unit, and (2) the establishment and fostering of horizontal formal and informal networks among the people working in different but related business units. The first mechanism helps build the necessary motivational context for business unit managers to become eager to search for synergies; on the other hand, the second mechanism helps build the necessary enabling links that would increase the effectiveness and reduce the bureaucratic costs of searching for and realizing the potential synergies.

Nucor Steel provides a persuasive example of using incentives to foster a self-driven search for synergies (Gupta and Govindarajan, 2000). Over the last three decades, Nucor has been the most efficient and profitable steel producer in the United States, even though it has no proprietary advantages in terms of raw materials, technologies, distribution channels, or brand image. What has distinguished Nucor is its ability to obtain significantly greater efficiencies from inputs that are equally available to competitors. Nucor has done this through a variety of mechanisms, including an unusual incentive system. At every level of the company, incentives are solely team based and very high powered. At the business unit level, Nucor has about 25 business units, each with a general manager. Annually, each general manager has the potential to earn a bonus up to 4–5 times his or her base salary. Yet this bonus is based on the financial performance of the entire company, rather than the focal business unit. The rather large and totally variable nature of this bonus creates a situation whereby it is considered enlightened self-interest for any general manager to eagerly look for opportunities where their business unit could either provide help to or get help from peer business units. Other general managers

simply have no basis to say, "Don't bother me. Go mind your own business." Historically, the use of stock options in many high technology companies has served a similar purpose.

As an example of establishing horizontal mechanisms in order to ensure direct linkages between relevant business units, take the case of Intel Capital, the corporate venture capital arm of Intel Corporation. Among high technology companies in particular (and, perhaps, all companies across industries), Intel Corporation has been the most aggressive in making venture capital investments in start-up companies whose technologies or products might be synergistic with Intel's. Yet Intel Capital has a rule. It will not invest in any new venture if one of Intel's existing business units is not willing to become a sponsor and champion of such an investment. This requirement reduces the need for corporate headquarters to invest in costly and bureaucratic coordination and control mechanisms while, at the same time, giving a relatively high degree of decision-making autonomy to the existing unit as well as the new venture.

As we look ahead at the future of business units, I would predict that the concept will continue to thrive. Further, as managers become more sophisticated in the design of incentive systems and the cultivation of formal and informal horizontal networks among peer units, there will be less reason to think of decision-making autonomy and pursuit of cross-business synergies as mutually incompatible.

Note

1   Consistent with the strategy and organization theory literature, as well as practice within companies, I use the terms "business unit" and "strategic business unit" synonymously.

Bibliography

Aguilar, F. J. and Hamermesh, R. (1981). *General Electric Strategic Position – 1981*. Boston, MA: Harvard Business School Case No. 381–174.

Govindarajan, V. (1986). Decentralization, strategy, and effectiveness of strategic business units in multibusiness organizations. *Academy of Management Review*, 11: 844–56.

Gupta, A. K. (1987). SBU strategies, corporate-SBU relations, and SBU effectiveness in strategy implementation. *Academy of Management Journal*, 30: 477–500.

Gupta, A. K. and Govindarajan, V. (1984). Business unit strategy, managerial characteristics, and business unit effectiveness at strategy implementation. *Academy of Management Journal*, 27 (1): 25–41.

Gupta, A. K. and Govindarajan, V. (2000). Knowledge management's social dimension: Lessons from Nucor Steel. *Sloan Management Review*, 71–80.

Porter, M. E. (1985). *Competitive Advantage*. New York: Free Press.

Ramanujam, V. and Varadarajan, P. (1989). Research on corporate diversification: A synthesis. *Strategic Management Journal*, 10: 523–551.

B

bankruptcy

Richard D'Aveni

A corporation is technically bankrupt under two conditions: insolvency or negative net worth. Insolvency occurs when a firm does not have the liquid assets to pay its currently due liabilities. Negative net worth is when the firm's total debts exceed the value of its total assets. While technically bankrupt, firms are not "in bankruptcy" unless either the firm's management or its creditors file a petition with the US Bankruptcy Court to place the firm in bankruptcy.

When placed in bankruptcy, the corporation's management is replaced by or placed under the supervision of a trustee in bankruptcy. Trustees are typical when the bankrupt is a large firm or management fraud is suspected. The bankruptcy judge may supervise the bankrupt firm directly without a trustee in smaller, more manageable cases and cases not involving management fraud. Unlike normal circumstances where the management has a duty to run a firm for the benefit of stockholders, once in bankruptcy, the firm is managed for the benefit of the creditors. The goal is to maximize the amount repaid to creditors, even at the expense of stockholders' interests.

In some cases, entrepreneurs establish their businesses as sole proprietorships or partnerships, rather than as corporations or corporate-like limited liability partnerships, because investors require the entrepreneurs to "put up" all their savings to show commitment to the success of the business. In the case of failed proprietorships and partnerships, the individual entrepreneurs may declare bankruptcy. They lose all their assets, except their "homestead" (their house and personal belongings up to a limited amount in value), but they gain a fresh start in life without any debts to repay.

In general, it is better to create a corporation or limited liability partnership to limit the entrepreneur's losses to only those assets invested in the business if a bankruptcy occurs. However, creditors and other investors may still ask for personal guarantees from the entrepreneurs, effectively extending an entrepreneur's losses to some of his or her personal assets if a bankruptcy occurs. In an attempt to protect assets from such potential losses, entrepreneurs may place some of their personal assets in the names of relatives, in trusts, or in foreign bank accounts that are hard to reach before there is any hint of bankruptcy. However, care must be taken to avoid fraud if such methods are used, especially if done to hide assets or deny their real ownership during a bankruptcy proceeding.

TYPES OF CORPORATE BANKRUPTCY

Two types of petitions may be filed in the case of corporate bankruptcies: liquidation or reorganization. A liquidation petition asks the court to cease business operations and sell all assets, distributing the proceeds to the highest priority creditors first, typically secured creditors. The remaining proceeds go to lower priority, unsecured creditors, and then to equity holders, if any funds are left over. Creditors rarely recover all their money in liquidation – otherwise, the firm would not be technically bankrupt.

A reorganization petition asks the court to continue some or all of the business operations of the bankrupt and to reorganize its debt and equity structure. In the reorganization, some debt holders may become stockholders. Some debt may be written off, or its interest rate or duration adjusted to make it easier to pay the debt after the firm emerges from bankruptcy.

New investors may be sought and some assets may be sold, so some debtors may be paid out of these proceeds. Many possible reorganization plans could be adopted by the court. So interested creditors – and often management – suggest different plans and a vote is taken among the creditors to advise the court. The vote is taken by class of debtors. That is, each group of secured, subordinated secured, and unsecured debtors votes separately. More fine grained classes may be created by the court if the interests of the creditors within a class differ substantially.

If all classes accept the plan, the judge generally accepts the plan. But this is rare, especially if the highest priority creditors get all the funds. So complex negotiations go on among the creditors, and plans are formulated to entice the lower priority creditors to vote for them by offering some funds to them that they would not receive under the normal priorities assigned to them. It is rare that agreement can be reached among all creditors, even after negotiations occur. In this case, the court looks at the plans which gathered the support of at least one class of creditors. That class of creditors then attempts to persuade the judge (based on the merits of the plan) to do what is called a "cram down," which is exactly what it sounds like – the plan is crammed down the throats of the other creditors and shareholders. The judge has some guidelines for selecting among plans if more than one gains the approval of at least one class of creditors, but these guidelines essentially give the judge a lot of discretion to cram any plan down on the parties that he or she wants.

Smaller and entrepreneurial firms are typically liquidated because there are few tangible assets left to be used in reorganization. Liquidation is especially likely if key managers, salespeople, or scientists have departed before or during the bankruptcy process. But complete liquidation is often wasteful because substantial intangible assets often reside in the heads of the entrepreneurial team. Thus, if a reorganization is to take place, special provisions must be made to secure the loyalty of key personnel. In larger scale bankruptcies, intangible assets often reside in systems and groups that are not so dependent upon any one individual, making reorganization and emergence as an ongoing concern easier.

INVOLUNTARY AND VOLUNTARY BANKRUPTCY

When the creditors file a bankruptcy petition, it is called an "involuntary" bankruptcy because the bankrupt has no choice in the matter. In practice, management can sometimes influence whether a bankruptcy petition is filed, and in most situations management can influence the timing of a filing. As a firm's financial condition deteriorates, management often attempts to "work-out" its problems with the creditors by reorganizing its debts, much the way the bankruptcy court would, but without the restrictive supervision of a court and the technical rules of bankruptcy law applying. Management can also try to turn around its operations and strategy while reassuring its employees and customers that everything will be all right after a few changes are made.

Impression management becomes very important for avoiding entering into a downward spiral that causes the firm's legitimacy and support to dry up. If management projects a credible impression that they can save the company, it often becomes a self-fulfilling prophecy, reducing the probability of failure and attracting new investors and allies that contribute to pulling the firm out of trouble. This is, of course, preferable to bankruptcy proceedings because it avoids the stigma and administrative costs of bankruptcy, as well as any potential decline in customer confidence that may be caused by even the hint of bankruptcy.

However, management can get into trouble during the process of managing impressions because management typically gives contradictory messages to different stakeholders – telling employees and customers to stick with the firm because things are improving, while telling unions and creditors that things are getting worse to convince them that they must make concessions to reorganize the firm's financial or cost structure. In the process, fraud or its appearance may be committed. This problem is especially acute for publicly traded firms, where SEC disclosure rules apply and securities fraud is easy to commit.

In smaller bankruptcies, creditors are often quicker to file an involuntary petition due to fears that entrepreneurs may strip assets illicitly from the firm, or because the entrepreneurs' impression management techniques are transparent or not credible given the small size of the firm and its lack of reserve resources. In the end, creditors must make a judgment about the "dependability" of the debtor's management – that is, its ability to turn around the company and the trustworthiness of the management's statements. Studies have shown that when creditors make judgments, it is not always a rational process based solely on the numbers. Creditors also base their decisions about whether and when to file bankruptcy on their personal relationships with management and the prestige of the debtor's management team. Teams filled with people with important memberships in or connections to elite aspects of society (such as military, social, or economic elites) are often given more time to work out their financial and strategic problems. Prestige provides a halo effect that makes impression management more effective.

When management files the petition, it is called "voluntary" bankruptcy. In practice, many so-called "voluntary" bankruptcies are not really voluntary at all. Many result from a race to the court house when management gets wind that creditors are going to file. Management may prefer a voluntary bankruptcy because if it files first it can determine if liquidation or reorganization will be pursued, and management may want to influence whether a trustee is chosen and if the management itself is replaced by the court or the trustee.

Some bankruptcies are truly voluntary and used in a strategic manner. "Strategic" bankruptcy has been used to void onerous union contracts, unneeded real estate leases for closed facilities, overwhelming pension liabilities, excessive legal judgments resulting from major product liability cases, as well as to reorganize the finances of firms with good operating cash flow but poor financial structures. Congress has put many restrictions on the use of the bankruptcy laws for strategic purposes, but strategic bankruptcies are still possible under certain circumstances.

BANKRUPTCY AVOIDANCE IN
ENTREPRENEURIAL FIRMS

Entrepreneurial firms often live on the edge of bankruptcy during their start-up period. In fact,

the vast majority of start-ups don't last two years. "Liabilities of newness" abound. As with most things new, customers, employees, and investors are often skeptical about whether the business model, the product or service, or the management, are legitimate, questioning whether they will succeed in the long run. The usual worries about cash flows, the ability to get that all important first customer, the risks of major customer defections, key employee departures and other factors affecting the survival of the firm all encourage fears that might drive creditors to file an involuntary bankruptcy petition prematurely.

To get by this period, entrepreneurs either need substantial funds of their own to assure everyone that the firm will survive or they must have extensive networks in the local community or industry. Studies have shown that the survival of entrepreneurial firms often depends upon their access to resources, relationships, and customer or technical knowledge. Entrepreneurs with wider networks of friends and colleagues – even non-elite connections within those communities – significantly decrease the chances of bankruptcy during the start-up phase because their centrality in the network provides them with options that they could not generate if they were isolated individuals.

Several other strategies for overcoming the liabilities of newness that cause most bankruptcies among entrepreneurial firms exist. For example, seeking a "strategic investor," an investor who promises to be the first customer, can reduce the worries about bankruptcy. Distribution alliances with potentially dangerous competitors, such as imitators who might become fast followers, can also reduce the risk of bankruptcy. In addition, affiliation with a particularly prestigious institution (such as a university) or a highly regarded venture capital firm are used to counter problems associated with illegitimacy, because the affiliate's implied endorsement extends their brand or reputation to the entrepreneurial firm.

BANKRUPTCY STIGMA

Bankruptcy carries a large stigma effect with it. The mere hint of a pending bankruptcy can cause the defection of key managers or customers. And managers who were in charge at the time of a bankruptcy often find it difficult to find another good job because they are tainted by their association with a bankrupt firm. At one time, failure to repay debts was a criminal offense, treated like theft.

In modern times, this stigma has lessened. In fact, in some entrepreneurial societies (such as Silicon Valley), entrepreneurs with histories of multiple failures are common. Working for a failed firm hurts, but does not destroy, an entrepreneur's resume or ability to raise capital. Two factors are important in avoiding the stigma effect of bankruptcy. First, don't go down with the ship. People who are in charge at the time of failure are stigmatized more than those who leave a year or two before the failure, even when the early leavers were responsible for the failure. If it happens on one's watch, the failure will be attributed by others to that person. Bailing out early also gives the entrepreneur deniability – the ability to say it's not my fault, subsequent actions and strategies of others could always have been better. Because this provides incentives to leave when the going gets tough, savvy investors often seek to lock up entrepreneurs with tough non-competition agreements and draconian employment contracts.

The second factor lessening the stigma effect associated with bankruptcy is the learning effect. Serial entrepreneurs can present what they have learned about why the venture failed, how they would do things differently this time around, and who they would get to join their team to avoid the previous problems. In addition, often a technology or product fails because the business model was wrong, or the business model fails because the technology or product was wrong. Or a technology could have been used for another purpose that other customers would have adopted faster. In such cases the value of the learning from the previous experience may overcome the stigma of being associated with bankruptcy. Nevertheless, it is still better to be successful the first time, rather than to have to argue why the stigma of bankruptcy shouldn't be attached to you.

bisociation

Patrick G. Maggitti and Ken G. Smith

Bisociation, a term coined by Arthur Koestler in his book *The Act of Creation* (1964), refers to the creative process through which two seemingly unrelated matrices of thought are combined to form a novel outcome (*see* CREATIVITY). Bisociation differs from logical associations of concepts that are in some way related or consistent with each other. For example, it is quite logical and consistent to associate the concepts of fire and light. That is, fire emits light. However, it took Edison to bisociate the concept of light with a previously unrelated concept, electricity. Outcomes of bisociation, such as the light bulb, are more radically creative than those resulting from routine, logical, and single dimension thought. Importantly, Koestler notes, and the light bulb example demonstrates, that the creative act does not result from fashioning some creative product from nothing. Rather, "it uncovers, selects, re-shuffles, combines, synthesizes already existing facts, ideas, faculties, (and) skills" (Koestler, 1964: 120). In fact, it is often the case that the most original creative discoveries are also those that, in retrospect, seem most obvious.

Koestler largely explores bisociation in the context of humor and satire. For example, he relates a joke in which a convict, caught cheating while playing cards with his fellow inmates, is kicked out of jail for cheating. The irony of the situation is based on the intersection of two ideas that, independently, are quite unremarkable (i.e., convicts are in jail and cheaters are kicked out). The bisociation of these two notions creates a novel and creatively humorous situation. Other researchers have explored the concept of bisociation in humor by suggesting its necessity for the humorous result of puns (Attardo, 1988) and conundrums (Dienhart, 1999). Punch lines in general are linguistic triggers that bisociate the semantics of two seemingly disparate ideas (Dienhart, 1999) or realms of meaning (Johnson, 1976).

Bisociation also occurs in other types of creative endeavors beyond humor, such as science, music, and art (Amabile, 1996). Koestler illustrates this point by maintaining that scientists bring together unrelated ideas while exploring problems in their field. Likewise, he also brings to light bisociation in the invention of new products. For example, he explains how Gutenberg invented type-casting by bringing together his knowledge of wine presses and coin stamping. Researchers have also used bisociation to describe creativity in other populations, such as children (Auerbach, 1972) and in specific individuals like Albert Einstein (Dreistadt, 1974).

Psychologists have examined bisociation as a tool in a variety of contexts. For example, humorous bisociations between love and career are used by career counselors to help clients clarify and confront their career choices in a creative manner (Nevo, 1986). Humorous bisociations were also shown to desensitize dentistry patients and create a playful-humorous environment (Nevo and Shapira, 1988). Psychoanalysts have used bisociation to develop the concept of hemispheric bisociation, the synthesis of two different cerebral planes, as an effective psychoanalytic technique to encourage creativity through the use of both symbols and verbalizations (Hoppe, 1988). Finally, with a sample of research and development scientists, Jabri (1988) developed and validated a scale, based on Koestler's concept of bisociation, to measure creative problem-solving approaches.

Management researchers are beginning to offer bisociation as an explanation to account for the creativity of market actors in a variety of contexts, such as entrepreneurial innovation (Sexton and Smilor, 1997). For example, Smith and Di Gregorio (2002) argue that entrepreneurs combine, or bisociate, preexisting but unrelated matrices of information concerning markets, customers, and resources. These researchers propose that individuals differ in their ability to bisociate more advanced and complex information based on their level of intrinsic motivation, an appropriate stimulus, domain knowledge, and creative skills. Further, they argue that the greater the diversity of information that is integrated in the bisociation process, the more novel and market disrupting their subsequent entrepreneurial actions. This perspective links the idea of bisociation with the concept of "creative

destruction" (Schumpeter, 1942). Creative destruction occurs when the market equilibrium is disrupted by the introduction of a new product, new service, new process, new market, new source of raw material, or new way of organizing – what Schumpeter called innovation. Schumpeter argued that these innovations are the creative result of new combinations of existing factors of production. It is possible, therefore, that the concept of bisociation can explain the level of creativeness and destructiveness of innovations based on the diversity of inputs or resources that are bisociated in the process of innovation.

Bibliography

Amabile, T. M. (1996). *Creativity in Context*. Boulder, CO: Westview Press.

Attardo, S. (1988). Trends in European humor research: Toward a text model. *Humor: International Journal of Humor Research*, 1: 349–69.

Auerbach, A. G. (1972). The bisociative or creative act in the nursery school. *Young Children*, 28: 27–31.

Dienhart, J. M. (1999). A linguistic look at riddles. *Journal of Pragmatics*, 31: 95–125.

Dreistadt, R. (1974). The psychology of creativity: How Einstein discovered the theory of relativity. *Psychology: A Journal of Human Behavior*, 11: 15–25.

Hoppe, K. D. (1988). Hemispheric specialization and creativity. *Psychiatric Clinics of North America*, 11: 303–15.

Jabri, M. M. (1988). A new scale for the measurement of individual innovativeness amongst research and development scientists. *Psychological Reports*, 62: 951–2.

Johnson, R. (1976). Two realms and a joke: Bisociation theories of joking. *Semiotica*, 16: 195–221.

Koestler, A. (1964). *The Act of Creation*. New York: Macmillan.

Nevo, O. (1986). Uses of humor in career counseling. *Vocational Guidance Quarterly*, 34: 188–96.

Nevo, O. and Shapira, J. (1988). The use of humor by pediatric dentists. *Journal of Children in Contemporary Society*, 20: 171–8.

Schumpeter, J. A. (1942). *Capitalism, Socialism, and Democracy*. New York: Harper and Row.

Sexton, D. L. and Smilor, R. W. (eds.) (1997). *Entrepreneurship 2000*. Chicago: Upstart Publishing.

Smith, K. G. and Di Gregorio, D. (2002). Bisociation, discovery, and the role of entrepreneurial action. In M. A. Hitt, R. D. Ireland, S. M. Camp, and D. L. Sexton (eds.), *Strategic Entrepreneurship*. Oxford: Blackwell.

board structure and composition

Catherine M. Daily and Dan R. Dalton

There is a rich tradition in corporate governance studies of examining the structure and composition of boards of directors. This is true whether the organizations of interest are entrepreneurial or otherwise. Importantly, the defining characteristics of board structure and composition are invariant across firm types, but their relationships with firm processes and outcomes are sometimes dependent on firm context (Dalton et al., 1998). These differences are salient to entrepreneurial firms, as adherence to board structure and composition configurations prescribed for traditional large corporations may yield different outcomes for entrepreneurial firms.

In brief, board structure refers to whether the chief executive officer (CEO) concurrently serves as chairperson of the board of directors. Board composition refers to the relative proportions of inside (management) and outside directors. While these two board configurations are most salient in the corporate context (i.e., firms whose stock is publicly traded), private firms, too, rely on boards of directors to enhance firm effectiveness.

BOARD STRUCTURE

Whether the CEO serves simultaneously as board chairperson (a condition commonly referred to as CEO duality when these positions are combined) is often regarded as an indicator of the potential for management to dominate the board of directors. This structure is most at issue for public firms where there is a separation between management and control. Under such conditions, management can become entrenched, thereby reducing the ability of the board of directors to effectively oversee firm management (Finkelstein and D'Aveni, 1994). This view is consistent with agency theory principles, which suggest that the board of directors is a necessary element in the system of checks and balances that ensure managers' interests are effectively aligned with those of shareholders (Jensen and Meckling, 1976). Formal separation between management and the board enables the board to better hold management accountable

for firm processes, and this should result in higher levels of firm performance (Shleifer and Vishny, 1997).

An alternative view is grounded in stewardship theory (e.g., Davis, Schoorman, and Donaldson, 1997). This perspective suggests that CEO duality provides for unified vision and leadership within the firm. Importantly, this unification has benefits both internally with organizational employees and externally with firms' stakeholders (e.g., customers, investors, suppliers). Absent ambiguity regarding who is responsible for marshaling the firms' resources, firms should achieve superior firm performance.

Interestingly, a meta-analysis of the relationship between board structure and firm performance indicates no significant relationship between these variables. This is true when the size of the firm (i.e., entrepreneurial/small firms vs. large firms) is considered, as well as when accounting versus market-based firm performance measures are considered (see Daily et al., 2002, for an overview specific to the entrepreneurial context). Reliance on CEO duality or the separate board leadership structure, then, appears to be a choice between the benefits to be gained as a function of unequivocal leadership as compared to separate (i.e., independent) board leadership.

BOARD COMPOSITION

While the classification of directors as insiders or outsiders may seem rather straightforward, there are a number of subtleties that underlie board composition. A common element of any board composition classification, however, is the level of independence afforded by the various categories of directors (Daily, Johnson, and Dalton, 1999).

A dominant theme in the configuration of any board of directors is how to comprise the board for effective oversight of firm management. This focus on independence through board composition has been a consistent theme for shareholder activists and the focus of recent legislation (i.e., Sarbanes-Oxley Act of 2002) and stock exchange guideline revisions (e.g., New York Stock Exchange and Nasdaq) in the United States. Greater board effectiveness through independence is also consistent with agency theory. Agency theory is premised on the view that managers may, given the opportunity, seek to satisfy their own interests at the expense of shareholders (Jensen and Meckling 1976). As a result, an appropriately comprised board of directors protects shareholders from managerial self-interest through effective monitoring.

Not all types of directors are believed to be equally suited for the oversight function. There is, however, little consistency in the classification of directors (Daily et al., 1999). Inside directors are typically operationalized as directors concurrently serving as firm officers. As noted by Daily et al. (1999), however, some researchers have expanded this definition to include former officers and relatives of management. Many observers would argue that inside directors are ill-suited for directors' oversight role. With regard to CEOs, they are, in effect, asked to monitor themselves. With regard to other inside directors, they are asked to monitor themselves, but more importantly the person to whom they report, the CEO (Fama and Jensen, 1983; Zahra and Pearce, 1989). There is, however, an alternative lens through which to consider inside directors. Some observers believe that inside directors have incentives to expose a poorly performing CEO and that they provide valuable firm-specific information to board deliberations (e.g., Baysinger and Hoskisson, 1990). For example, insiders often possess superior firm-specific information that can be valuable in strategic decision-making processes. Outsiders are generally not privy to the operational functioning of the firms they serve and, as a result, are less able to contribute to strategic deliberations at the same level as insiders.

Outside director classification is substantially more complex than that for insiders. Outside directors have been segmented into independent, affiliated, and interdependent categories, each with differing degrees of independence from management. Here, too, however, there is little consistency in measurement within each of these categories (see Daily et al., 1999, for an overview). Independent outside directors include those directors who maintain no personal or professional relationship with the firm or firm management. As a result, these directors are

believed best capable of fulfilling the monitoring function.

Affiliated (also referred to as grey or SEC6[b]) directors include outside directors with some form of personal or professional relationship with the firm or firm management (Daily and Dalton, 1994; Johnson, Hoskisson, and Hitt, 1993). Examples of affiliated relationships include outside board members who directly provide or whose employer provides legal counsel, investment banking services, or consulting services. Also included are board members representing major customers or suppliers, as well as board members with familial relationships with firm management. In agency theory terms, the issue is that these directors may not effectively monitor firm management and risk their board positions.

While affiliated directors are not generally believed to be effective monitors, they are perhaps effectively positioned to fulfill an alternative board role – that of resource acquisition (e.g., Pfeffer and Salancik, 1978). Affiliated directors who maintain professional relationships with the firm or firm management are positioned to assist in the acquisition of critical resources and provide valuable expertise as a function of their external contacts and professional expertise.

A third category of outside directors is that of interdependent directors. The distinction here is based on the timing of directors' appointments to the board. Interdependent directors are appointed during the tenure of the standing CEO (Wade, O'Reilly, and Chandratat, 1990). Here the issue is the extent to which interdependent directors maintain a sense of obligation to the CEO (the individual who almost certainly extended the invitation to join the board), which mitigates their propensity to effectively monitor firm management.

Incorporating the multiple means by which board composition has been measured, Dalton et al. (1998) conducted a meta-analysis of the relationship between board composition and firm performance. Their findings did not support the view that greater board independence will result in superior firm performance. This conclusion is true regardless of the measurement of board composition (i.e., inside, outside, etc.), and regardless of the type of performance indicator (i.e., accounting, market). Importantly, this relationship does not differ for entrepreneurial/small versus large firms. While boards might be constructed to fulfill a variety of needs, the level of independence is apparently not the path to better performance (see Daily et al., 2002, for an overview of studies supporting a relationship between various aspects of boards of directors and firm performance in entrepreneurial contexts).

Board structure and composition can be especially critical issues for entrepreneurial firms. It is in this organizational context that boards of directors are uniquely positioned to facilitate organizational processes and outcomes. Strategic leaders often have a greater influence in entrepreneurial firms, as they are less constrained by more complex or established systems and structures typically found in larger, more traditional corporations (see Daily et al., 2002, for an overview) *(see* BOARDS OF DIRECTORS IN NEW VENTURES).

Bibliography

Baysinger, B. D. and Hoskisson, R. E. (1990). The composition of boards of directors and strategic control: Effects on corporate strategy. *Academy of Management Review*, 15: 72–87.

Daily, C. M. and Dalton, D. R. (1994). Bankruptcy and corporate governance: The impact of board composition and structure. *Academy of Management Journal*, 37: 1603–17.

Daily, C. M., Johnson, J. L., and Dalton, D. R. (1999). On the measurement of board composition: Poor consistency and a serious mismatch of theory and operationalization. *Decision Sciences*, 30: 83–106.

Daily, C. M., McDougall, P. P., Covin, J. G., and Dalton, D. R. (2002). Governance and strategic leadership in entrepreneurial firms. *Journal of Management*, 28: 387–412.

Dalton, D. R., Daily, C. M., Ellstrand, A. E., and Johnson, J. L. (1998). Meta-analytic reviews of board composition, leadership structure, and financial performance. *Strategic Management Journal*, 19: 269–90.

Davis, J. H., Schoorman, F. D., and Donaldson, L. (1997). Toward a stewardship theory of management. *Academy of Management Review*, 22: 20–47.

Fama, E. F. and Jensen, M. C. (1983). Agency problems and residual claims. *Journal of Law and Economics*, 26: 327–49.

Finkelstein, S. and D'Aveni, R. A. (1994). CEO duality as a double-edged sword: How boards of directors balance entrenchment avoidance and unity of command. *Academy of Management Journal*, 37: 1079–108.

Jensen, M. C. and Meckling, W. H. (1976). Theory of the firm: Managerial behavior, agency costs and ownership structure. *Journal of Financial Economics*, 3: 305–60.

Johnson, R. A., Hoskisson, R. E., and Hitt, M. A. (1993). Board of director involvement in restructuring: The effects of board versus managerial controls and characteristics. *Strategic Management Journal*, 14 (summer special issue): 33–50.

Pfeffer, J. and Salancik, G. R. (1978). *The External Control of Organizations: A Resource-Dependence Perspective*. New York: Harper and Row.

Shleifer, A. and Vishny, R. W. (1997). A survey of corporate governance. *Journal of Finance*, 52: 737–83.

Wade, J., O'Reilly, C. A., and Chandratat, I. (1990). Golden parachutes: CEOs and the exercise of social influence. *Administrative Science Quarterly*, 35: 587–603.

Zahra, S. A. and Pearce, J. A. (1989). Boards of directors and corporate financial performance: A review and integrative model. *Journal of Management*, 15: 291–334.

boards of directors in new ventures

Dan R. Dalton and Catherine M. Daily

The appropriate roles and responsibilities of boards of directors and their influence on corporate financial performance have been subject to extensive empirical examination and discussion for many years. In fact, many elements of the Sarbanes-Oxley Act and guidelines enacted by the Securities and Exchange Commission (SEC), the New York Stock Exchange (NYSE), American Stock Exchange (AME), and Nasdaq focus on these issues.

The overwhelming majority of that body of work, however, has been focused on large-scale, traditional organizations (e.g., *Fortune* 500, *S&P* 500 firms). Smaller firms have received far less attention, and new ventures even less (for a notable exception, see Daily et al., 2002). In subsequent sections, we describe a few key concepts and suggest some potentially interesting aspects of boards of directors that have special application to new ventures.

Any discussion of boards of directors would certainly include the notion of independence. The issue here is the extent to which a board can, or will, provide a dispassionate assessment of the CEO. Many observers of corporate governance would argue that a board comprised of inside directors (officers of the firm) and affiliated directors (non-employee directors who have close personal or professional relationships with the firm or its executives) may have a tendency to support the CEO somewhat more unconditionally than a board comprised of outside directors (directors without those relationships with the firm or its executives).

Another aspect of board independence is whether the CEO concurrently serves as board chairperson. The potential problem is straightforward: Can a board effectively monitor the CEO when the chairperson of the board *is* the CEO? Imagine also the extreme scenario: a board comprised of a preponderance of inside and affiliated board members with its CEO serving as board chairperson. There is a long-standing view, often referred to as agency theory, that the lack of independence in the governance structures of companies will be reflected in poor financial performance for the firm. This is based on the central principle of agency theory: high-ranking corporate officers, acting as the agents of shareholders, can pursue courses of action inconsistent with the interests of owners (for a review of agency theory and corporate governance, see Shleifer and Vishny, 1997). In the following sections, then, when we mention independence, it is these dimensions regarding the composition of the board and the CEO/board chairperson issue to which we refer.

Board independence is an important element in the perception of the quality of a firm's governance. This issue, however, can be exacerbated for new ventures because the CEOs are often the founders. For the new venture, then, it is possible that (1) the founder is the CEO; (2) the founder is also the board chairperson; and (3) the board is not independent. Importantly, the perceived lack of independent governance in a new venture can adversely affect its relationship with external constituencies – constituencies that may be critical for the new venture's growth and success.

Consider, for example, the venture capital community. Many venture firms will seek the support of venture capitalists (VCs). Obviously, VCs are a source of funds, but it is also true that the survival rates of venture-backed firms are much higher than for firms without VC funding.

VC firms, however, are extremely selective in choosing which firms to support. Among the factors that VCs will carefully evaluate are the overall governance of the firm, the nature of its board, and whether the founder is CEO. In fact, VC firms will often "nominate" board members to be added to the firm, often insisting that they have representation on the boards in which they invest.

An initial public offering (IPO) is another means of raising funds for new ventures' growth and development. This process, too, will be informed by the governance structures of the firm. While the IPO process, managed by an investment bank (IB) is complex (for an overview of the IPO process, see Certo, Daily, and Dalton, 2002; Ritter, 1998), a critical step is setting the price at which the IPO firm's stock will be offered to the public. Board independence, given the value placed on independent governance structures by key shareholder groups such as institutional investors, may serve as a proxy for firm quality, enabling the IB and the firm's owners to extract a higher value when setting the opening price. This is, of course, in the interests of the new venture firm that is going public.

Interestingly, there is also a synergistic effect of VC involvement in the IPO process. VC participation in a new venture can serve as a powerful signal to potential investors about the quality of the firm going public (e.g., Megginson and Weiss, 1991) and this, in turn, is related to more capital raised through the IPO process for the firm's treasury.

Equity holdings by the members of the board is another factor that may affect the new venture leaders' ability to raise funds, particularly in the IPO context. Agency theory suggests that when outside board members hold substantial equity positions in the firms they serve, they are more likely to act in shareholders' interests (for a discussion of equity holding by board members, see Dalton et al., 2003). Individuals and institutions that might purchase stock in an IPO company would be much more comfortable knowing that the board's interests and theirs are similar (i.e., all are shareholders in the firm).

The size of the board of directors may also be of interest to those considering an investment in the new enterprise (for a discussion of board size and financial performance, see Dalton et al.,

1999). Specifically, larger boards may signal that the firm has access to a wider range and quality of critical resources: information, people, capital, raw materials, services (for a comprehensive discussion of "resource dependence," see Pfeffer and Salancik, 1978). This perspective is also consistent with "social capital" theory, the notion that social networks (e.g., the people you know and to whom you have access) can increase the venture's overall resources as well as effectively leverage its current resources (e.g., Florin, Lubatkin, and Schulze, 2003). It has been demonstrated that board size is related to the financial performance of the firm; notably, that relationship is even larger in the case of smaller firms (Dalton et al., 1999). It is also interesting that larger boards are associated with greater net returns for IPO firms (Certo, Daily, and Dalton, 2002).

In fairness, board networking can be a mixed blessing. An obvious means to secure high-quality comparative information about best practices, for example, is when board members serve on multiple boards. The number of directorships held by directors, however, has been subject to sharp criticism by the business/financial press and shareholder activists. Their point is that, beyond some threshold (e.g., memberships in more than three or four boards), additional directorships compromise directors' attendance, attention, and effectiveness.

The current environment of corporate governance appreciably shapes both the mature company as well as the new venture, but at different stages. The governance structures of large-scale, publicly traded corporations have *never* been under the current level of scrutiny. Interestingly, the new venture is unlikely to grow, develop, and become a public company without focused attention on its governance structures as well.

Who cares about governance structures in new ventures?	Issues that may be of concern
Venture capital firms	Independence of the board of directors
Investment banks	Same person serving as CEO and chairperson of the board
IPO investors	
Securities and Exchange Commission	Founder of the firm as CEO and/or chairperson of the board
Stock exchanges	Extent of equity holdings in the firm by board members Size of the board of directors

Bibliography

Certo, S. T., Daily, C. M., and Dalton, D. R. (2002). Signaling firm value through board structure: An investigation of initial public offerings. *Entrepreneurship Theory and Practice*, 26: 33–50.

Daily, C. M., McDougall, T., Covin, J. G., and Dalton, D. R. (2002). Governance and strategic leadership in entrepreneurial firms. *Journal of Management*, 28: 387–412.

Dalton, D. R., Daily, C. M., Certo, S. T., and Roengpitya, R. (2003). Meta-analyses of corporate financial performance and the equity of CEOs, officers, boards of directors, institutions, and blockholders: Fusion or confusion? *Academy of Management Journal*, 46: 13–26.

Dalton, D. R., Daily, C. M., Johnson, J. L., and Ellstrand, A. E. (1999). Number of directors on the board and financial performance: A meta-analysis. *Academy of Management Journal*, 42: 674–86.

Florin, J., Lubatkin, M., and Schulze, W. (2003). A social capital model of high-growth ventures. *Academy of Management Journal*, 46: 374–84.

Megginson, W. L. and Weiss, K. A. (1991). Venture capitalist certification in initial public offerings. *Journal of Finance*, 46: 879–903.

Pfeffer, J. and Salancik, G. R. (1978). *The External Control of Organizations: A Resource-Dependence Perspective*. New York: Harper and Row.

Ritter, J. R. (1998). Initial public offerings. *Contemporary Finance Digest*, 2: 5–30.

Shleifer, A. and Vishny, R. W. (1997). A survey of corporate governance. *Journal of Finance*, 52: 737–83.

business angel network

Saras D. Sarasvathy and Robert Wiltbank

INTRODUCTION

Informal venture capital (VC) (i.e., angel investing) is the largest single source of private equity capital in new venture development. Angel investors are so named because in the early 1900s wealthy individuals provided capital to help launch new theatrical productions. As patrons of the arts, these investors were considered by theater professionals as "angels." Estimates of the number of active angel investors in the US vary widely. By triangulation of various estimates it is at least four or five times larger than the formal VC market (Freear, Sohl, and Wetzel, 1995; Mason and Harrison, 2002). For example, while 36,000 companies received $20 billion of angel funding for the year 2002,[1] approximately only 3,000 companies received capital from VC firms in 2002.[2] Of the latter, only 22 percent was invested in early stage companies.

A recent trend in angel investing consists of the formation of business angel "networks," such as the Band of Angels in Silicon Valley and the Alliance of Angels in the Pacific Northwest. It is estimated that there are over 150 business angel networks in the USA and several in European and Asian countries. Books and websites on business angels continue to proliferate. From a research standpoint, however, in spite of the considerably larger magnitude of business angels when compared to VCs, we know less about the former than the latter. The current state of the art in early stage investing consists almost exclusively of research into formal VCs, including descriptions of practices, calculations of returns, and theories that explain both.

AN INTRIGUING PUZZLE

From a theoretical standpoint, extant research identifies two key problems of interest with regard to early stage private equity financing, both of which embody elements of information asymmetry between investor and entrepreneur.

The investor does not know the entrepreneur's ability. There are at least three sets of theoretical arguments that set this up as a major source of risk in both angel and VC investing. First, as summarized in Berger and Udell (1998), no one will fund early stage entrepreneurial firms because of moral hazard problems – so they have to depend on internal funding. Second, the ones that do get funding will not be the best ones because of adverse selection problems (Amit, Glosten, and Muller, 1990). Third, when VCs do manage to discover a high-potential entrepreneurial venture, they will face a free-rider problem from other VCs due to non-excludability of the information (Anand and Galetovic, 2000).

The investor does not know the entrepreneur's motivation. Added to the problems due to theories based on information asymmetry and agency is the onerous fact that these problems cannot be "contracted" away. Theories of incomplete contracting therefore suggest that the above theories are inadequate at describing the risks involved in early stage financing, because they all assume both investors and entrepreneurs are motivated by the same thing – i.e., cash flows (Hart, 2001). But when "private benefits" other than cash flows matter to the entrepreneur, decision (control) rights become extremely important.

Given these enormous problems identified by theoretical and empirical examinations of formal VC funding practices and the early investment histories of entrepreneurial firms, we would expect that business angels, even more than VCs, would have developed an elaborate set of practices to overcome these problems. Yet the research that does look at the practices of angel investors suggests that they often use none or considerably less of the types of practices that formal VCs use to overcome the above-mentioned problems. A pithy saying in the popular lore on entrepreneurship points to the earliest investors as consisting of three Fs: *friends, family, and fools*, angels being the last of the three. More seriously, as Prowse (1998) discusses, angel investors focus their investments in earlier stages of venture development than do VCs, do significantly less due diligence, source deals very locally through largely personal networks, do not have comparable levels of portfolio diversification (if any at all), rarely take positions of controlling interest, and regularly avoid detailed contracts and incentive schemes.

While the predominance of VC investment occurs in the later stages of the development of a venture, angels largely concentrate their investments in very early stages, providing seed and start-up capital primarily (Amis and Stevenson, 2001; Prowse, 1998; Gupta and Sapienza, 1992). This earlier angel investment stage is regularly considered to be broadly associated with higher risks of failure (Shepherd, Douglas, and Shanley, 2000) and also subject to higher risks from information asymmetries (Triantis, 2001). Most angels tend to insist on previous personal knowledge of the entrepreneur and consider business plans and forecasts secondary to their own knowledge about the proposals and comfort levels with the entrepreneur. In fact, angels routinely reject "promising" proposals due to lack of first hand knowledge of the venture concept and/or the principals involved (Prowse, 1998).

In a more recent empirical study of the differences between angels and VCs, Mason and Harrison (2002) contrast the two types of investors in terms of their approaches to investment appraisal, due diligence, and contracting as follows:

> Many of these arise because business angels, unlike venture capital fund managers, decide on the worth of a potential investment as principals, rather than as agents and/or employees (Feeney, Haines, and Riding, 1999; Prasad, Bruton, and Vozikis, 2000). Business angels are less concerned with financial projections and are less likely to calculate rates of return. They do less detailed due diligence, have fewer meetings with entrepreneurs, are less likely to take up references on the entrepreneur, and are less likely to consult other people about the investment. Conversely, business angels are more likely to invest on "gut feeling."

When looking at the differences between these investment types, angels and VCs, it seems that angels make investments that are at greater risk of failure than the firms in which venture capitalists invest. In every category of practice for dealing with the challenges of private equity investing, angel investors tend to be on the higher end of the risk spectrum. At the same time, however, the only clear empirical research comparing the return distributions of formal and informal venture capital suggests that their relationship to failure is in fact the reverse! In no small deviation from expectations based on previous theorizing, Mason and Harrison (2002), combining their own surveys with those of Murray (1999), arrive at the conclusion that angels are 60 percent *less* likely to fail (exit at a loss) than VCs. Additionally, angels' rate of "home run" investments essentially equaled that of the VC group.

This sets up an interesting puzzle for future theorizing about financing of entrepreneurial ventures: What could be the theoretical rationale for this observed empirical anomaly?

A POSSIBLE ANSWER TO THE PUZZLE

One possible answer is suggested by recent studies of expert entrepreneurs (Sarasvathy, 2001a, 2001b; Dew, 2002). Together, these studies argue that not only do external stakeholders such as angels and VCs not know the abilities and motivations of entrepreneurs, but, in fact, the entrepreneurs themselves do not know their own capabilities and motivations. They discover and formulate them in the very process of building new firms and markets. Curiously, it is their ability to plow forth in the face of considerable goal ambiguity that allows them to create frame-breaking demand-side innovations and new social artifacts such as new markets and new organizations. Furthermore, this tolerance of goal ambiguity may actually help overcome the problems in early stage equity financing based on information asymmetry, agency, and incomplete contracts.

This "effectual" view of equity investing takes a position diametrically opposed to that of "causal" agency theories. Causal theories cast entrepreneurs and angels as two sides of an adversarial relationship, where each is trying to out-guess the other in terms of what each brings to the table and what each (really) wants. Effectuation instead posits both as partners seeking to construct new possibilities in a world where neither can predict what the future will be, and both strive for as long as feasible to remain untethered to specific goals to be achieved in that future. In this view, agents do not come with *a priori* well-ordered preferences. In fact each stakeholder remains tentative in many relevant preferences that may need to be traded off in making an acceptable future happen. In other words, angels and entrepreneurs negotiate, not for pieces of the predicted future pie, but for what the pie can possibly be, given what each is willing to commit to the enterprise in the face of Knightian uncertainty (Knight, 1921). Therefore, they undertake the venture together as principals, not as principal and agent, a fact that is evidenced also by the extraordinary emphasis that angels explicitly place upon entrepreneurial human capital, while they tend to under-weight or even ignore other predictive elements of the actual business proposal. Once they are satisfied with the potential of the entre-preneurial team, they base their investment decisions not on expected return, but on affordable loss, and their strategies seek to leverage positive contingencies, rather than to avoid negative ones.

CONCLUSION

Whether current theories suggesting the overwhelming implausibility or even impossibility of "rational" early stage equity financing are more useful than the new "effectual" perspective that endorses the wisdom of specific principles of decision-making that embrace both environmental uncertainties and motivational ambiguities, is at present an open question. In the meantime, however, it is very clear that business angels constitute a fascinating unexplored landscape – a phenomenon of high practical importance and intriguing intellectual potential – for future researchers.

Notes

1 Estimate by the Center for Venture Research at the University of New Hampshire.
2 Estimate by *Venture Economics* and the National Venture Capital Association.

Bibliography

Amis, D. and Stevenson, H. (2001). *Winning Angels: The Seven Fundamentals of Early Stage Investing*. Harlow: Pearson Educational.

Amit, R., Glosten, L., and Muller, E. (1990). Entrepreneurial ability, venture investments, and risksharing. *Management Science*, 36: 1232–45.

Anand, B. N. and Galetovic, A. (2000). Information, non-excludability, and financial market structure. *Journal of Business*, 73 (3): 357–402.

Berger, A. N. and Udell, G. F. (1998). The economics of small business finance: The roles of private equity and debt markets in the financial growth cycle. *Journal of Banking and Finance*, 22: 613–73.

Dew, N. (2002). Lipsticks and razorblades: How the Auto-ID Center used pre-commitments to build the "Internet of Things." Unpublished dissertation, University of Virginia.

Feeney, L., Haines, G. H., and Riding, A. L. (1999). Private investors' investment criteria: Insights from qualitative data. *Venture Capital: International Journal of Entrepreneurial Finance*, 1: 121–45.

Freear, J., Sohl, J. E., and Wetzel, W. E., Jr. (1995). Angels: Personal investors in the venture capital market. *Entrepreneurship and Regional Development*, 7: 85–94.

Gupta, A. K. and Sapienza, H. J. (1992). Determinants of venture capital firms' preferences regarding the industry diversity and geographic scope of their investments. *Journal of Business Venturing*, 7: 347–62.

Hart, O. (2001). Financial contracting. *Journal of Economic Literature*, 39 (4): 1079–100.

Knight, F. H. (1921). *Risk, Uncertainty and Profit*. Cambridge, MA: Riverside Press.

Mason, C. M. and Harrison, R. T. (2002). Is it worth it? The rates of return from informal venture capital investments. *Journal of Business Venturing*, 17: 211–36.

Murray, G. (1999). Seed capital funds and the effect of scale economies. *Venture Capital: International Journal of Entrepreneurial Finance*, 1: 351–84.

Prasad, D., Bruton, G. D., and Vozikis, G. (2000). Signaling value to business angels: The proportion of the entrepreneur's net worth invested in a new venture as a decision signal. *Venture Capital: International Journal of Entrepreneurial Finance*, 2: 167–82.

Prowse, S. (1998). Angel investors and the market for angel investments. *Journal of Banking and Finance*, 22: 785–92.

Sarasvathy, S. D. (2001a). Causation and effectuation: Toward a theoretical shift from economic inevitability to entrepreneurial contingency. *Academy of Management Review*, 26: 243–63.

Sarasvathy, S. D. (2001b). Effectual reasoning in entrepreneurial decision-making: Existence and bounds. Best paper proceedings, Academy of Management. Washington, DC, August 3–8.

Shepherd, D. A., Douglas, E. J., and Shanley, M. (2000). New venture survival: Ignorance, external shock, and risk reduction strategies. *Journal of Business Venturing*, 15: 393–410.

Triantis, G. G. (2001). Financial contract design in the world of venture capital. *University of Chicago Law Review*, 68: 305–22.

business model

Christoph Zott and Raphael Amit

INTRODUCTION

What is a business model? While the term "business model" has become prevalent in the entrepreneurship and management literatures, there is a divergence of views among scholars and practitioners as to its meaning. The concept of the business model first appeared in the ABI Inform database in 1975. Between 1975 and

1994, there were 166 articles that cited the term, while 1,563 articles referred to it in the period 1995–2000 (Ghaziani and Ventresca, 2002). In some applications, the concept of the business model is invoked in the context of value capture, answering such questions as: How does the venture make money? In other contexts, the term is used to describe value creation, answering such questions as: How does the firm conduct business with its stakeholders?

This article seeks to show that the design of the business model is central to the entrepreneurship domain. We review the main scholarly work on business models, and provide clarity on the construct and its relation to value creation and value capture. Our main conclusion is that one can think of a business model as a template for how a firm designs and conducts economic exchanges across its boundaries, to link resource and product markets in the quest for wealth creation.

Wealth creation is one of the central functions of entrepreneurship (Knight, 1921). The perspective of the business model promises to further our understanding of wealth creation by pointing to the design of economic exchanges as a potential locus of innovation. The perspective portrays the entrepreneur as the architect of the business system, and as a creative designer (and, potentially, innovator) of economic exchanges, which complements received notions of entrepreneurs as product and process innovators.

In designing their business models, entrepreneurs throughout the world have been able to leverage recent advances in information and communication technologies. This has contributed to a shift in the locus of competitive advantage from the new venture and its internal stakeholders (e.g., management, shareholders, employees) to its ecosystem, which includes external stakeholders such as partners, vendors, and customers. Indeed, advances in digital technologies have opened up new opportunities for the design of boundary-spanning exchange relationships among firms, partners, and customers. As a result, business models have become a possible source of value creation.

LITERATURE REVIEW

At this early stage in the development of the business model perspective, a dominant view

has not yet emerged, as different conceptualizations of the business model emphasize various aspects of wealth creation. Broadly speaking, some concepts center on value creation, while others focus more on value appropriation through, for example, revenue generation. Some authors propose a more encompassing definition of the term, embracing aspects of both value creation and appropriation.

Based on the observation that no single entrepreneurship or strategic management theory can fully explain the value creation potential of highly interconnected firms, Amit and Zott (2001) conceptualize the business model as a unit of analysis that captures the value creation potential arising from the design of transactions between a focal firm and external stakeholders such as partners, vendors, and customers. The business model spans firm and industry boundaries. This perspective integrates the theoretical views of the value chain framework (Porter, 1985), Schumpeter's theory of creative destruction (Schumpeter, 1942), the resource-based view of the firm (Amit and Schoemaker, 1993), strategic network theory (Gulati, 1998), and transaction cost economics (Williamson, 1975). The sources of value creation suggested by these theories refer to factors that enhance the total value created in transactions (Brandenburger and Stuart, 1996), and which give rise to four distinct themes (novelty, efficiency, complementarities, and lock-in) that can be used to describe and measure business model design (Zott and Amit, 2003).

Building on the value creation perspective, Magretta (2002: 87) conceptualizes business models as "stories that explain how enterprises work" and that center on a value-creating insight. The main questions a business model answers are: Who is the customer? What does the customer value? What is the underlying logic that explains how a firm can deliver value to customers at an appropriate cost? According to this view, the business model is distinct from strategy, because it describes how a firm does business, while strategy describes how the firm deals with competition (see Zott and Amit, 2003).

Other researchers suggest that the business model refers more to questions about value appropriation. Eisenmann, for example, views the business model as "a hypothesis about how a company will make money over the long term: what the company will sell, and to whom; how the company will collect revenue; what technologies it will employ; when it will rely on partners; and, following from the last two points, how its costs will 'scale' with growth" (2002: xii). (Amit and Zott, 2001, denote some of these characteristics as the revenue model, which "refers to the specific modes in which a business model enables revenue generation.") Applying this conceptualization to e-businesses, Eisenmann presents and analyzes eight generic types of business models: access providers, portals, content providers, retailers, brokers, market makers, networked utility providers, and application service providers.

Combining both value creation and value appropriation perspectives, Afuah and Tucci (2000), as well as Chesbrough and Rosenbloom (2002), propose more encompassing views of the business model. Afuah and Tucci suggest: "A business model can be conceptualized as a system that is made up of components, linkages between the components, and dynamics" (2000: 4). The components of the business model are customer value, customer segments, scope of products and services, pricing, revenue sources, connected activities, implementation, capabilities, and sustainability. In a similar vein, building on the technology management literature, Chesbrough and Rosenbloom (2002: 533–4) present the business model as a construct that mediates between technological inputs and economic outputs. The functions of a business model are to (1) articulate the value proposition; (2) identify a market segment, as well as the revenue generation mechanism for the firm; (3) define the structure of the value chain; (4) estimate cost structure and profit potential; (5) describe the position of the firm within the network linking suppliers, customers, complementors, and competitors; and (6) formulate a competitive strategy.

The various approaches offered in the academic literature are a clear indication that research on business models could be advanced by a convergence of the field to a common understanding of the construct. Promising ideas that could serve as catalysts for such a convergence might be the notions of inter-organizational

architecture (Mendelson, 2000) and design (Hargadorn and Yellowlees, 2001; Romme, 2003; Zott and Amit, 2003). Mendelson maintains that the performance of the firm depends on the "architecture of the entire business network" (2000: 519). Examining how entrepreneurs market innovations, Hargadorn and Yellowlees point to the central role of the design of the business system, which is centered on "a particular set of understandings and interactions" (2001: 494) between different stakeholders, such as the firm and its customers. Romme (2003) notes that the purpose of design is to produce systems that do not yet exist, and Zott and Amit (2003) show how the design of the business model is central to wealth creation through entrepreneurship. Next, we elaborate in more detail on one theoretically rigorous conceptualization of the business model which is consistent with these ideas, and which has proven useful for empirical analysis.

OUR CONCEPTUALIZATION

Consistent with the theoretical development in Amit and Zott (2001), the business model can be defined as depicting the content, structure, and governance of transactions designed to create value through the exploitation of business opportunities. Transaction content refers to the goods or information that are being exchanged, and to the resources and capabilities that are required to enable the exchange. Transaction structure refers to the parties that participate in the exchange, and to the ways in which these parties are linked (including the sequencing of exchanges, and the adopted exchange mechanisms). Transaction governance refers to the ways in which relevant parties control the flows of information, resources, and goods (including the legal form of organization, and the incentives for exchange participants).

This conceptualization of a business model encompasses transaction efficiency (emphasized by TCE; see Williamson, 1975), novelty in transaction content, structure, and governance (Schumpeterian innovation; see Schumpeter, 1996), complementarities among resources and capabilities (advocated by RBV; see Amit and Schoemaker, 1993), and network effects (inherent in strategic networks; see Gulati, 1998). It also integrates important entrepreneurship and strategy theories, and thus potentially heightens our understanding of the complex processes and mechanics that drive wealth creation (Hitt et al., 2001).

The proposed construct is parsimonious, distinct from competitive business-level strategy, and it can be operationalized and measured. Zott and Amit (2003), for example, develop and test hypotheses about the impact of business model design on wealth creation by entrepreneurial firms. Their content analysis of firms' IPO prospectuses shows that novelty-centered business model design matters most to the equity value created by these firms. It also points to a potential differential impact of business model design themes under varying resource munificence regimes, and to potential diseconomies of scope in design. Thus, the business model holds promise for advancing entrepreneurship research, both theoretically and empirically.

RESEARCH OPPORTUNITIES

Research on business models, then, could benefit from a convergence of the field to a common understanding of the construct, through both theory development and empirical research. Consensus on the theoretical foundation and fundamental properties could lead to the emergence of broadly accepted typologies of business models, which are currently lacking. Further research on the relationship between the business and revenue models of firms is needed to extend both theory and practice. Such research will help deepen our understanding of the linkages between value creation and value appropriation. Empirical research on the measurement of business model design, structured to capture all lines of a firm's business that have revenue potential, holds great promise to enhance our understanding of business models. Examining the dynamics of business model evolution, how they emerge, and how they are shaped and adapted over time, as well as how business models co-evolve with strategy and organization design, reflects an important research program that will substantially solidify the business model as a unit of analysis that is pivotal to our understanding of wealth creation.

In summary, we are at the very beginning of a long journey to identifying and evaluating a new level of analysis for entrepreneurial firms. Theoretical, empirical, and field research on the foundations and evolutions of business models promises to broaden our understanding of wealth creation through entrepreneurship.

Bibliography

Afuah, A. and Tucci, C. L. (2000). *Internet Business Models and Strategies: Text and Cases.* New York: Irwin/McGraw-Hill.

Amit, R. and Schoemaker, P. (1993). Strategic assets and organizational rent. *Strategic Management Journal*, 14: 33–46.

Amit, R. and Zott, C. (2001). Value creation in e-business. *Strategic Management Journal*, 22: 493–520.

Brandenburger, A. M. and Stuart, H. (1996). Value-based business strategy. *Journal of Economics and Management Strategy*, 5: 5–25.

Chesbrough, H. and Rosenbloom, R. (2002). The role of the business model in capturing value from innovation: Evidence from Xerox Corporation's technology spinoff companies. *Industrial and Corporate Change*, 11: 529–55.

Eisenmann, T. R. (2002). *Internet Business Models.* New York: Irwin/McGraw-Hill.

Ghaziani, A. and Ventresca, M. J. (2002). Discursive fields, boundary objects, and the categorical structuring of discourse: Evidence from frame analysis of business model public talk, 1975–2000. Working Paper, Northwestern University, April.

Gulati, R. (1998). Alliances and networks. *Strategic Management Journal*, 19: 293–317.

Hargadorn, A. B. and Yellowlees, D. (2001). When innovations meet institutions: Edison and the design of the electric light. *Administrative Science Quarterly*, 46: 476–501.

Hitt, M. A., Ireland, R. D., Camp, S. M., and Sexton, D. L. (2001). Strategic entrepreneurship: Entrepreneurial strategies for wealth creation. *Strategic Management Journal*, 22: 479–91.

Knight, F. H. (1921). *Risk, Uncertainty and Profit.* Cambridge, MA: Riverside Press.

Magretta, J. (2002). Why business models matter. *Harvard Business Review*, May: 86–92.

Mendelson, H. (2000). Organizational architecture and success in the information technology industry. *Management Science*, 46: 513–29.

Porter, M. E. (1985). *Competitive Advantage: Creating and Sustaining Superior Performance.* New York: Free Press.

Romme, A. G. L. (2003). Making a difference: Organization as design. *Organization Science*, 14: 558–73.

Schumpeter, J. A. (1942). *Capitalism, Socialism, and Democracy.* New York: Harper.

24 business plan

Schumpeter, J. A. (1996) [1934]. *The Theory of Economic Development: An Inquiry Into Profits, Capital, Credit, Interest, and the Business Cycle.* Cambridge, MA: Harvard University Press.

Williamson, O. E. (1975). *Markets and Hierarchies: Analysis and Antitrust Implications.* New York: Free Press.

Zott, C. and Amit, R. (2003). Business model design and the performance of entrepreneurial firms. INSEAD Working Paper 2003/94/ENT/SM/ACGRD 4.

business plan

Donald F. Kuratko

A business plan is a written document that details a proposed venture. It must illustrate the current status, expected needs, and projected results of the new business (Fry and Stoner, 1985). Every aspect of the venture should be described: the project, marketing, research and development, manufacturing, management, critical risks, financing, and milestones or timetable. A description of all these facets of the proposed venture is necessary to give a clear picture of the venture, its intended direction, and the actions to be taken to reach its goals. Thus, the business plan represents the entrepreneur's roadmap for a successful enterprise (Kuratko and Cirtin, 1990).

The business plan is also called a venture plan, a loan proposal, or investment prospectus. Whatever its name, this document is initially required by any financial source. Although it may be utilized as a working document once the venture is established, the business plan's major purpose is to encapsulate strategic developments of the project in a comprehensive document for scrutiny by outside investors.

The business plan describes to potential investors and financial sources all of the events that may affect the proposed venture, including its projected actions and their associated revenues and costs. It is vital to explicitly state the assumptions on which the plan is being based. For example, changes in the economy or the venture's target market(s) during the start-up period should be indicated. Successful launching of the venture is what the plan should emphasize. In other words, it is not just the writing of an effective plan that is important, but also the

translation of that plan into a successful enterprise (Perry, 2001). Thus, a business plan should:

- describe every aspect of a particular business;
- include a marketing plan;
- clarify and outline financial needs;
- identify potential obstacles and alternative solutions;
- serve as a communication tool for all financial and professional sources.

The business plan is the major tool used to guide the venture's formation as well as the primary document needed to manage it. It is also more than a written document: it is an ongoing process that begins when the entrepreneur gathers information and then continues as projections are made, implemented, measured, and updated.

BENEFITS OF A BUSINESS PLAN

The entire business planning process forces an entrepreneur to analyze all aspects of the venture and prepare effective strategies to deal with unexpected uncertainties. Thus, a business plan may help an entrepreneur avoid failure. The benefits derived from a business plan for both the entrepreneur and the financial source that will evaluate it include the following.

Financing. Venture capitalists and most banks require business plans. Generally, when the national economy declines, it becomes more difficult to obtain financing, and financiers increase their demands for documentation.

Increased knowledge. For many entrepreneurs, the process of actually putting the plan together is just as important as obtaining financing. Writing the plan forces them to review the business critically, objectively, and thoroughly.

Preventing poor investments. Business plans help entrepreneurs avoid projects that are poor investments. It is better not to begin a project that is destined to fail.

Planning. Business plans force planning. Because all aspects of the venture must be addressed in the plan, the entrepreneur develops and examines operating strategies and their expected results. Goals and objectives are quantified so that forecasts can be compared with actual results, facilitating the making of appropriate adjustments (Kuratko, 1991).

Entrepreneurs who prepare all or most of the business plan themselves tend to benefit the most, while those who delegate this job tend to gain the least. If an entrepreneurial team is involved in planning, all key members should help write the plan, although it is important that the lead entrepreneur understand each member's contribution. If consultants are sought to help prepare a business plan, the entrepreneur must remain the driving force behind the process. Seeking the advice and assistance of outside professionals is always wise, but owners need to understand every aspect of the business plan because they, not the consultants, will be scrutinized by financial sources. Thus, the business plan stands as the entrepreneur's description and prediction for the venture.

DEVELOPING A WELL-CONCEIVED BUSINESS PLAN

Most investors agree that only a well-conceived business plan garners the support that results in financing. The business plan should enthusiastically (yet accurately) describe the new venture. A brief description of the ten components of a business plan is presented next (Kuratko and Hodgetts, 2004). See Table 1 for a complete outline.

Table 1 Outline of a business plan for entrepreneurial ventures

Section I: Executive summary

Section II: Description of the business
A General description of the business
B Industry background
C Company history or background
D Goals and potential of the business and milestones (if any)
E Uniqueness of product or service

Section III: Marketing segment
A Research and analysis
  1 Target market (customers) identified
  2 Market size and trends
  3 Competition
  4 Estimated market share

B Marketing plan
  1 Market strategy: sales and distribution
  2 Pricing
  3 Advertising and promotions

Section IV: Operations segment
A Research and design results (if applicable)
B Development costs
C Identify location
  1 Advantages
  2 Zoning
  3 Taxes
D Proximity to supplies/transportation

Section V: Management segment
A Management team: key personnel
B Legal structure: stock agreements, employment agreements, ownership, etc.
C Board of directors, advisors, consultants, etc.

Section VI: Financial segment
A Financial forecast
  1 Profit and loss
  2 Cash flow
  3 Breakeven analysis
  4 Cost controls
  5 Budgeting plans

Section VII: Critical risks segment
A Potential problems
B Obstacles and risks
C Alternative courses of action

Section VIII: Harvest strategy segment
A Transfer of assets
B Continuity of business strategy
C Identify successor

Section IX: Milestone schedule
A Timing and objectives
B Deadlines and milestones
C Relationship of events

Section X: Appendix

Source: Kuratko, Montagno, and Sabatine (2002)

COMPONENTS

Executive summary. The executive summary is the most important section because it must convince readers that the business will succeed. In three pages or less, the plan's highlights should be summarized. Because investors who review many business plans may read only the executive summary, it must stand on its own. Executive summaries failing to attract the investor's attention often lead to non-acceptance of the business plan. Because this section summarizes the plan, it is often best to write it last.

Description of the business.   This section should provide background information about the industry, the venture's history, and a general description of the new product or service's unique qualities and value to consumers.

Marketing segment.   This section has two major parts. The first part is the research and analysis section in which the entrepreneur discusses the target customer/market in terms of size and anticipated trends and projects sales revenue. Additionally, competitors are identified and examined in terms of their strengths and weaknesses and the competitive advantage of the proposed venture relative to competitors is specified.

The second part is a *marketing plan.* This section details a marketing strategy in terms of sales, distribution, pricing, advertising, promotion, and public awareness. The primary purpose of this material is to highlight how the marketing plan will support the venture's competitive advantage(s).

Operations segment.   This section includes *developmental research* leading to the design of the product (good or service), as well as the costs associated with these activities. This section should also describe the advantages of the proposed venture's location in terms of zoning, tax laws, wage rates, labor availability, and proximity to suppliers and transportation systems. Anticipated expenses for facilities and equipment are also specified in this section.

Management segment.   Here, the entrepreneur describes the venture's *management team*, its unique qualifications, and plans for their compensation (including salaries, employment agreements, stock purchase plans, levels of ownership, and other considerations). In addition to presenting the venture's legal and organizational structures, the potential contribution of the board of directors, advisors, and consultants are described in this section.

Financial segment.   Commonly covering a three-year period, three key financial statements are presented in this section: a *balance sheet*, an *income statement*, and a *cash flow statement*. Preparing these documents allows the entrepreneur to specify the stages at which the venture will require external financing and identify the expected financing sources (both debt and equity). In addition, the expected return on investment is highlighted, as well as the revenue and cost structures necessary to earn the projected return. These statements serve as a standard to measure actual operating results and become a valuable tool for managing and controlling the venture in its first few years.

Critical risks segment.   Here, entrepreneurs identify the venture's *potential risks* as well as approaches to deal with them. Strong pricing tactics by competitors, potentially unfavorable industry-wide trends, design or manufacturing costs that exceed estimates, failure to meet sales projections, production delays, difficulties or long lead times in procuring parts or raw materials, and greater-than-expected innovation and development costs are examples of risks entrepreneurs may encounter. The objective of this section is anticipation and control of risks.

Harvest strategy segment.   It is important for entrepreneurs to plan the orderly transition of the venture. Thus, this section deals with change management issues such as the orderly transfer of the company assets if ownership of the business changes, continuity of the business strategy during such a transition, and the designation of key individuals to run the business if the current management team changes. With foresight, entrepreneurs keep their dreams alive, ensure the security of their investors, and usually strengthen their businesses in the process.

Milestone schedule.   Here, the entrepreneur specifies batches of tasks that are to be completed within certain time lines. A network of the activities associated with the venture's launching and subsequent actions results from a careful and tightly integrated set of milestones.

Appendix.   This section presents important background information that was not included in other sections. It should include such items as resumes of the management team, names of references and advisors, drawings, documents, agreements, and sources from which information was gathered.

Bibliography

Fry, F. L. and Stoner, C. R. (1985). Business plans: Two major types. *Journal of Small Business Management*, 1–6.

Kuratko, D. F. (1991). Demystifying the business plan process: An introductory guide. *Small Business Forum*, 33–40.

Kuratko, D. F. and Cirtin, A. (1990). Developing a business plan for your clients. *National Public Accountant*, 24–8.

Kuratko, D. F. and Hodgetts, R. M. (2004). *Entrepreneurship: Theory, Process, Practice*, 6th edn. Mason, OH: Thomson South-Western Publishing, 304–13.

Kuratko, D. F., Montagno, R. V., and Sabatine, F. J. (2002). *The Entrepreneurial Decision*. Muncie, IN: Midwest Entrepreneurial Education Center, College of Business, Ball State University.

Perry, S. C. (2001). The relationship between written business plans and the failure of small businesses in the US. *Journal of Small Business Management*, 39 (3): 201–8.

C

championing corporate venturing

Shaker A. Zahra

Corporate venturing (CV) is the process by which an organization enters a new market, either domestically or internationally. This process can be undertaken internally or externally. Internal CV refers to those formal and informal activities that foster new business creation within an organization. External CV focuses on those activities that enable the firm to gain access to new business fields through acquisitions and alliances. Internal and external CV activities often take the organization into fields in which it typically does not have extensive skills or competencies. Developing these competencies requires patient investments in building the organizational infrastructure and complementary assets. It also requires building and expanding the firm's absorptive capacity that allows it to spot, identify, acquire, and assimilate new knowledge. These activities entail considerable risks for the firm, a factor that can make executives reluctant to support CV. Therefore, champions are needed to spur CV efforts and build momentum for them among senior executives (Sathe, 2003).

Champions are individuals who recognize the importance of an idea for organizational success and then expend their energy and political capital to refine this idea, make it visible to management, and ensure that the CV idea is considered and fairly evaluated (Schon, 1963). Champions undertake these activities because they believe in an idea or see its potential value for the company. Many of these champions do so voluntarily and, oftentimes, take important career risks in pursuit of CV ideas. Backing projects that have little strategic merit or that fail to gain the support of senior management might damage the reputation of the champion.

ROLES CV CHAMPIONS PLAY

Research suggests that different champions play different but complementary roles in positioning and promoting CV initiatives (Shane, 1994). Early in the CV process, a champion may work to revise an idea to match an important challenge facing the organization or ensure that the opportunity associated with the initiative is relevant to the firm. Once this is accomplished, another champion may dedicate their energies to make senior executives aware of the strategic implications of the opportunity. Toward this end, the champion may explore ways to test the idea and conduct market analyses that will show the magnitude of the opportunity implied in the initiative. A champion may also work to develop awareness of the idea among colleagues, setting the stage for gaining the political support needed for the project to flourish. The champion may use their position to gain access to senior executives and formally or informally draw their attention to the merits of considering and evaluating ideas.

Some champions opt to work within the system and do so diligently to make their organization receptive to radical CV ideas. These champions excel in building and using their social capital to garner and maintain support for their ideas. They build bridges and networks across organizational boundaries and gain the trust and support of others. However, other champions may find it essential to challenge the prevailing culture and existing systems to bring about change that favors CV. These renegade champions have an important role to play in promoting strategic change, especially when the proposed CV initiative represents a radical shift in the organizational mindset (Shane, Venkataraman, and MacMillan, 1995).

Renegade champions often put their careers and reputations on the line, risking counter-attacks by existing units and others in the organization who disagree with or fear the proposed change.

ESSENTIAL CHAMPIONING SKILLS

Champions need different skills in order to succeed in promoting CV initiatives. They need to envision the firm's future and the changes that are likely to occur in their firm's competencies should CV initiatives receive approval. This capability, in turn, requires an understanding of the firm's strategy, markets, and capabilities. Champions need also to understand how CV initiatives may influence different organizational units quite differently and how to work around these issues. The resource implications of pursuing new initiatives are also another area of great importance for CV champions, who not only have to consider the resources needed but also the sources from which these resources can be obtained.

Building momentum for the CV idea also requires social intelligence, meaning the ability to understand the motives and priorities of different actors throughout the organization. This social intelligence is an important component of the social capital champions develop and use to gain support for their entrepreneurial initiatives. Champions have to create support for CV projects and neutralize opposition throughout the organization. Social intelligence is also important for choosing the right approach to draw the attention of senior managers to gain their confidence and support. The champions' timing is influenced by their social intelligence when approaching senior executives with the idea for the CV project.

THE DARK SIDE OF CHAMPIONING

Though championing behavior is essential for the success of entrepreneurial activities within a company, it has serious organizational costs. Renegade champions, for example, can create serious tensions throughout the organization and these tensions can escalate into dysfunctional conflicts and hostility between units. Such conflicts can stifle, rather than promote, cooperation and the flow of information necessary for CV ideas to take hold in the firm. These conflicts are often exacerbated by re-

negade champions' dispositions to go around the existing systems, undermining managers' existing power bases. Some champions also work to neutralize opposition to their ideas, creating acrimony and distrust. Further, to prove the worthiness of their ideas, some champions may siphon resources away from ongoing operations to support their proposed CV projects, creating serious misalignments between existing goals and resource allocations.

Finally, some champions do not know when to let go of a successful CV idea. While champions may excel in positioning and promoting an idea, they may lack the managerial skills needed to manage the new business that is sanctioned by the firm. When this occurs, some champions are unable to distance themselves from their idea and let other and perhaps more capable managers assume leadership of the new units. This urge to remain in control can undermine champions' credibility and ability to have any influence in the new venture's operations.

NURTURING CHAMPIONS

The role champions play in fostering innovation and promoting receptivity to CV projects suggests a need for senior executives to develop a strategy that will encourage these individuals to lead strategic change. Many of these champions are middle managers who are well positioned to understand the changing dynamics of competition and shifting customer expectations. Middle managers serve at the nexus of information flows at a central position in their firms, making it possible for them to spot promising opportunities and innovative ideas. Given their access to important resources and information, middle managers are uniquely positioned to champion new initiatives in their companies. Therefore, sharing the firm's vision with middle managers is an important initial step towards encouraging championing behavior. Empowering these managers to support experimental CV activities is also essential. The use of seed funds that allow champions to explore innovative CV ideas is one useful approach. Tying formal CV programs, if they exist, to informal championing behavior is another important step in creating the context that encourages exploration and implementation of CV efforts. This link is an important framework within which to assess CV efforts.

Providing incentives to support champions' hard work to encourage CV projects is also important. Likewise, punitive and retaliatory actions by established power centers should be reduced. Finally, given that CV activities are complex and require considerable patient investments, it would be useful to capture the experiences, skills, and competencies of successful champions. Similarly, it is useful to examine the experiences of unsuccessful champions and identify lessons to be learned from these experiences.

Bibliography

Sathe, V. (2003). *Corporate Entrepreneurship: Top Managers and New Business Creation.* Cambridge: Cambridge University Press.

Schon, D. A. (1963). Champions of radical new inventions. *Harvard Business Review*, 41 (2): 77–86.

Shane, S. A. (1994). Are champions different from non-champions? *Journal of Business Venturing*, 9: 397–421.

Shane, S. A., Venkataraman, S., and MacMillan, I. C. (1995). Cultural differences in innovation championing strategies. *Journal of Management*, 21: 931–52.

Chinese entrepreneurship: today and tomorrow

Garry D. Bruton and David Ahlstrom

The People's Republic of China is one of the fastest growing economies in the world, with a growth rate in terms of GDP that has exceeded 7 percent annually for over two decades. China now has the world's seventh largest economy, behind the United States, Japan, and several Western European countries. On a purchasing-power parity basis, China is thought to have the second highest country GDP, only behind the United States (Central Intelligence Agency, 2003). The growth in China has come in large measure from foreign direct investment by firms from the developed economies of Asia and the West, as they financed businesses to produce products for export. Additionally, much growth has also been promoted by reform in the state-owned sector, such as the conversion of commune-brigade organizations into township and village enterprises and private companies upon the initiation of economic liberalization in the late 1970s (Naughton, 1995).

Today, however, recently founded private enterprises are an increasingly important part of economic development in China. It is estimated that there are now over a million such enterprises (Xinhua News Agency, 1998). These enterprises initially developed illegally, since citizens' right to own private property in China was not formally recognized until 2000. However, in 2002, private entrepreneurs had attained such status that they were invited to join the Chinese Communist Party for the first time.

While entrepreneurs and private enterprises have both increased in number in recent years, the investigation of entrepreneurs in China has remained largely anecdotal. The existing research literature can be viewed along four dimensions: the broad environment in China for entrepreneurs; entrepreneur orientation; entrepreneurial strategies; and the financing of entrepreneurial firms and venture capital. We briefly review each of these research streams in this article, before offering an agenda for future research in this domain.

BROAD ENVIRONMENT

There have been limited efforts to discuss the broad environment for entrepreneurs in China. These efforts include the initial investigation of entrepreneurship in China. Specifically, Tsang (1994, 1995) provided the groundwork for investigation of the domain by highlighting the existence of entrepreneurs in China despite the fact they were technically still not legal at that time. These initial investigations helped to draw attention to the unique and influential institutional environment facing entrepreneurs in China (Peng and Heath, 1996). Chow and Fung (1996) extended this earlier work by generating additional detail about private entrepreneurs. However, again, their study principally provided insight into the nature of the individuals who were entrepreneurs and their backgrounds. More recently, researchers have investigated the institutional environment and its effect on entrepreneurship in China (Peng, 2000, 2001; Ahlstrom and Bruton, 2001). Institutional theory introduces a broad range of variables to explain how the institutional environment affects organizations (Powell and DiMaggio, 1991). Institutions in a country also fundamentally influence how organizations evolve and which ones come into existence (North, 1990).

ENTREPRENEURIAL ORIENTATION

Another widely examined topic within the entrepreneurship domain in China is the orientation of entrepreneurs in that country. The three principal articles that have examined the orientations of Chinese entrepreneurs have focused on how these entrepreneurs personally approach China's unique institutional environment. Some evidence suggests that there are a few similarities between entrepreneurs in mature economies and those in China. For example, Lau and Busentiz (2001) found that the entrepreneur's commitment, need for achievement, and the nature of the social environment affected the entrepreneur's orientation toward firm growth. They found that the relative importance of these factors may be different from that of mature economies, but the focus on growth by private firms in China was the same as in mature economies.

Other researchers found some similarities, but also began to identify differences. For example, Holt (1997) pointed out that the Confucian philosophy so common in China resulted in differences in entrepreneurial behavior, such as giving greater weight to tradition. Tan (2001) continued with this perspective by highlighting that risk taking among Chinese entrepreneurs was lower than among entrepreneurs from the West. The negative view of failure in Confucian philosophy is substantial and likely contributed to this risk aversion. Tan, Luo, and Zhang's (1998) results supported the view that entrepreneurial strategies in China typically reflect this lower risk-taking orientation.

ENTREPRENEURIAL STRATEGIES

A large number of articles have focused on the actual strategies that entrepreneurial firms in China have used in the pursuit of commercial success. The distinguishing factor here is that the institutional setting in China results in unique strategies that may not have companion strategies in more developed economies. For example, in mature economies, start-up firms and new industries must generate an acceptance or legitimacy among those with whom they deal. Tsang (1996) points out that many private firms

in China generate legitimacy for themselves in ways that do not occur in the West. For example, such entrepreneurial firms often have to hide the fact they are private firms by associating themselves with government entities through various methods.

The absence of resources such as financing for expansion, managerial talent, and information about the market in a transitional economy such as China also leads to unique strategies (e.g., networking) to generate needed resources. Both Peng (2001) and Zhao and Aram (1995) highlight the benefit to entrepreneurial ventures in generating resources by networking with other firms and key individuals in the environment. Recent research has also examined how private firms in China can actively manage the institutional environment to build legitimacy and better secure their position (Ahlstrom and Bruton, 2001).

ENTREPRENEURIAL FINANCING

A small body of literature is beginning to examine the financing of private ventures in China. The financing of new ventures is known to be critical to their success. However, in an environment where there is no (or a very limited) legitimacy for private entrepreneurs and no institutions that may lead to the financing of such ventures, the question of resource acquisition is critical. Chow and Fung (2000) detail some of the initial liquidity constraints that face private entrepreneurs. Bruton and colleagues (Bruton et al., 1999; Ahlstrom, Bruton, and Chan, 2000; Bruton and Ahlstrom, 2003) examined the development and practice of venture capital in China. They found that while there is a nascent venture capital industry in China, the industry there is closer to what is called private equity in the United States and actually provides little financing to start-up firms. China's venture capital industry funds buyouts and provides mezzanine financing to expanding businesses and infrastructure projects.

FUTURE RESEARCH NEEDS

As highlighted by our discussion of financing, the existing research evidence about entrepreneurship in China points to a range of issues that are not always relevant to entrepreneurial success. Thus, future research should examine how entrepreneurs actually start their firms in China. The sources of funds are very different – some would say more varied. How do entrepreneurs get started and how do they sustain growth in the absence of an extensive venture capital industry, but in the presence of financing from a number of non-traditional sources such as government bureaus and state-owned enterprises? Also, the growth stage of Chinese entrepreneurial firms can be very different. Entrepreneurs in China are often reticent to grow; they often prefer to shift money out of the firm and store it safely (and out of sight). How do they maintain reasonable firm growth while balancing this perceived need to conceal their success to some extent? What is the relationship with the central government and local governments? At a higher level of analysis, why do entrepreneurs in China often exhibit the need to conceal their (and their firms') success? How do entrepreneurs minimize interference from the many potential "mother-in-law" organizations that are able to extract resources from the firm (Ahlstrom, Bruton, and Lui, 2000)? What are the exit options available to entrepreneurs in China? Equity markets are still not as open and liquid as those in the US. How do entrepreneurs make money (i.e., generate returns) in such markets? Should entrepreneurs in China go overseas for financing and a listing? If so, what are the implications of this, given the legal regulations in China, and how do entrepreneurs manage this apparent balancing act?

Bibliography

Ahlstrom, D. and Bruton, G. (2001). Learning from successful local private firms in China: Establishing legitimacy. *Academy of Management Executive*, 15 (4): 72–83.

Ahlstrom, D., Bruton, G., and Chan, E. S. (2000). Venture capital in China: Ground-level challenges for high technology investing. *Journal of Private Equity*, 3 (2): 1–10.

Ahlstrom, D., Bruton, G., and Lui, S. (2000). Navigating China's changing economy: Strategies for private firms. *Business Horizons*, 43 (1): 5–15.

Bruton, G. and Ahlstrom, D. (2003). An institutional view of China's venture capital industry: Explaining the difference between China and the West. *Journal of Business Venturing*, 18: 233–59.

Bruton, G., Dattani, M., Fung, M., Chow, C., and Ahlstrom, D. (1999). Private equity in China: Differences and similarities with the Western model. *Journal of Private Equity*, 2 (2): 7–14.

Central Intelligence Agency (2003). *The World Factbook 2003*. Washington, DC: Central Intelligence Agency.

Chow, C. K. W. and Fung, M. K. Y. (1996). Firm dynamics and industrialization in the Chinese economy in transition: Implications for small business policy. *Journal of Business Venturing*, 11: 489–505.

Chow, C. K. W. and Fung, M. K. Y. (2000). Small businesses and liquidity constraints in financing business investment: Evidence from Shanghai's manufacturing sector. *Journal of Business Venturing*, 15: 363–83.

Holt, D. H. (1997). A comparative study of values among Chinese and US entrepreneurs: Pragmatic convergence between contrasting cultures. *Journal of Business Venturing*, 12: 483–505.

Lau, C. M. and Busenitz, L. W. (2001). Growth intentions of entrepreneurs in a transitional economy: The People's Republic of China. *Entrepreneurship: Theory and Practice*, 26 (1): 5–20.

Naughton, B. (1995). *Growing Out of the Plan: Chinese Economic Reform, 1978–1993*. New York: Cambridge University Press.

North D. (1990). *Institutions, Institutional Change and Economic Performance*. New York: Norton.

Peng, M. W. (2000). *Business Strategies in Transition Economies*. Thousand Oaks, CA: Sage.

Peng, M. W. (2001). How entrepreneurs create wealth in transition economies. *Academy of Management Executive*, 15 (1): 95–108.

Peng, M. W. and Heath, P. (1996). The growth of the firm in planned economies in transition: Institutions, organizations, and strategic choice. *Academy of Management Review*, 21: 492–528.

Powell, W. W. and DiMaggio, P. J. (eds.) (1991). *The New Institutionalism in Organizational Analysis*. Chicago: University of Chicago Press.

Tan, J. (2001). Innovation and risk taking in a transitional economy: A comparative study of Chinese managers and entrepreneurs. *Journal of Business Venturing*, 16: 359–76.

Tan, J., Luo, Y., and Zhang, Y. (1998). Comparative strategies under regulatory environment: A study of Chinese private entrepreneurs. *International Journal of Management*, 15 (2): 141–50.

Tsang, E. W. K. (1994). Threats and opportunities faced by private business in China. *Journal of Business Venturing*, 9: 451–69

Tsang, E. W. K. (1995). Ideology, policy, and the private entrepreneurs in China. *Journal of Asian Business*, 10: 1–17.

Tsang, E. W. K. (1996). In search of legitimacy: The private entrepreneur in China. *Entrepreneurship: Theory and Practice*, 21 (9): 21–30.

Xinhua News Agency (1998). China has almost one million private enterprises. *Weekly Economic Report*, 5 August (broadcast – Beijing).

Zhao, L. and Aram, J. D. (1995). Networking and growth of young technology-intensive ventures in China. *Journal of Business Venturing*, 10: 349–70.

cognitive biases and venture formation

Mark Simon

Many possible types of actions might be considered a venture. Consistent with this article's focus on entrepreneurship, it considers those actions that are high in innovation, risk, and proactiveness (Lumpkin and Dess, 1996), including forming a start-up company and introducing a pioneering product.

Many factors, including culture, demographics, and economics, promote the formation of a venture. Several scholars, however, have argued that one must understand the entrepreneur to understand why ventures are formed (e.g., Shaver and Scott, 1991). For instance, why out of hundreds who are laid off will only one person start a venture? Researchers initially addressed this question by examining whether entrepreneurs were more likely than others to have certain personality traits, a direction that has been characterized as a "dead end" by some (e.g., Gartner, 1985). More recent studies have explored the role of entrepreneurial cognitive processes on venture formation (e.g., Krueger, 1993). This approach led to the conclusion that an individual's perceptions regarding the feasibility and desirability of a venture influence the decision to form the venture. This finding, however, does not explain why individuals develop positive perceptions, even though many ventures fail and there is a paucity of reliable information upon which to reach a favorable conclusion.

To address this issue, researchers began conceptually and empirically to explore the relationship between cognitive biases and venture formation. Cognitive biases arise because people's cognitive capacity is limited, so they can neither comprehensively search for, nor accurately interpret, information. They occur when individuals apply a rule of thumb that systematically violates the rules of probability and may lead to deviations from normatively derived answers (Hogarth, 1980). They also, however, assist people when making judgments

that involve high levels of uncertainty, novelty, and time pressure – the very conditions surrounding the decision to launch a new venture.

RESEARCH EXPLORING THE RELATIONSHIP BETWEEN COGNITIVE BIASES AND VENTURE FORMATION

The findings from three early empirical studies (Cooper, Folta, and Woo, 1995; Cooper, Woo, and Dunkelberg, 1988; Palich and Bagby, 1995) strongly suggest that a relationship between cognitive biases and venture formation might exist. Employing categorization theory, Palich and Bagby (1995) found that, when interpreting ambiguous scenarios, entrepreneurs were more likely than managers to perceive strengths and opportunities and less likely to perceive weaknesses and threats. The authors explained that these types of categorizations can often lead to distortion in information processing and might cause entrepreneurs to be excessively optimistic. This study, however, did not involve perception regarding the feasibility of a venture, but instead focused on interpretation of technological changes, international trends, and competitive environments. An earlier study by Cooper, Woo, and Dunkelberg (1988) directly suggested that entrepreneurs were excessively confident of venture success, finding that over 80 percent believed that their ventures had a better than a seven out of ten chance of succeeding and a remarkable 33 percent were convinced there was no chance of venture failure. Furthermore, the authors' analyses tentatively suggested that these inflated expectations were a function of cognitive biases. The authors found that the vast majority of the entrepreneurs rated their chances of success higher than that of entrepreneurs in similar businesses, suggesting they might suffer from a cognitive bias known as "ignoring base rates" (Tversky and Kahneman, 1974). Their predictions of success were also completely unrelated to objective factors typically associated with venture success, which could indicate that they suffer from an illusion of control. An illusion of control refers to an overestimation of one's skills and consequently one's ability to cope with and predict future events (Langer, 1975). A later study by Cooper, Folta, and Woo (1995) also suggested that entrepreneurs might not be employing fully rational decision processes. The research found that, the more unfamiliar entrepreneurs were with a field they were venturing into, the less information they searched for. This was especially true for novice entrepreneurs. These three studies, however, did not explicitly measure cognitive biases.

Three later studies addressed this issue. Busenitz and Barney (1997) examined overconfidence, that is, the failure to know the limits of one's own knowledge, and representativeness, which is the willingness to generalize about a person or phenomenon based on only a few attributes of that person or phenomenon. The study found that entrepreneurs, compared with managers, displayed these biases to a greater degree. Baron (2000) extended this stream by examining a cognitive phenomenon known as counterfactual reasoning. Counterfactual reasoning refers to reflecting on outcomes and events that might have occurred if the persons in question had acted differently or if circumstances had somehow been different. Similar to sunk costs, these thoughts about the past should not influence future decision-making. The study compared differences in the extent to which entrepreneurs (persons who had recently started their own ventures), potential entrepreneurs (persons who expressed a strong desire to start their own ventures), and non-entrepreneurs engaged in counterfactual reasoning. Results indicated that entrepreneurs engaged in counterfactual reasoning less than other groups did, and experienced fewer regrets over past events. The article went on to propose that these tendencies generated positive affect states that may have led entrepreneurs to interpret situations positively, thereby contributing to their decision to start a venture.

In contrast, Markman, Balkin, and Baron (2002) determined that the patent inventors who founded ventures exhibited stronger regrets than those patent inventors who did not. The contradictory findings of the two studies could stem from the fact that non-entrepreneurs in Markman and colleagues' study were skilled and proactive enough to file a patent, so may have relatively little to regret in life. In contrast, the sample of potential entrepreneurs in Baron's (2000) study included teachers, students, government employees, and individuals working in retail, who might have been less successful, suggesting greater possible regrets. Importantly, all three of the studies compared biases of entrepreneurs with non-entrepreneurs well after the venture was formed. While it is quite possible, and arguably even probable, that these biases played a role in the decision to form the venture, such an assertion nevertheless requires a leap of logic. The question arises, could the biases have arisen after the venture was formed? For example, Cooper, Woo, and Dunkelberg (1988) proposed that entrepreneurs overestimate the probability of success because they exhibit a bias known as post-decision bolstering, whereby they exaggerate the attractiveness of an option after a decision is made.

This concern was addressed by three studies that measured biases at roughly the same time as the decision to form a venture. All three utilized subjects' reactions to cases and/or scenarios. Using Masters of Business Administration (MBA) students, the first study (Simon, Houghton, and Aquino, 2000) examined the illusion of control, overconfidence, and the belief in law of small numbers. This latter bias is closely related to representativeness and occurs when an individual uses a limited number of informational inputs (a small sample of information) to draw firm conclusions (Tversky and Kahneman, 1974). The research examined individual decision-makers and found that both the illusion of control and the belief in the law of small numbers were associated with the decision to form a start-up company. The study also determined that the relationship was mediated by risk perception. A follow-up study by Houghton et al. (2000) compared the strength of these relationships at the individual level to their strength at the group levels by examining the responses of individual MBAs and teams of MBAs. Also, unlike the initial study, this research used the decision to introduce pioneering products rather than the decision to form a start-up. Nevertheless, the basic relationships held across levels of analysis and with different dependent variables. In fact, at the group level, the belief in the law of small numbers generated even stronger relationships. Finally, Keh, Foo, and Lim (2002) returned to testing the relationships at the individual level, but utilized entrepreneurs rather than MBAs. They also added planning fallacy as an independent variable and used opportunity evaluation as the dependent variable. Despite these changes, the study generated findings that were similar to the earlier studies of Simon and colleagues. Planning fallacy, however, was not related to any of the variables in the model.

None of the three studies found a significant relationship between overconfidence and risk perception or between overconfidence and the dependent variable. The authors suggested this might have occurred because overconfidence was measured using diverse items that were not directly associated with the case decision. McNamara and Bromiley (1999) argued that researchers might make drastic errors in the design and interpretation of risk-taking models if they fail to examine the issues managers actually attend to. This assertion not only indicates that the measure of overconfidence should reflect the decision being considered, but also suggests the need for field studies that examine decisions in their natural environments.

A study by Simon and Houghton (2003) addressed these issues. It examined data from managers of small computer companies around the time each company launched a new product to assess the extent to which the product was pioneering, the success factors the manager was focusing on, and the manager's level of certainty in achieving each success factor. Eighteen months later the authors collected data to determine whether the new product introduction had achieved the specified success factors. If they were initially certain that they would achieve a success factor and did not, they were judged to be overconfident. The study found that overconfidence was positively related to the degree to which product introductions were pioneering. While this study greatly advanced our knowledge of cognitive biases and their effect on entrepreneurial behavior, it should be noted that they examined only one cognitive bias, namely overconfidence, and one type of venture, namely pioneering a new product, and failed to address the mediating factor uncovered in previous studies.

CONCLUSION

Collectively, the discussion above strongly suggests that cognitive biases do play a role in venture formation, but also indicates how much research is yet to be done in this area. For example, a theoretical article by Baron (1998) made a compelling case that researchers need to explore the effects of counterfactual reasoning, planning fallacy, affect infusion, attribution style, and self-justification on venture formation. Five years later, entrepreneurship research has empirically examined only two of these five biases. A more recent theory piece by Simon and Houghton (2002) not only adds reasoning by analogy to the list of unexplored biases, but also more importantly suggests that the relationship between biases and deciding to pursue a venture is much finer grained than previously suggested. The authors propose that the illusion of control, belief in the law of small numbers, and reasoning by analogy contribute to underestimating competition, overestimating demand, and overlooking requisite assets. These misperceptions, in turn, lead to the decision to introduce a pioneering product. Even out of the biases and relationships examined, only the relationship between overconfidence and pioneering has been explored in its natural decision environment at roughly the time the decision was made. It is our hope that this review not only illustrates what has been learned, but also serves to spur others to begin to further examine this rich area.

Bibliography

Baron, R. A. (1998). Cognitive mechanisms in entrepreneurship: Why and when entrepreneurs think differently than other people. *Journal of Business Venturing*, 13: 275–94.

Baron, R. A. (2000). Counterfactual thinking and venture formation: The potential effects of thinking about "What might have been." *Journal of Business Venturing*, 15: 79–91.

Busenitz, L. W. and Barney, J. (1997). Biases and heuristics in strategic decision-making: Differences between entrepreneurs and managers in large organizations. *Journal of Business Venturing*, 12: 9–30.

Cooper, A. C., Folta, T. B., and Woo, C. (1995). Entrepreneurial information search. *Journal of Business Venturing*, 10: 107–20.

Cooper, A. C., Woo, C. Y., and Dunkelberg, W. C. (1988). Entrepreneurs' perceived chances for success. *Journal of Business Venturing*, 3: 97–108.

Gartner, W. B. (1985). A conceptual framework for describing the phenomenon of new venture creation. *Academy of Management Review*, 10: 696–706.

Hogarth, R. M. (1980). *Judgment and Choice: The Psychology of Decision*. New York: John Wiley.

Houghton, S., Simon, M., Aquino, K., and Goldberg, C. (2000). No safety in numbers: Persistence of biases and their effects on team risk perception and team decision-making. *Group and Organization Management: An International Journal*, 25 (4): 325–53.

Keh, H., Foo, M., and Lim, B. (2002). Opportunity evaluation under risky conditions: The cognitive processes of entrepreneurs. *Entrepreneurship: Theory and Practice*, 27 (2): 25–149.

Krueger, N. (1993). The impact of prior entrepreneurial exposure on perceptions of new venture feasibility and desirability. *Entrepreneurship: Theory and Practice*, 18 (1): 5–21.

Langer, E. J. (1975). The illusion of control. *Journal of Personality and Social Psychology*, 32 (2): 311–28.

Lumpkin, G. T. and Dess, G. G. (1996). Clarifying the entrepreneurial orientation construct and linking it to performance. *Academy of Management Review*, 21 (1): 135–73.

McNamara, G. and Bromiley, P. (1999). Risk and return in organization decision-making. *Academy of Management Journal*, 42: 330–9.

Markman, G., Balkin, D., and Baron, R. (2002). Inventors and new venture formation: The effects of general self-efficacy and regretful thinking. *Entrepreneurship: Theory and Practice*, 27 (2): 149–65.

Palich, L. E. and Bagby, D. R. (1995). Using cognitive theory to explain entrepreneurial risk taking: Challenging conventional wisdom. *Journal of Business Venturing*, 10: 425–38.

Shaver, K. G. and Scott, L. (1991). Person, process, choice: The psychology of new venture creation. *Entrepreneurship: Theory and Practice*, 16 (2): 23–45.

Simon, M. and Houghton, S. M. (2002). The relationship among biases, misperceptions and introducing pioneering products: Examining differences in venture decision contexts. *Entrepreneurship: Theory and Practice*, 27 (2): 105–24.

Simon, M. and Houghton, S. M. (2003). The relationship between overconfidence and the introduction of risky products: Evidence from a field study. *Academy of Management Journal*, 46: 139–50.

Simon, M., Houghton, S. M., and Aquino, K. (2000). Cognitive biases, risk perception, and venture formation: How individuals decide to start companies. *Journal of Business Venturing*, 15: 113–34.

Tversky, A. and Kahneman, D. (1974). Judgment under uncertainty: Heuristics and biases. *Science*, 185: 1124–31.

competitive advantage

Morgan P. Miles

Competitive advantage is the foundation on which a firm competes. When a firm gains competitive advantage, it holds a favorable market position based upon its ability to create superior customer value through product differentiation, lower-cost alternatives, more rapidly satisfying its customers, or through a symbiotic combination of these factors. Competitive advantage pertains to the ability of a firm to strategically deploy its set of resources and distinctive competencies to create a unique value-creating strategy that outperforms its competitors in the market (see Barney, 1991, 2001).

In markets where customers enjoy the freedom to select from a marketplace of goods and entrepreneurs enjoy the freedom to exploit attractive economic opportunities, firms compete for the opportunity to engage in profitable transactions with customers. Exchange is based on the customer's perception of value. Those customer segments that demand need-satisfying products enter into exchange relationships with firms that offer superior value solutions for these specific needs. In market-based economies, firms that most efficiently create the highest need-satisfying value offering will prosper (Hunt, 2000). Firms must constantly seek out opportunities to create additional value for customers through ongoing radical and incremental innovation initiatives, thereby gaining and sustaining competitive advantage.

The capability of some firms to outperform their peers has been a topic of great interest to academics and executives. Since Ricardo, scholars have considered the topic of "rent" to understand why some firms enjoy superior economic performance over their competitors (see Lewin and Phelan, 2000). Those firms that are able to leverage proactive, radical customer-centered innovation and exploit reactive competitor-focused innovation to generate superior economic returns (rent), enhance customer satisfaction, establish market leadership, and strengthen customer loyalty, are considered to possess a competitive advantage (Day and Wensley, 1988; Hunt, 2000).

Entrepreneurship involves a firm leveraging innovation to exploit new opportunities, renew its current position, or create new product-market domains, and is an antecedent required to gain and sustain a competitive advantage (see Covin and Miles, 1999; Miles, Paul, and Wilhite, 2003). However, for a firm to sustain a competitive advantage, it must also be both effective and efficient in continuing to exploit innovation. Competitive advantage is based on the assumption that firms possess unique strategic resources and competencies that are valuable, scarce, imperfectly imitable, and largely immutable (Barney, 1991). In a market economy, firms face demand that is dynamic and heterogeneous across and within industries (Hunt, 2000). While firms may leverage resources to create a competitive advantage based on economies of scale or scope, or the ability to develop unique business models, all competitive advantages are dynamic and based on a specific set of market and environmental conditions (Christensen, 2001).

When other entrepreneurs perceive that a firm is enjoying superior financial performance (or rent), they enter the market with innovative or lower-cost products and rents are dissipated, making any competitive advantage transitory. For a firm to sustain competitive advantage, it must constantly renew its ability to more effectively and more efficiently exploit resources by proactive, radical, industry altering, market creating, Schumpeterian innovation (Schumpeter, 1934; Hunt, 2000). Figure 1 illustrates how firms may leverage corporate entrepreneurship strategically to gain and sustain competitive advantage.

The three major tenets of competitive advantage include (1) the firm's resources (Barney, 1991), (2) the firm's ability to establish an advantageous market position (Porter, 1985), and (3) the firm's decision rules and processes that drive the pursuit of opportunities (Eisenhardt and Sull, 2001). Competitive advantage requires that resources are more effectively and

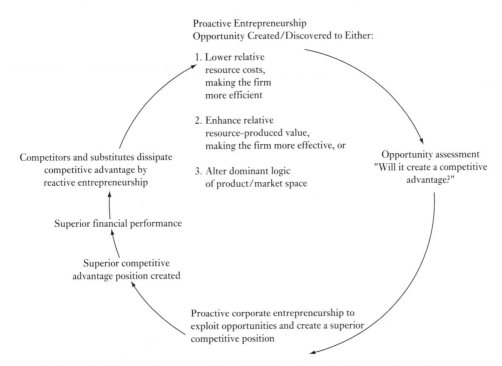

Figure 1   Innovation, Corporate Entrepreneurship, and the Path to Competitive Advantage Renewal

efficiently deployed to create a superior market position. However, without ongoing entrepreneurial initiatives to leverage radical Schumpeterian innovation in the pursuit of attractive opportunities, a firm's competitive advantage will be dissipated by competitors and is not renewable. Therefore, the entrepreneurial decision processes and rules that enable firms to recognize or create, evaluate, and successfully exploit opportunities are a source of competitive advantage (see Shane and Venkataraman, 2000).

In summary, why customers choose to purchase from Firm A over Firm B rests on the firm's transitory ability to harness entrepreneurship to create superior value for its customers through product differentiation, cost leadership, quick response, or some combination of these bases for competitive advantage (see Porter, 1985; Bhide, 1986; Prahalad and Hamel, 1990). Firms wishing to gain and sustain a competitive advantage must consistently employ entrepreneurship to rejuvenate, renew, and redefine the firm, its markets, its strategies, or its industries (Covin and Miles, 1999). While a firm may be entrepreneurial and, thus, leverage innovation to gain a competitive advantage, it must continually be entrepreneurial in order to sustain that competitive advantage.

Bibliography

Barney, J. (1991). Firm resources and sustained competitive advantage. *Journal of Management*, 17 (1): 99–120.

Barney, J. (2001). Resource-based theories of competitive advantage: A ten-year retrospective on the resource-based view. *Journal of Management*, 27 (6): 643–50.

Bhide, A. (1986). Hustle as a strategy. *Harvard Business Review*, 64 (5): 59–65.

Christensen, C. M. (2001). The past and future of competitive advantage. *MIT Sloan Management Review*, 42 (2): 105–10.

Covin, J. G. and Miles, M. P. (1999). Corporate entrepreneurship and the pursuit of competitive advantage. *Entrepreneurship: Theory and Practice*, 23 (3): 47–63.

Day, G. S. and Wensley, R. (1988). Assessing advantage: A framework for diagnosing competitive superiority. *Journal of Marketing*, 52: 45–57.

Eisenhardt, K. M. and Sull, D. N. (2001). Strategy as simple rules. *Harvard Business Review*, 79 (1): 107–16.

Hunt, S. D. (2000). *A General Theory of Competition*. Thousand Oaks, CA: Sage.

Lewin, P. and Phelan, S. E. (2000). An Austrian theory of the firm. *Review of Austrian Economics*, 13 (1): 59–80.

Miles, M. P., Paul, C. W., and Wilhite, A. (2003). Modeling corporate entrepreneurship as rent-seeking competition. *Technovation*, 23 (5): 393–400.

Porter, M. E. (1985). *Competitive Advantage: Creating and Sustaining Superior Performance*. New York: Free Press.

Prahalad, C. K. and Hamel, G. (1990). The core competence of the corporation. *Harvard Business Review*, 68 (3): 79–91.

Schumpeter, J. A. (1934). *The Theory of Economic Development*. Cambridge, MA: Harvard University Press.

Shane, S. and Venkataraman, S. (2000). The promise of entrepreneurship as a field of research. *Academy of Management Review*, 25 (1): 217–26.

competitive dynamics among entrepreneurial firms

Ming-Jer Chen

How entrepreneurial firms compete has received some attention from strategic management and entrepreneurship scholars alike. Strategy researchers have approached this issue by focusing on how firms with low market shares compete against their larger rivals and by offering such normative advice as "be flexible and move fast" (Hambrick, MacMillan, and Day, 1982). Chen and Hambrick (1995) found that relatively smaller industry players differ from their larger counterparts in their competitive behaviors, as typified by such attributes as propensity for action and response speed. The entrepreneurship literature has applied Porter's (1980) and Miles and Snow's (1978) typologies of strategy to examine competition in the context of small and medium-size firms. Extending from Miller (1983), Lumpkin and Dess (1996) formalized the construct of entrepreneurial orientation and highlighted the importance of competitive aggressiveness and proactiveness in such vital entrepreneurial activities as new entry and new-venture creation.

Consistent with Hitt et al. (2001), this essay stresses the integrative nature between entrepreneurial and strategic actions in competition research. Its purpose is twofold. It first reviews some of the key concepts and findings advanced in competitive dynamics research in the strategy literature. Second, and more importantly, it shows how these concepts can be used to facilitate entrepreneurship research in the study of competition. The discussion below considers entrepreneurial firms both from the "orientation perspective" of Lumpkin and Dess (1996) and from the more conventional view that incorporates firm size and age as the key organizational features in the entrepreneurship research domain. Hence, the ideas here apply equally to emerging, or new, firms and to those small and medium-size firms that may tend to be more limited in market scope and constrained by their resources.

COMPETITIVE DYNAMICS

Over the last decade, strategy scholars, taking the Austrian and Schumpeterian perspective, have produced some useful ideas in the study of competitive dynamics (see the review by Smith, Ferrier, and Ndofor, 2001). First, by using the individual competitive move as the unit of analysis, researchers are able to analyze competition by studying the exchange of actions and responses. Likewise, this approach enables analysis of competitors through pairwise comparison between each rival in an industry with a focal firm along some market and resource dimensions (Chen, 1996). Second, researchers have developed a set of variables (such as likelihood and speed) that can be used to characterize competitive actions and responses. Research has shown that the exchange of actions and responses affects firm performance (Smith, Ferrier, and Ndofor, 2001) and that a firm's responses can be predicted by such factors as the defender's dependence on the markets under attack and the signaling of an attacker's actions (Chen and MacMillan, 1992).

Extended from the firm-specific perspective, Chen (1996) proposed the idea of competitive asymmetry: the notion that a given pair of firms may not pose an equal threat to each other. The idea that each competitive relationship is unique and not necessarily symmetrical derives in part from the resource-based view of the firm and, more importantly, from Tversky's (1977) seminal work on the features of similarity. The basic idea is that similarity between two objects should not be treated as a symmetric relation: statements of similarity are directional and depend on which element of the comparison is the "subject" and which the "referent" (Tversky, 1977: 328). The metric distance function, then, states that

$d(a, b) \neq d(b, a)$. Market and resource conditions, such as firm size and structure, are important contributing factors for competitive asymmetry.

RESEARCH IMPLICATIONS

Competitive dynamics research has tended to sample from large established firms. Its central ideas and premises, however, can be extended to an array of research issues that are pertinent to the study both of entrepreneurially oriented organizations and of firms that are relatively smaller or younger, or which are limited in market scope or resource endowment. For example, competitive dynamics research has frequently found that a bias for actions (or launching lots of actions) is positively related to performance. Does the same phenomenon hold for entrepreneurial ventures – or are they better off initiating fewer actions, due to size and resource issues and possible needs for stealth?

Similarly, competitive dynamics research has found beneficial effects of a broad competitive repertoire. Does this apply to entrepreneurial ventures? Or, due to liabilities of age and size, are entrepreneurial ventures better off relying on a simple, narrow, competitive repertoire, until they have overcome the early-stage limitations of age and size and have the resources and legitimacy to expand their competitive repertoire?

One of the key issues for entrepreneurial ventures is how to anticipate incumbent firm response. Market commonality (the degree of a competitor's presence in the markets in which it overlaps with a given entrepreneurial firm) and resource similarity (the extent to which a given rival possesses comparable strategic endowments to those of the firm) hold promise as analytical tools for anticipating response. To what extent can an entrepreneurial firm plan the extent of its market commonality with rivals in an attempt to "manage" incumbent response?

An entrepreneurial firm often seeks to undertake innovative actions or expand into untapped or unrecognized markets where it has the opportunity to create local dominance. How can it protect such niches when established firms decide to move in? Specifically, how can it undertake actions that may escape the attention of established industry players, delay their reactions, exploit their response barriers, and minimize the magnitude of their responses?

An entrepreneurial venture, by virtue of its flexibility, often can create competitive asymmetry vis-à-vis its established rivals. What are some conditions under which it can maintain and take advantage of such asymmetry? To what extent can it defend itself by counterattacking in the established firm's home market, rather than in its own home market under attack? An entrepreneurial firm may also undertake actions to redirect (or even misdirect) its larger rivals so they will invest or expand in businesses or markets that will be potentially beneficial to the firm. What are some market conditions and strategic considerations for making this kind of competitive maneuvering?

In many cases, an entrepreneurial firm is under pressure to compete or cooperate with entrenched firms. How should market and resource considerations (i.e., market commonality and resource similarity) affect the firm's timing in cooperative moves and its decisions for partner selection? How can the firm utilize its social capital and network to expand its market scope and resource profile in its fight with larger rivals, or take advantage of government policy to help it compete overseas?

Investigation of these issues should advance competition research in the entrepreneurial context. Moreover, it has the potential to contribute equally to competitive dynamics research, which so far – due largely, perhaps, to data and information constraints – have not given adequate attention to the study of entrepreneurial firms. Such investigation may help broaden the conventional consideration of competition as a head-on, war-like activity. In light of globalization, development of an expansive view of competition may be especially pressing. The notion of indirect competition, for instance, may lead to the treatment of competition as non-confrontational, subtle rivalrous behavior. Accordingly, the study of such ideas as competitive–cooperative interdependence may open new frontiers for both entrepreneurship and strategic management researchers.

Bibliography

Chen, M.-J. (1996). Competitor analysis and interfirm rivalry: Toward a theoretical integration. *Academy of Management Review*, 21 (1): 100–34.

Chen, M.-J. and Hambrick, D. C. (1995). Speed, stealth, and selective attack: How small firms differ from large firms in competitive behavior. *Academy of Management Journal*, 38 (2): 453–82.

Chen, M.-J. and MacMillan, I. C. (1992). Non-response and delayed response to competitive moves: The roles of competitor dependence and action irreversibility. *Academy of Management Journal*, 35 (3): 539–70.

Hambrick, D. C., MacMillan, I. C., and Day, D. L. (1982). Strategic attributes and performance in the BCG matrix: A PIMS-based analysis of industrial product businesses. *Academy of Management Journal*, 25 (3): 510–31.

Hitt, M. A., Ireland, R. D., Camp, S. M., and Sexton, D. L. (2001). Strategic entrepreneurship: Entrepreneurial strategies for wealth creation. *Strategic Management Journal*, 22 (6/7): 479–91.

Lumpkin, G. T. and Dess, G. G. (1996). Enriching the entrepreneurial orientation construct: A reply to entrepreneurial orientation or pioneer advantage. *Academy of Management Review*, 21 (3): 605–7.

Miles, R. and Snow, C. (1978). *Organizational Strategy, Structure, and Process*. New York: McGraw-Hill.

Miller, D. (1983). The correlates of entrepreneurship in three types of firms. *Management Science*, 29 (7): 770–91.

Porter, M. E. (1980). *Competitive Strategy: Techniques for Analyzing Industries and Competitors*. New York: Free Press.

Smith, K. G., Ferrier, W., and Ndofor, H. (2001). Competitive dynamics research: Critique and future directions. In M. A. Hitt, R. Freeman, and J. Harrison (eds.), *Handbook of Strategic Management*. Oxford: Blackwell, 315–61.

Tversky, A. (1977). Features of similarity. *Psychological Review*, 84 (4): 327–52.

contingent earnouts

Jeffrey J. Reuer and Roberto Ragozzino

A contingent earnout is a contractual agreement stipulating a schedule of variable payments that an acquirer is to make to a seller following an acquisition. While payment for an acquisition typically occurs at the time of a deal's completion, a bidder can turn to a contingent earnout in order to defer payouts and make them dependent on the attainment of pre-specified performance objectives for a certain time interval (e.g., 3–5 years). Therefore, one of the features of contingent earnouts that makes them attractive in acquisitions is that acquirers facing uncertainty about the value of the targeted resources are able to transfer a portion of the valuation risk to the target firm (Reuer, Shenkar, and Ragozzino, 2004).

The valuation problem for acquirers has been noted by scholars researching acquisitions deal structures and the determinants of merger and acquisition (M&A) failure. Fundamentally, the model is an extension of the widely known "market for lemons" model, which is discussed by Nobel prizewinner George Akerlof in the context of product markets (Akerlof, 1970). Specifically, he discusses how information asymmetries that exist between buyers and sellers can lead to the problem of adverse selection. When information asymmetries exist, buyers of products are unable to separate the good ones from the lemons in an efficient manner, and because sellers are aware of their advantageous informational position, they have an incentive to misrepresent the value of their products. Asocial institutions (e.g., warranties) and social institutions (e.g., trust) can therefore take on importance in rectifying the failure of product markets affected by asymmetric information.

In M&A markets, target firms may likewise hold privileged information about their resources and be unable to convey it to prospective bidders in a credible fashion. Under these circumstances, earnouts can serve as contractual remedies that allow the acquisition to take place despite parties' potential valuation disagreements. For example, bidders may agree to pay for the amount reflecting their valuation upfront, and disburse the excess amount claimed by targets if and only if the value of these resources is borne out in the future. Furthermore, targets are provided with an opportunity to signal the veracity of their claims by agreeing to enter into these contractual arrangements (Spence, 1974). This suggests that earnouts will be helpful in acquiring less related targets with disparate knowledge bases vis-à-vis the acquirer.

Another distinct advantage of contingent earnouts is that they can ensure that a target firm's managers stay on board after an acquisition, and earnouts also incentivize them to perform. There is evidence in finance and strategy research that acquisitions often fail due to losses in human capital in the acquired firm, particularly in high-tech acquisitions or other acquisitions reliant on intangible assets. By implementing earnouts, acquirers find a way to address this additional risk and increase their chances for a successful deal.

While contingent earnouts can be an efficient way to mitigate *ex ante* information asymmetry problems, as well as the risk of *ex post* management departures, their characteristics also present a number of drawbacks that can limit their usefulness. First, earnouts will tend to be unsuited for acquisitions requiring immediate integration of the target firm's resources. This is because the seller's assets must be kept separate in order for acquirers to measure the target's performance and determine whether the deferred payments are to occur. More generally, it is implicit in the earnout contract that the buying firm should minimize its supervision in the operations of the target firm over the contract life, so as to avoid ambiguity in the cause-and-effect linkage between the target firm's activities and performance outcomes. Targets subject to earnouts therefore will require significant autonomy after the acquisition has been completed.

A second important disadvantage of earnouts is that they may give rise to moral hazard problems for acquirers which, like the problem of adverse selection, can thwart the success of a deal. In general, the precise specification of earnout terms (e.g., performance benchmarks, durations, etc.) can encourage target management to behave in some ways that are inconsistent with the long-term, wealth maximization objectives of the acquiring firm. For example, target management may choose investments with a horizon less than that of the earnout contract, while other projects with longer durations may have superior long-term cash flow prospects or embedded options. As another illustration, if the performance benchmark chosen for the earnout is based on accounting measures such as ROA, target management may elect to reduce expenses that may nevertheless be in the business's long-term interests. Along the same lines, lack of clarity and completeness in the earnout contract may induce acquirers to behave opportunistically in order to avoid deferred payments. For instance, disagreements may arise regarding inconsistent accounting practices or depreciation methods, which in turn increase the risk of costly litigation.

Given their characteristics, contingent earnouts can be attractive deal structuring devices for some entrepreneurial acquisitions for several reasons. Recent research in entrepreneurship has found that entrepreneurs tend to exhibit a number of behavioral biases that can exacerbate valuation disagreements with acquirers. Entrepreneurs have been noted to be overconfident about their prospects, underestimate their future challenges, and generalize erroneously from prior experiences. As targets, entrepreneurial firms may therefore hold exaggerated expectations about their own value, which likely increases the chances of valuation disagreements with prospective acquirers. Under these circumstances, earnouts are attractive in allowing deals to go forward, even when bidders and sellers hold divergent valuations for the targeted resources.

Aside from some of the heuristics that have been associated with entrepreneurs, there are a number of other reasons why contingent earnouts can be useful in acquisitions of entrepreneurial firms. First, many entrepreneurial firms are privately held and have yet to undergo the IPO process. Privately held targets pose higher informational hazards for bidders, owing to the lack of credible information available on private targets (Shen and Reuer, forthcoming). By undertaking an IPO, the target firm can provide signals to would-be acquirers by bearing the direct costs of going public, as well as the indirect costs of underpricing and associating with reputable third parties (Reuer and Shen, 2004). Second, entrepreneurial firms are often new ventures that lack codified historical information on their operations. Third, entrepreneurial firms can have unique capabilities that differ from those of more established bidders. Often the know-how in entrepreneurial firms is embodied in the entrepreneur, and it can be in the best interest of the acquiring firm to ensure his or her continued presence in the target firm for a transitional period after the acquisition has been completed.

The above rationales suggest that contingent earnouts can be particularly useful in acquisitions of entrepreneurial firms. Recent research has brought evidence that contingent earnouts are in fact most useful in the acquisitions of firms that are privately held rather than publicly traded, newly incorporated versus more established, and that have different knowledge bases from those of acquirers. Earnouts may also provide substitute remedies vis-à-vis governance solutions such as equity collaborations to the problem of adverse selection in the market for firm resources (Reuer and Koza, 2000). This emerging research presents a broad array of choices for entrepreneurs seeking to grow or exit, ranging from going public to forming various types of alliances, to going forward with acquisitions with particular deal structures tailored to firms' needs. Given that entrepreneurial firms also engage in acquisitive growth and may find it difficult to evaluate targets (Zahra, Ireland, and Hitt, 2000), future research might also consider the conditions under which earnouts might be useful deal structuring devices for these firms.

Bibliography

Akerlof, G. A. (1970). The market for "lemons": Qualitative uncertainty and the market mechanism. *Quarterly Journal of Economics*, 84: 488–500.

Reuer, J. J. and Koza, M. P. (2000). Asymmetric information and joint venture performance: Theory and evidence for domestic and international joint ventures. *Strategic Management Journal*, 21: 81–8 .

Reuer, J. J. and Shen, J.-C. (2004). Sequential divestiture through initial public offerings. *Journal of Economic Behavior and Organization*, 54: 249–66.

Reuer, J. J., Shenkar, O., and Ragozzino, R. (forthcoming). Mitigating risk in international mergers and acquisitions: The role of contingent payouts. *Journal of International Business Studies*, 35: 19–32.

Shen, J.-C. and Reuer, J. J. (forthcoming). Adverse selection in acquisitions of small manufacturing firms: A comparison of private and public targets. *Small Business Economics*.

Spence, A. M. (1974). *Market Signaling*. Cambridge, MA: Harvard University Press.

Zahra, S. A., Ireland, R. D., and Hitt, M. A. (2000). International expansion by new venture firms: International diversity, mode of market entry, technological learning, and performance. *Academy of Management Journal*, 43: 925–50.

corporate entrepreneurship

Shaker A. Zahra

The concept of corporate entrepreneurship (CE) has gained considerable recognition over the past two decades. The concept's popularity stems from the varied contributions CE can make to a company's financial and non-financial performance (Zahra, Jennings, and Kurtako, 1999). CE can improve financial indicators of performance, such as return on assets and company growth, especially in highly dynamic markets. CE provides an opportunity for different groups to collaborate and create new products and goods, thus improving the company's competitive position. CE activities also create opportunities to learn new skills that allow the company to renew its operations and compete effectively. This learning is crucial for acquiring new competencies and capabilities that make it possible for the firm to explore new growth options beyond its traditional markets and industries (Zahra, 1991).

DIMENSIONS OF CE

The concept of CE has been the subject of much discussion, leading to the proliferation of different classifications of its dimensions (Sharma and Chrisman, 1999). One of the most popular definitions views CE as the sum of the firm's product innovation, proactiveness, and risk taking (Miller, 1983). Product innovation refers to the creation of goods and services. Proactiveness means being at the forefront of change in the industry – leading, rather than imitating other companies in their industries. Risk taking denotes a willingness to invest in projects that are deemed essential for the company's survival and successful performance, even when the outcomes of those investments are uncertain.

There is a growing consensus in the literature that CE consists of three major dimensions: innovation, venturing, and strategic renewal. While the strategic value of these dimensions appears to vary from one industry (and country) to the next, the three dimensions form a constellation of activities that keep the organization innovative.

Innovation is the first dimension of CE; it refers to the firm's commitment to and investment in creating new products, goods, and services. It also refers to the firm's creation of new business models. Miller (1983) highlights the importance of radical innovation as a key indicator of organizational risk taking, which is important for successful CE. Covin and Slevin (1989) argue the importance of pioneering radical innovation, suggesting that it requires serious organizational resource commitment and specialized managerial and organizational skills.

Venturing is the second component of CE (Guth and Ginsberg, 1990). It centers on the creation of new businesses in existing or new markets. Internal venturing refers to those situations where new creation occurs within exiting markets. Innovation is one of most important routes to internal venturing. External venturing occurs when new business creation takes place outside the boundaries of current business units. Alliances and acquisitions are commonly used in external corporate venturing. Corporate venturing activities serve multiple purposes, such as creating new businesses, developing new organizational competencies and capabilities, learning about distant markets and industries, and keeping the organization alert to various opportunities outside their current operations.

Corporate venturing is risky because it often takes the firm away from its traditional core competencies, leaving it vulnerable to competitive attacks. It is also difficult to integrate new and existing businesses due to differences in cultures, goals, and strategic priorities. New ventures also take away resources from established operations, creating another source of tension within the organization. Some companies may also lack the managerial skills to nurture new ventures and invest in them patiently over a period of time. Therefore, successful corporate venturing requires clear and specific goals, coupled with milestones. It also demands establishing and sharing a set of criteria by which new ventures' success is evaluated. New ventures need time to develop and influence the organization's financial performance; therefore, the sustained and visible support of senior executives is also needed. Finally, because many new ventures cross divisional lines, their success demands the broad representation of various units in the firm.

Strategic renewal is the third and final dimension of CE. It refers to the various activities intended to revitalize a company's operations, build new competitive skills, or change its strategic thrust in fundamental ways. Strategic renewal begins with a vision for the company's future and the skills necessary to actualize this vision. Senior management should lead the rest of the organization in developing this vision and share it with other managers and employees. Strategic renewal embodies system-wide changes that alter the technological base of the firm, revise its systems and processes, and challenge prevailing cultural assumptions about the market and competition. The effect of strategic renewal on a company's financial performance might be slow to materialize because it requires significant changes in corporate cultures and managerial decision-making.

CENTRALIZED VS. DISPERSED CE

Given the advantages associated with CE, companies have considered effective ways to stimulate and foster these activities. Some companies opt to formalize their CE efforts by creating units that support and champion these activities. This centralized approach has major pluses, including the coherence of the company's various activities. This approach also makes it easier for companies to track their investments and evaluate the results gained from CE efforts.

Other companies follow a more dispersed approach to CE, where they use seed money and incentives to encourage entrepreneurial activities. These efforts capitalize on and stimulate employees' interest in developing and championing innovative ideas that benefit their units and the organization as a whole. These informal initiatives often complement existing formal systems and fill voids that exist in them. Some refer to informal CE activities as "intrapreneurship" (Pinchot, 1985). Once their viability has been proven, informal activities may receive management support and then be integrated into the company's formal CE projects. Thus, these informal initiatives are often the forerunners of formal CE venture programs.

Still, conflicts might arise between formal and informal intrapreneurial activities where employees pursue ideas that clash with the formal organizational agenda. Alternatively, managers may suppress informal initiatives that they do not understand or like. It is important, therefore, to create a system within the organization to evaluate informal initiatives and determine which projects have the potential to influence company performance. These projects should be integrated into existing CE systems, units, and structures. In conducting these reviews, managers should be aware that radical ideas often fall well beyond existing business lines or concepts. In these cases, new business creation units (or similar units) might be used to foster the development of these initiatives.

PROMOTING INTRAPRENEURSHIP

Several factors stimulate and spur intrapreneurship. A sense of autonomy gives employees and managers the freedom to take initiative and act. Political, organizational, and financial support from managers – especially when ideas fail – allows employees to explore innovative ideas without fearing the loss of their jobs or damaging their status or reputation. The availability of slack resources also encourages experimentation and exploration of innovative ideas, which are essential to discovering relevant opportunities and proving their market viability. "Slack" refers to organizational resources that exceed the firm's current needs to accomplish its goals. Slack resources may include excess inputs (e.g., extra employees and unused capacity) and unexploited opportunities (Nohria and Gulati, 1996). Given that they are not committed to ongoing operations, these resources could be used to explore new ideas and prove their viability. The existence of an organic organization structure also promotes discovery and risk taking, which are crucial for successful intrapreneurship. Organic structures facilitate informal as well as formal communication across divisional boundaries, building support and momentum for new ideas within the firm. The existence of strong and persistent champions also makes it easier for employees to undertake intrapreneurial efforts.

Bibliography

Covin, J. and Slevin, D. (1989). Strategic management of small firms in hostile and benign environments. *Strategic Management Journal*, 10: 75–87.
Guth, W. D. and Ginsberg, A. (1990). Guest editors' introduction: Corporate entrepreneurship. *Strategic Management Journal*, 11: 5–15.
Miller, D. (1983). The correlates of entrepreneurship in three types of firms. *Management Science*, 29: 770–91.
Nohria, N. and Gulati, R. (1996). Is slack good or bad for innovation? *Academy of Management Journal*, 39: 1245–64.

Pinchot, G. (1985). *Intrapreneuring: Why You Don't Have to Leave the Corporation to Become an Entrepreneur.* New York: Harper and Row.

Sathe, V. (2003). *Corporate Entrepreneurship: Top Managers and New Business Creation.* Cambridge: Cambridge University Press.

Sharma, P. and Chrisman, J. J. (1999). Toward a reconciliation of the definitional issues in the field of corporate entrepreneurship. *Entrepreneurship: Theory and Practice*, 23: 11–27.

Zahra, S. (1991). Predictors and financial outcomes of corporate entrepreneurship: An exploratory study. *Journal of Business Venturing*, 6: 259–85.

Zahra, S., Jennings, D., and Kuratko, D. (1999). The antecedents and consequences of firm-level entrepreneurship: The state of the field. *Entrepreneurship: Theory and Practice*, 24: 45–65.

corporate ventures and knowledge

William C. Bogner

The roles of knowledge, learning new knowledge, and searching for new knowledge are critical components to understanding successful corporate venturing (CV). This essay examines some of the recent insights in each of these areas and how they tie to entrepreneurial activities in established firms. In discussing these issues, I regularly contrast two very different types of corporate entrepreneurial activities that firms could pursue: continual rejuvenation and domain redefinition (Covin and Miles, 1999). These two approaches represent end points on a continuum capturing the relative uniqueness of the resulting new knowledge, and hence competitive advantage, that a firm seeks through CV and they require very different choices on managers' parts.

This discussion is built on the resource-based view of the firm (Barney, 1997) and its core ideas of how firms gain advantage in otherwise open and competitive markets. The important role of knowledge and learning in this view is grounded in the tenets of the knowledge-based view of the firm (Grant, 1996; Spender, 1996). These interrelationships are briefly outlined below. Based on these views, an assumption I make is that the key goal of corporate venturing is the creation of new knowledge for building and sustaining competitive advantage. I posit that in existing firms,

entrepreneurial success is driven by the development of new knowledge that the firm can actually exploit, and that its exploitation is dependent on choices that increase the likelihood of new knowledge being acquired, assimilated, and transformed into exploitable form (Zahra and George, 2002).

KNOWLEDGE IN THE RESOURCE-BASED VIEW OF THE FIRM

The role of learning and knowledge in organizations has long been an issue of scholarly interest; it is the tie to dynamic competitive advantage that is relatively new. The Carnegie school's behavioral view of the firm (e.g., March and Simon, 1958; Cyert and March, 1963), the work of Joseph Schumpeter (1934), and Nelson and Winter's (1982) evolutionary view of economics all contributed to our understanding of knowledge's key role in dynamic markets, the importance of developing new knowledge, and the difficulties firms encounter in searching for and processing new knowledge. In the early 1990s, scholars (e.g., Nonaka, 1994) began developing sophisticated models of how learning can effectively take place so that the firm can change and adapt to its environment. Spender (1996), Grant (1996), and others argued that organizational learning is the genesis for the knowledge-based resources and capabilities that firms are able to exploit in unique ways. Thus, the unique knowledge about products and markets, and about the skills, processes, and capabilities for effectively reaching those markets (Makadok and Walker, 1996), became the critical point of focus in the firm.

The role of this knowledge-based view fits tightly with contemporary perspectives of entrepreneurial behavior. Effective entrepreneurship includes the process of discovering and exploiting opportunities that are not obvious to others (Shane and Venkataraman, 2000). This is exactly the type of behavior the knowledge-based view suggests is the key to understanding how firms build and sustain competitive advantage.

SEARCH CHOICES

The process of discovery first involves choices about search. Regardless of the firm's subsequent ability to learn, transmit, and utilize information, a firm can only learn that to which its search routines expose it. In CV, the type of search initiated must fit the type of venturing pursued. Issues such as the search breadth and depth, and the age of the search target, are all important considerations that will determine the quantity of new insights the firm will develop, as well as the relative uniqueness those insights provide when compared to the firm's current products, services, and capabilities.

Breadth is the primary consideration in aligning CV strategy with new knowledge search. How broadly a firm searches for a solution to a problem determines the learning opportunities it will encounter. For basic problem solving, firms prefer local searches and minimally satisfying, or "satisficing," solutions (Cyert and March, 1963). This type of search is often called exploitive search and this is the type of search seen in corporate venturing that seeks sustained regeneration with limited opportunities for new competitive postures (Stuart and Podolny, 1996). More far-ranging searches are exploratory searches (March, 1991). These searches deliberately go into market or technology domains where the firm lacks significant knowledge and understanding.

As firms move their CV focus toward domain redefinition, emphasis on this latter type of search needs to increase. The main challenge in conducting exploratory search is that it has a high failure rate in producing entrepreneurial opportunities. This is because such opportunities arise when existing knowledge of a firm complements the new data that is brought in by the search. As will be discussed further in the next section, the less overlap a firm's existing knowledge and understandings have with the new information coming in, the less likely it is that an opportunistic insight will emerge. However, when these exploratory searches do produce insights, they can be quite valuable. This is due to the relative uniqueness for the knowledge that the combination produces. Consistent with the knowledge-based view of the firm, the relative uniqueness of a firm's capabilities should be related to the degree of success the insight will produce. Still, while there is a high potential payoff for exploratory searches, the large number of failures leaves average returns far below those of exploitive searches.

On this point, however, some important observations need to be made. First, it is an exploratory or "outlier" search that will produce the major breakthrough into a new market or business configuration. Thus, along Covin and Miles' (1999) continuum, a search approach that is a rational preference for sustained regeneration will likely be of limited effect in strategic renewal, and will almost surely fail to provide sufficient change in domain redefinition.

Second, managers can moderate these odds through the leadership choices they make in their CV activities. In CV units, searches may be wide ranging, but they also are directed. Fleming and Sorenson (2000, 2001) studied the effects of different search approaches, emphasizing the role of a search leader who is processing information on an ongoing basis and redirecting search resources accordingly. Thus, someone who has a strong sense of the search terrain and of how to process information as the search progresses leads the wide-ranging search. The search direction is in constant flux. For firms instituting domain redefinition, however, it must be recognized that a trade-off exists. On the one hand, the greater the break that is sought with current firm configurations, the broader the search will have to be. Yet, on the other hand, at any level of search breadth, the one leading the search will bias or limit the search process and, eventually, the entrepreneurial opportunities to which the firm will be exposed. The search leader's knowledge of the terrain to be searched, as well as the cognitive schema the search leader holds in processing the stimuli encountered, will determine these opportunities. Thus, the search leader in a venture unit becomes a key moderator of the flow of new knowledge acquisition into the firm.

The second dimension of search that is tied to the learning that will occur is scope depth. The increased use of the same knowledge leads to deeper understanding of that knowledge, with a resulting level of predictability and reliability in the knowledge that is used (Katila and Ahuja, 2002). This type of search increases the number of similar new products firms develop; however, it also limits the likelihood of moving from a firm's existing technological trajectory and may even help reinforce existing routines (Argyris and Schon, 1978). Thus, in CV, deep search is only suited for sustained rejuvenation goals.

Age is a final search dimension that affects both knowledge sought and venturing success. Katila (2002) showed that searching new knowledge to stimulate learning is most effective only in domains close to existing knowledge and understanding. As a firm moves into new domains, as it would in CVs seeking domain redefinition, searching in older knowledge of the target domain will be more helpful. Older knowledge is still new to the firm, and more is likely to positively affect performance. To understand this further, some aspects of entrepreneurial learning have to be considered.

LEARNING

The ability of a firm to observe stimuli is only the first step in creating new knowledge; that stimulus has to be understood in some way. Nahapiet and Ghoshal (1996) take a Schumpeterian idea and argue that this occurs through "exchange and combination." Exchange occurs when knowledge held by a firm or individual is transferred to another firm or individual. Combination occurs when that newly received information is combined with the existing knowledge base of the recipient. New knowledge and entrepreneurial opportunities emerge from this interaction. An important part of this process is the interpretive schema, a firm's "dominant logic" (Prahalad and Bettis, 1986). Because no two firms' interpretive schemata are the same, each firm can uniquely understand the same information. These entrepreneurial opportunities emerge from learning knowledge that is new to the firm, although others already know it.

Such a description of how new knowledge is created also shows why dramatically new opportunities that are far from a firm's current product/market base are harder to create. Stimuli that come into the firm from new domains do not encounter existing knowledge structures that can help in the exchange and combination processes of interpretation. Thus, although the firm may be able to understand the stimuli on a very basic level, the insight, or "conjecture" (Shane and Venkataraman, 2000), that would enable the firm to see rich and unique entrepreneurial opportunities is more difficult to construct due to the limited prior information about the domain held by the firm.

Zahra and George (2002) make a similar point in discussing bisociation (see BISOCIATION) (Koestler, 1966) as another perspective on how new knowledge emerges from learning after search. Like combination and conjecture, bisociation addresses bringing newly acquired knowledge together with existing knowledge. Here, however, the focus is on the act of recognizing incompatibilities between new and existing knowledge, and developing some knowledge from reconciliation is seen as shaping entrepreneurial action within the firm (McGrath and MacMillan, 2000).

From all of the above, it can also be understood why entrepreneurial activities that rely on local searches produce new knowledge that is close to that already known and why it can be produced with a high degree of success. When new stimuli carry many of the traits of existing knowledge, they can be easily manipulated in the context of existing routines and heuristics (March and Simon, 1958).

Similarly, to build richness in new areas, Katila's (2002) suggestion that firms search old knowledge touches on the important distinction between tacit and explicit knowledge (Polanyi, 1966) and the effect of that distinction on a firm's ability to learn. Older knowledge has more often been made explicit in a way that is easier for others to understand. Moreover, this explicated, older knowledge should already be linked in more complex ways to other pieces of competitive information, creating increased likelihood that a firm encountering it will develop a richer understanding of how it can benefit its competitive situation. By bringing in such well-developed knowledge, a firm increases the likelihood of bridging a domain. Indeed, Katila's (2002) research shows that searches in old knowledge that are outside a firm's domain are more fruitful in producing new products than searches on the new knowledge in the same domains.

How new opportunities, once discovered, are integrated into the firm presents many challenges to successful CV. Christensen (1997) described how firms in a number of industries were able to develop new technologies that should have allowed them to penetrate new markets, but then failed to do so because of the power of the routines and culture that surround existing products and services. Entrepreneurial activities had discovered the opportunity, but systems and structures outside of the CV activity prevented exploitation. Importantly, he also showed how firms can avoid these difficulties and manage a venture successfully, even if the venture could be perceived as cannibalizing existing products and customers.

Bibliography

Argyris, C. and Schon, D. (1978). *Organizational Learning*. Reading, MA: Addison-Wesley.

Barney, J. (1997). *Gaining and Sustaining Competitive Advantage*. Reading, MA: Addison-Wesley.

Christensen, C. (1997). *The Innovator's Dilemma*. Cambridge, MA: Harvard University Press.

Covin, J. and Miles, M. (1999). Corporate entrepreneurship and the pursuit of competitive advantage. *Entrepreneurship: Theory and Practice*, 23 (3): 47–63.

Cyert, R. and March, J. (1963). *A Behavioral Theory of the Firm*. Englewood Cliffs, NJ: Prentice-Hall.

Fleming, L. and Sorenson, O. (2000). Science as a map in technological search. UCLA/NBER working paper.

Fleming, L. and Sorenson, O. (2001). Technology as a complex adaptive system: Evidence from patent data. *Research Policy*, 30: 1019–39.

Grant, R. (1996). Toward a knowledge-based theory of the firm. *Strategic Management Journal*, 17 (winter special): 109–22.

Katila, R. (2002). New product search over time: Past ideas in their prime? *Academy of Management Journal*, 45: 995–1010.

Katila, R. and Ahuja, G. (2002). Something old, something new: A longitudinal study of search behavior and new product introduction. *Academy of Management Journal*, 45: 1183–94.

Koestler, A. (1966). *The Act of Creation*. London: Hutchinson.

McGrath, R. and MacMillan, I. (2000). *The Entrepreneurial Mindset*. Cambridge, MA: Harvard University Press.

Makadok, R. and Walker, G. (1996). Search and selection in the money market fund industry. *Strategic Management Journal*, 17 (summer special): 39–54.

March, J. (1991). Exploration and exploitation in organizational learning. *Organization Science*, 2: 71–87.

March, J. and Simon, H. (1958). *Organizations*. New York: Wiley.

Nahapiet, J. and Ghoshal, S. (1996). Social capital, intellectual capital, and organizational advantage. *Academy of Management Review*, 23: 242–66.

Nelson, R. and Winter, S. (1982). *An Evolutionary View of Economic Change*. Cambridge, MA: Harvard University Press.

Nonaka, I. (1994). A dynamic theory of organizational knowledge creation. *Organization Science*, 5: 14–37.

Polanyi, M. (1966). *The Tacit Dimension*. Garden City, NJ: Doubleday Anchor.

Prahalad, C. and Bettis, R. (1986). The dominant logic: A new linkage between diversity and performance. *Strategic Management Journal*, 7: 485–501.

Schumpeter, J. (1934). *The Theory of Economic Development*. Cambridge, MA: Harvard Economic Studies.

Shane, S. and Venkataraman, S. (2000). The promise of entrepreneurship as a field of research. *Academy of Management Review*, 25: 217–26.

Spender, J. (1996). Making knowledge the basis of a dynamic theory of the firm. *Strategic Management Journal*, 17 (winter special): 45–62.

Stuart, T. and Podolny, J. (1996). Local search and the evolution of technological capabilities. *Strategic Management Journal*, 17 (summer special): 21–38.

Zahra, S. and George, G. (2002). Absorptive capacity: A review, reconceptualization and extension. *Academy of Management Review*, 27: 185–203.

creating value

Charles E. Bamford

Value creation is the act of obtaining rents (widely defined as financial, social, or personal) that exceed the total costs (which may or may not include average rates of return for a particular industry) associated with that acquisition. More specifically, value creation is any outcome that has a positive utility (which may be economic or non-economic in nature) for any member of the subsystem (Habbershon, Williams, and MacMillan, 2003). A more micro-financial value assessment of value would include economic profits that refer to income above and beyond the cost of production, including interest and a normal return on capital. "Value is created by transforming inputs into products. The product is the medium for transferring value between the firm and its customers" (Stabell and Fjeldstad, 1998: 416).

The opportunity for creating value lies within market response timing under the assumption of market equilibrium, with unique resource bundles under the assumption of market disequilibrium, or as a result of creative discovery under an approach that examines the results of an individual or group of individuals' exploitation of an opportunity.

Three conditions underlie the ability to create value under conditions of market equilibrium. The first condition of general equilibrium is that the products within a market are relatively homogeneous (Hayek, 1948). Under this scenario, few differences exist between the characteristics of the products sold by each market participant; consequently, buyers distinguish between alternative offerings solely on the basis of price. A second condition is the relatively static quality of markets, where it is assumed that any changes in the supply or demand characteristics are quickly and efficiently matched by the reactions of consumers and/or producers. These rapid moves depend upon a third condition: perfectly competitive markets and, therefore, complete information (Hayek, 1948). Consumers must have perfect knowledge of market offerings, and producers must have complete information on market characteristics, production technologies, and sources of supply.

The outcome of these three conditions is that price quickly moves to marginal cost and no value is attainable after a short period of time. The quantity supplied is assumed to be equal to the quantity demanded, and thus the market clears in a quick manner. The value creation under these circumstances exists solely with market timing.

As we relax these assumptions, deterministic predictions become less applicable. The removal of the assumption of homogeneous demand and supply has a number of implications for the character of markets. Within economics, the basic unit of analysis is the industry and the presence of differences in demand curves within an industry (heterogeneous demand) implies that some producers will attempt to serve that heterogeneity through product differentiation (Porter, 1980). Thus, the existence of heterogeneous demand will lead to heterogeneous supply, whereby producers offer products which vary from those of other producers according to the desires of separate market groups. Likewise, economic actors may have unique characteristics that differentiate them from others who serve the same market. Therefore, under this approach, value is created through superior knowledge of the characteristics of demand, unique methods of production,

sources of supply, unique information, or means of distribution.

A third approach to value creation assumes that the value is created by entrepreneurs who discover an opportunity and exploit that within the market (Schumpeter, 1934). That is, Schumpeter saw the entrepreneur as the initiator of creative destruction and as the cause of constant change in the economy. Thus, rather than reacting to changes in the market, the entrepreneur is the creator of change that pushes the market into a state of disequilibrium.

Under this scenario, the entrepreneur, as the innovator within a market, achieves creative destruction in one of five ways (Schumpeter, 1934: 66):

- the introduction of a new good or level of quality;
- the introduction of a new method of production;
- the opening of a new market;
- the conquest of a new source of supply;
- the carrying out of the new organization of any industry.

This approach implicitly assumes imperfect information, without which there would be no opportunity to obtain entrepreneurial rents.

> An entrepreneurial discovery occurs when someone makes the conjecture that a set of resources is not put to its "best use" (i.e., the resources are priced "too low," given a belief about the price at which the output from their combination could be sold in another location, at another time, or in another form). If the conjecture is acted upon and is correct, the individual will earn an entrepreneurial profit. (Shane and Venkataraman, 2000: 220)

One of the truly compelling elements of entrepreneurship research is a systematic examination of *value creation*. While it has generally been examined as a financial construct, value would appear to be a condition that would extend beyond the financial to include social and personal positive utility. It is also fundamentally grounded in the starting position/perspective of the entrepreneur.

> The exploitation of an entrepreneurial opportunity requires the entrepreneur to believe that the

expected value of the entrepreneurial profit will be large enough to compensate for the opportunity cost of other alternatives (including the loss of leisure), the lack of liquidity of the investment of time and money, and a premium for bearing uncertainty. (Shane and Venkataraman, 2000: 223)

There have been some very promising, well-designed research efforts in this area of value creation. Erkko and Yli-Renko (1998) developed an innovative examination of value creation that is grounded in both transaction cost economics and the resource-based view of the firm. They provide a series of value creating mechanisms for entrepreneurs. Vozikis et al. (1999) examined value creation as a function of firm outputs rather than primarily accounting measures. Zahra and George (2002) utilized dynamic capabilities to generate wealth by upsetting the equilibrium of markets. Finally, Young, Sapienza, and Baumer (2003) found that value creation depended upon both innovation and knowledge sharing with strategic partners. This creative destruction enables new knowledge to replace less capable knowledge systems and provide positive value along multiple dimensions for new firms. The investigation of value creation by direct entrepreneurial endeavors has the potential to open a window onto the examination of opportunity analysis, persistence, and perhaps even existence.

Bibliography

Erkko, A. and Yli-Renko, H. (1998). New technology-based firms as agents of technological rejuvenation. *Entrepreneurship and Regional Development*, 10 (1): 71–93.

Habbershon, T., Williams, M., and MacMillan, I. (2003). A unified systems perspective of family firm performance. *Journal of Business Venturing*, 18 (4): 451–65.

Hayek, F. A. (1948). *Individualism and Economic Order*. Chicago: University of Chicago Press.

Porter, M. (1980). *Competitive Strategy: Techniques for Analyzing Industries and Competitors*. New York: Free Press.

Schumpeter, S. (1934). *Capitalism, Socialism, and Democracy*. New York: Harper and Row.

Shane, S. and Venkataraman, S. (2000). The promise of entrepreneurship as a field of research. *Academy of Management Review*, 25 (1): 217–26.

Stabell, C. and Fjeldstad, O. (1998). Configuring value for competitive advantage: On chains, shops and networks. *Strategic Management Journal*, 19: 413–37.

Vozikis, G., Bruton, G., Prasad, D., and Merikas, A. (1999). Linking corporate entrepreneurship to financial theory through additional value creation. *Entrepreneurship: Theory and Practice*, 24 (2): 33–43.

Young, G., Sapienza, H., and Baumer, D. (2003). The influence of flexibility in buyer–seller relationships on the productivity of knowledge. *Journal of Business Research*, 56: 443–51.

Zahra, S. and George, G. (2002). The net-enabled business innovation cycle and the evolution of dynamic capabilities. *Information Systems Research*, 13 (2): 147–50.

creative destruction

Michael D. Pfarrer and Ken G. Smith

Coined by Austrian economist Joseph Schumpeter in *Capitalism, Socialism, and Democracy* (*CSD*) (1942), creative destruction is an evolutionary process within capitalism that "revolutionizes the economic structure *from within*, incessantly destroying the old one, incessantly creating the new one." It is this "perennial gale" that every firm operates in, and in that "every piece of business strategy acquires its true significance" (1942: 83; original emphasis).

From his definition, one can conclude that Schumpeter viewed the market and competition as dynamic and in flux. Educated in Vienna at the turn of the century, Schumpeter was a student of the Austrian school of economics, a loose-knit group of researchers and acolytes that studied in the tradition of Carl Menger. Unlike traditional economists, who focus on equilibrium and a static form of competition, the Austrians view the market as a dynamic process (Smith, Ferrier, and Ndorfer, 2002). Whereas classic economic theory believes the key to competitive advantage and sustainable profits lies in the dampening of competition through barriers to entry and strategic positioning (Porter, 1980), the Austrians believe that abnormal profits and competitive advantage are fleeting, due to the perennial gale of firm actions and rival reactions. Innovation and firm success lead to imitation, which leads to erosion of profits.

Whereas classic economic theory largely ignores change, uncertainty, and disequilibrium, the Austrians emphasize innovation, flexibility, and heterogeneity (Jacobson, 1992: 784). Central to this debate is the role of the entrepreneur. The ideas of perfect competition and efficient markets, bulwarks to classic economic theory, downplay the role of the entrepreneur in market development and the accrual of profits (Jacobson, 1992). Schumpeter and the Austrians, however, see the entrepreneur as the central player in the market process. For Schumpeter, the entrepreneur is any manager or decision-maker who innovates (Allen, 1991, I: 104). These innovations, or "new combinations," include new goods, new methods, new markets, new sources of supply, and new industry organizations (Schumpeter, 1934: 66). Other Austrians, notably Kirzner (1973), have focused on the entrepreneur's use of idiosyncratic information to take advantage of opportunities not noticed by others. Different entrepreneurs will thus discover different opportunities because they possess different knowledge (Shane, 2000). Therefore, developments of new combinations will not be evenly distributed among industries and over time; instead, they will appear in "discrete rushes" or "swarms" (Schumpeter, 1934, 1942).

Schumpeter and other Austrian economics adherents view the market as never reaching equilibrium, due to the role of entrepreneurial innovation (Smith, Ferrier, and Ndorfer, 2002). These innovations, or "new combinations," direct the flow of resources toward fulfillment of consumer needs as opportunities arise, and when an innovating firm takes action that generates profits, competitors will respond (Schumpeter, 1942). The response leads to an inability of the innovators (first movers) to sustain profits (competitive advantage) due to imitation (Lee et al., 2000; Ferrier, Smith, and Grimm, 1999; Grimm and Smith, 1997). As the value of the new creation is destroyed, market leaders lose their advantage, and profit margins slow. Imitation increases, and overall market expansion slows, moving the business cycle toward equilibrium – until another innovation shatters the status quo (Schumpeter, 1934; Jacobson, 1992). The successful firm, then, must constantly be innovating to sustain profitability, and to avoid the perennial gale of creative destruction.

Schumpeter's idea of creative destruction is borne from the ideas he put forth in his two best-known works, the *Theory of Economic Development* (*TED*) and *CSD*. Schumpeter's concept of creative destruction is explored in chapter 7 of *CSD*, "Can capitalism survive?" Ironically, many of today's modern Austrians, as well as other strategy researchers, use creative destruction as support for capitalism's unique ability to reincarnate itself, but fail to focus on the negative impact that such a process might have. In order to fully understand the definition of creative destruction and its impact on current research, it is important to understand the context within which its author placed it.

Robert Loring Allen's biography of Schumpeter, *Opening Doors* (1991), expertly explains Schumpeter's affection for capitalism, but also his belief in its demise. Schumpeter argued capitalism's success would "inevitably lead to the throttling of innovation and a transition to socialism" (1991: xi). His thesis states that capitalism, "while economically stable... creates... a mentality and a style of life incompatible with its own fundamental conditions. [It] will be changed... although not by economic necessity and probably even at some sacrifice of economic welfare, into an order of things which it will be merely a matter of taste and terminology to call Socialism or not" (Schumpeter, 1928: 385–6). Loring goes on to elaborate on Schumpeter's expectations, saying that capitalism's success removes the entrepreneurial stimulus to gain profit (1991, II: 27). Whereas success may breed success, profit gainers also tend to become sated after a while. Schumpeter did not deny capitalism's role in the economic progress of the last two centuries, but he also felt that its overemphasis on profits would eventually fail to make people better or happier (Loring, 1991, II: 123–4). Indeed, as innovation becomes routine, growth will slow, and the entrepreneur will not feel the urge to challenge the status quo. The capitalists will thus become the bureaucrats and the ruling class, and the disenfranchised will eventually lash out against the "system" (Schumpeter, 1942). In the end, capitalism will fail because it has done its job too well – "it has created the institutions and conditions... that can easily be transformed into socialism" (Loring, 1991, II: 126). Interestingly enough, Schumpeter did not foresee the role of creative destruction in continually renewing the innovative and capitalist process, thus permitting capitalism to be reborn again and again.

While Schumpeter initially insisted that innovations typically originated in new, small firms (1934), he later argues in *CSD* that it is large, established enterprises frequently enjoying monopoly power that play the role of innovative leaders (1942). Schumpeter claims that because technical innovation is inherently risky, risk bearing appears to be more likely when firms are able to deploy an array of restrictive practices to protect their investments. He also argues that perfect competition is not only impossible but also inferior, and should not be set up as a model of ideal efficiency. Challenging the microeconomic theory assertion that monopolies' pricing behavior distorts socially beneficial resource allocation, Schumpeter claims that monopolies have to exercise their power cautiously, both in pricing and product policy, out of fear that they could stimulate another wave of monopoly-eroding changes. Therefore, monopolies are not nefarious, but rather have greater incentive to develop innovations, and thus benefit consumers (Conner, 1991). As one would expect, there continues to be challenges to this notion and other Schumpeterian ideas among economic, organizational, and strategic researchers (see Scherer, 1992, for a review).

Perhaps the greatest challenges, however, to Schumpeter's ideas of innovation, disequilibrium, and the role of the entrepreneur have come from fellow Austrian adherents. Israel Kirzner (1973, 1997) has long argued that innovation induces an "equilibrating" change to the status quo, in contrast to Schumpeter's more "disequilibrating," radical upheaval. Frank Knight, in his theory of entrepreneurship, argues that the innovator and capitalist are intertwined, whereas Schumpeter believes that their functions are separate (Evans and Jovanovic, 1989). Because of that, Knight argues entrepreneurs have to be responsible for their own capital funding. Schumpeter, thinking the entrepreneur is not a risk taker (1934: 77), feels that there are no liquidity constraints to being an entrepreneur, and that eventually the capital markets will bear the financial risk of discovery.

Schumpeter's ideas have flourished among his disciples and today's researchers. Many argue that Austrian economics is still radical and beyond the mainstream (Jacobson, 1992), but its vestiges can be seen in several fields, including competitive dynamics (cf. Smith, Ferrier, and Ndorfer, 2002; D'Aveni, 1994), dynamic capabilities (cf. Eisenhardt and Martin, 2000; Teece, Pisano, and Shuen, 1997), evolutionary theory (cf. Nelson and Winter, 1982), and the entrepreneurship-based (cf. Shane and Venkataraman, 2000) and resource-based view literatures (cf. Barney, 1986). Definitions of creative destruction and the "perennial gale" also abound: "Inevitable and eventual market decline of leading firms through the process of competitive action and reaction" (Smith, Ferrier, and Ndorfer, 2002); "Advantage is created and destroyed. Eventually every advantage will be eroded as realization of profits invite imitation. Firms that attempt to maintain the status quo are doomed" (Grimm and Smith, 1997); "Technological change occurring in upheavals" (Waldman and Jensen, 2001); "Invention of a new technology creates market disequilibrium" (Shane, 2000); and so on.

If "no general laws of business exist," as Jacobson writes, and "business success is a 'science of the specific'" (1992. 803, 804), then Austrian economics in general, and Joseph Schumpeter's idea of creative destruction in particular, should serve well the modern researcher who believes that markets are always changing, and that the pursuit of innovation is paramount to firm survival.

Bibliography

Allen, R. L. (1991). *Opening Doors: The Life and Work of Joseph Schumpeter*, 2 vols. London: Transaction Publishers.

Barney, J. B. (1986). The types of competition and the theory of strategy: Toward an integrative framework. *Academy of Management Review*, 11: 791–800.

Conner, K. (1991). A historical comparison of resource-based theory and five schools of thought within industrial organization economics: Do we have a new theory of the firm? *Journal of Management*, 17: 121–54.

D'Aveni, R. (1994). *Hypercompetition*. New York: Free Press.

Eisenhardt, K. and Martin, J. (2000). Dynamic capabilities: What are they? *Strategic Management Journal*, 21: 1105–21.

Evans, D. and Jovanovic, B. (1989). An estimated model of entrepreneurial choice under liquidity constraints. *Journal of Political Economy*, 97: 808–27.

Ferrier, W. J., Smith, K. G., and Grimm, C. M. (1999). The role of competition in market share erosion and dethronement: A study of industry leaders and challengers. *Academy of Management Journal*, 42: 372–88.

Grimm, C. M. and Smith, K. G. (1997). *Strategy as Action: Industry Rivalry and Coordination*. Cincinnati, OH: South-Western College Publishing.

Jacobson, R. (1992). The "Austrian" school of strategy. *Academy of Management Review*, 17: 782–807.

Kirzner, I. M. (1973). *Competition and Entrepreneurship*. Chicago: University of Chicago Press.

Kirzner, I. M. (1997). Entrepreneurial discovery and the competitive market process. *Journal of Economic Literature*, 35: 60–85.

Lee, H., Smith, K. G., Grimm, C. M., and Schomburg, A. (2000). Timing, order and durability of new product advantages with imitation. *Strategic Management Journal*, 21: 23–30.

Nelson, R. and Winter, S. (1982). *An Evolutionary Theory of Economic Change*. Cambridge, MA: Harvard University Press.

Porter, M. E. (1980). *Competitive Strategy*. New York: Free Press.

Scherer, F. M. (1992). Schumpeter and plausible capitalism. *Journal of Economic Literature*, 30: 1416–33.

Schumpeter, J. A. (1928). The instability of capitalism. *Economic Journal*, 38: 361–86.

Schumpeter, J. A. (1934). *The Theory of Economic Development*. Cambridge, MA: Harvard University Press.

Schumpeter, J. A. (1942). *Capitalism, Socialism, and Democracy*, 3rd edn. New York: Harper.

Shane, S. (2000). Prior knowledge and the discovery of entrepreneurial opportunities. *Organization Science*, 11: 448–69.

Shane, S. and Venkataraman, S. (2000). The promise of entrepreneurship as a field of research. *Academy of Management Review*, 25: 217–26.

Smith, K. G., Ferrier, W., and Ndorför, H. (2002). Competitive dynamics research: Critique and future directions. In M. Hitt, J. Harrison, and E. Freeman (eds.), *Handbook of Strategic Management*. Oxford: Blackwell, 315–61.

Teece, D., Pisano, G., and Shuen, A. (1997). Dynamic capabilities and strategic management. *Strategic Management Journal*, 18: 509–33.

Waldman, D. E. and Jensen, E. J. (2001). *Industrial Organization: Theory and Practice*. Boston, MA: Addison Wesley.

creativity

Jing Zhou

Creativity refers to the generation of novel and useful ideas concerning products, services, work methods, processes, and procedures by an individual or a small group of individuals working together (Amabile, 1996). This definition is outcome instead of process oriented. We judge the extent to which an idea is creative, instead of judging the extent to which an individual's mental process through which an idea is produced is creative. In addition, both novelty and usefulness are necessary conditions for an idea to be considered creative. An idea that is novel but has no potential value or usefulness would not be considered creative. By definition, individual creativity is different from organizational innovation, in that the former involves the idea generation stage, whereas the latter includes both the idea generation and implementation stages. Thus, individual creativity often provides a starting point for organizational innovation (Amabile, 1988).

Creativity can be seen as a continuum ranging from low levels to relatively high levels (Mumford and Gustafson, 1988). Whereas lower level creativity often involves incremental modifications and adjustments, reconfigurations of existing ideas, or combination of two or more previously unrelated ideas or material in a novel and useful fashion (*see* BISOCIATION), higher level creativity involves more frame-breaking and radical contributions.

Anyone with a normal level of intelligence can be somewhat creative (Barron and Harrington, 1981). To a certain degree, most individuals' creative abilities can be improved over time, through training and actual experience of participating in creative activities (Zhou and Shalley, 2003). However, different individuals may be capable of being creative in different domains (Amabile, 1996). For example, whereas one person may tend to express creativity in artistic designs in advertising, another person may be particularly good at coming up with new and useful ideas to improve business processes.

MEASUREMENT

The outcome-oriented definition of creativity facilitates empirical research because it allows researchers to measure and quantify creativity. In the behavioral laboratory, creativity is often measured by using the consensual assessment technique in which two or more qualified judges independently rate the extent to which an idea or solution is creative (Amabile, 1996). If the judges' ratings are found to be reliable and in agreement, then a creativity score is computed as an average of the creativity ratings for each individual across judges and the ideas rated (Shalley, 1991; Zhou, 1998).

In field studies, creativity is often measured by asking supervisors to rate the creativity of their employees (Oldham and Cummings, 1996; Zhou and George, 2001). Some studies involving R&D employees have also used objective measures such as the number of patents, patent disclosures, research papers and technical reports, and ideas submitted to employee suggestion programs (see Zhou and Shalley, 2003, for a review). Many studies have found similar results between objective measures and supervisory ratings of creativity, yet some studies have found varying results, and still other studies have found varying results between different objective measures. Thus, more research is needed to examine relations between supervisor ratings and objective measures, and among different objective measures of creativity (Zhou and Shalley, 2003).

FACTORS INFLUENCING CREATIVITY

Early creativity research took a person-centered approach, focusing on identifying personalities that characterize creative individuals (Barron and Harrington, 1981). However, despite the enormous effort spent on identifying key personalities that determine creativity across subject areas, empirical results have been inconclusive and inconsistent (Barron and Harrington, 1981). The answer to the question of what personalities are determinants of creativity in the workplace remains elusive. Thus, contemporary research has emphasized the need to identify and examine contextual factors that facilitate or inhibit creativity (Zhou and Shalley, 2003). More recently, researchers have come to realize that a fuller and more comprehensive understanding of how creativity is enhanced or restricted would require an interactional approach, in which both personal and contextual factors are taken into consideration (Oldham and Cummings, 1996; Woodman, Sawyer, and Griffin, 1993; Zhou, 2003).

A great deal of research concerning effects of contextual factors on creativity has been facilitated by an intrinsic motivation principle (Zhou and Shalley, 2003). This principle is the key part of the componential model of creativity, which posits that individuals exhibit the highest level of creativity when they possess domain-relevant knowledge and skills, creativity-relevant skills and strategies, and most importantly, task motivation (Amabile, 1988, 1996). Contextual factors are theorized to affect creativity via influencing individuals' task motivation, especially their intrinsic motivation. Factors that boost intrinsic motivation are theorized to enhance creativity, whereas factors that reduce intrinsic motivation are said to diminish creativity, particularly during idea generation (Amabile, 1996). This principle has received some direct and indirect support. For example, transformational leadership has been shown to enhance creativity partially through boosting intrinsic motivation (Shin and Zhou, 2003).

More conceptual advances have been made in recent years. For example, Zhou and George (2001) developed a voice perspective of creativity. They theorized and found that employees with high job *dissatisfaction* exhibited the highest creativity when continuance commitment was high and when (1) useful feedback from co-workers, or (2) co-worker helping, or (3) perceived organizational support for creativity was high. Shalley (1991) highlighted the importance of creativity goals in directing one's attention and effort toward creativity. Shalley and Perry-Smith (2001) and Zhou (2003) developed a social learning perspective of creativity. These and other new conceptual advances hold considerable promise for achieving richer and more in-depth understanding of how a wide variety of contextual factors affect creativity.

Examining issues related to creativity might be particularly interesting and important in the context of entrepreneurship, because creativity in entrepreneurship goes far beyond simply coming up with a new business idea. In fact, to the extent that entrepreneurship involves the creation, discovery, evaluation, exploration, and exploitation of opportunities (Shane and Venkataraman, 2000), either within established firms or as new ventures, creativity exhibited by individuals, groups, and organizations is an indispensable part of the entire entrepreneurial process. As such, investigating antecedents and consequences of creativity at the individual, group, and organization levels in the entrepreneurial process presents a rich and exciting opportunity for researchers and practitioners interested in understanding, promoting, and engaging in entrepreneurship.

Bibliography

Amabile, T. M. (1988). A model of creativity and innovation in organizations. In B. M. Staw and L. L. Cummings (eds.), *Research in Organizational Behavior*, 10: 123–67. Greenwich, CT: JAI Press.

Amabile, T. M. (1996). *Creativity in Context*. Boulder, CO: Westview Press.

Barron, F. and Harrington, D. M. (1981). Creativity, intelligence, and personality. *Annual Review of Psychology*, 32: 439–76.

Mumford, M. D. and Gustafson, S. B. (1988). Creativity syndrome: Integration, application, and innovation. *Psychological Bulletin*, 103: 27–43.

Oldham, G. R. and Cummings, A. (1996). Employee creativity: Personal and contextual factors at work. *Academy of Management Journal*, 39: 607–34.

Shalley, C. E. (1991). Effects of productivity goals, creativity goals, and personal discretion on individual creativity. *Journal of Applied Psychology*, 76: 179–85.

Shalley, C. E. and Perry-Smith, J. E. (2001). Effects of social-psychological factors on creative performance: The role of informational and controlling expected evaluation and modeling experience. *Organizational Behavior and Human Decision Processes*, 84: 1–22.

Shane, S. and Venkataraman, S. (2000). The promise of entrepreneurship as a field of research. *Academy of Management Review*, 25: 217–26.

Shin, S. and Zhou, J. (2003). Transformational leadership, conservation, and creativity: Evidence from Korea. *Academy of Management Journal*, 46: 703–14.

Woodman, R. W., Sawyer, J. E., and Griffin, R. W. (1993). Toward a theory of organizational creativity. *Academy of Management Review*, 18: 293–321.

Zhou, J. (1998). Feedback valence, feedback style, task autonomy, and achievement orientation: Interactive effects on creative performance. *Journal of Applied Psychology*, 83: 261–76.

Zhou, J. (2003). When the presence of creative co-workers is related to creativity: Role of supervisor close monitoring, developmental feedback, and creative personality. *Journal of Applied Psychology*, 88: 413–422.

Zhou, J. and George, J. M. (2001). When job dissatisfaction leads to creativity: Encouraging the expression of voice. *Academy of Management Journal*, 44: 682–96.

Zhou, J. and Shalley, C. E. (2003). Research on employee creativity: A critical review and directions for future research. In J. J. Martocchio and G. R. Ferris (eds.), *Research in Personnel and Human Resource Management*, Vol. 22. Oxford: Elsevier Science, 165–217.

D

disruptive innovations

Gautam Ahuja and PuayKhoon Toh

Disruptive innovations refer to technologies that introduce a different, and often initially inferior, performance package from the mainstream technology but manage to gain dominance over and displace the superior technology in the market. Christensen (1997) pioneered the notion of disruptive innovations while studying phenomena in the hard disk drive industry. The key idea and the irony underlying this phenomenon is that the new technological trajectory, created by the disruptive technology that supersedes the old one, is actually initially poorer in terms of performance attributes valued by traditional customers.

To demonstrate this notion, Christensen (1997) provides the example of the 3.5-inch hard drives overtaking the original state-of-the-art 5.25-inch hard disk drive in the market, despite their lower capacity and higher cost per megabyte. IBM's dominance in the mainframe industry and its subsequent missing out on the minicomputer architecture and market, despite the two products' similarity in technology and the mainframe computer's superiority in terms of technological performance attributes, is another example of the disruptive innovations phenomenon (Christensen and Bower, 1996). One main reason put forth to explain such phenomena is the concept of "performance oversupply." Consumers switch to the disruptive technology when their requirements for the principal functional attribute of the technology has been satisfied, and they shift their emphasis and evaluation criteria towards the less important secondary attributes. The original mainstream technology oversupplies in terms of the principal attribute (e.g., performance), but loses out on

the secondary ones (e.g., overall cost of the packaged product). Implicit in such analysis is the idea of decreasing marginal returns to consumers of the principal attribute beyond a certain threshold. The incremental value, to consumers, of superior performance along the main attribute dimension is low beyond a certain point. When such incremental value does not supersede the other product attributes such as overall cost, then consumers may actually choose the products with lower performance capabilities along the principal dimension. The concept of disruption is different from that of a technological discontinuity (*see* RADICAL INNOVATIONS). Disruptive innovations do not necessarily create a discontinuity in the technological trajectory, but rather displace whole paradigms with new, and in some respects, possibly inferior paths.

The idea of disruptive innovations draws upon the theory that the resource allocation of the firm with respect to inventive activities is heavily influenced by main customers. Typically, firms with a superior mainstream technology that are subsequently overtaken by disruptive technologies do not necessarily suffer from managerial myopia or organizational lethargy. Rather, they fail to recognize their situation of oversupply on the principal performance attribute, not because they are inattentive to market demands, but because they listen too closely to their main customers. These main customers are typically the most sophisticated ones who demand the maximum performance for the principal attribute.

In the early phase of development, the subsequently disruptive technology is significantly inferior on the principal performance attribute, and hence only serves a niche market, while firms with the superior mainstream technology predominantly serve the bulk of the consumer demand. At this stage, the emphasis is still on principal performance of the technology and the subsequently disruptive technology cannot yet serve the technological needs of the more sophisticated customers. Further, at this time, mainstream firms compete actively along the dimension of technological performance, as they fight to satisfy the needs of their most sophisticated customers in order to remain industry leaders. Subsequently, however, when further development raises the performance level of the inferior disruptive technology to a level that is sufficient to satisfy the bulk of the customers, customers switch to such disruptive technologies as they provide better value along other dimensions such as price.

The difficulties of operationalizing consumer utility pose challenges to empirical research in this area. The demand-based view of technological evolution underlying the concept of disruptive innovation necessitates the operationalization of the utility function in one form or the other in most empirical studies of this concept. For example, in answering the question "when are technologies disruptive and when do they remain merely inferior?" one would need to determine, conceptually or otherwise, the point where technological performance of the "disruptive" innovation exceeds the needs of the mainstream consumers. Without an accurate estimate of the consumer's utility function, it is difficult to form an ex-ante expectation of the disruptive potential of an inferior technology. Thus, empirically explaining the occurrence of technological disruptions by inferior technologies requires a proper characterization of the demand function; for example, the extent of decreasing marginal utility, heterogeneity of demand, or similarity and symmetry of preferences between different consumer groups (Adner, 2002; Adner and Levinthal, 2001). Simulation techniques have been used to study disruptive technologies, and such simulations circumvent the need to operationalize consumer utility by explicitly modeling them. To date, the challenge of empirically examining the dynamics of disruptive technologies still remains.

Bibliography

Adner, R. (2002). When are technologies disruptive? A demand-based view of the emergence of competition. *Strategic Management Journal*, 23: 667–88.

Adner, R. and Levinthal, D. A. (2001). Demand heterogeneity and technology evolution: Implications for product and process innovation. *Management Science*, 47: 611–28.

Christensen, C. M. (1997). *The Innovator's Dilemma*. Boston, MA: Harvard Business School Press.

Christensen, C. M. and Bower, J. L. (1996). Customer power, strategic investment, and the failure of leading firms. *Strategic Management Journal*, 17: 197–218.

Pfeffer, J. and Salancik, G. R. (1978). *The External Control of Organizations: A Resource Dependence Perspective*. New York: Harper and Row.

E

emergent strategy

Dennis P. Slevin and Jeffrey G. Covin

Emergent strategy can be defined as internally consistent patterns of competitive actions and reactions that spontaneously arise over time as organizations navigate within their operating environments. This definition recognizes that emergent strategies may occupy one end of a deliberate–emergent continuum which represents different fundamental behaviors concerning the strategic process (Mintzberg and Waters, 1985). Deliberate strategies involve a well articulated and formalized planning process. Commonly with deliberate strategies, assumptions are checked; SWOT analyses are conducted; specific plans are formulated; and then the organization tracks its performance according to plan. Deliberate strategies reflect a Newtonian philosophical approach to the universe and are characteristic of much of the scholarly thinking concerning strategic planning in the 1960s and 1970s (Newman and Logan, 1971; Ansoff, 1965; Steiner, 1969; Andrews, 1971).

Emergent strategies, in contrast, are more sporadic, short time-frame, reactive, and opportunistic responses to environmental conditions. Mintzberg and Waters have suggested a five-part model in which intended strategy eventually develops into realized strategy (Mintzberg and Waters, 1985; Mintzberg, 1994). The starting point is the *intended* strategy, but things do not always go as planned and *unrealized* strategies drop off the intended strategic menu. This generates the *deliberate* strategy of the firm, which is then augmented by the *emergent* strategy, and the confluence of deliberate strategy and emergent strategy results in the *realized* (actual) strategy of the firm.

In the simplest of worlds the intended strategy would become the realized strategy, and life would be mechanistic and predictable. In the most complex and challenging of worlds there might not even be an intended strategy, but merely an emergent strategy in response to variously anticipated environmental and competitive challenges. Mintzberg and Waters (1985) suggest not only a deliberate–emergent strategy continuum, but also the fact that various strategy types can exist within this continuum. These include planned, entrepreneurial, ideological, umbrella, process, unconnected, consensus, and imposed strategy types.

The propensity of firms to exhibit emergent strategies will likely be related to the extent to which those firms seek to recognize and exploit entrepreneurial opportunity. For example, high-growth new ventures often follow emergent strategies to cope with the high rates of change they are facing. It has been proposed that "time . . . exerts unrelenting forward pressure on successful entrepreneurial ventures for continuous adaptation" (Slevin and Covin, 1997a: 58). Emergent strategy can enable new ventures to meet the needs of continuous adaptation. Likewise, long-established firms that wish to engage in entrepreneurial activity must similarly cope with rapid change via emergent strategic processes. However, the need for and potential benefit of emergent strategy may be somewhat diminished, in a relative sense, among firms that are generally less inclined to act entrepreneurially. This is so because the absence of an entrepreneurial orientation among such firms will correspond with less felt need for strategic responsiveness, as enabled through emergent strategy, to recognized entrepreneurial opportunities.

THE WORD "EMERGENT"

"Emergent" is an interesting word because it captures some of the spontaneity and reactivity of the strategy formation (vs. formulation) process. The word "emergent" is often used in the context of budding flowers or sprouting trees. Synonyms include "appearing," "budding," "coming," "developing," "efflorescent," "emanant," "emanating," "emerging," "issuing forth," "outgoing," and "rising." However, as a word, it may not capture much of the desperation that often accompanies firms' efforts to reorient their strategic focus. It would be interesting to find some label that more accurately denotes the reactivity and spontaneity of the emergent strategy process. Perhaps the expression "responsive strategy" captures more of the characteristics, or at least additional connotations, of the phenomenon.

Nonetheless, it appears as though "emergence" is increasingly recognized as a useful construct in strategic management and organizational behavior research. As Goldstein (1999: 68) suggests: "Emergence is not an entirely new topic. Conceptual constructs resembling emergence can be found in Western thought since the time of the ancient Greeks, and have at times had significant impact on intellectual culture. However, emergence is emerging today as a construct of complex, dynamical systems." Certainly, the prior observations on the relevance of emergent strategy for entrepreneurial firms would support this contention.

DEFINING THE EMERGENT-TO-PLANNED STRATEGY CONTINUUM

Percy W. Bridgman (1927), a US physicist and the father of operationalism, suggested that concepts are defined by the behaviors used to measure them. In this spirit, it may be useful to specify items that have been used in empirical research to measure the Emergent-to-Planned Strategy Scale (Slevin and Covin, 1997b). The following items are all measured on a seven-point "strongly disagree" to "strongly agree" Likert scale.

- We typically don't know what the content of our business strategy should be until we engage in some trial and error actions. (Reverse scored)
- My business unit's strategy is carefully planned and well understood before any significant competitive actions are taken.
- Formal strategic plans serve as a basis for our competitive actions.
- My business unit's strategy is typically not planned in advance, but, rather, emerges over time as the best means for achieving our objectives become clearer. (Reverse scored)
- Competitive strategy for my business unit typically results from a formal business planning process (i.e., the formal plan precedes the action).

It appears clear from the above items that there are two ends of the continuum:

Deliberate: Environmental analysis – Formulation – Implementation – Evaluation and control
Emergent: Purposefully maneuver toward desired end state – Evaluate progress – Incrementally adapt – Purposefully maneuver toward desired end state

There is no reason to believe that the firm must stay at either the deliberate or the emergent end of the strategy continuum. It makes sense that one could start with a deliberate planning process based on core competencies and resources of the firm and then apply emergent "patches" as needed to respond to environmental exigencies. These emergent "patches" could be metaphorically compared to the numerous software patches that we work with as we engage our computer systems. The entire software system is not rewritten, but rather a "patch" is applied to cope with a virus or some other environmental contingency. Other conditions may call for the development of a much more comprehensive emergent strategy. Moreover, there is no reason to suggest that deliberate and emergent strategic planning processes cannot exist simultaneously in the same firm. According to Mintzberg (1994: 111): "All viable strategies have emergent and deliberate [i.e., planned] qualities, since all must combine some degree of flexible learning with some degree of cerebral control." In a recent

study, Fletcher and Harris (2002) used participants in a Graduate Enterprise Programme in
the UK to determine their frequency of participation in deliberate versus emergent planning
processes. The results, in brief, suggest "the
emergent category appeared most frequently
(95 instances within 24 of the 25 firms), followed
by planning (53 instances within 20 firms). The
integrated category occurred less frequently (36
instances in 15 firms), while the 'neither planning nor integrated' category appeared in only
16 instances and 10 firms" (Fletcher and Harris,
2002: 304).

These results and intuition suggest that firms
cycle on the deliberate–emergent strategy continuum and that strategic processes at both
ends of the continuum can possibly occur
simultaneously (Fletcher and Harris, 2002:
304). An important matter, regardless of whether
the strategy is deliberate or emergent, is the issue
of consistency. It makes sense to argue that
the essence of most good strategies is *consistency*
in decisions concerning markets, customers, production, design, service, and so on (Argyreis and
McGahan, 2002). As noted by Mintzberg (1987:
29), "strategy is a concept rooted in stability."

Research into the phenomenon of emergent
strategy might productively focus on the
following questions.

What are the organizational architecture attributes that enable companies to effectively carry
out emergent strategies? Organizational architecture is the conduit through which strategies
are enacted, so architectures must be created
with the needs of strategy in mind. Given the
increasingly recognized need for companies to
exhibit strategic flexibility (Eisenhardt and
Brown, 1999), contributing to a better understanding of how organizational architecture facilitates or inhibits the exhibition of emergent
strategy should be a high priority for researchers.

How can emergent strategy be harnessed or
directed to best leverage entrepreneurial opportunities? Entrepreneurial opportunities are often
autonomously and serendipitously recognized
by an organization's members (Burgelman,
1984). The effective exploitation of entrepreneurial opportunities would, therefore, seem to
be dependent upon the organization's ability
to craft an emergent strategy designed with

the objective of entrepreneurial growth in
mind. Studies of how the most innovative
companies exhibit strategic responsiveness to
recognized entrepreneurial opportunities are
suggested.

How is emergent strategy managed from an
organizational-level perspective? Relevant challenges here would include determining (1) how
the control function is manifested in firms whose
strategies are emergent; (2) how the parameters
of acceptable or desirable strategic behaviors
are communicated within firms with emergent
strategies; and (3) how the pattern of strategic
behavior that represents emergent strategy is
established and sustained over time.

Bibliography

Andrews, K. (1971). *The Concept of Corporate Strategy.*
Homewood, IL: Dow Jones-Irwin.
Ansoff, H. I. (1965). *Corporate Strategy.* New York:
McGraw-Hill.
Argyreis, N. and McGahan, A. M. (2002). An interview
with Michael Porter. *Academy of Management Execu-
tive*, 16 (2): 43–52.
Bridgman, Percy W. (1927). *The Logic of Modern Physics.*
New York: Macmillan.
Burgelman, R. A. (1984). Managing the internal corporate
venturing process: Some recommendations from prac-
tice. *Sloan Management Review*, 25 (2): 33–48.
Eisenhardt, K. M. and Brown, S. L. (1999). Patching:
Restitching business portfolios in dynamic markets.
Harvard Business Review, 77 (3): 72–82.
Fletcher, M. and Harris, S. (2002). Seven aspects of
strategy formation: Exploring the value of plan-
ning. *International Small Business Journal*, 20 (3):
297–313.
Goldstein, J. (1999). Emergence as a construct: History
and issues. *Emergence*, 1 (1): 49–73.
Mintzberg, H. (1987). Strategy concept II: Another look
at why organizations need strategies. *California Management Review*, 30 (1): 25–32.
Mintzberg, H. (1994). The fall and rise of strategic planning. *Harvard Business Review*, 72 (1): 107–14.
Mintzberg, H. and Waters, J. A. (1985). Of strategies,
deliberate and emergent. *Strategic Management Journal*, 6: 257–72.
Newman, W. A. and Logan, J. P. (1971). *Strategy, Policy,
and Central Management.* Cincinnati, OH: Southwest-
ern Publications.
Slevin, D. P. and Covin, J. G. (1997a). Time, growth,
complexity, and transitions: Entrepreneurial challenges
for the future. *Entrepreneurship: Theory and Practice*, 22
(2): 53–68.

Slevin, D. P. and Covin, J. G. (1997b). Strategy formation patterns, performance, and the significance of context. *Journal of Management*, 23 (2): 189–209.

Steiner, G. A. (1969). *Strategic Planning: What Every Manager Must Know*. New York: Free Press.

entrepreneur

James J. Chrisman and Franz Kellermanns

"Entrepreneurs are individuals or groups of individuals, acting independently, or as part of a corporate system, who create new organizations, or instigate renewal or innovation within an existing organization" (Sharma and Chrisman, 1999: 17). As the definition suggests, entrepreneurs can act either independently or in affiliation with an existing organization (*see* CORPORATE ENTREPRENEURSHIP), although the former is more prevalent and has received the most attention.

The notion that entrepreneurs are key to a nation's economic development and recovery has been suggested by prominent scholars in the field (e.g., Schumpeter, 1934; Stevenson and Jarillo, 1990). However, the use of the term "entrepreneur" (see ENTREPRENEURSHIP) has been the subject of much debate. Judgments range from rejection or skepticism about universally acceptable definitions, to a clear stated need for a definition in order to further understanding among researchers and practitioners (Gartner, 1988; Sharma and Chrisman, 1999).

An early definition by Richard Cantillon (1734) characterizes entrepreneurs as individuals driven by profit, who have the ability to realize such profit by buying low and selling high. In his *Treatise on Political Economy*, Jean Baptiste Say (1816) also focuses on the quest for profit as characteristic of entrepreneurs, while emphasizing that entrepreneurs use periods of change and uncertainty to reallocate resources. Thus, Say describes the entrepreneur as a person involved in creating newness. These early definitions of the term focus on entrepreneurial creation and thus are behavioral in nature. However, entrepreneurs were always regarded as individuals with unique qualities. For example, Say (1816) attributes special qualities like judgment, perseverance, and knowledge to entrepreneurs (*see* HISTORY OF THE ACADEMIC STUDY OF ENTREPRENEURSHIP).

By contrast, the most important contemporary theory of entrepreneurship focused exclusively on the behavioral aspects of an entrepreneur. Schumpeter (1934) conceptualized the entrepreneur as an innovator (*see* INNOVATIONS), who realizes new means of production without necessarily being an owner. In fact, Schumpeter argues that risk bearing is inherent to owners and capitalists and is not an entrepreneurial function (*see* ENTREPRENEURIAL RISK). To Schumpeter, an individual is an entrepreneur only when he or she is engaged in the development of new combinations. An individual ceases to be an entrepreneur once that set of tasks is completed and the individual turns to new occupations, most typically the management of the enterprise created to exploit a new combination.

Two economic perspectives contribute to an appreciation of the economic role of entrepreneurs. For Schumpeter (1934), the entrepreneurial act, termed creative destruction (*see* CREATIVE DESTRUCTION), disturbs existing equilibrium situations in an economy. By contrast, the Austrian school suggests that the economy is in disequilibrium and that entrepreneurs take advantage of imperfections in the market to guide the economy toward an equilibrium situation (Kirzner, 1973). Thus, entrepreneurs can create new ventures under diverse market conditions, be it by exploiting inefficiencies or by creating new resource combinations.

Schumpeter (1934) focuses on innovative behavior as the defining characteristic of entrepreneurs. Kirzner (1973), on the other hand, highlights the ability to perceive opportunities in the environment as the factor that distinguishes entrepreneurs from non-entrepreneurs (*see* ENTREPRENEURIAL DISCOVERY). His notion of entrepreneurial alertness (*see* ENTREPRENEURIAL ALERTNESS) goes beyond the assumption that entrepreneurs possess superior information; instead, alertness refers to the ability to find market information that helps exploit opportunities. Both of these viewpoints suggest that being an entrepreneur is a behavior an individual might display at certain points in his or her life. Ronstadt (1988) has further shown that this behavior may be recurring and can expose individuals to ideas and opportunities that make it likely that they will display that behavior again in the future. An implication of Ronstadt's work is that habitual entrepreneurs (*see* HABITUAL ENTREPRENEURS) learn from their venturing efforts, making the likelihood of a successful entrepreneurial career higher than the likelihood of success with any single venturing foray.

However, until recently, research on entrepreneurship outside of economics focused largely upon personal and psychological characteristics of entrepreneurs. Labeled the "trait approach" (Gartner, 1988), this school of thought often presented entrepreneurs as great inspirational leaders. Among others, risk taking propensity, need for achievement, perceived locus of control, autonomy, perseverance, commitment, vision, creativity, single-mindedness, physical attractiveness, popularity, sociability, intelligence, diplomacy, decisiveness, and birth order were considered important determinants of whether an individual became an entrepreneur as well as whether the individual was successful in that endeavor (Gartner, 1988).

Among the most prominent of the adherents to this perspective was McClelland (1961). His book *The Achieving Society*, and others like it, helped set the direction of the field for approximately a quarter of a century. He argued that individuals with a high need for achievement compared to other members of society are prone to engage in entrepreneurial activities, since opportunity exploitation (*see* OPPORTUNITY EXPLOITATION) satisfies their need for accomplishment. However, subsequent studies with more careful control features demonstrated that the trait approach was limited in its ability to distinguish entrepreneurs from managers or members of the general population (Gartner, 1988).

By contrast, the "behavioral approach" does not concentrate on personality characteristics, but regards contextual factors, such as the way entrepreneurs find opportunities, acquire resources, and formulate entry strategies, as more important. Thus, this line of research focuses on the decisions an entrepreneur makes and what an entrepreneur does, not who he or she is (Gartner, 1988). Most scholars have moved toward the behavioral approach, as it appears to be more fruitful for addressing why entrepreneurs act, how entrepreneurs seek, discover, and pursue opportunities, and what the consequences are of their actions (Stevenson and Jarillo, 1990). For example, research has suggested that individuals who procrastinate or plan too extensively are less likely to start businesses than individuals who are prepared to act, albeit with imperfect information, to find out if their ideas are feasible (Carter, Gartner, and Reynolds, 1996).

On the other hand, more recent attempts to understand how personal attributes affect entrepreneurial success have been reframed to focus on factors such as entrepreneurial networks (*see* ENTREPRENEURIAL NETWORKS), industry, management, and venturing experience, skills and abilities, and educational background. This revised focus is consistent with the conventional wisdom of venture capitalists (*see* VENTURE CAPITAL) who believe that the behaviors and characteristics of an entrepreneur are more important than a venture's strategy (*see* BUSINESS PLAN; STRATEGIC ENTREPRENEURSHIP). In fact, research has indicated that the initial size, survival, and growth of a venture are each related to some of the following characteristics: the number of entrepreneurs involved in a start-up, education levels, management experience, industry experience, age, entrepreneurial experience, goals, and parental role models (Cooper, Gimeno-Gascon, and Woo, 1994; Cooper, Woo, and Dunkelberg, 1989).

See also *entrepreneurial decisions; entrepreneurial growth; entrepreneurial leadership; nascent entrepreneur*

Bibliography

Cantillon, R. (1734). *Essai sur la nature du commerce en general.* [*Essay on the nature of general commerce*]. London: Macmillan.

Carter, N. M., Gartner, W. B., and Reynolds, P. D. (1996). Exploring start-up event sequences. *Journal of Business Venturing*, 11: 151–66.

Cooper, A. C., Gimeno-Gascon, F. J., and Woo, C. Y. (1994). Initial human and financial capital predictors of new venture performance. *Journal of Business Venturing*, 9: 371–95.

Cooper, A. C., Woo, C. Y., and Dunkelberg, W. C. (1989). Entrepreneurship and the initial size of firms. *Journal of Business Venturing*, 4: 317–32.

Gartner, W. B. (1988). "Who is an entrepreneur?" is the wrong question. *American Journal of Small Business*, 12 (4): 11–32.

Kirzner, I. M. (1973). *Competition and Entrepreneurship*. Chicago: University of Chicago Press.

McClelland, D. C. (1961). *The Achieving Society*. Princeton, NJ: Van Nostrand.

Ronstadt, R. (1988). The corridor principle. *Journal of Business Venturing*, 3: 31–40.

Say, J. B. A. (1816). *A Treatise on Political Economy*. London: Sherwood, Neeley and Jones.

Schumpeter, J. A. (1934). *The Theory of Economic Development*. Cambridge, MA: Harvard University Press.

Sharma, P. and Chrisman, J. J. (1999). Toward a reconciliation of the definitional issues in the field of corporate entrepreneurship. *Entrepreneurship: Theory and Practice*, 23 (3): 11–27.

Stevenson, H. H. and Jarillo, J. C. (1990). A paradigm of entrepreneurship: Entrepreneurial management. *Strategic Management Journal*, 11 (summer): 11–27.

entrepreneurial alertness

Sharon A. Alvarez and Jay B. Barney

Entrepreneurial alertness is the ability that some people have to recognize competitive imperfections in markets. Competitive imperfections exist in markets when information about technology, demand, or other determinants of competition in an industry is not widely understood by those operating in that industry. The existence of competitive imperfections in markets suggests that it is possible for at least some economic actors in these markets to earn economic profits. Thus, entrepreneurial alertness can be thought of as the ability of some people to recognize opportunities to earn economic profits.

However, as developed by Kirzner (1989), entrepreneurial alertness does not imply that individuals are systematically and rationally searching their environment for competitive imperfections. Rather, these individuals become aware of these competitive imperfections through their day-to-day activities. Indeed, they are often surprised that these imperfections exist, and that they have not been previously exploited by someone else.

Kirzner developed these perspectives about entrepreneurial alertness in connection with other theorists, including Hayek (1948) and Mises (1949), in response to traditional neoclassical theories in economics. Neoclassical theory admits the possibility that information asymmetries might exist in markets. However, this theory adopts the assumption that such asymmetries can, in principle, always be reduced by rational and costly search. That is, all information is, in principle, knowable, although it may be costly to produce. In this sense, there can be no entrepreneurial alertness – in the way this concept is defined by Kirzner – in the markets described by neoclassical theory, because there can be no "surprise" information in such markets.

Hayek (1948) argued that information asymmetries often persist in markets. Indeed, for Hayek, each person in a market has unique information that is costly for others in that market to obtain. Market processes have the effect of aggregating the unique information held by different individuals in a market. Market imperfections – and thus, opportunities for profit – are created when a person's information is substantively different than the aggregate information created by the market.

Mises (1949) developed this point of view further by arguing that individuals in markets are not simply price takers – at the mercy of aggregate market forces over which they have no control. Rather, he suggested that some people – what he called entrepreneurs – engage in activities that give them influence over how a market will evolve. For Mises, entrepreneurs drive market forces, rather than just market forces driving entrepreneurial behavior.

In this context, Kirzner's notion of entrepreneurial alertness is a logical predecessor to entrepreneurial action. Entrepreneurial action is defined as entrepreneurial discovery (*see* ENTREPRENEURIAL DISCOVERY). Without the ability to recognize competitive imperfections, entrepreneurial activity cannot exist. And without entrepreneurial action, the arguments put forward by Hayek and Mises about how markets work have no validity.

The work of Hayek, Mises, and Kirzner are all examples of what has come to be called Austrian economics (*see* AUSTRIAN ECONOMICS).

However, while traditional Austrians abandoned all notions of equilibrium in their analysis, modern Austrians – starting with Hayek and Mises, and continuing with Kirzner – include some equilibrium notions in their analysis.

Future research questions might be concerned with issues such as the degree to which entrepreneurial alertness exists. If entrepreneurial alertness does exist, what is its nature? Is entrepreneurial alertness cognitive or is it a personality difference? Do only entrepreneurs have entrepreneurial alertness or are others characterized by this phenomenon as well? And, does entrepreneurial alertness manifest itself in other ways? If so, what are those ways? Finally, can entrepreneurial alertness be acquired or is an individual born entrepreneurially alert?

Bibliography

Hayek, F. A. von (1948). *Individualism and Economic Order*. London: Routledge and Kegan Paul.

Kirzner, I. M. (1989). *Discovery, Capitalism, and Distributive Justice*. Oxford: Blackwell.

Mises, Ludwig von (1949). *Human Action*. New Haven, CT: Yale University Press.

entrepreneurial alliances

Jeffrey J. Reuer

An entrepreneurial alliance may be defined simply as a collaborative agreement undertaken by a firm for an entrepreneurial purpose. Typically, these alliances will involve at least one entrepreneurial firm, but this need not be the case, just as some entrepreneurial firms might utilize alliances for more routine activities.

The first question that this definition raises, then, is what distinctive content does the adjective "entrepreneurial" add? For example, in what ways do entrepreneurial alliances differ from "strategic" alliances or other types of interfirm collaborations, and what insights might such distinctions yield?

Based on alliance investment patterns over the past few decades, one may argue that such adjectives are of no small consequence and are becoming increasingly relevant as alliances have become more pervasive and have also changed in character. Historically, the typical alliance tended to be an equity joint venture used for the purpose of entering a developing country while responding to a government's restrictions on foreign investment. Technology transfer often was unilateral, from a multinational firm to a venture in the host country, and the foreign investor primarily sought access to the local market on a stand-alone basis.

Today, however, alliances often crop up between actual or potential competitors, involve bilateral knowledge sharing while using more complex deal structures, and have global market objectives in a variety of sectors. Alliances often figure prominently in new ventures' internationalization initiatives, are an investment vehicle by which corporate entrepreneurship proceeds, and are often an important means by which entrepreneurial firms can achieve their growth and financing objectives.

When thinking about how entrepreneurial alliances potentially differ from other types of alliances, it is useful to consider separately a number of differences in *degree* versus differences in *kind*. Both types of differences pose fruitful avenues of research that can enrich the entrepreneurship literature as well as the developing body of research on alliances.

Like other forms of collaborations, entrepreneurial alliances are becoming more important components of firms' growth initiatives and are seen as risky endeavors. Although these characteristics apply to various types of collaborative agreements, they can take on particular importance for an entrepreneurial firm with a proclivity to take risks and assume a more aggressive competitive posture. Thus, research comparing and contrasting entrepreneurial alliances with other forms of collaboration should consider the focus of the collaboration, such as whether the alliance is with a foreign versus domestic partner, in a high-tech domain or in a more tranquil environment, and so forth, in order to account for the risk-taking propensities and more aggressive competitive stances of entrepreneurial firms. Like other forms of collaborations, alliances can also be instrumental for an entrepreneurial firm seeking to access complementary resources and leverage the upstream capabilities that it possesses.

Indeed, many of the features of other collaborative agreements can be more pronounced for an entrepreneurial firm, often simply because an alliance represents a larger portion of the firm's activities. As another example of differences in degree, research on alliance structuring emphasizes the need to develop an appropriate interface between collaborators, and this can be especially challenging for entrepreneurial firms engaged in alliances with established firms. The entrepreneurial firm, for instance, might wish for the operational responsibility for the alliance to rest at a high level in a larger firm, while the latter for its part might have concerns that its complex organizational structure might provide ambiguities that the entrepreneurial firm can exploit.

These and other differences in degree can have several implications for how one thinks about and studies alliances. First, they raise the basic question of whether interpretations drawn from samples of non-entrepreneurial firms can extend to the alliances formed by entrepreneurial firms. It may be the case that many of the insights obtained in other fields such as strategic management and international business are fungible, but bounds on generalizability are likely to exist for many issues and need to receive research attention.

Second, these differences suggest that some more fundamental theoretical issues might be overlooked by simply pooling together entrepreneurial alliances with other collaborative agreements rather than exploiting interesting sources of variance. For instance, consider a set of theories or variables that explain some important alliance phenomenon or outcome. When we consider the vector of differences that have been attributed to entrepreneurial versus established firms in many studies, it is then possible to investigate how these core theoretical mechanisms potentially play out differently for entrepreneurial and other firms. For instance, due to their relative lack of administrative capabilities and slack resources, entrepreneurial firms may find it more difficult to operate their alliances efficiently and adapt these relationships as needed in the face of various exchange hazards (Leiblein and Reuer, 2004; Reuer and Ariño, 2002).

Whereas many differences in degree might be identified and their implications traced out for entrepreneurial alliances, differences in kind are more challenging to isolate due to the substantial heterogeneity that exists in firms' collaborative agreements, as well as in the motives that lead firms to engage in partnering. With this caveat in mind, however, it appears that entrepreneurial alliances have several fundamental features that do not figure significantly in prior writings on strategic alliances. Below I highlight two.

First, the impact of entrepreneurial alliances extends well beyond the collaboration itself, due to the signals conveyed to other organizations, whether potential bidders, customers, capital providers, etc. For instance, recent research relying on information economics to study firms' exit strategies shows that firms with resources that are difficult to value often find it useful to undertake an IPO prior to divestiture. Essentially, bidders find it valuable to rely on the stock market to serve as a screening device, and the direct and indirect costs borne by entrepreneurial firms going public enable them to signal their quality to would-be buyers. However, such hard to value firms that also have been engaged in strategic alliances see less need to rely upon a two-stage divestiture rather than an outright sale, since alliances themselves can reduce information asymmetries directly or mitigate the effects of adverse selection (Reuer and Koza, 2000; Reuer and Shen, 2004).

Second, the financial context of alliances looms large for entrepreneurial firms. Narrowly speaking, alliances may be used to obtain financial resources from a partner or indirectly substitute for shortfalls in capital. When the firm is not able to acquire the capital it needs, the alliance also may be designed in such a way that equity positions or other features reflect more transitory financial considerations in new ventures (Lerner, Shane, and Tsai, 2003). Outside of the scope of the alliance proper, because of the signaling aspects of collaboration for entrepreneurial firms noted above, alliances may also have longer term implications for the firm seeking to overcome liquidity constraints and make needed strategic investments.

Although these considerations are more speculative, they can have implications for how one thinks about and studies entrepreneurial alliances. For instance, the signaling considerations noted above suggest that attention to entrepreneurship and alliances can add new insights to the literature on corporate strategy that has focused on buy-side considerations in M&A without giving sell-side processes their due. Such work could also contribute to the literature on IPOs that has often depicted the going-public decision as an end-state addressing a purely financial objective. In broader terms, the IPO, M&A, and alliance markets interact, just as capital markets, product markets, and markets for partners have potential spillover effects on one another, and these relationships are interesting to study in the entrepreneurship context. For example, giving attention to the financial context of alliances raises new questions concerning the interplay between financial markets and firms' governance decisions, as well as the implications of alliances for financing choices. Although alliance research in strategic management and other fields has predominantly focused on ex-post contracting issues using the Williamsonian framework, the discussion above on entrepreneurial firms' alliances raises some new research possibilities on search processes and information asymmetries that are also very relevant sources of transaction costs in these markets.

Whether one emphasizes the differences in degree or differences in kind that exist across entrepreneurial alliances and collaborative agreements of other types, it is apparent that the developing literature on alliances has much to add to many issues of interest to entrepreneurship scholars (e.g., financing growth, exit strategies, corporate entrepreneurship, internationalization strategies, etc.), just as entrepreneurship scholars can enrich alliance research in new directions by emphasizing novel aspects of entrepreneurial firms and their collaborative agreements.

Bibliography

Leiblein, M. J. and Reuer, J. J. (2004). Building a foreign sales base: The roles of capabilities and alliances for entrepreneurial firms. *Journal of Business Venturing*, 19: 285–307.

Lerner, J., Shane, H., and Tsai, A. (2003). Do equity financing cycles matter? Evidence from biotechnology alliances. *Journal of Financial Economics*, 67: 411–46.

Reuer, J. J. and Ariño, A. (2002). Contractual renegotiations in strategic alliances. *Journal of Management*, 28: 51–74.

Reuer, J. J. and Koza, M. P. (2000). Asymmetric information and joint venture performance: Theory and evidence for domestic and international joint ventures. *Strategic Management Journal*, 21: 81–8.

Reuer, J. J. and Shen, J.-C. (2004). Sequential divestiture through initial public offerings. *Journal of Economic Behavior and Organization*, 54: 249–66.

entrepreneurial archetypes

Danny Miller

Miller and Friesen (1984) defined archetypes as very commonly occurring configurations among organizational qualities. These types were richly characterized along numerous dimensions of strategy, structure, process, context, and performance, and each appeared to reflect a core theme, such as spry adaptiveness, constant innovation, determined efficiency, or relentless expansion. The authors used methods of numerical taxonomy to discover empirically the most common successful and unsuccessful types that emerged out of their broad sample of companies. The significance of the archetypes was that a rather few types could describe in a fine-grained way a large fraction of the organizations that were studied. Therefore, a few variables could be used to categorize a firm into one of the types, and from that categorization numerous predictions could be made about other variables, their relationships, and financial performance.

Speaking more broadly, the notion of archetypes also applies to *a priori* conceptually (as opposed to empirically) derived typologies of firms, again characterized by strategies, modes of organization, etc. Porter's (1980) generic strategies, and Miles and Snow's (1978) typologies, are prominent among these.

The utility of empirically and conceptually derived types is that they segment the complex world of organizations into more homogeneous and analytically tractable compartments. They allow researchers to make key distinctions among the different types, and more powerful generalizations and predictions within them. Meyer, Tsui, and Hinings (1993), Miller (1983, 1996), and Mintzberg, Ahlstrom, and Lampel (1997) have referred to this study of archetypes as the "configuration approach."

This approach has benefited the field of entrepreneurship in two major ways. First, it distinguishes among the varieties of entrepreneurship that can arise, as well as their determinants and performance drivers. Second, it identifies the contexts that give rise to, support, and benefit from the various types of entrepreneurship.

In their reviews, Miller (1983) and Covin and Slevin (1986) found that researchers tended to concentrate on three different dimensions of entrepreneurship: *risk taking* – a willingness to take chances in committing resources, *innovation* in processes and products, and *proactiveness* – a striving to "beat rivals to the punch" and be the first mover. Miller (1983) found these dimensions to correlate positively, collectively composing an "entrepreneurship factor" or scale. He also found, however, that the nature and drivers of entrepreneurship varied greatly among organizational archetypes. The significance of entrepreneurial types thus became apparent – it was important to distinguish among the forms of entrepreneurship, the organizational contexts in which these emerged, and the organizational determinants of entrepreneurial effectiveness within those contexts (see also Shane and Venkataraman, 2000).

Although much work remains to be done to isolate the most relevant and predictive entrepreneurial archetypes, it will be useful to show their potential power by discussing some *representative* types. What follows, therefore, are three entrepreneurial archetypes, conceptual composites of organizational qualities based on the work of Miller (1983, 1990), Mintzberg, Ahlstrom, and Lampel (1997), and others. These are chosen because of their recurrence in the literature, and because their striking differences illustrate (a) a diverse array of entrepreneurial objectives; (b) their different potential drivers, contexts, and organizational co-requisites; and (c) their different challenges. And because they represent an amalgam of findings from different studies, the descriptions that follow should be taken as suggestive rather than factual. Table 1 summarizes the types.

Table 1 Proposed features of some common entrepreneurial archetypes

Core dimension of entrepreneurship	Business creation	Innovation	Proactive expansion
Common firm type	Newly founded	Pioneer	Builder
Key drivers	Owner personality	Substantive mission	Strategic plans
Firm characteristics	Small, young	Informal, dynamic	Large, diversified
Key actors	Founder	Leaders and technocrats	Planners and middle managers
Strategy requirements	Disciplined financial management, ability to deliver value distinctively	Steep investment in R&D and competency building	Disciplined strategic plan; profound understanding of core competencies and ability to leverage
Organization requirements	Clear allocation of responsibility and authority, delegation, good controls	Organic adhocracy, informality, excellent liaison devices, expert empowerment	Divisionalized structure, sharp controls, relevant incentives
Dangers	Cash crunch, competition	Irrelevance of offerings	Expansion beyond area of expertise
Context	Hostile	Turbulent	Complex
Key strategy school	Traditional entrepreneurship literature	Resource-based and dynamic competency views	Competitive analysis and strategic planning literature

BUSINESS CREATION: THE FOUNDING
ENTREPRENEUR

The organization of a founding entrepreneur is
the type most often discussed in the traditional
literature on entrepreneurship. The organization is characterized by owner management, administrative simplicity, and usually, small size
and youth. Entrepreneurship here takes the
form of building a viable business. Owners do
this by combining the factors of production in a
way that adds value for the market. Strategy is
driven primarily by the personality and objectives of the owner. The major strategic objective
often is to do something distinctive well enough
to command a price that will afford adequate
returns to capital and allow for growth. Strategic
priorities typically revolve around product development and identifying a niche of the market
that is inadequately served. Critical functions
are product-service design, niche identification,
business getting, financing, and infrastructure
development (Kubicek and Isbester, 1983).
Organizational requirements have mostly to
do with ensuring that owners implement appropriate financial controls, delegate enough authority to others in the firm, and define tasks
and accountabilities clearly. Major challenges
are cash shortages and competition from
larger, more powerful rivals. Common problems
are a dearth of funds, inadequate functional
capability or managerial talent, and poor
controls.

INNOVATION: THE PIONEERING ENTERPRISE

In highly innovative organizations, entrepreneurship takes quite a different form. Here it is
not so much about creating a new business as
about pioneering product, process, or technological innovations – the kind that can establish
new niches, markets, and occasionally even industries. Firms are driven not by survival objectives so much as a desire to be first movers in
accomplishing a substantive scientific or technological or even social mission. For many of
today's high-technology companies, this pioneering type of entrepreneurship is central.
Recent research has suggested that innovation
is facilitated by deep investment in research and
development, constant and cumulative core
competency building within a focused know-

ledge domain, and an ability to leverage discoveries across different niches of the market (Yi-
Renko, Autio, and Sapienza, 2001; Zahra, Jennings, and Kuratko, 1999). Alliances and network formation, too, are key activities here (Lee,
Lee, and Pennings, 2001). Organization designs
are especially helpful to innovation when characterized by empowering cultures, organic and
flexible organization structures, excellent liaison
devices across functions, and selective recruit-
ment. Pioneering entrepreneurship is most frequently to be found in turbulent environments
and industries. Its particular performance challenges are the idealistic pursuit of innovations
that are overly ambitious, impractical, too far
ahead of their time, or unattractive to the market
(Miller, 1990). Excessive expenditure and difficulties with commercialization also tend to be
important dangers.

EXPANSION: THE CORPORATE BUILDER

In large, multi-product firms, a "corporate expansion" mode of entrepreneurship often pre-
vails. Here, entrepreneurship takes the form
mostly of product-market diversification ventures, usually into established markets, with the
primary objective being to grow the company.
The strategy is supported by an explicit set of
strategic plans, much of it the result of competitive market analysis. A good deal of the writing
on "intrapreneurship" reflects this planning
mode (Mintzberg, Ahlstrom, and Lampel
1997). Typically, the building mode is supported by a strong market scanning and intelligence gathering function, a bottom-line and
growth driven set of performance standards,
and a divisionalized structure that makes much
use of formal controls and information technologies. Expansion may take place by leveraging
products and abilities across new markets and
by mergers and acquisitions. Thus, the environmental context of the organization is often a
complex one, with the firm operating in many
different markets, often across different countries, and even different businesses. Performance is apt to be governed by a disciplined
approach to diversification, specifically, an ability to avoid over-expansion and areas of ignorance (Miller, 1990), and an excellent post-
merger integration capability. Builders, too,
must have a deep understanding of their core

competencies in order to determine how these can be leveraged in the growth trajectory.

In short, configuration scholars argue it is useful to identify and make clear distinctions among such different types of entrepreneurship in order to better study their drivers, performance requirements, and common contexts (Meyer, Tsui, and Hinings, 1993; Miller, 1983, 1996; Mintzberg, Ahlstrom, and Lampel, 1997). They would also suggest that firms be studied holistically, believing it far more revealing to examine entrepreneurship within a rich human, organizational, and market context than to study it a few variables at a time. Only then, configurationists believe, will scholars begin to truly appreciate the range, drivers, and challenges of the vital economic engine that is entrepreneurship.

Bibliography

Covin, G. and Slevin, D. (1986). The development and testing of an organization-level entrepreneurship scale. In *Frontiers of Entrepreneurship*. Wellesley, MA: Babson College, 628–39.

Kubicek, T. and Isbester, F. (1983). *Managing Canadian Business*, Toronto: Prentice-Hall.

Lee, C., Lee, K., and Pennings, J. (2001). Internal capabilities, external networks, and performance. *Strategic Management Journal*, 22: 615–40.

Meyer, A., Tsui, A., and Hinings, C. (1993). Configurational approaches to organizational analysis. *Academy of Management Journal*, 36: 1175–95.

Miles, R. and Snow, C. (1978). *Organizational Strategy, Structure and Process*. New York: McGraw-Hill.

Miller, D. (1983). The correlates of entrepreneurship in three kinds of firms. *Management Science*, 29: 770–91.

Miller, D. (1990). *The Icarus Paradox*. New York: Harper Business.

Miller, D. (1996). Configurations revisited. *Strategic Management Journal*, 17: 505–12.

Miller, D. and Friesen, P. H. (1984). *Organizations: A Quantum View*. Englewood Cliffs, NJ: Prentice-Hall.

Mintzberg, H., Ahlstrom, B., and Lampel, J. (1997). *Strategy Safari*. New York: Basic Books.

Porter, M. (1980). *Competitive Strategy*. New York: Free Press.

Shane, S. and Venkataraman, S. (2000). The promise of entrepreneurship as a field of research. *Academy of Management Review*, 25: 217–26.

Yi-Renko, H., Autio, E., and Sapienza, H. (2001). Social capital, knowledge acquisition and exploitation in young, technology-based firms. *Strategic Management Journal*, 22: 587–614.

Zahra, S., Jennings, D., and Kuratko, A. (1999). Guest editorial: Entrepreneurship and the acquisition of dynamic organizational capabilities. *Entrepreneurship: Theory and Practice*, 23 (3): 5–10.

entrepreneurial decisions

Jeffrey A. Martin and George P. Huber

That the term "entrepreneurial decision" is given a variety of meanings creates ambiguity in the research, scholarship, and communication necessary to advance understanding in the entrepreneurship field. To help reduce this obstacle to progress, we provide a definition of the term that fulfills three requirements: (1) it is sufficiently precise that it conveys clear meaning; (2) it is parsimonious; (3) it satisfies the range of definitions implied in the writings of most of those who practice or study in the entrepreneurship field. First, we examine the matter of range. We then examine the two foremost attributes of any decision: the decision context and the decision maker's motivation(s) for engaging in an entrepreneurial enterprise. From these efforts we distill a definition that meets the three requirements just noted.

RANGE OF PRIMARY MEANINGS

The adjective "entrepreneurial" in the term "entrepreneurial decision" is used almost exclusively to indicate either the nature of the decision itself (as are the adjectives in "strategic decision" or "risky decision") or the nature of the decision-maker (as is the adjective in "presidential decision"). In the first case, to make an entrepreneurial decision means to decide to initiate an entrepreneurial enterprise, an organization or unit that exploits a new product (broadly defined to include a good, service, process, and business model), or that enters a new market or environment with either a new or existing product. A frequently occurring decision of this type is to initiate a new enterprise within an existing organization. This can be a top-down decision, where a high level initiator assigns the responsibility for organizing and managing the new enterprise to someone else, or it can be a bottom-up decision, where an intrapreneur champions or promotes an idea, sells it to upper management, and then organizes and manages the resultant enterprise. In contrast is the decision, sometimes taken by venture capitalists, philanthropists, and other resource controllers, to initiate an entirely new enterprise, one not associated with an existing organization, and to induce others to organize and manage it. Taking these two types of decisions together, and focusing on the nature of the decision as contrasted with the nature of the decision-maker, it seems reasonable to define an *entrepreneurial decision* as "a decision to initiate an entrepreneurial enterprise."

In the second case, where the adjective "entrepreneurial" is used to indicate the decision-maker's nature, it is important to be clear on what is meant by "entrepreneur." The common denominators of the primary dictionary definitions of an entrepreneur describe a person who "organizes" and "manages" an "enterprise," usually under conditions of "risk" and with considerable "initiative" (*Random House Webster's Unabridged Dictionary*, 2001) (*see* ENTREPRENEUR). It seems important also not to define an entrepreneurial decision simply as a decision made by an entrepreneur. Entrepreneurs make many decisions. Is each and every one an entrepreneurial decision? Hardly! Which, then, are the entrepreneurial decisions? In keeping with the above paragraph, it seems reasonable to accept as a second definition of an *entrepreneurial decision*, "a person's decision to personally initiate, organize, and manage an enterprise."

To provide a richer understanding of the term, let us turn now to examining the context of entrepreneurial decisions. It will be convenient and yet not unduly restrictive to focus on the decision of a person to personally initiate, organize, and manage an enterprise.

THE CONTEXT OF ENTREPRENEURIAL DECISIONS

Entrepreneurship involves novelty and newness, as well "organizing" and "risking" and "managing" in an environment where the product is unfamiliar. Here, and henceforth, we mean for "novel" to be context determined; i.e., for a product or enterprise to be novel means only that it needs to be novel in the specific context or environment, rather than necessarily being novel to the world. In particular, when the nature of an enterprise is novel to a certain environment, it is a "novel enterprise," even if the enterprise's nature or product is not novel in another environment.

Risk and uncertainty are not unique to the decision contexts of entrepreneurs. Entrepreneurs – either as organizers of new enterprises or as managers of novel enterprises – have, however, a qualitatively different form of uncertainty with which to deal. That is, whereas the manager of an existing enterprise can draw on the enterprise's recent past as one basis for making predictions about the enterprise's near or intermediate term future, the manager of a new enterprise cannot. In this way, the decision contexts of decisions made by entrepreneurs are more uncertain, risky, and unknowable than are the decision contexts of managers of existing enterprises. The newness of the entrepreneur's enterprise causes extrapolation to be unavailable for reducing uncertainty about the future and the novelty of the enterprise causes reasoning by analogy to be more problematic as a basis for reducing such uncertainty. For these two reasons, whatever the volatility of an enterprise's environment, the contexts of entrepreneurial decisions are less predictable and therefore necessarily riskier than are the contexts of decisions made by managers of non-entrepreneurial enterprises.

Unfortunately, the term "risk-seeking" has been suggested as an attribute of entrepreneurs, as if it were a goal or motivation for engaging in entrepreneurial activity (Brockhaus, 1980). But as described above, risk is simply an outcome of engaging in entrepreneurship. This suggests that an observed association between the decision to engage in entrepreneurial ventures and the riskiness of an entrepreneurial decision context is not necessarily an indication that risk seeking is an entrepreneurial attribute. That risk does *not* serve as an attraction for entrepreneurs is suggested by the research of Brockhaus (1980) and seems to be demonstrated by observing that entrepreneurs, like other managers, are diligent and creative in reducing, controlling, and distributing risk (see, for example, Rangan, 1994; Rivkin and Meier, 2000; Stevenson and Mossi, 1985).

If entrepreneurial decisions are inherently risky, and therefore subject the entrepreneur to failure, why do people engage in entrepreneurial ventures?

DECISION-MAKER MOTIVATIONS

In the United States, especially, the popular press portrays successful entrepreneurs as heroes. They take risks, they fight hard, and they often win. Published instances of successful entrepreneurship suggest both (1) that successful entrepreneurs obtain large amounts of personal wealth as a result of their venture and (2) that the possibility of a large increase in their personal wealth is their primary motivation for engaging in (i.e., initiating, organizing, and managing) the venture. Should we assume that a defining feature for the definition of an entrepreneurial decision is that it is a decision to organize and manage a venture for the purpose of increasing the decision-maker's wealth? Attending to stories in the popular press, we might assume that the answer is "yes." But it may be that accumulating wealth is not as primary a motivation for engaging in an entrepreneurial venture as the frequency of its mention would suggest. Because there is little, if any, systematic research that documents these motivations, we infer the following motivations from the broader organizational science and strategic management literatures (and, more specifically, from the innovation and entrepreneurship literatures) and from histories and biographies of Lee Iacocca, John DeLorean, and Govindappa Venkataswamy (Fallon and Srodes, 1983; Haddad, 1985; Levin, 1995; Levin, 1983; Rangan, 1994; Rubin, 2001).

At least initially, entrepreneurs (and especially intrapreneurs) might have as motivations for initiating an enterprise:

1 Facilitating the evolution of a novel product (broadly defined) with which they identify and that they feel has value for others.
2 Contributing to the health of an organization with which they strongly identify and feel a high level of commitment.
3 Acquiring a positive image in the eyes of valued peers or the organization's high-level executives.
4 Acquiring the authority to manage the new unit or enterprise created to exploit the novel product.
5 Increasing their financial well-being.

The histories of DeLorean and Iacocca suggest that this last motivation is prone to surface when satiation is reached on the other four motivations, or when compensation becomes an important measure of the level of achievement on motivations (1), (2), or (3). It might also be, of course, that entrepreneurs have as their motivation simply the passion to engage in novel or challenging endeavors (as suggested by the remarks of serial entrepreneurs quoted in the *New York Times*, 2003).

Examining the careers of Lee Iacocca (before he was forced out as chief executive of Chrysler), John DeLorean (before his legal troubles surfaced), and Govindappa Venkataswamy has the potential to provide some insights about the nature and expression of entrepreneurial/intrapreneurial motivations. Well-researched analyses (Abodaher, 1982; Levin, 1995) and his own autobiographical works (Iacocca, 1984, 1988) indicate that Lee Iacocca, the promoter of the Mustang and Cougar at Ford and the K-cars and LeBaron convertible at Chrysler, was strongly motivated by (1) his commitment to products in which he believed, (2) his commitment to the firms for which he worked, (3) the need for recognition, and (4) the ambition to manage an enterprise. While satisfying these motivations was undoubtedly instrumental to his obtaining high levels of firm-provided compensation, it appears that Iacocca valued these motivations themselves. For Ford and for Chrysler, Iacocca managed an enterprise, showed considerable initiative, and took risks – with innovative products and with his decision to accept the opportunity to head Chrysler, a failing company. Was the possibility of obtaining a large increase in his personal wealth Iacocca's primary motivation for engaging in the ventures he chose? Relevant facts are that when he left Ford for Chrysler, Iacocca forfeited Ford's $1 million a year incentive not to work for a competitor for two years after leaving Ford, and upon arriving at Chrysler he cut his salary to $1 a year. On the other hand, near the end of his career with Chrysler, as he was being eased out by Chrysler's board, Iacocca exhibited a strong craving for financial compensation. It appears, however, that this apparent craving was prompted by the fact that his political enemy, Robert Lutz, was scheduled to receive a larger pension than was he (Levin, 1995). It seems, then, that Iacocca's attempt to increase his personal wealth might actually have been an attempt to maintain his image.

Next we consider John DeLorean, a would-be intrapeneur and entrepreneur. DeLorean was well known as an outstanding engineer as well as an ambitious seeker of a favorable image. He attempted to satisfy both his creative needs and his status needs by seeking to manage an entrepreneurial enterprise. For example, he promoted the idea of his managing the manufacturing and marketing, through GM's Pontiac Division, of a sports car having an innovative combination of features. But GM's engineering policy group rebuffed his proposal. Later events moved DeLorean from a would-be intrapreneur in this instance to become a would-be entrepreneur promoting another sports car with unusual features, his dream car the DeLorean. Fallon and Srodes (1983) and Levin (1983) indicate that DeLorean's attempts at intrapreneurship and entrepreneurship were motivated primarily by his commitment to the features of the cars he promoted, by his desire to manage the enterprises that would have produced and marketed the cars, and by his need for a favorable image, rather than by the desire to increase his personal wealth. Indeed, it seems that he began focusing primarily on attaining wealth when his career took a sharp downward trend (Haddad, 1985), although it is not clear which were the causal directions of the several forces at work near the end of his career.

Finally, we consider the entrepreneurial decision made by Dr. Govindappa Venkataswamy, a retired eye surgeon in India, to found the not-for-profit Aravind Eye Hospitals (Rangan, 1994). Dr. Venkataswamy was motivated to address the problem of blindness among India's poor by his expressed motivation to "serve humanity and God" (Rangan, 1994: 4). Upon his retirement as a head of Ophthalmology at a major hospital in 1976, he established a 12-bed eye hospital to provide quality eye care for those with little or no resources to pay. Using a variety of creative approaches that mirror those used in for-profit businesses (Rangan, 1994), he "grew the business." By 2001, Dr. Venkataswamy was managing five hospitals that performed more than 180,000 eye operations per year (Rubin, 2001).

To summarize, we offer the following observations: (1) An entrepreneurial decision can be defined either as "a decision to initiate an enterprise for someone else to organize and manage" or as "a person's decision to initiate and personally organize and manage an enterprise"; (2) whatever the actual volatility of the enterprise's environment, because the newness of the entrepreneur's enterprise causes extrapolation to be unavailable for reducing uncertainty about the future and because the novelty of the enterprise makes reasoning by analogy more problematic, the contexts of decisions made by entrepreneurs are more uncertain and riskier than are the contexts of decisions made by managers of existing enterprises; and (3) the motivations to initiate, organize, or manage entrepreneurial enterprises vary across entrepreneurs and vary across time for specific entrepreneurs.

Bibliography

Abodaher, D. (1982). *Iacocca*. New York: Macmillan.

Brockhaus, R. H. (1980). Risk taking propensity of entrepreneurs. *Academy of Management Journal*, 23: 509–20.

Fallon, I. and Srodes, J. (1983). *Dream Maker: The Rise and Fall of John Z. DeLorean*. New York: Putnam and Sons.

Haddad, W. (1985). *Hard Driving: My Years with John DeLorean*. New York: Random House.

Iacocca, L. (1984). *Iacocca: An Autobiography*, with W. Novak. New York: Bantam Books.

Iacocca, L. (1988). *Talking Straight*, with S. Kleinfield. New York: Bantam Books.

Levin, D. P. (1995). *Behind the Wheel at Chrysler: The Iacocca Legacy*. New York: Harcourt Brace.

Levin, H. (1983). *Grand Delusions: The Cosmic Career of John DeLorean*. New York: Viking Press.

New York Times (2003). Bouncing from start-up to start-up, and loving it. December 11: C6.

Rangan, V. K. (1994). Aravind eye hospital, Madurai, India: In service for sight. Harvard Business School Case 9-593-098 (revised May 1994).

Rivkin, J. W. and Meier, G. (2000). BMG Entertainment. Harvard Business School Case 9-701-003.

Rubin, H. (2001). The perfect vision of Dr. V. *Fast Company*, February: 146–57.

Stevenson, H. H. and Mossi, J.-C. J. (1985). R&R. Harvard Business School Case 9-386-019 (revised November 1987).

entrepreneurial discovery

Sharon A. Alvarez and Jay B. Barney

Entrepreneurial alertness is the ability that some people have to recognize market imperfections that have the potential for generating economic profits (*see* ENTREPRENEURIAL ALERTNESS). Entrepreneurial discovery is concerned with the actions people take to exploit the competitive imperfections they see in the market.

At the point that an individual experiences entrepreneurial alertness, the actions that need to be taken to exploit a market imperfection are only known imperfectly. As individuals begin to take actions designed to exploit an imperfection, they discover those actions that enable this exploitation and those that do not enable this exploitation. Thus, this series of actions, where individuals learn what must be done to exploit a market imperfection, can appropriately be called entrepreneurial discovery.

The concept of entrepreneurial discovery was originally developed by Hayek (1948) and Mises (1949) in response to perfect information assumptions in neoclassical economics. In neoclassical theory, all relevant information about technologies, demand, and other determinants of market competition are known to be available, but may be costly to produce. The concept of entrepreneurial discovery suggests that the actions that need to be taken to exploit imperfect competition are not knowable *a priori* and must be discovered over time through efforts to exploit these imperfections.

However, the act of learning what actions need to be taken to exploit a market imperfection often has the effect of informing others in the market of the existence of this imperfection. Thus, while alert entrepreneurs may be able to keep their recognition of a market imperfection – and the profit opportunities associated with that imperfection – proprietary, the act of trying to exploit these imperfections through entrepreneurial discovery often informs others about this opportunity.

The work of Hayek, Mises, and Kirzner are all examples of what has come to be called Austrian economics (*see* AUSTRIAN ECONOMICS). However, while traditional Austrians abandoned all notions of equilibrium in their analysis, modern Austrians – starting with Hayek and Mises, and continuing with Kirzner – include some equilibrium notions in their analysis.

Entrepreneurial discovery is the process by which market imperfections are exploited. Future research might be conducted in order to determine if some processes are more effective at exploiting market imperfections than others and, if so, how those attempting to exploit these opportunities know how to chose the most desirable/effective process.

Bibliography

Hayek, F. A. von (1948). *Individualism and Economic Order*. London: Routledge and Kegan Paul.

Kirzner, I. M. (1989). *Discovery, Capitalism, and Distributive Justice*. Oxford: Blackwell.

Mises, Ludwig von (1949). *Human Action*. New Haven, CT: Yale University Press.

entrepreneurial dominant logic

Kurt A. Heppard and G. Dale Meyer

Entrepreneurial dominant logic is a constantly evolving information filter that is economically and managerially oriented and is based on organizational processes, schemas, or mental maps. This filter attenuates the complexity of information in the firm's external environment and shapes the conceptualization and execution of wealth creation within the context of the existing firm and its businesses. Entrepreneurial dominant logic is at the heart of corporate entrepreneurship and drives or guides the configuration or reconfiguration of internal resources and capabilities to reactively or proactively support environmentally related change or diversification via growth into new ventures in order to create or capture entrepreneurial rents in the new competitive landscape. When combined with analytic procedures used by corporate entrepreneurs, it forms the entrepreneurial intelligence or entrepreneurial mindset, of the firm.

Entrepreneurial dominant logic is derived from the concept of dominant logic designated by Prahalad and Bettis (1986) to link patterns of diversification and performance . More specifically, dominant logic was said to consist of "the mental maps developed through experience in the core business and sometimes applied inappropriately in other businesses" (1986: 485). The concept was refined by Bettis and Prahalad (1995) when they extended the notion of dominant logic to environmentally driven change and conceptualized the dominant logic as an information filter. This filter determines relevant data for the analytic procedures used by managers, which are incorporated into competitive strategies, values and expectations, measures of performance, and reinforced behaviors (Bettis and Prahalad, 1995). Organizational learning and unlearning links these organizational functions with the dominant logic in a recursive feedback loop. This feedback system linking organizational learning and unlearning to the need to change or shift an organization's dominant logic to meet the challenges of an ever-changing competitive landscape is vital. The basic concept of dominant logic is illustrated in figure 1.

Entrepreneurial dominant logic places these concepts in the context of strategic entrepreneurship and provides a fundamental link between scholarly research in the strategic management and entrepreneurship literatures (Meyer and Heppard, 2000; Hitt et al., 2001). The concept also creates a relationship that is valuable for future studies of entrepreneurial strategies. In fact, dominant logic consensus among top managers has recently been identified as an important research issue in the investigation of corporate entrepreneurship (Dess et al., 2003).

Entrepreneurial dominant logic (information filter), combined with entrepreneurial analytics (managerial procedures) of a firm, makes up the entrepreneurial intelligence of a firm. This entrepreneurial intelligence is, most basically, an organization's ability to learn and unlearn (Bettis and Prahalad, 1995; Hitt and Reed, 2000), but in the entrepreneurial context is perhaps the most widely referred to as an "entrepreneurial mindset" (McGrath and MacMillan, 2000) or entrepreneurial cognition (Mitchell et al., 2002). Strategic managers play a key role in developing this information filter in that they state a strategic vision and make important decisions about firm strategies, structures, and overall organizational form (Miles et al., 2000; Covin and Slevin, 2001).

A key aspect of entrepreneurial dominant logic is that it favors information regarding the potential for wealth creation. Wealth creation is at the heart of both strategic management and entrepreneurship research (Ireland et al., 2001). It is shaped by an organization's competitive strategy, values and expectations, measures of performance, and reinforced behavior. Wealth creation has also been related to supernormal profitability, economic profits, or economic rents. Four basic economic rents are generally recognized as monopoly rents, quasi-monopoly rents, Ricardian rents, and entrepreneurial rents.

Entrepreneurial dominant logic is focused specifically on entrepreneurial rents.

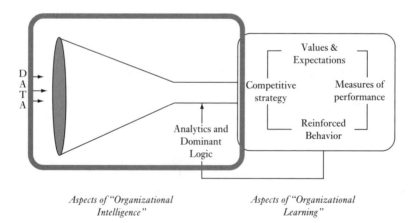

Aspects of "Organizational Intelligence"

Aspects of "Organizational Learning"

Figure 1
Source: Bettis and Prahalad (1995)

Entrepreneurial rents arise from new combinations of resources in environments of great uncertainty (Rumelt, 1987). Rumelt defines entrepreneurial rent as "the difference between a venture's ex-post value (or payment stream) and the ex-ante cost (or value) of the resources combined to form the venture" (Rumelt, 1987: 143). Entrepreneurial rent, then, is the reward or result of expected uncertainty in returns of a new venture. These rents are also typically considered non-sustainable, given the assumption that other competitors will erode profitability. This assumption forces firms to transition to other information filters and managerial analytics that focus on sustainable competitive advantage and supernormal profitability in the face of eroding entrepreneurial rents.

Entrepreneurial dominant logic is related most closely with two key streams of strategic management research related to wealth creation: adaptation and diversification. Adaptation or strategic fit (Zajac, Kraatz, and Bresser, 2000), in the rapidly changing external environment described by Bettis and Hitt (1995) as the new competitive landscape, is particularly important. The new competitive landscape is characterized as an environment of great uncertainty and opportunities for many new and innovative resource combinations. Hitt and Reed (2000) further specify an "entrepreneurial zone" in this new competitive landscape, in which market opportunities for entrepreneurial rent must be immediately spotted and explored, where increases in productivity and innovation must occur quickly, where organizational structures can be changed almost immediately, and where learning and unlearning occur very quickly. Eisenhardt, Brown, and Neck (2000) extended this notion further by proposing that entrepreneurial adaptation is proactive rather than reactive and allows firms to compete on the entrepreneurial edge of chaos and time.

The second key concept is growth-related diversification through the creation of new ventures (Burgleman, 1983). The objectives of this entrepreneurial diversification are twofold, in that it provides internal diversity for a corporation and seeks entrepreneurial rents in the marketplace. The links between entrepreneurship and diversification are well established. Teece (1982) provided important reasons why entre-

preneurial activities would lead to firm diversification and why there could be economic returns associated with such activities. Burgelman (1983: 1349) formally defines corporate entrepreneurship as "the process whereby firms engage in diversification through internal development." He goes on to stress the importance of new resource combinations in entrepreneurial diversification and refers to corporate entrepreneurship as the "corporate analog" of individual entrepreneurship. More recently, Alvarez and Barney (2000) have developed a resource-based view of asset combinations and recombinations associated with entrepreneurial strategies.

In summary, fully understanding the components of entrepreneurial dominant logic requires a synthesis of ideas related to the concepts of information filtering, selection, and processing found in studies of strategic management, entrepreneurship, managerial and organizational cognition, organizational learning, entrepreneurial cognition, and knowledge creation. As the components of the entrepreneurial dominant logic are more fully refined, it is important for researchers to recognize that entrepreneurial dominant logic is specifically the information filtering component of the overall entrepreneurial intelligence or entrepreneurial mindset of a firm. Entrepreneurial dominant logic is most appropriately described as a component of corporate entrepreneurship and is most closely related to strategic adaptation to a rapidly changing competitive landscape and growth through diversification by the creation of new ventures.

Bibliography

Alvarez, S. A. and Barney, J. B. (2000). Entrepreneurial capabilities: A resource-based view. In G. D. Meyer and K. A. Heppard (eds.), *Entrepreneurship as Strategy: Competing on the Entrepreneurial Edge*. Thousand Oaks, CA: Sage, 63–81.

Bettis, R. A. and Hitt, M. A. (1995). The new competitive landscape. *Strategic Management Journal* (summer special issue), 16: 7–20.

Bettis, R. A. and Prahalad, C. K. (1995). The dominant logic: Retrospective and extension. *Strategic Management Journal*, 16: 5–14.

Burgelman, R. A. (1983). Corporate entrepreneurship and strategic management: Insights from a process study. *Management Science*, 29 (12): 1349–64.

Covin, J. G. and Slevin, D. P. (2001). The entrepreneurial imperatives of strategic leadership. In M. A. Hitt et al. (eds.), *Strategic Entrepreneurship: Creating a New Mindset*. Oxford: Blackwell.

Dess, G. G., Ireland, R. D., Zahra, S. A., Floyd, S. W., Janney, J. J., and Lane, P. L. (2003). Emerging issues in corporate entrepreneurship. *Journal of Management*, 29 (3): 351–78.

Eisenhardt, K. M., Brown, S. L., and Neck, H. M. (2000). Competing on the entrepreneurial edge. In G. D. Meyer and K. A. Heppard (eds.), *Entrepreneurship as Strategy: Competing on the Entrepreneurial Edge*. Thousand Oaks, CA: Sage, 49–62.

Hitt, M. A., Ireland, R. D., Camp, S. M., and Sexton, D. L. (2001). Strategic entrepreneurship: Entrepreneurial strategies for wealth creation. *Strategic Management Journal*, 22: 479–91.

Hitt, M. A. and Reed, T. S. (2000). Entrepreneurship in the new competitive landscape. In G. D. Meyer and K. A. Heppard (eds.), *Entrepreneurship as Strategy: Competing on the Entrepreneurial Edge*. Thousand Oaks, CA: Sage, 23–45.

Ireland, D. R., Hitt, M. A., Camp, S. M., and Sexton, D. L. (2001). Integrating entrepreneurship and strategic management actions to create firm wealth. *Academy of Management Executive*, 15 (1): 49–63.

McGrath, R. G. and MacMillan, I. (2000). *The Entrepreneurial Mindset*. Boston, MA: Harvard Business School Press.

Meyer, G. D. and Heppard, K. A. (2000). *Entrepreneurship as Strategy: Competing on the Entrepreneurial Edge*. Thousand Oaks, CA: Sage.

Miles, G., Heppard, K. A., Miles, R. E., and Snow, C. C. (2000). Entrepreneurial strategies: The critical role of top management. In G. D. Meyer and K. A. Heppard (eds.), *Entrepreneurship as Strategy: Competing on the Entrepreneurial Edge*. Thousand Oaks, CA: Sage, 101–14.

Mitchell, R. K., Busenitz, L., Lant, T., McDougal, P. P., Morse, E. A., and Smith, J. B. (2002). Toward a theory of entrepreneurial cognition: Rethinking the people side of entrepreneurship research. *Entrepreneurship Theory and Practice*, 27 (2): 93–104.

Prahalad, C. K. and Bettis, R. A. (1986). The dominant logic: A new linkage between diversity and performance. *Strategic Management Journal*, 7: 485–501.

Rumelt, R. P. (1987). Theory, strategy, and entrepreneurship. In D. J. Teece (ed.), *The Competitive Challenge: Strategies for Industrial Innovation and Renewal*. Cambridge, MA: Ballinger Publishing, 137–58.

Teece, D. J. (1982). Towards an economic theory of the multi-product firm. *Journal of Economic Behavior and Organization*, 3: 39–63.

Zajac, E. J., Kraatz, M. S., and Bresser, R. K. F. (2000). Modeling the dynamics of strategic fit: A normative approach to strategic change. *Strategic Management Journal*, 21: 429–53.

entrepreneurial expertise

Saras D. Sarasvathy and Stuart Reed

INTRODUCTION

Entrepreneurship has traditionally been viewed as an individual characteristic. Besides investigating personality traits and attributes, studies have examined gender differences (Carter et al., 2003), risk aversion (Miner, Smith, and Bracker, 1994), and even sociopathy as possible traits or characteristics of entrepreneurs (Winslow and Solomon, 1987). Unfortunately, these efforts have returned little more than inconclusive results on what defines an entrepreneur and sustains him or her through a continuing career in entrepreneurship. Recently, however, there is a move to study entrepreneurship as expertise: a set of skills, models, and processes that can be acquired with time and deliberate practice. For example, Mitchell (1997) sought to understand the nature of entrepreneurial expertise in management, while Reuber and Fischer (1994) showed an empirical relationship between entrepreneurial expertise and firm performance.

Expertise has traditionally been studied in cognitive science using protocol analysis (Ericsson and Simon, 1993). This method consists of having experts solve typical problems from their domain of expertise while continuously thinking aloud. The think-aloud protocols are usually recorded on tape and the contents of the transcribed protocols are analyzed in order to extract the baseline models used by the expert. Sarasvathy (1998) used this time-tested method on a subject pool consisting of 27 founders of companies ranging in size from $200 million to $6.5 billion to induce a baseline model of entrepreneurial expertise called "effectuation."

EFFECTUATION, ENTREPRENEURIAL EXPERTISE, AND EXPERTISE IN GENERAL

The word "effectual" is the inverse of "causal." In general, in MBA programs across the world, students are taught causal or predictive reasoning – in every functional area of business.

Causal rationality begins with a predetermined goal and a given set of means, and seeks to identify the optimal – fastest, cheapest, most efficient, etc. – alternative to achieve the given goal. The make-vs.-buy decision in production, or choosing the target market with the highest potential return in marketing, or picking a portfolio with the lowest risk in finance, or even hiring the best person for the job in human resources management, are all examples of problems of causal reasoning. A more interesting variation of causal reasoning involves the creation of additional alternatives to achieve the given goal. This form of creative causal reasoning is often used in strategic thinking.

Effectual reasoning, or expert entrepreneurial reasoning, however, does not begin with a specific goal. Instead, it begins with a given set of means and allows goals to emerge contingently over time from the varied imagination and diverse aspirations of the founders and the people they interact with (Sarasvathy 2001a, 2001b). While causal thinkers are like great generals seeking to conquer fertile lands (Genghis Khan conquering two-thirds of the known world), effectual thinkers are like explorers setting out on voyages into uncharted waters (Columbus discovering the new world). It is important to point out, though, that the same person can use both causal and effectual reasoning at different times, depending on what the circumstances call for.

As depicted in figure 1, expert entrepreneurs begin the effectual process with three categories of means; namely, who they are, what they know, and whom they know. Based on these, they come up with a list of possible actions they *can* do, including taking their ideas to people they know or meet. Soon, particular stakeholders commit particular resources to come on board the enterprise; in the process of negotiating these commitments, they (both founder and subsequent stakeholder) reformulate each other's preferences for particular features of the firm and market they end up creating. Each commitment makes available new means to the enterprise, setting in motion an expanding cycle of resources; at the same time, however, each commitment also reshapes extant goals and fabricates new ones, setting in motion a converging cycle of constraints on what the artifact that the stakeholders end up building may look like. In other words, the new firm and market that come to be are a residual of the dual dynamics of the effectual process – on the one hand, expanding resources available to the network of stakeholders, and on the other, contracting what exactly the network can do with those resources.

This baseline model of entrepreneurial expertise embodies several key characteristics of expertise in general, as identified by the vast expertise literature in cognitive science (Read,

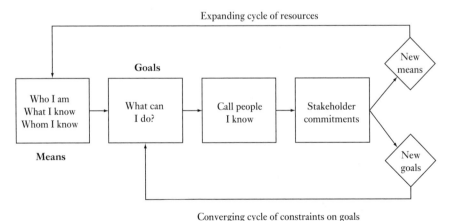

Both new means and new goals are changes in constraints

Figure 1

Sarasvathy, and Wiltbank, 2003). This literature has investigated expertise in a wide variety of domains, including chess, mathematics, scientific discovery, medical diagnosis, music, and so on. The four significant parallels between entrepreneurial expertise and expertise in general include the following.

Eschewing prediction. The literature on expert decision-making shows us that experts amass and organize the knowledge (Glaser, 1996) necessary to make good decisions without a great reliance on external inputs, particularly predictive inputs (Rikers et al., 2002). Similarly, expert entrepreneurs ignore predictive information, as it is based on the existing environment and does not account for the actions that the entrepreneur will take (Sarasvathy, 2001a).

Focus on "can." Experts automatically store information according to outcomes (Ericsson and Kintsch, 1995); they then match and recognize stored patterns against existing situations (Reingold et al., 2001) to retrieve strategies whose elements they already know how to implement (Kalakoski and Saariluoma, 2001). Expert entrepreneurs do the same thing, matching current opportunities with past experiences (Sarasvathy, 2001a).

Means-based action. While novices are likely to use goals as the basis for taking action, experts allow their knowledge of means to provide alternative rationales for taking action that simply are not available to novices (Larkin et al., 1980; Shanteau, 1992). Likewise, expert entrepreneurs facing goal ambiguity and environmental uncertainty craft means-driven strategies based on who they are, what they know, and whom they know (Sarasvathy, 2001a).

Strategies that leverage contingencies. Experts intuitively realize from past experiences where failure is possible (Schenk, Vitalari, and Davis, 1998), and work to frame problems in such a way that they build contingency into their strategies (Glaser, 1996). Expert entrepreneurs frame decisions in the same way, replacing elaborate planning toward a single outcome with strategies that enable many different paths that are contingent on intermediate outcomes (Sarasvathy, 2001a).

Entrepreneurial Expertise and Performance: Hypothesized Relationships

In further developing research on entrepreneurship as a form of expertise, the next step obviously is to compare expert entrepreneurs with novices and demonstrate the relationship of entrepreneurial expertise to performance. Entrepreneurial performance, however, is not a simple matter of firm performance. In fact, in the domain entrepreneurship, there exist two performance spaces: that of firm performance and that of the performance of the entrepreneur over a career of firm formation (Sarasvathy and Menon, 2002). Furthermore, entrepreneurial performance and the performance of any given firm they start may be related in complicated ways. With a view to delineating the subtleties underlying the relationship between entrepreneurial expertise and performance, Read, Sarasvathy, and Wiltbank (2003) propose the following four hypotheses that are graphically represented in figure 2:

Proposition 1	While novices may vary in their use of causal and effectual action, they will move toward a more effectual position as their expertise grows. Furthermore, both highly causal and highly effectual novices will move toward a more balanced position before developing a clear preference for highly effectual strategies as their expertise grows.
Proposition 2	The more resources available to novices, the more causal their actions are likely to be. In the case of expert entrepreneurs, availability of resources will not affect their use of highly effectual action
Proposition 3	Successful firms are more likely to have begun through effectual action and grown through causal action as they expand and endure over time.
Proposition 4	Only a small subset of expert entrepreneurs will successfully make the transition from an entrepreneurial firm to a large corporation.

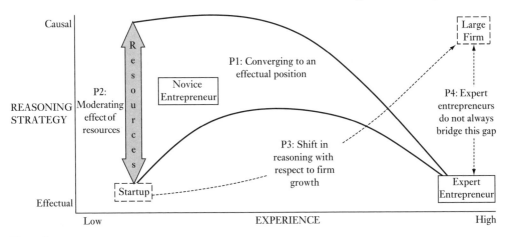

Figure 2

CONCLUSION

Studying entrepreneurship as a form of cognitive expertise has rich potential for future research. It provides empirically testable propositions for clarifying differences between novices and experts, and relating those differences to firm performance. Furthermore, there is much current interest in the education of entrepreneurship, and developing a body of information to be shared with aspiring entrepreneurs is a valuable goal for scholarship and pedagogy alike, particularly in schools of business management. Understanding the processes used by expert entrepreneurs offers the potential to provide a foundation for that body of knowledge. We know from the expert/novice literature that teaching expert rules results in expertise and that the performance of experts can be predicted accurately from knowledge of the rules they claim to use (Holyoak, 1991). Studying entrepreneurship as a form of expertise promises to shed light not only on how new businesses and markets are created, but also on the current holy grail of how to make existing enterprises more entrepreneurial.

Bibliography

Carter, N. M., Gartner, W. B., Shaver, K. G., and Gatewood, E. (2003). The career reasons of nascent entrepreneurs. *Journal of Business Venturing*, 18 (1): 13–39.

Ericsson, K. A. and Kintsch, W. (1995). Long-term working memory. *Psychological Review*, 102 (2): 211–45.

Ericsson, K. A. and Simon, H. A. (1993). *Protocol Analysis: Verbal Reports as Data*. Cambridge, MA: MIT Press.

Glaser, R. (1996). Changing the agency for learning: Acquiring expert performance. In K. A. Ericsson (ed.), *The Road to Excellence: The Acquisition of Expert Performance in the Arts and Sciences, Sports, and Games*. Mahwah, NJ: Erlbaum, 303–11.

Holyoak, K. (1991). Symbolic connectionism: Toward third-generation theories of expertise. In K. A. Ericsson, and J. Smith (eds.), *Toward a General Theory of Expertise: Prospects and Limits*. New York: Cambridge University Press, 301–36.

Kalakoski, V. and Saariluoma, P. (2001). Taxi drivers' exceptional memory of street names. *Memory and Cognition*, 29 (4): 634–8.

Larkin, J., McDermott, J., Simon, D. P., and Simon, H. A. (1980). Expert and novice performance in solving physics problems. *Science*, 208: 1335–42.

Miner, J. B., Smith, N. R., and Bracker, J. S. (1994). Role of entrepreneurial task motivation in the growth of technologically innovative firms: Interpretations from follow-up data. *Journal of Applied Psychology*, 79 (4): 627–30.

Mitchell, R. K. (1997). Oral history and expert scripts: Demystifying the entrepreneurial experience. *International Journal of Entrepreneurial Behaviour and Research*, 3 (2): 122.

Presley, M. and McCormick, B. (1995). Social interactional theories of learning and development: Vygotsky's sociocultural approaches to mind. In M. Presley, and B. McCormick (eds.), *Cognition, Teaching and Assessment*. New York: Harper Collins.

Read, S., Sarasvathy, S. D., and Wiltbank, R. (2003). What do entrepreneurs really learn from experience? The difference between expert and novice entrepreneurs. *2003 Frontiers of Entrepreneurship Research*.

Reingold, E. M., Charness, N., Schultetus, R. S., and Stampe, D. M. (2001). Perceptual automaticity in expert chess players: Parallel encoding of chess relations. *Psychonomic Bulletin and Review*, 8 (3): 504–10.

Reuber, A. R. and Fischer, E. M. (1994). Entrepreneurs' experience, expertise, and the performance of technology-based firms. *IEEE Transactions on Engineering Management*, 41 (4): 365–74.

Rikers, R. M. J. P., Schmidt, H. G., Boshuizen, H. P. A., Linssen, G. C. M., Geert, J. W., and Paas, F. G. W. C. (2002). The robustness of medical expertise: Clinical case processing by medical experts and subexperts. *American Journal of Psychology*, 115 (4): 609–29.

Sarasvathy, S. D. (1998). How do firms come to be? Towards a theory of the prefirm. Unpublished doctoral dissertation, Carnegie Mellon University.

Sarasvathy, S. D. (2001a). Causation and effectuation: Toward a theoretical shift from economic inevitability to entrepreneurial contingency. *Academy of Management Review*, 26 (2): 243–63.

Sarasvathy, S. D. (2001b). Effectual reasoning in entrepreneurial decision-making: Existence and bounds. *Academy of Management Best Paper Proceedings*.

Sarasvathy, S. D. and Menon, A. R. (2002). Failing firms and successful entrepreneurs: Serial entrepreneurship as a simple machine. Paper presented at the 2002 Academy of Management Conference in Denver, CO.

Schenk, K. D., Vitalari, N. P., and Davis, K. S. (1998). Differences between novice and expert systems analysts: What do we know and what do we do? *Journal of Management Information Systems*, 15 (1): 9–51.

Shanteau, J. (1992). Competence in experts: The role of task characteristics. *Organizational Behavior and Human Decision Processes*, 53 (2): 252–66.

Winslow, E. K. and Solomon, G. T. (1987). Entrepreneurs are more than non-conformists: They are mildly sociopathic. *Journal of Creative Behavior*, 21 (3): 202–13.

entrepreneurial growth

Per Davidsson

Although entrepreneurship and growth are frequently associated, the concept of *entrepreneurial growth* is not (yet) a firmly established term in theory, be it economic, organizational, or strategic. This work, however, focuses on entrepreneurial growth of the micro level units – firms or ventures. Therefore, while referring to the aggregate level economic growth that results from entrepreneurial action on the micro level would be a legitimate use of the concept of entre-

preneurial growth, this is not our focus here. On the micro level, entrepreneurial growth has different meanings, depending on the conceptualization of entrepreneurship employed (*see* ENTREPRENEURSHIP). Three partly overlapping perspectives on entrepreneurship are considered: (1) entrepreneurship is starting and running one's own firm; (2) entrepreneurship is the creation of new organizations; and (3) entrepreneurship is (economic development through) the creation of new-to-the-market economic activity. It can be argued that these three perspectives collectively exhaust the possible meanings of entrepreneurial growth on the micro level.

The notion that entrepreneurship is about starting and running one's own firm is explicit or implicit in much empirical research conducted under the entrepreneurship label. Under this conceptualization, entrepreneurial growth means, simply, the growth of independently owned and managed firms (*see* ENTREPRENEURIAL GROWTH). It is irrelevant whether the growth is achieved proactively or reactively and whether it is obtained though market penetration, market expansion, or the development and launch of new products and services. It is likewise irrelevant whether these forms of growth occur organically or through acquisition. What makes the growth entrepreneurial is that it occurs in a firm run by an entrepreneur, understood as a founder-manager of a business. This perspective, then, offers a straightforward interpretation of the concept of entrepreneurial growth. This view is closely linked to the configuration argument in stages-of-development models (e.g., Churchill and Lewis, 1983), which highlight among other things the changing demands on the founder-manager as the firm grows and matures.

While seemingly straightforward, this notion of entrepreneurial growth is problematic. An enterprising individual may start and run several business operations. If independent ownership is the vantage point for defining entrepreneurial growth, it can be argued to be the growth of the total set of business operations that are associated with an individual – and not that of one particular firm – that should be the basis for a discussion of entrepreneurial growth (Davidsson and Wiklund, 2000). Moreover, with the aging and maturing of entrepreneurship as an academic field of study, the association between entrepreneurship and small (owner-managed) business has been weakened. This is arguably because we have learned that many small, independent businesses do not excel at other characteristics associated with entrepreneurship (e.g., proactiveness, innovativeness, risk taking), while many larger and/or non-independent business organizations do. As a result, interpreting entrepreneurial growth as the growth of owner-managed firms is losing popularity.

The notion that entrepreneurship is the creation (or emergence) of new organizations is strongly associated with the works of William Gartner (e.g., Gartner, 1988). This notion is also embraced by population ecologists and organizational sociologists. One of the main missions for entrepreneurship research under this paradigm is to explain how and why organizations come into being, thus covering a topic that has been largely neglected in economic and organizational theories. This perspective does not allow for the concept of entrepreneurial growth. Entrepreneurship is about organizational emergence; the growth of established organizations is a different phenomenon, outside the entrepreneurial realm. However, most real world firms become operational at a much smaller size and with much less of a structure, systems, and functional division than the firm as we know it from organization theory. Therefore, in order to fill the gap and fulfill its theoretical mission, research conducted from this perspective may have to include not only pre-launch processes but also the "early growth" phase of businesses.

The notion that entrepreneurship is (economic development through) the creation of new-to-the-market economic activity has been embraced in some form by economic theorists who have taken an interest in entrepreneurship. With slightly different wording this view has recently been propagated in an influential article by Shane and Venkataraman (2000). Under this conceptualization, entrepreneurial growth is firm- or venture-level growth that has been obtained through offering a market something new (Davidsson, 2003; Davidsson, Delmar, and Wiklund, 2002). This new offer (product or service innovation, new business model, or just a new, marginally dissimilar product or service) gives customers new choice alternatives; it pro-

vides incumbent firms with a reason to take counter-action, and it may inspire other potential entrants to follow suit – possibly with a slightly improved offer. An established firm growing as a result of entering a new market is also an instance of entrepreneurial growth, even if the market offerings are the same as previously offered by the same firm in other markets. This is because the market effects (on customers, incumbents, and potential followers) are the same as if a new firm had entered the same market with a corresponding offer. By contrast, growth obtained through market penetration is not entrepreneurial growth, because there is no creation of new-to-the-market economic activity. The same is true for a firm that grows by acquiring other firms. In itself, this transfer of ownership does not change anything in the marketplace, and therefore the acquiring firm's expansion is not an example of entrepreneurial growth.

In summary, this article has suggested two micro-level interpretations of the concept of entrepreneurial growth. The first equates this concept with the expansion of founder-managed firms. This is consistent with defining entrepreneurship as starting and owning one's own firm. The second interpretation associates the term with organic growth through new product development or market expansion. This is consistent with defining entrepreneurship as (economic development through) the creation of new-to-the-market economic activity. According to the third main perspective on entrepreneurship – concerning the creation of new organizations – firm growth takes place after the entrepreneurial process of emergence is completed.

Bibliography

Churchill, C. and Lewis, V. L. (1983). The five stages of small business growth. *Harvard Business Review*, 61 (3): 30–50.

Davidsson, P. (2003). The domain of entrepreneurship research: Some suggestions. In J. Katz and S. Shepherd (eds.), *Advances in Entrepreneurship, Firm Emergence and Growth*, Vol. 6. Oxford: Elsevier/JAI Press, 315–72.

Davidsson, P., Delmar, F., and Wiklund, J. (2002). Entrepreneurship as growth; growth as entrepreneurship. In M. A. Hitt, R. D. Ireland, S. M. Camp, and D. L.

Sexton (eds.), *Strategic Entrepreneurship: Creating a New Integrated Mindset*. Oxford: Blackwell, 328–42.

Davidsson, P. and Wiklund, J. (2000). Conceptual and empirical challenges in the study of firm growth. In D. Sexton and H. Landström (eds.), *The Blackwell Handbook of Entrepreneurship*. Oxford: Blackwell, 26–44.

Gartner, W. B. (1988). "Who is an entrepreneur" is the wrong question. *American Small Business Journal*, 12 (spring): 11–31.

Shane, S. and Venkataraman, S. (2000). The promise of entrepreneurship as a field of research. *Academy of Management Review*, 25: 217–26.

entrepreneurial human capital

Russell Coff

The term "human capital" originates from the economics literature, where it is explored primarily as an investment that individuals make in knowledge and skills (Becker, 1964). It is an important distinction from the term "labor," which is treated as an undifferentiated commodity. It also marks recognition that knowledge and skills are a critical form of capital that affects firms' and individuals' productive capabilities. In this literature, much of the work has focused on the return on individuals' investments in the form of wages. Most of this research has focused narrowly on education as a measure of human capital because individuals make a conscious decision whether or not to seek a college education and advanced degrees.

However, education is clearly not the only form of knowledge or skills with economic value. Indeed, the knowledge literature focuses decidedly on more tacit knowledge that is unlikely to be part of formal education (Nonaka, 1994; Polanyi, 1966). While there has been some study in the economics literature of training and experience, it represents a relatively small portion of that literature and is subject to coarse-grained measures (Glick and Feuer, 1984).

Entrepreneurial human capital, then, is linked to the broader concept of human capital. Specifically, entrepreneurial human capital is the *set of knowledge and skills that individuals can bring to bear to create and exploit market opportunities*. Just as the central issue for the human capital literature is return on investment, a key question for entrepreneurial human capital is what is the

value of the asset? Put another way, to what extent do increases in entrepreneurial human capital lead to successful new ventures in both corporate and entrepreneurial settings?

As a research construct, a critical question is how to differentiate this construct from related concepts (especially human capital and social capital). Since human capital is, by definition, valuable in enhancing productive capabilities for individuals and firms, it is not surprising to find that it also contributes to new venture success (Gimeno et al., 1997). This finding does not, in itself, demonstrate the existence of a new construct distinct from traditional conceptualizations of human capital. To do this, it is necessary to identify how the human capital required in entrepreneurial settings might differ. The discussion below explores three issues critical to identifying entrepreneurial human capital as a distinct construct: (1) What knowledge and skills are uniquely relevant to successful new ventures? (2) How does one invest in entrepreneurial human capital? (3) How is entrepreneurial human capital differentiated from social capital?

WHAT TYPE OF KNOWLEDGE AND SKILLS?

We are immediately faced with the question of what knowledge and skills are uniquely relevant to creating new business ventures. This is critical to distinguish the term *entrepreneurial human capital* from the broader concept of human capital. That is, the traditional measures, education, training, and work experience, are important, but do these address the knowledge and skills that are most critical for entrepreneurial success? What knowledge and skills are most important in identifying and exploiting new market opportunities? Furthermore, do corporate settings demand a different set of skills to promote entrepreneurial ventures?

Iyigun and Owen (1998) identify professional and entrepreneurial human capital and explore their role in economic development. Here, professional human capital refers to traditional education-based learning or managerial experience, while entrepreneurial human capital refers specifically to entrepreneurial experience. Their model suggested that both types of human capital are important for economic development.

Gimeno et al. (1997) tested similar hypotheses empirically, using a survey of more than 1,500 entrepreneurs. They found that human capital did influence a venture's economic performance. The most significant measures of human capital included education, managerial experience, supervisory experience, experience in a similar business, and prior number of jobs held – all are generally forms of professional human capital. That is, they are known to enhance productivity in most business settings and are not specific to an entrepreneurial context. This is consistent with Lerner and Haber's (2001) finding that managerial skills had a very strong association with new venture performance.

However, Gimeno et al. (1997) found that prior entrepreneurial experience was important to a much lesser extent. Their results suggest that experience in a similar business, supervisory experience, and formal education are all more important than specific experience running a business – perhaps casting some doubt on the importance of entrepreneurial human capital as a distinct construct from professional human capital.

Another interpretation may be that some prior entrepreneurial experience is more valuable than others and that Gimeno et al. (1997) do not distinguish the type of prior entrepreneurial experience. This highlights an important avenue for further research on what entrepreneurial experience is most valuable. Ultimately, the ability to create and exploit market opportunities is a creative endeavor. It is unclear how or where potential entrepreneurs could enhance their skills in such creativity independently from traditional sources of professional human capital (e.g., education and work experience).

INVESTMENTS IN ENTREPRENEURIAL HUMAN CAPITAL

Thus, acquiring entrepreneurial human capital, apart from professional human capital, is complicated by the fact that not all entrepreneurial experience is necessarily valuable. It would appear that there is some causal ambiguity concerning exactly in which knowledge or skills would-be entrepreneurs should invest. Accordingly, noted labor economist Walter Oi (1999) concludes that entrepreneurship is sufficiently risky as to be effectively gambling. That is, one

can win with the first hand, or not win after playing many hands, or have a winning streak. While there are certainly instances of serial entrepreneurship (Wright, Robbie, and Ennew, 1997a), it is less clear how much of their success is due to experience (e.g., previous successful and/or failed ventures) as opposed to other sources of knowledge and skills – an intuitive sense of what ideas will be effective. Indeed, Wright, Robbie, and Ennew (1997b) found that experienced entrepreneurs did *not* outperform novice entrepreneurs who also got venture capital financing. If an entrepreneur envisions a value-creating formula, there is no guarantee that he or she will be able to reproduce those results. In this context, Oi (1999) argues that entrepreneurial human capital is *not* a useful construct separate and distinct from professional human capital because individuals cannot make rational decisions about how much to invest.

In order to counter this gambling argument, further exploration is warranted concerning what knowledge is critical for entrepreneurial success and how this knowledge is obtained. Nevertheless, to the extent that past entrepreneurial experience of some type is valuable, it is reasonable to view it as a form of capital. This would be true even if the type of experience needed were sufficiently causally ambiguous as to make systematic investing impossible for individuals. This is the case for many resources underlying the resource-based view and they are still clearly viewed as assets (Reed and DeFillippi, 1990).

However, even causally ambiguous assets might be acquired using approaches suited to investment under uncertainty, such as real options (Dixit, 1989). Generally, this heuristic involves making multiple initial investments and fully funding only those that are revealed as having merit based on subsequent information. This may recast the high rate of entrepreneurial failure in a more favorable light as "options that were not exercised" (McGrath, 1999). Of course, this is a very different model for human capital investment than that normally explored in the literature – initiating new ventures specifically for the purpose of developing scarce skills. Additional research on this topic is certainly warranted.

A final problem in analyzing investments in entrepreneurial human capital is that entrepreneurs are known to have a mixture of economic and non-economic objectives. Thus, while an investment approach might explore the impact of human capital on outcomes such as venture capital, market penetration, or financial performance, a given entrepreneur may have other objectives that are not captured by these measures (Bird, 1988).

ENTREPRENEURIAL SOCIAL CAPITAL

Finally, entrepreneurial human capital is strongly linked to social capital. The human capital literature has spawned a related area in sociology and management that focuses on individuals' use of social ties as a form of capital. Whereas human capital is "what you know," social capital addresses the question of "who you know." This distinction has increased in importance as the economics literature focused heavily on empirical measures of education and experience to the detriment of social ties. However, as Coleman (1988) identifies, the two are often closely linked in practice. Such is the case in an entrepreneurial context. Certainly, social capital has an important impact on new venture success (Shane and Stuart, 2002). Social ties are an important source of essential resources, including information, employees, customers, and venture capital (Sacks, 2002). Indeed, social capital may be relatively more important than human capital in this context (Davidsson and Honig, 2003).

However, the distinction may be especially blurred for entrepreneurial human capital to the extent that it refers specifically to experience in previous entrepreneurial ventures. Whereas education may ultimately be loosely linked to one's professional networks, experience may be more closely related. Indeed, the most important and valuable social ties may have been forged as a result of prior entrepreneurial experience. In practice, it may be hard to empirically differentiate the two constructs.

Bibliography

Becker, G. S. (1964). *Human Capital*. New York: Columbia.

Bird, B. J. (1988). Implementing entrepreneurial ideas: The case for intention. *Academy of Management Review*, 13 (3): 442–53.

Coleman, J. S. (1988). Social capital in the creation of human capital. *American Journal of Sociology*, 94 (summer): 95–120.

Davidsson, P. and Honig, B. (2003). The role of social and human capital among nascent entrepreneurs. *Journal of Business Venturing*, 18 (3): 301–31.

Dixit, A. (1989). Entry and exit decisions under uncertainty. *Journal of Political Economy*, 97 (3): 620–38.

Gimeno, J., Folta, T. B., Cooper, A. C., and Woo, C. Y. (1997). Survival of the fittest? Entrepreneurial human capital and the persistence of underperforming firms. *Administrative Science Quarterly*, 42: 750–83.

Glick, H. A. and Feuer, M. J. (1984). Employer-sponsored training and the governance of specific human capital investments. *Quarterly Review of Economics and Business*, 24 (2): 91–104.

Iyigun, M. F. and Owen, A. L. (1998). Risk, entrepreneurship, and human capital accumulation. *American Economic Review*, 88 (2): 454–8.

Lerner, M. and Haber, S. (2001). Performance factors of small tourism ventures: The interface of tourism, entrepreneurship and the environment. *Journal of Business Venturing*, 16 (1): 77–100.

McGrath, R. G. (1999). Falling forward: Real options reasoning and entrepreneurial failure. *Academy of Management Review*, 24 (1): 13–30.

Nonaka, I. (1994). A dynamic theory of organizational knowledge creation. *Organization Science*, 5 (1): 14–37.

Oi, W. Y. (1999). The hearty and cheery state. *Contemporary Economic Policy*, 17 (1): 138–47.

Polanyi, M. (1966). *The Tacit Dimension*. New York: Anchor Day Books.

Reed, R. and DeFillippi, R. J. (1990). Causal ambiguity, barriers to imitation, and sustainable competitive advantage. *Academy of Management Review*, 15 (1): 88–102.

Sacks, M. A. (2002). The social structure of new venture funding: Stratification and the differential liability of newness. *Research in the Sociology of Organizations*, 19: 263–94.

Shane, S. and Stuart, T. (2002). Organizational endowments and the performance of university start-ups. *Management Science*, 48 (1): 154–71.

Wright, M., Robbie, K., and Ennew, C. (1997a). Serial entrepreneurs. *British Journal of Management*, 8 (3): 251–69.

Wright, M., Robbie, K., and Ennew, C. (1997b). Venture capitalists and serial entrepreneurs. *Journal of Business Venturing*, 12 (3): 227–50.

entrepreneurial human resource strategy

Christopher J. Collins, Matthew Allen, and Scott Snell

Entrepreneurship is the process by which "opportunities to create future goods and services are discovered, evaluated, and exploited" (Shane and Venkataraman, 2000: 218). In other words, it is the process by which organizations and individuals convert new knowledge into new opportunities in the form of new products and services. Strategic human resource management (SHRM) has been defined as the system of organizational practices and policies used to manage employees in a manner that leads to higher organizational performance (Wright and McMahan, 1992). Further, one perspective suggests that sets of HR practices do not themselves create competitive advantage; instead, they foster the development of organizational capabilities which in turn create such advantages (Lado and Wilson, 1994; Wright, Dunford, and Snell, 2001). Specifically, this body of literature suggests that HR practices lead to firm performance when they are aligned to work together to create and support the employee-based capabilities that lead to competitive advantage (Wright and Snell, 2000; Wright, Dunford, and Snell, 2001). Thus, entrepreneurial human resource strategy is best defined as the set or sets of human resources practices that will increase the likelihood that new knowledge will be converted to new products or services.

STRATEGIC HUMAN RESOURCE MANAGEMENT AND KNOWLEDGE CREATION

Based on the above definition of entrepreneurship, new knowledge creation is key to the entrepreneurial process. Further, organizational researchers have pointed to both the ability to diffuse and exploit current knowledge and the ability to create new knowledge as critical capabilities for organizational success (Kogut and Zander, 1992). This is especially true for entrepreneurial firms whose success and survival are dependent upon identifying and exploiting opportunities in rapidly changing markets (Christiansen, 1997). Nahapiet and Ghoshal (1998) argued that for exchange and combination to take place, parties must have access to one an-

other, be capable of combining and exchanging ideas and information, and perceive value from the exchange and combination process. Most studies of organizational learning recognize initial knowledge of employees as a key factor in organizational learning and employees as a primary repository of organizational knowledge (Argote, 1999). Further, the ability of firms to create new knowledge is dependent upon the social capital that exists inside the firm, because the social connections between employees lead to productive exchanges and combinations of ideas and information (Nahapiet and Ghoshal, 1998).

Further, research on SHRM suggests that companies can build and reinforce a knowledge creation capability by aligning HR practices to create the employee-based capabilities necessary for knowledge creation. For example, Snell, Youndt, and Wright (1996) noted that HR practices can be used to increase the transfer of knowledge between employees and institutionalize knowledge in the form of processes and procedures. As noted above, one of the key elements in creating new organizational knowledge is the human capital of the company, defined as abilities, intelligence, and skills acquired from informal and formal education and job experience of key employees in the firm (Becker, 1964). There is some evidence that firms can systematically affect the human capital of the firm through systems of HR practices. For example, firms create higher levels of employee human capital by implementing multiple recruiting sources, extensive selection practices, paying above-market starting salaries, investing more in training and development, etc. (Koch and McGrath, 1996; Snell and Dean, 1992).

Nahapiet and Ghoshal (1998) argued that social capital is another key employee-based resource that both increases the ability and motivation of employees to exchange and combine knowledge. Leana and Van Buren (1999) argued that different human resource practices can be used to build social capital between the employees within an organization. In a recent empirical study, Collins and Clark (2003) found that several bundles of HR practices were related to the internal and external social networks of top management team members in high-technology firms. Similarly, Collins (2003) found that a high-performance bundle of HR practices was related to measures of core employee social capital (measured as trust and shared norms).

While these two empirical studies are promising, future research in SHRM must continue to explore the relationships between bundles of HR practices and the employee-based resources that lead to knowledge creation. Recently, Kang, Morris, and Snell (2004) posited two different forms of social capital – or relational archetypes – that represent different approaches to knowledge exchange. On the one hand, the entrepreneurial archetype is characterized by sparse networks of loosely coupled parties whose exchange relationships are based on personal dyadic trust and common component knowledge. This archetype is more closely aligned with the requirements of exploratory learning for absorbing novel and diverse knowledge in new and unfamiliar domains (March, 1991). Kang, Morris, and Snell suggested it would be facilitated through HR practices that support flexible work structures, multiple career (boundaryless) development strategies, trans-specialist skill development, and results-based incentives and performance management systems.

In contrast, the cooperative archetype is characterized by strong and dense social networks where relationships are reinforced by generalized trust and common architectural knowledge. This type of archetype is perhaps best for combining and integrating fine-grained and in-depth knowledge in familiar knowledge domains (March, 1991). The cooperative archetype is perhaps best supported by HR practices that focus on interdependent work structures, staffing, and socialization systems that reinforce organizational values, employment security, cross-functional skill development, and performance management systems that emphasize collective achievements.

Based on these types of frameworks, there appear to be multiple bundles of HR practices that firms can implement to increase knowledge creation among employees. Further, as suggested by the SHRM literature (e.g., Wright, Dunford, and Snell, 2001), firms should use different sets of HR practices depending upon the type of knowledge sharing and requisite

social networks that the firm is attempting to foster. As noted above, Kang, Morris, and Snell (2004) agued that firms should implement a more individualistic set of HR practices that lead to sparse and broad-reaching individual employee networks in order to foster novel combinations of previously unconnected knowledge; whereas firms seeking to foster the recombination of existing knowledge should implement team- and organizational-based HR practices that lead to dense employee networks. While these theoretical proposals are interesting, additional empirical research is needed to specifically link HR practices to hard measures of knowledge creation through employee-based capabilities.

STRATEGIC HUMAN RESOURCES AND KNOWLEDGE EXPLOITATION

While knowledge creation is important, by itself it is not enough to ensure that the entrepreneurial process occurs in companies. Instead, HR practices must also create and reinforce an environment in which employees convert that new knowledge into new products and services. Further, there is some empirical research to suggest that HR practices can lead to greater innovation in the form of the introduction of new products and services. For example, Chandler, Keller, and Lyon (2000) also found that reward systems could positively affect the performance of entrepreneurial organizations that face a rapidly changing environment when the rewards are aligned to create a culture that is supportive of innovation. In a paper that more closely follows the SHRM approach, Collins (2003) found that multiple sets of practices led to innovation in high-technology firms. Specifically, he found that both high-commitment and network-building bundles of HR practices were related to firm innovation (measured as the number of new products and services) through their effects on an organizational climate of cooperation and core employee internal and external social networks.

As with the effects of HR on knowledge creation, these papers suggest that there are multiple sets of HR practices that can be used to facilitate the exploitation of knowledge in the form of actual product or service innovations. Further, as is suggested by the theoretical work on SHRM (e.g., Wright, Dunford, and Snell,

2001; Wright and Snell, 2000), it appears that firms can positively affect their competitive advantage by designing their HR systems to support employee-based resources. Specifically, firms can design and implement HR practices to create the organizational climates, culture, and employee network relationships that support innovation. Again, while these studies are useful, additional empirical research is needed to explore the array of possible relationships between HR practices and knowledge exploitation in the form of new products and services.

Bibliography

Argote, L. (1999). *Organizational Learning: Creating, Retaining and Transferring Knowledge*. Boston: Kluwer Academic Publishers.

Becker, G. S. (1964). *Human Capital*. New York: Columbia University Press.

Chandler, G. N., Keller, C., and Lyon, D. W. (2000). Unraveling the determinants and consequences of an innovation-supportive organizational culture. *Entrepreneurship: Theory and Practice*, 25 (1): 59–76.

Christiansen, C. (1997). *The Innovators' Dilemma*. Cambridge, MA: Harvard Business School Press.

Collins, C. J. (2003). Human resource practices, core employee social capital, and firm innovation. Presented at the Academy of Management Meetings, Seattle, WA.

Collins, C. J. and Clark, K. D. (2003). Strategic human resource practices, top management team social networks, and firm performance: The role of HR practices in creating organizational competitive advantage. *Academy of Management Journal*, 46: 740–52.

Kang, S., Morris, S., and Snell, S. S. (2004). Relational archetypes, organizational learning, and value creation: Extending the human resource architecture. Unpublished manuscript.

Koch, M. J. and McGrath, R. G. (1996). Improving labor productivity: Human resource management policies do matter. *Strategic Management Journal*, 17: 335–54.

Kogut, B. and Zander, U. (1992). Knowledge of the firm, combination capabilities, and the replication of technology. *Organization Science*, 3: 383–97.

Lado, A. A. and Wilson, M. C. (1994). Human resource systems and sustained competitive advantage: A competency-based perspective. *Academy of Management Review*, 19: 699–727.

Leana, C. R. and Van Buren, H. J. (1999). Organizational social capital and employment practices. *Academy of Management Journal*, 24: 538–55.

March, J. G. (1991). Exploration and exploitation in organizational learning. *Organization Science*, 2: 71–87.

Nahapiet, J. and Ghoshal, S. (1998). Social capital, intellectual capital, and the organizational advantage. *Academy of Management Review*, 23: 242–66.

Shane, S. and Venkataraman, S. (2000). The promise of entrepreneurship as a field of research. *Academy of Management Review*, 25: 217–26.

Snell, S. A. and Dean, J. W. (1992). Integrated manufacturing and human resource management: A human capital perspective. *Academy of Management Journal*, 35: 467–504.

Snell, S. A., Youndt, M. A., and Wright, P. M. (1996). Establishing a framework for research in strategic human resource management: Merging resource theory and organizational learning. In G. R. Ferris (ed.), *Research in Personnel and Human Resource Management*, 14: 61–90. Greenwich, CT: JAI Press.

Wright, P. M., Dunford, B. B., and Snell, S. A. (2001). Human resources and the resource-based view of the firm. *Journal of Management*, 27: 701–21.

Wright, P. M. and McMahan, G. C. (1992). Theoretical perspectives for strategic human resource management. *Journal of Management*, 18: 295–320.

Wright, P. M. and Snell, S. A. (2000). Toward a unifying framework for exploring fit and flexibility in strategic human resource management. *Academy of Management Review*, 23: 756–72.

entrepreneurial identity

Ha Hoang and Javier Gimeno

Entrepreneurial identity refers to a person's set of meanings, including attitudes and beliefs, attributes, and subjective evaluations of behavior, that define him- or herself in an entrepreneurial role. The construct of entrepreneurial identity encompasses how a person defines the entrepreneurial role, and whether he or she identifies with that role. Individuals with different entrepreneurial identities behave differently in similar environmental contexts. Therefore, a focus on entrepreneurial identity can help answer questions such as: Why do some people actively search their environments for entrepreneurial opportunities, while others ignore the opportunities available to them? Why do some individuals become entrepreneurs while others in similar contexts never try or give up in their efforts? It is because entrepreneurial activity depends in part on whether the individual defines him or herself as entrepreneurial. Thus far, entrepreneurship scholars have focused on objective, economic factors, such as human and financial capital or environmental opportunities, that facilitate entrepreneurial activity, while largely ignoring subjective, sociocognitive factors such as identity. A mismatch between a person's behaviors and identity may lead to disengagement from the entrepreneurial role. Therefore, attention to the formation and commitment to an entrepreneurial identity complements and extends our understanding of successful entrepreneurial behavior.

Identity, a part of a person's self-concept, is important because it moderates a person's interactions with the environment. Individuals with different identities may respond differently to similar contextual clues. Because of its role in motivating behavior, interest in identity in the social sciences is strong (Gecas, 1982) and has shed light on a number of diverse phenomena, such as career transitions (Ibarra, 2003), racial and gender identities (Burke and Tully, 1977; Sellers et al., 1998), language assimilation in former Soviet republics (Laitin, 1998), and perceptions of racial discrimination (Sellers and Shelton, 2003). Our conceptualization of entrepreneurial identity draws on research in the sociology and social psychology literature that links identity to roles (Gordon, 1968). Roles are social positions that carry expectations for behavior as well as values and beliefs that are internalized through socialization and identification processes. Understanding entrepreneurial identity thus requires an exploration of the entrepreneurial role, and how identification with that role evolves over time.

DIMENSIONS OF ENTREPRENEURIAL IDENTITY

Research in the conceptualization and measurement of roles commonly argues that identities are multi-dimensional constructs (Hoelter, 1985). Accordingly, we identify four dimensions that characterize entrepreneurial identity. An important dimension that consistently characterizes roles is the set of attributes and traits that an individual uses to describe the role (Burke and Tully, 1977; Burke, 1980). Hence, one dimension of entrepreneurial identity is perceived attributes or distinguishing traits usually associated with people who occupy the entrepreneurial role. For example, entrepreneurs may be

characterized as "dynamic," "opportunistic," or "risk-taking." These characteristics are perceived traits that in turn may be based on an individual's direct experience in the role, on relationships with entrepreneurs, or on ideal types propagated by the media. Individuals may differ in their attribution of entrepreneurial traits, although social processes may achieve some shared social meaning. The overlap between traits attributed to the entrepreneurial role and traits that individuals believe that they possess, can provide insight into the strength of an entrepreneurial identity.

Because there is no widely held definition of entrepreneurship, attributes ascribed to entrepreneurs may depend in part on what the individual defines as entrepreneurial activity. The research literature reflects the diversity of definitions of entrepreneurship. The most common definitions are starting a business, self-employment, and building a business around a novel product or technology. Moreover, some researchers argue that opportunity identification and exploitation are the principal activities of entrepreneurs (Shane and Venkataraman, 2000). Thus, another relevant dimension of entrepreneurial identity encompasses an individual's perceptions of what constitutes entrepreneurial activity. In turn, the definition can help to frame the way in which the person defines him or herself and serve as a guide for action. For example, individuals who associate the entrepreneurial role with the creation of inventions or new patents may fulfill their identity without creating new businesses. Because different definitions may have different implications for behavior, a better understanding of content attributions helps to explain variation across individuals in the entrepreneurial activities that they undertake.

The previous dimensions outline an individual's meanings ascribed to an entrepreneurial role, but do not capture the extent to which the person defines him or herself as entrepreneurial. The third dimension, identity centrality, reflects the importance of an entrepreneurial identity to one's self-definition. The notion implies that the entrepreneurial identity occupies a salient position within a hierarchy of multiple social identities (e.g., "father," "neighbor," "citizen," etc.) that forms the self-concept or "the totality of an individual's thoughts and feelings having reference to oneself as an object" (Rosenberg, 1979: 7). More central identities are those that are enacted across a wider variety of social relations (Stryker, 1968). Thus, individuals with central entrepreneurial identities may enact that identity in other social contexts, such as with family and friends, or among church or school acquaintances.

The last dimension, identity regard, acknowledges that the traits and activities associated with the role may be viewed positively or negatively. Research has found that personal evaluative judgments can differ from what individuals believe are the broader society's view of the role identity (Sellers et al., 1998). Thus, we differentiate between public and private regard, reflecting the positive to negative attributions of being entrepreneurial that an individual holds (private regard), which may differ from the individual's perception about society's evaluation of the entrepreneurial role (public regard). Positive or negative evaluations of the entrepreneurial role may naturally explain the extent of the individual's identification with the role. Given that these judgments carry a valence, they are likely to have motivational power if both private and public regard of entrepreneurial activity is positive. However, some individuals may view entrepreneurship as a revolutionary act, and may gain motivation from a perceived negative public regard for entrepreneurship.

Building on this multi-dimensional model of entrepreneurial identity, a number of relationships across the dimensions are possible and worthy of empirical study. It is expected that those with central entrepreneurial identities would have more positive opinions of entrepreneurs and their activities. Thus, the relationship between identity centrality and private regard should be positive. A high regard for entrepreneurs should also be related to positive attributions of entrepreneurs. High private regard may also be related to a definition of entrepreneurial activity that emphasizes its socially beneficial role, for example, in the creation of novel technologies, products, or services. Finally, because personal opinions are influenced by the views of others, private regard will also tend to be correlated with public regard.

FORMATION OF ENTREPRENEURIAL IDENTITY

How does an entrepreneurial identity take root and develop? Although more research is needed to answer this question, social networks are likely to be an important facilitator of entrepreneurial identity. Thus far, the role of social ties in entrepreneurial activity has emphasized the concrete resources that contacts can provide in the start-up effort. Greater attention to identity dynamics suggests that network contacts may also be important in defining and adapting to an entrepreneurial role. In particular, ties to *role models* help to make the entrepreneurial activity more concrete and to illuminate what entrepreneurs do. Direct links to role models serve as a referent for appropriate role behavior, attributes, and attitudes. The importance of role models may explain a consistent finding in longitudinal studies of entrepreneurial activity that link the likelihood that an individual will be self-employed to having parents, friends, or family members who owned a business (Carroll and Mosakowski, 1987; Evans and Leighton, 1989). Moreover, evidence suggests that entrepreneurs whose parents owned a business are not necessarily more economically successful, but are more likely to persist in the role (Gimeno et al., 1997).

Two other types of network contacts that we term *cheerleaders* and *coaches* may also support the development of an entrepreneurial identity. Cheerleaders provide social and emotional support, which is important for maintaining high self-esteem in the process of role transition. Coaches, through their knowledge of the individual gained from past interactions, help individuals evaluate the potential for fit with the entrepreneurial role. Coaches are trusted advisors whose past experience can provide an important source of input as to whether the individual has the knowledge and personal attributes thought to be important for the entrepreneurial undertaking at hand. The emergence of an entrepreneurial identity may also be hindered by social relationships anchored in previous identities, such as former colleagues in a previous job, who are critical of such transitions (Ebaugh, 1988).

In contrast to personality traits previously studied in entrepreneurship research, which are viewed as stable over time (e.g., need of achievement, locus of control, and risk orientation), entrepreneurial identity is a dynamic construct. In particular, individuals moving into entrepreneurship must grapple with the identity implications of their activities, resulting in assessments of whether they want to be and can be an entrepreneur. This notion is supported by research on individuals making significant role transitions that find identities change in adapting to role changes (Ebaugh, 1988; Ibarra, 1999; Markus and Nurius, 1986). As the discussion of social networks suggests, a key element of the transition process focuses on the development of new social relationships and a reconfiguration of existing ties to support an identity change.

CONSEQUENCES OF ENTREPRENEURIAL IDENTITY

Clearly, an entrepreneurial identity is not sufficient for success in entrepreneurial activities, but may influence the choice of activities and the commitment to realizing the venture. Entrepreneurial identity may influence the set of entrepreneurial behaviors emphasized in the early stages of venture formation. As captured in the activity dimension, entrepreneurial identity includes perceptions of important entrepreneurial activities that are influenced by the individual's past experiences and skills, as well as by role models and coaches. Thus, nascent entrepreneurs with different identities may place different emphases on technical, financial, and marketing activities that in turn have consequences for the venture's subsequent performance.

Entrepreneurial identity may also influence the continuation or dissolution of ventures through its role in generating commitment to the entrepreneurial process. Individuals with high private regard for entrepreneurship will likely experience an increase in self-esteem when performing entrepreneurial activities that encourages them to remain in entrepreneurial roles even if alternatives with better economic outcomes exist. Indeed, identity can mediate the consideration and evaluation of alternatives; individuals with strongly held entrepreneurial identities may not evaluate alternative roles. The consequences of identity for continuation

may be particularly critical during the early stages of a venture (nascent and founding stages), because identity may encourage exploration and discovery in contexts of high uncertainty about future outcomes. In those situations, feedback signals from the environmental stakeholders may not be entirely positive. Individuals with a central entrepreneurial identity may be more willing to persist in those early activities, while those with a less central identity may give up earlier. Thus, an identity-based perspective suggests that researchers could benefit from increased attention to the process of entrepreneurial identity formation and its facilitators in order to shed light on why some, and not others, become entrepreneurs.

Bibliography

Burke, P. J. (1980). The self: Measurement requirements from an interactionist perspective. *Social Psychology Quarterly*, 43: 18–29.

Burke, P. J. and Tully, J. C. (1977). The measurement of role identity. *Social Forces*, 55: 881–97.

Carroll, G. R. and Mosakowski, E. (1987). The career dynamics of self-employment. *Administrative Science Quarterly*, 32: 570–89.

Ebaugh, H. R. F. (1988). *Becoming an Ex: The Process of Role Exit*. Chicago: University of Chicago Press.

Evans, D. S. and Leighton, L. S. (1989). Some empirical aspects of entrepreneurship. *American Economic Review*, 79 (5): 19–35.

Gecas, V. (1982). The self concept. *Annual Review of Sociology*, 8: 1–33.

Gimeno, J., Folta, T. B., Cooper, A. C., and Woo, C. Y. (1997). Survival of the fittest? Entrepreneurial human capital and the persistence of underperforming firms. *Administrative Science Quarterly*, 42: 750–83.

Gordon, C. (1968). Self-conceptions: Configurations of content. In C. Gordon and K. Gergen (eds.), *The Self in Social Interaction*. New York: Wiley, 115–32.

Hoelter, J. W. (1985). The structure of self-conception: Conceptualization and measurement. *Journal of Personality and Social Psychology*, 49: 1392–407.

Ibarra, H. (1999). Provisional selves: Experimenting with image and identity in professional adaptation. *Administrative Science Quarterly*, 44: 764–91.

Ibarra, H. (2003). *Working Identity: Unconventional Strategies for Reinventing Your Career*. Boston, MA: Harvard Business School Press.

Laitin, D. (1998). *Identity in Formation: The Russian-Speaking Populations in the Near Abroad*. Ithaca, NY: Cornell University Press.

Markus, H. and Nurius, P. (1986). Possible selves. *American Psychologist*, 41: 954–69.

Rosenberg, M. (1979). *Conceiving the Self*. New York: Basic Books.

Sellers, R. M., Smith, M. A., Shelton, J. N., Rowley, S. A. J., and Chavous, T. M. (1998). Multidimensional model of racial identity: A reconceptualization of African-American racial identity. *Personality and Social Psychology Review*, 2: 18–39.

Sellers, R. M. and Shelton, J. N. (2003). The role of racial identity in perceived racial discrimination. *Journal of Personality and Social Psychology*, 84: 1079–92.

Shane, S. and Venkataraman, S. (2000). The promise of entrepreneurship as a field of research. *Academy of Management Review*, 25: 217–26.

Stryker, S. (1968). Identity salience and role performance. *Journal of Marriage and the Family*, 30: 558–64.

entrepreneurial intensity

Michael Morris

"Entrepreneurial" is an adjective increasingly applied to people, projects, organizations, geographic regions, and countries. Considerable research has been done at the organizational level. Terms such as entrepreneurial intensity, entrepreneurial orientation, entrepreneurial posture, organic emphasis, entrepreneurship level, and entrepreneurial aggressiveness have been employed to describe levels of entrepreneurship in established organizations. The present discussion is an exploration of the concept of entrepreneurial intensity (EI).

Underlying Dimensions of Entrepreneurship

What does it mean to characterize an organization as entrepreneurial? While one might be tempted to think in either–or terms, entrepreneurship is a variable. There is some level of entrepreneurship in every organization. Even within the largest, highly conservative company or the most bureaucratic government organization, elements of entrepreneurial behavior can be found. The question becomes one of determining in the aggregate how entrepreneurial a given organization is.

It has been argued that entrepreneurship has three underlying dimensions: innovativeness, risk taking, and proactiveness (Covin and Slevin,

1989; Krieser, Marino, and Weaver, 2002; Wiklund, 1999). Innovativeness is concerned with the relative emphasis on novel or unique products, services, and processes. Product and service innovations can range from radical breakthroughs that address a need not previously addressed, to minor enhancements of existing products. Process innovations can include new production techniques, distribution approaches, selling methods, procurement programs, or administrative systems, among others.

Risk concerns the likelihood that actual results will differ from expectations. Risk taking involves a willingness to pursue opportunities that have a reasonable likelihood of producing major losses or significant performance discrepancies. Entrepreneurship does not entail reckless decisions and extreme risks, but instead involves calculated risk taking. "Calculated" implies a reasonable awareness of the risks involved and an attempt to mitigate and manage these risks.

Proactiveness has been associated with assertiveness and action. Miller (1987) sees entrepreneurial firms as *acting on* rather than *reacting to* their environments, by leading rather than following competitors in innovation; favoring growth, innovation, and development over the tried and true; and attempting to undo competitors. Bateman and Grant (1993) speak of a disposition to take action to influence one's environment. Venkatraman (1989) refers to continuous experimentation. Behaviorally, proactiveness is concerned with doing what is necessary to bring an entrepreneurial concept to fruition, and typically entails considerable perseverance, adaptability, and a willingness to assume responsibility for failure.

Although these three dimensions have received the greatest amount of attention from researchers, Lumpkin and Dess (2001) suggest autonomy and competitive aggressiveness are also dimensions of entrepreneurship. Autonomy refers to independent action by a team or individual aimed at developing and implementing a new business concept or vision. Competitive aggressiveness involves a combative posture vis-à-vis the firm's competitors. While the empirical evidence regarding autonomy is scant, these authors found support for distinguishing competitive aggressiveness from proactiveness, although the latter has a much clearer impact on company performance than the former.

ENTREPRENEURIAL INTENSITY: COMBINING DEGREE AND FREQUENCY

A given entrepreneurial event (new product, service, or process) might be characterized as being higher or lower on each of these three dimensions. Accordingly, "degree of entrepreneurship" refers to the extent to which events are more innovative, risky, and proactive. Just as important is the question of how many entrepreneurial events take place within a company over a given period of time. This number of events can be referred to as the frequency of entrepreneurship. Some companies produce a steady stream of new products, services, and processes over time, while others very rarely introduce something new or different.

This brings us to the concept of entrepreneurial intensity. To assess the overall level of entrepreneurship in an organization, the concepts of degree and frequency must be considered together. Any number of combinations can result. Thus, a firm may be engaging in many entrepreneurial initiatives (high on frequency),

but perhaps none of them are all that innovative, risky, or proactive (low on degree). Another company may pursue a path that emphasizes breakthrough developments (high degree) that are done every four or five years (low frequency). To better understand the EI concept, consider figure 1. Here, a two-dimensional matrix presents the number, or frequency, of entrepreneurial events on the vertical axis, and the extent or degree to which these events are innovative, risky, and proactive on the horizontal axis. This matrix can be termed the entrepreneurial grid. For illustration purposes, five sample scenarios have been identified in figure 1, and these have been labeled Periodic/incremental, Continuous/incremental, Periodic/discontinuous, Dynamic, and Revolutionary. For example, where few entrepreneurial events are produced, and these events are only nominally innovative, risky, and proactive, the organization can be described as periodic/incremental in terms of its (modest) level of EI. Similarly, an organization that is responsible for numerous entrepreneurial events that are highly innovative, risky, or proactive will fit into the revolutionary segment of the grid, reflecting the highest levels of EI.

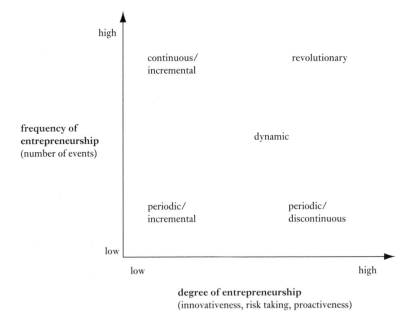

Figure 1   The entrepreneurial grid

MEASUREMENT APPROACHES

Reliable and valid scales have long existed for the measurement of entrepreneurship's underlying dimensions, and these have been employed to address a wide range of research questions, as discussed below. Criticisms have been raised, however, in that most of the published work relies on managerial perceptions (Lumpkin and Dess, 2001). Another approach involves relying on measures of actual firm behavior, such as new product or process introduction. A third measurement approach examines how the firm allocates resources, such that a firm that is more financially leveraged is taking higher risks, and one with a higher proportion of R&D expenditures is more innovative.

Measurement of EI also has important managerial implications. For instance, Morris and Kuratko (2002) have reported on a measure that illustrates where a given company falls in the grid presented in figure 1. Relying on both perceptual data averaged across multiple respondents and behavioral data on new products, services, and processes, their entrepreneurial performance index has been applied to hundreds of companies. These firms (and divisions within) are able to first benchmark their overall performance, and then track it over time and compare it to other firms in their industry. Management can determine where the firm falls in the entrepreneurial grid, the relative importance of frequency and degree, and the specific types of innovation, risk taking, and proactive behaviors that are consistent with the firm's strategic direction.

THINGS WE KNOW AND DON'T KNOW ABOUT ENTREPRENEURIAL INTENSITY

Where a company falls on the entrepreneurial grid will vary depending on a number of internal and external factors. Internally, entrepreneurship is more evidenced where company structures are flatter, control systems contain a measure of slack, appraisal systems include innovation and risk-taking criteria, jobs are broader in scope, reward systems encourage individual achievement, and cultures emphasize a balance of individualism and group orientation (Morris and Jones, 1993; Morris, Davis, and Allen, 1994; Zahra and Covin, 1995). Another

stream of research has demonstrated a strong positive correlation between the level of entrepreneurial intensity demonstrated by a firm and its market orientation (Miles and Arnold, 1991).

Externally, where industries are highly concentrated, competitors are cooperative, demand is fairly captive and homogeneous, technologies rarely change, economic conditions are stable, and margins are comfortable, companies will demonstrate lower EI scores (Davis, Morris, and Allen, 1991; Dickson and Weaver, 1997). One possibility may be that frequency of entrepreneurship is directly related to the intensity of competition and amount of market heterogeneity, while degree of entrepreneurship is more a function of the rate of technological change in an industry and amount of product heterogeneity.

Perhaps the most significant research finding to date concerns this question: "Do companies with stronger entrepreneurial orientations perform better?" The answer is generally "yes," with some exceptions. Researchers have found significant relationships between EI and multiple indicators of company performance (e.g., Miller and Friesen, 1983; Zahra and Covin, 1995). Examples of such indicators include profits, the income-to-sales ratio, rates of growth in revenue, assets, and employment, and a composite measure of financial and non-financial criteria. Morris and Sexton (1996) found the relationship was strongest where weights of .7 and .3 were applied respectively to degree and frequency. This linkage between EI and performance appears to be especially strong for firms that operate in highly turbulent environments, but is also modified by the fit between company strategy, structure, and the external environment (Naman and Slevin, 1993). The linkage also gets stronger over time (Wiklund, 1999).

This does not mean that more entrepreneurship is inherently better. There are industry norms for entrepreneurial intensity. Such norms suggest there is no best place to be in the entrepreneurial grid – the ideal point is industry-, market-, and time-specific. Better performing firms are those that demonstrate a stronger entrepreneurial orientation than their counterparts in the same industry. But norms for industries vary widely. One might expect a grocery retail chain to be higher on frequency, lower on degree, with a heavier emphasis on process innovation. Alternatively, leading pharmaceutical companies will likely approach the dynamic sector of the grid, with high frequency of new products, and a portfolio of innovations that includes both incremental advances and breakthrough products.

How do the dimensions relate to one another? Although most studies have shown innovativeness, risk taking, and proactiveness to be correlated, the relationships can be quite complex, and each dimension can vary independently. A firm could be quite proactive without being very innovative, or proactive behavior could only involve a modicum of risk. One might assume that doing more innovative things means taking higher risks, when the relationship actually may be curvilinear. Risk is high when the company engages in little to no innovation, but also when the company pursues breakthrough innovations that create new markets. Risk is lower and more manageable in between these two endpoints, where the firm manages a balanced portfolio of innovation projects. The combinations of the dimensions that are optimal in terms of company performance will likely vary depending on the environment in which a firm operates.

Within companies, entrepreneurial orientations can be expected to differ significantly among various divisions, units, departments, and areas. No patterns exist such that marketing departments in companies are relatively more entrepreneurial, or procurement departments are always less entrepreneurial. Not only will it differ by company, but also an entrepreneurial manager can guide a staid, conservative unit of any kind towards a more entrepreneurial profile. At the same time, the more a given unit must operate under turbulent or threatening conditions, the more one would expect it to have a higher entrepreneurial profile.

Finally, it is not clear that high levels of EI are sustainable. It may be that there are patterns to a company's entrepreneurial performance over time. One theory is that companies alternate, or "cycle," between fairly dynamic periods of higher entrepreneurial intensity, and periods where innovations are more incremental and intensity is lower (Slevin and Covin, 1990). During these less intense periods, the focus is more on consolidation and administrative control.

CONCLUSIONS

While progress has been made, our understanding of entrepreneurial intensity in organizations is in its infancy. Yet, it is a concept that holds immense potential for researchers and managers alike. Researchers can use measures of EI to better determine the types of work environments that induce more innovative, risk-taking, and proactive behaviors on the part of managers. EI can help in calibrating the appropriate fit between external variables such as competitive intensity or technological turbulence and internal variables including strategy, structure, culture, controls, and human resource management practices. As a case in point, firms experiencing higher levels of environmental turbulence may require higher levels of EI to survive and grow, which in turn generate corporate strategies that are more aggressive (e.g., focusing on new product and market development), as well as structures that are more flexible, decentralized, and open.

For executives, EI can become a key activity ratio that is monitored on an ongoing basis within organizations. Assessment at the level of the organization can be used to benchmark levels of entrepreneurship, establish norms and draw industry comparisons, establish entrepreneurship goals, develop strategies, and assess relationships between EI and company performance variables over time. Assessments can be useful in helping managers and others to examine and refine their own leadership styles. Ultimately, entrepreneurial intensity can serve as an integral component of the dominant logic of a company.

Bibliography

Bateman, T. S. and Grant, J. M. (1993). The proactive component of organizational behavior: A measure and correlates. *Journal of Organizational Behavior*, 14 (March): 103–18.

Covin, J. G. and Slevin, D. P. (1989). Strategic management of small firms in hostile behavior. *Entrepreneurship: Theory and Practice*, 16 (fall): 7–25.

Davis, D., Morris, M., and Allen, J. (1991). Perceived environmental turbulence and its effect on selected entrepreneurship, marketing, and organizational characteristics in industrial firms. *Journal of the Academy of Marketing Science*, 19 (spring): 43–51.

Dickson, P. H. and Weaver, K. M. (1997). Environmental determinants and individual-level moderators of alliance use. *Academy of Management Journal*, 40 (2): 404–26.

Krieser, P. M., Marino, L. D., and Weaver, K. M. (2002). Assessing the psychometric properties of the entrepreneurial orientation scale. *Entrepreneurship: Theory and Practice*, 26 (4): 71–94.

Lumpkin, G. T. and Dess, G. (2001). Linking two dimensions of entrepreneurial orientation to firm performance: The moderating role of environment and industry life cycle. *Journal of Business Venturing*, 16 (4): 429–51.

Miles, M. P. and Arnold, D. R. (1991). The relationship between marketing orientation and entrepreneurial orientation. *Entrepreneurship: Theory and Practice*, 15 (4): 49–65.

Miller, D. (1987). Strategy making and structure: Analysis and implications for performance. *Academy of Management Journal*, 30 (1): 7–32.

Miller, D. and Friesen, P. H. (1983). Innovation in conservative and entrepreneurial firms: Two models of strategic momentum. *Strategic Management Journal*, 3 (1): 1–25.

Morris, M. H., Davis, D., and Allen, J. (1994). Fostering corporate entrepreneurship: Cross-cultural comparisons of the importance of individualism versus collectivism. *Journal of International Business Studies*, 25 (1): 65–89.

Morris, M. H. and Jones, F. (1993). Human resource management practices and corporate entrepreneurship. *International Journal of Human Resources Management*, 4 (4): 873–96.

Morris, M. H. and Kuratko, D. (2002). *Corporate Entrepreneurship*. Fort Worth, TX: Harcourt.

Morris, M. H. and Sexton, D. L. (1996). The concept of entrepreneurial intensity. *Journal of Business Research*, 36 (1): 5–14.

Naman, J. L. and Slevin, D. P. (1993). Entrepreneurship and the concept of fit: A model and empirical test. *Strategic Management Journal*, 14 (2): 137–53.

Slevin, D. P. and Covin, J. G. (1990). Juggling entrepreneurial style and organization structure: How to get your act together. *Sloan Management Review* (winter): 43–53.

Venkatraman, N. (1989). Strategic orientation of business enterprises: The construct, dimensionality, and measurement. *Management Science*, 35 (August): 942–62.

Wiklund, J. (1999). The sustainability of the entrepreneurial orientation–performance relationship. *Entrepreneurship: Theory and Practice*, 24 (1): 37–48.

Zahra, S. A. and Covin, J. G. (1995). Contextual influences on the corporate entrepreneurship–performance relationship: A longitudinal analysis. *Journal of Business Venturing*, 10 (1): 43–58.

entrepreneurial leadership

Jeffrey G. Covin and Dennis P. Slevin

Entrepreneurial leadership can be defined as a social influence process intended to facilitate the discovery, evaluation, and exploitation of entrepreneurial opportunities. This definition recognizes that, consistent with myriad writings on the topic, leadership is inherently a social influence process (e.g., Bass, 1985; Finkelstein and Hambrick, 1996; Kotter, 1990). It also recognizes that entrepreneurship is a process defined by the discovery, evaluation, and exploitation of entrepreneurial opportunities (Shane and Venkataraman, 2000), or "situations in which new goods, services, raw materials, markets, and organizing methods can be introduced through the formation of new means, ends, or means–ends relationships" (Eckhardt and Shane, 2003: 336).

The preceding definition suggests that entrepreneurial leadership is a specific type or dimension of leadership and not simply a context in which leadership is exercised. Regarding this latter point, the term entrepreneurial leadership is often used loosely to refer to leadership within the context of an "entrepreneurial firm," where entrepreneurial firm is variously defined, for example, as an independent company (e.g., Nicholson, 1998), a start-up firm/new venture (e.g., Swiercz and Lydon, 2002), or an innovative, established firm (e.g., Clifford and Cavanagh, 1985). Used in this latter sense, the term entrepreneurial leadership implies nothing inherently unique about the nature of the leadership being exhibited; only that leadership is being exhibited in a particular type of firm. To define entrepreneurial leadership as leadership within an entrepreneurial firm context is an insufficient representation of the concept.

The proposed definition is also broader in scope than the definitions offered by others. Ireland, Hitt, and Sirmon (2003), for example, define entrepreneurial leadership as "the ability to influence others to manage resources strategically in order to emphasize both opportunity-seeking and advantage-seeking behaviors."

This definition contains the two essential elements of entrepreneurial leadership as proposed in the current conceptualization (i.e., social influence and entrepreneurial opportunity), but adds "advantage-seeking behaviors" to the list of defining elements. Thus, these authors adopt a definition of entrepreneurial leadership that is part of the concept as proposed herein, but that layers additional qualifications onto the concept as currently defined.

In the interests of further delineating the conceptual domain of entrepreneurial leadership, this phenomenon will be contrasted with the phenomenon of entrepreneurial management and observations will be offered concerning how entrepreneurial leadership can be exhibited as a pre-organization phenomenon, a phenomenon that occurs throughout the organizational hierarchy, and a phenomenon that is exhibited by multiple levels or units of analysis.

DIFFERENTIATING ENTREPRENEURIAL LEADERSHIP FROM ENTREPRENEURIAL MANAGEMENT

Just as it is appropriate to differentiate between leadership and management (see House and Aditya, 1997; Kotter, 1990), it is appropriate to differentiate between entrepreneurial leadership and entrepreneurial management. As mentioned, the two essential elements of entrepreneurial leadership as proposed in the current conceptualization are social influence and entrepreneurial opportunity. Entrepreneurial opportunity is also core to many definitions of entrepreneurial management. Social influence is not. Rather, the acquisition and management of entrepreneurial resources, broadly defined to include those human, social, financial, physical, technological, and organizational resources that enable the pursuit of entrepreneurial opportunity (see Brush, Greene, and Hart, 2001), are elements more typically acknowledged in definitions of entrepreneurial management. Stevenson (1983: 3) linked opportunities and resources in his early definition of entrepreneurial management: "the pursuit of opportunity without regard to resources currently controlled." Others have more directly suggested that resource *acquisition* and *management* are central to the concept of entrepreneurial management (e.g., Alvarez and Barney, 2002; Amit, Brigham,

and Markman, 2000; Ireland, Hitt, and Sirmon, 2003). Consistent with this view of entrepreneurial management, Thompson (1999: 286) has described entrepreneurial managers as those who "obtain resources and exploit organizational competencies and capabilities to seize or even open windows of opportunity in their selected environments."

Thus, while entrepreneurial leadership can be defined as a social influence process intended to facilitate the discovery, evaluation, and exploitation of entrepreneurial opportunities, entrepreneurial management is more appropriately conceptualized as a style, process, or system of operating through which entrepreneurial resources are identified, acquired, configured, and/or deployed in the interests of facilitating the discovery, evaluation, and exploitation of entrepreneurial opportunities.

ENTREPRENEURIAL LEADERSHIP AS A PRE-ORGANIZATION PHENOMENON

Entrepreneurial leadership can be exhibited in any form of enterprise including, for example, profit-seeking and not-for-profit organizations, small sole proprietorships to large, global corporations, and recently founded ventures to mature business organizations. Such leadership can also be exhibited before a venture's operating organization has been formally created. That is, a formal organization need not exist as a prerequisite to the conduct of entrepreneurial leadership. During the processes of entrepreneurial opportunity discovery, evaluation, and exploitation, entrepreneurial actors will characteristically exert social influence over prospective venture stakeholders in an effort to effect conditions favorable to the formation of the venture organization. The creation and management of a social network, for example, is critical to the establishment of an enterprise system whose viability depends upon information and other resources accessible through that network (Johannisson, 2000). Significantly, networking tasks undertaken to align resources and stakeholder commitment with the entrepreneur's vision and enterprise agenda will often require the exhibition of entrepreneurial leadership. Thus, entrepreneurial leadership is exercised in the pre-organization as well as the post-organization stages of venture development.

ENTREPRENEURIAL LEADERSHIP AS A PHENOMENON EXHIBITED THROUGHOUT THE ORGANIZATIONAL HIERARCHY

Entrepreneurial leadership has been described as "the most important job" in an organization (McGrath and MacMillan, 2000). However, this job is not the sole responsibility of any given individual or set of individuals. Rather, entrepreneurial leadership can be exercised throughout the organizational hierarchy by managers and non-managers at any organizational level. A common result of such leadership is the emergence of an entrepreneurial orientation (Covin and Slevin, 1991) or a high level of entrepreneurial intensity (Morris, 1998) as reflected in the behavior of the organization's membership. While it is, perhaps, most common to conceive of senior executives as potentially or ideally exhibiting entrepreneurial leadership (Nadler and Tushman, 1999), the exhibition of such leadership is increasingly depicted as a collective responsibility of the organization's membership (e.g., Miles et al., 2000). As argued by Cohen (2002: 8): "Entrepreneurial contributors do not have to be appointed and designated as leaders; they can be at any level or in any job and spot an opportunity that they help to bring to fruition, no matter how the organization is arranged."

ENTREPRENEURIAL LEADERSHIP AS A MULTI-LEVEL/UNIT OF ANALYSIS PHENOMENON

Entrepreneurial leadership is frequently evident in the actions of venture founders as well as established-firm CEOs. However, other units of analysis beyond the individual can also exhibit strategic leadership. Groups or teams of individuals, organizational subunits, and entire organizations can exercise entrepreneurial leadership as this phenomenon is herein defined. The adoption of technological standards within industries often occurs, for example, as a result of what can be accurately described, using the current definition, as entrepreneurial leadership by the pioneering firm (Hill, 1997). It may even be meaningful to conceive of entire industries or other collective entities as potentially exhibiting entrepreneurial leadership. In short, the domain of entrepreneurial leadership is not bound within a particular unit of analysis.

In summary, entrepreneurial leadership is not simply leadership within an entrepreneurial firm, nor is it the conceptual equivalent of entrepreneurial management. Rather, entrepreneurial leadership – as a social influence process intended to facilitate the discovery, evaluation, and exploitation of entrepreneurial opportunities – is a distinct phenomenon that is manifested by a wide variety of actors and observable in a wide variety of contexts, both within and beyond the bounds of organizations.

Given the frequency with which anecdotal evidence has suggested a positive effect of entrepreneurial leadership on such desirable outcomes as wealth creation (e.g., Ireland et al., 2002), the enhancement of firm competitiveness (e.g., Hamel, 2000), and social welfare improvement (e.g., Oliver and Paul-Shaheen, 1997), the continued conduct of research into the phenomenon of entrepreneurial leadership is certainly warranted. Of particular importance will be the development and validation of measures of entrepreneurial leadership. Being able to examine entrepreneurial leadership not only as a theoretical concept but also as an empirically measurable research variable will open many avenues of potentially promising inquiry. Three questions suggested for further research consideration are: Can organizations systematically foster and sustain entrepreneurial leadership as a "normal," ubiquitous phenomenon and, if so, how? What are the effects of entrepreneurial leadership as exhibited by various levels of an organization's membership on measures commonly used to assess organizational performance? How is entrepreneurial leadership typically manifested in the words and actions of those parties who use this type of leadership to greatest effect?

Bibliography

Alvarez, S. A. and Barney, J. B. (2002). Resource-based theory and the entrepreneurial firm. In M. A. Hitt, R. D. Ireland, S. M. Camp, and D. L. Sexton (eds.), *Strategic Entrepreneurship: Creating a New Mindset.* Oxford: Blackwell, 89–105.

Amit, R. H., Brigham, K., and Markman, G. D. (2000). Entrepreneurial management as strategy. In G. D. Meyer and K. A. Heppard (eds.), *Entrepreneurship as Strategy.* Thousand Oaks, CA: Sage, 83–99.

Bass, B. M. (1985). *Leadership and Performance Beyond Expectation*. New York: Free Press.

Brush, C. G., Greene, P. G., and Hart, M. M. (2001). From initial idea to unique advantage: The entrepreneurial challenge of constructing a resource base. *Academy of Management Executive*, 15 (1): 64–78.

Clifford, D. K., Jr. and Cavanagh, R. E. (1985). The entrepreneurial corporation. *McKinsey Quarterly*, 3 (autumn): 2–13.

Cohen, A. R. (2002). Mainstreaming corporate entrepreneurship: Leadership at every level of organizations. *Babson Entrepreneurial Review* (October): 5–15.

Covin, J. G. and Slevin, D. P. (1991). A conceptual model of entrepreneurship as firm behavior. *Entrepreneurship: Theory and Practice*, 16 (1): 7–25.

Eckhardt, J. T. and Shane, S. A. (2003). Opportunities and entrepreneurship. *Journal of Management*, 29: 333–49.

Finkelstein, S. and Hambrick, D. (1996). *Strategic Leadership: Top Executives and Their Effects on Organizations*. St. Paul, MN: West.

Hamel, G. (2000). *Leading the Revolution*. Boston, MA: Harvard Business School Press.

Hill, C. W. L. (1997). Establishing a standard: Competitive strategy and technological standards in winner-take-all industries. *Academy of Management Executive*, 11 (2): 7–25.

House, R. J. and Aditya, R. N. (1997). The social scientific study of leadership: Quo vadis? *Journal of Management*, 23 (3): 409–73.

Ireland, R. D., Hitt, M. A., Camp, S. M., and Sexton, D. L. (2001). Integrating entrepreneurship and strategic management action to create firm wealth. *Academy of Management Executive*, 15 (1): 49–63.

Ireland, R. D., Hitt, M. A., and Sirmon, D. G. (2003). A model of strategic entrepreneurship: The construct and its dimensions. *Journal of Management*, in press.

Johannisson, B. (2000). Networking and entrepreneurial growth. In D. L. Sexton and H. Lanstrom (eds.), *The Blackwell Handbook of Entrepreneurship*. Oxford: Blackwell, 368–86.

Kotter, J. P. (1990). *A Force for Change: How Leadership Differs from Management*. New York: Free Press.

McGrath, R. G. and MacMillan, I. (2000). *The Entrepreneurial Mindset*. Boston, MA: Harvard Business School Press.

Miles, G., Heppard, K. A., Miles, R. E., and Snow, C. C. (2000). Entrepreneurial strategies: The critical role of top management. In G. D. Meyer and K. A. Heppard (eds.), *Entrepreneurship as Strategy*. Thousand Oaks, CA: Sage, 101–14.

Morris, M. H. (1998). *Entrepreneurial Intensity*. Westport, CT: Quorum Books.

Nadler, D. A. and Tushman, M. L. (1999). The organization of the future: Strategic imperatives and core competencies for the 21st century. *Organizational Dynamics*, 28 (1): 45–60.

Nicholson, N. (1998). Personality and entrepreneurial leadership: A study of the heads of the UK's most successful independent companies. *European Management Journal*, 16 (5): 529–39.

Oliver, T. R. and Paul-Shaheen, P. (1997). Translating ideas into actions: Entrepreneurial leadership in state healthcare reforms. *Journal of Health Politics, Policy and Law*, 22 (3): 721–88.

Shane, S. and Venkataraman, S. (2000). The promise of entrepreneurship as a field of research. *Academy of Management Review*, 25: 217–26.

Stevenson, H. H. (1983). A perspective on entrepreneurship. Harvard Business School Note 9-384-131.

Swiercz, P. M. and Lydon, S. R. (2002). Entrepreneurial leadership in high-tech firms: A field study. *Leadership and Organization Development Journal*, 23 (7): 380–9.

Thompson, J. L. (1999). A strategic perspective of entrepreneurship. *International Journal of Entrepreneurial Behavior and Research*, 5 (6): 279–96.

entrepreneurial networks

Arnold C. Cooper and Xaoli Yin

Entrepreneurial networks are concerned with how the social relations of entrepreneurs and entrepreneurial teams influence the processes of formation and development for new ventures. Johannisson (1990: 41) described the entrepreneurial network as "the strategically most significant resource of the firm."

Granovetter (1985) suggested that economic actions are embedded in social relations. Social capital is defined by the relational and structural resources attained by individuals/firms through a network of social relationships (Coleman, 1988) (*see* SOCIAL CAPITAL). Entrepreneurs vary in their levels of social capital, with some having strong ties with resource providers and others having little in the way of relationships which can be utilized. Different from human capital, social capital inheres in the structure of relations between and among individuals and organizations. While human capital emphasizes inequality generated by individual attributes and capabilities, social capital emphasizes differences in the structure and nature of relationships among individual actors (Coleman, 1988).

Social capital is often analyzed from two competing perspectives: strong, cohesive relationships vs. weak ties and structural holes. Strong, cohesive personal relationships are found to be important in generating competitive advantage. The strength of a tie is "a combination of the amount of time, the emotional intensity, the intimacy, and the reciprocal services which characterize the tie" (Granovetter, 1973: 1361). Uzzi (1997) studied the impact of embedded ties ("close or special relationships") and arm's-length ties ("market relationships") on the competitive advantage of 23 entrepreneurial firms. The study found that embedded ties, with higher levels of trust, fine-grained information transfer, and joint problem-solving skills, create competitive advantages for the entrepreneurial firms. An entrepreneur who shares a close, personal relationship with an exchange partner will be less likely to act opportunistically and will be more likely to share more detailed information, work through problems, and get direct feedback. Arm's-length ties, while greater in frequency, have less influence upon company success. Ruef, Aldrich, and Carter (2003) studied how network constraints affect the group composition of entrepreneurial founding teams. The study found that prior network ties among group members, particularly strong ties (family members), influence the founding team's choice of members.

Weak ties and structural holes, on the other hand, generate opportunities for entrepreneurs by bridging contacts between different groups and circles. Burt (1992) defined a structural hole as a relationship of non-redundancy between two contacts. An example would be an entrepreneur who has ties with two different people who do not know each other. The structural hole indicates an opportunity to broker the flow of information between disconnected people, such as "who knows about the opportunities, when they know, and who gets to participates in them" (Bart 1992: 30). The structural hole also generates control benefits as the *tertius gaudens* ("the third who benefits") benefits from brokering the connection between others. The structural hole argument is consistent with Granovetter's (1973) weak ties concept – that the spread of novel information, resources, and opportunities must come through weak ties that integrate otherwise disconnected contacts (Burt, 1992: 25–30). Granovetter (1973) found that American blue-collar workers found out about

new jobs more through weak ties than close contacts. An example of a weak tie would be an entrepreneur who has a contact with whom he or she talks only occasionally. The weak ties that an entrepreneur has are more likely to be with people of different circles who have access to information different from that which an entrepreneur normally receives.

In the setting of entrepreneurship, the importance of strong cohesive ties and weak ties and structural holes in venture formation and success depends on the competitive and relational characteristics of the network and industry structure. Rowley, Behrens, and Krackhardt (2000) studied the conditions under which strong/weak ties are positively related to firm performance. They proposed and found that the effect of strong/weak ties is contingent upon the relational structures and industry context. Specifically, strong ties are more advantageous when the firm is situated in a sparse network of alliances. Weak ties are more advantageous when the firm is situated in a dense network. An entrepreneur, for instance, will benefit less from forming and maintaining strong ties when its partners are highly interconnected. Rowley, Behrens, and Krackhardt (2000) found that the degree of uncertainty and required rate of innovation of the environment influenced the effect of strong/weak ties. The number of weak ties a firm has is more advantageous in environments demanding relatively high levels of exploration (such as the semiconductor industry). Walker, Kogut, and Shan (1997) compared cohesive networks and structural holes in the formation of relational networks of biotechnology start-ups. They found that social capital has positive effects in bringing about cooperation between biotechnology start-ups and their partners (mostly established firms). Biotechnology start-ups in cohesive networks are subjected to pressure to perform according to their partners' expectations, which leads to more relationships with new partners in the following time periods. For the biotechnology start-ups, relationships in biotechnology networks tended to last a long time and were based on mutual dependence, which facilitated cohesion and subsequent new cooperation. The complementary resources shared by biotechnology start-ups and their established firm partners prevent one from gaining control over another. The implication is that structural hole theory may apply more to networks of market transactions than to networks of cooperative relationships. In a network where relationships are of shorter duration, such as market transactions, firms are not required to collaborate over time and thus firms may not experience the constraints to behave cooperatively in their relationships. In such situations, careful partner selection to exploit the structural holes between dense regions of relationships, rather than cohesive networks, might determine effective cooperation between firms.

While there is a considerable body of research on the role of networks of relations in mature, established firms, research on the impact of social networks on entrepreneurial activities is relatively immature. Many issues remain unresolved. These include consideration of the processes of network formation for new firms and the examination of the extent to which individuals can utilize their previous network ties and access resources in the context of new organizations. For example, it is important to investigate the processes by which entrepreneurs vary in their ability to develop strong ties or networks with structural holes. Future research should also identify the particular challenges in doing research on entrepreneurial firms. Entrepreneurial firms often change rapidly, with additions and departures to their founding teams. They are often located in rapidly changing industries in which relationships may not be stable. All of this means that the individual ties which benefit the organization are often changing. Networks appear to play a central role in the establishment and development of entrepreneurial firms and there appear to be many opportunities to do research on these important relationships.

Bibliography

Burt, R. (1992). *Structural Holes.* Cambridge, MA: Harvard University Press.

Coleman, J. S. (1988). Social capital in the creation of human capital. *American Journal of Sociology*, 94: S95–S120.

Granovetter, M. S. (1973). The strength of weak ties. *American Journal of Sociology*, 78: 1360–80.

Granovetter, M. S. (1985). Economic action and social structure: The problem of embeddedness. *American Journal of Sociology*, 91 (3): 481–510.

Johannisson, B. (1990). Economies of overview: Guiding the external growth of small firms. *International Small Business Journal*, 9 (1): 32–44.

Rowley, T., Behrens, D., and Krackhardt, D. (2000). Redundant governance structures: An analysis of structural and relational embeddedness in the steel and semiconductor industries. *Strategic Management Journal*, 21: 369–86.

Ruef, M., Aldrich, H. E., and Carter, N. M. (2003). The structure of founding teams: Homophily, strong ties, and isolation among US entrepreneurs. *American Sociological Review*, 68: 195–222.

Walker, G., Kogut, B., and Shan, W. (1997). Social capital, structural holes and the formation of an industry network. *Organization Science*, 8 (2): 109–25.

Uzzi, B. (1997). Social structure and competition in interfirm networks: The paradox of embeddedness. *Administrative Science Quarterly*, 42: 35–67.

entrepreneurial opportunity

Sankaran Venkataraman and Troy Harting

An entrepreneurial opportunity is the chance for an individual (or a team) to offer new value to society, often by introducing new products or services. This chance arises at the nexus of an enterprising individual(s), unfolding macro forces, and changing human needs and preferences – a nexus that permits the crystallization of a business idea in the mind of a person and the motivation to take action on this idea. Entrepreneurial opportunities contain possibilities for both an economic gain and a loss for the entrepreneur pursuing the idea. Knight (1921) pointed out an important quality about entrepreneurial opportunities: there is a fundamental uncertainty about them. He observed that one cannot collect more information or perform more analysis before making key investments to reduce uncertainty. Rather, only the collective actions of competing entrepreneurs, resource suppliers, and customers can reduce uncertainties. There is no meaningful way in which to predict the future economic prospects of an entrepreneurial opportunity and then act on it. Knight pointed out this important distinction between *uncertainty* (outcomes that cannot be imagined and are unknowable) and *risk* (both outcomes and their probabilities can be subjectively assigned). You can insure against or diversify away risk, but you cannot insure against or diversify away uncertainty.

The *Oxford English Dictionary* defines opportunity as "a time, juncture, or condition of things favorable to an end or purpose, or admitting of something being done or effected." Thus, an opportunity involves a purpose, and conditions favorable to the achievement of it. For purpose to exist there must be an "original mind." Norbert Wiener has commented that at the beginning stages of a new idea, the effectiveness of the individual is enormous: "Before any new idea can arise in theory and practice, some person or persons must have introduced it in their own minds" (1993: 7).

In the case of an entrepreneurial opportunity, the "things favorable" for the "original mind" consist of two categories: (a) forces and trends in society conducive to entrepreneurship; and (b) the "original mind's" beliefs about these forces and trends.

The Raw Material of Opportunities: Macro Forces and Trends

We can identify three classes of forces or trends that are the raw materials of opportunities. In the first class are forces *endogenous* to existing organizations in an economy. These include inefficiencies, limits to knowledge, and incongruities. Inefficiencies arise because of (1) structural rigidities within a system such that it is difficult to remove poorly used resources from where they are currently employed and reapply them in ways that are more useful; and (2) when information does not flow easily and reliably within any system. When different people have different information and conjectures about the nature, quality, value, and price of resources, products, customer needs and preferences, supplier capabilities, distribution, and so forth, "inefficiencies" arise and offer a rich pool of opportunities for value creation. Practically every industry has pockets of such inefficiencies.

Similarly, every industry faces knowledge frontiers and this presents new opportunities for value creation. For example, every industry faces technological limits in design, manufactur-

ing, distribution, sales, marketing, logistics, quality, etc. and these are sources of both known and unexpected opportunities.

Finally, we have incongruities. According to Drucker (1985: 57), an incongruity is a "discrepancy, a dissonance, between what *is* and what *could* be." Incongruities exist when the reality of an industry clashes with the assumptions about it (when the things people within the industry "know" and "think" about themselves, are different from the things people outside "know" and "think" about them). Whenever and wherever these incongruities are large, there is an opportunity for some to carve out profitable new enterprises.

The second class of trends is the *exogenous* changes in social, political, demographic, and economic forces that are largely outside the control of individuals. These large-scale macro forces give rise to fundamental changes in how we live, where we live, and what we prefer, thus providing numerous opportunities for entrepreneurs to create and market new products and services. Indeed, these changes also provide opportunities to renew and reinvent existing products and services. When existing firms cannot or will not adapt to these changes, opportunities are created for entrepreneurs in new firms.

The third class of forces or trends is inventions and discoveries that produce *new knowledge*. Technological developments and breakthroughs in science, arts, crafts, and music present conditions for fashioning entrepreneurial opportunities. These developments may occur in scientific labs as much as in craft shops, garages, studios, and basements.

Almost all technological breakthroughs first begin as scientific or artistic discoveries or inventions. When knowledge is embodied in products of everyday use the intellectual property of the artist, scientist, or the lab becomes a tradable item, and can be produced and exchanged for profit. Whenever and wherever artistic and scientific breakthroughs occur, conditions are created for converting the new knowledge into products and processes either to solve existing problems or to create new needs and markets for these needs.

Social, political, and technological changes alter existing needs, change preference structures for existing products and services, and create new needs in society. More important, such changes make people open-minded to change and to new possibilities. This open-mindedness is very useful for entrepreneurs because people are more willing to try new things and to experiment. Further, it allows the entrepreneur to shape new needs and preferences.

As consumers, change provides information to all of us about new possibilities – new ways of solving old problems – and creates new problems and therefore opportunities for new solutions. Thus, change induces new needs or alters existing needs in a wide variety of areas, including health, education, entertainment, financial security, housing, travel, etc. Changing needs present conditions that are favorable to the creation of something new.

ORIGINAL MINDS, FORCES, AND NEEDS: THE NEXUS OF OPPORTUNITY AND THE INDIVIDUAL

In an open society, where market forces are allowed to work, the conditions for creating something new are ubiquitous and abundant. But it is never clear beforehand which new ideas will lead to economic gains and which to losses. It is not the macro forces themselves that are interesting from the point of view of entrepreneurial opportunities. Rather, it is the individualism and idiosyncrasy that each individual brings to the forces that makes entrepreneurial opportunities compelling. Just as, starting with exactly the same set of objects, a Degas, a Dali, and a novice would create completely different still-life paintings, it is conceivable that with the exact same set of macro forces, different entrepreneurs might create entirely different business possibilities for themselves and their stakeholders. Thus, a major source of variation in the nature of opportunities are the differences among people and their life experiences.

For example, three people pass by a vacant storefront on Main Street. The first person, who worked for a number of years as an equipment distributor to restaurants, sees the storefront and envisions an Italian restaurant comfortably filling that space. The second, who just moved from another city where an eclectic furniture store was popular, sees an opportunity for a similar store to open here and repeat the success.

The third, having just read about the tough economic times hitting the town, sees no opportunity at all in the storefront, since it is almost sure to fail whatever it becomes, and continues walking.

Because these three people carry different sets of information and attitudes, their impression of the vacant storefront ranges from a strong opportunity for profit to a money sinkhole. This fictional example highlights several other points. First, individual differences matter. People's values, experiences, and the information they carry shapes what they see in the world. If all three individuals saw the same possibility for the vacant storefront, it wouldn't be vacant for long. Second, for creation to take place, resources need to come together with the right individual in what is a nexus of the entrepreneur and the opportunity. Even if the two potential entrepreneurs considered other uses for the storefront, the former equipment distributor may make a poor retail manager, and the person who saw the furniture store opportunity might not have the skills to run a restaurant. Third, there is no guarantee that an opportunity will be noticed. Perhaps the storefront is an ideal place for a copy center, given its close proximity to the city's university, dormitories, and many local businesses, but no one has thought of it yet.

In the words of Sarasvathy (2001), "entrepreneurship is a function of individuality: who you are, what you know, and who you know." We cannot imagine how certain firms could have come to be aside from the particularity of certain individuals: Disney without Walt Disney, Ford without Henry Ford, General Electric without Thomas Edison, Wal-Mart without Sam Walton, and Microsoft without Bill Gates.

Thus, entrepreneurial opportunities are very much a function of the specific individuals who pursue them. In other words, the potential economic gain or loss from pursuing an idea is only partly a function of the macro forces. In large part it is a function of the specific social, human, moral, and intellectual capital of the pursuer and even more importantly the *manner in which the pursuer combines and leverages* this capital. The same idea when pursued and executed by two different individuals or teams will unfold differently and have very different outcomes because of the differences in the endowments and the manner in which they use this endowment.

Endowments and the manner of combining endowments can vary due to a variety of circumstances. Sometimes it can be because of blind luck. This happens by virtue of a particular person being in a particular place at a particular time and interacting with particular individuals. She does not consciously search or plan for this experience; rather, she acts on it serendipitously. For example, Bill Gates receives a visit from IBM executives who are looking for an operating system for their proposed personal computer business and think that Microsoft has such an operating system. Not finding such a product at Microsoft, the IBM executives visit another company in Silicon Valley who they understand has such a product. When the Silicon Valley firm is not able to meet IBM's requirement, the executives come back to Microsoft requesting them to develop such an operating system. Using his social network, Paul Allen, a co-founder of Microsoft, identifies another company in Seattle that has a rudimentary operating system (DOS), and negotiates to buy it outright for $50,000. By modifying this operating system platform, Microsoft creates a new operating system for the IBM PC. Thus, by pure chance, Microsoft has become involved in an entrepreneurial venture of IBM. Although there is little people can do to specifically receive contingent experience, the size and characteristics of their networks, their habits, attitudes, and behavioral patterns can influence the type of contingent experience they are likely to encounter.

Sometimes the development of the nexus is influenced by the idiosyncratic experiences and social networks that a particular person encounters simply by virtue of being that person. For example, a new immigrant from India who lives in the US will encounter experiences that are different from that of a person who was born and brought up in the US. The Indian immigrant will have a social and professional network of Indian friends and acquaintances and will access ethnic sources of information (such as the Indian media), in addition to having an incipient social and professional network of non-Indians. Even within the group of Indian immigrants, there are individual-level heterogeneities such as previous education, professional experience, family back-

ground, and certain stable psychological characteristics.

Finally, specialized knowledge that comes from particular educational training and professional experience also influences the development of the nexus. Renaissance man aside, depth of knowledge tends to occur at the expense of breadth of knowledge. This phenomenon is attributable, of course, to our cognitive limitations as human beings. Specialized knowledge makes it possible for individuals to "know more and more about less and less."

Such knowledge is explicit and tacit. Specialization leads to each of us operating in knowledge corridors, which means that we tend to see opportunities in our areas of specialization. For example, Shane (2000) found that eight entrepreneurial teams pursued eight different and totally unrelated opportunities from a single innovation that they all had access to, a three-dimensional printing process, that came out of the MIT labs. The original inventors never imagined the many possibilities that eventually transpired.

Thus, the individuality of a person dictates how the person perceives macro forces and trends, acts on them, and endows specificity to entrepreneurial opportunities. In summary, an entrepreneurial opportunity as discussed above transcends purely subjective and purely objective notions. An opportunity presupposes actors *for whom* it is *perceived* as an opportunity; at the same time, the opportunity has no meaning unless the actor/s actually act upon the real world of interacting forces within which the opportunity eventually has to be given shape.

Bibliography

Drucker, P. (1985). *Innovation and Entrepreneurship*. New York: Harper and Row.
Knight, F. H. (1921). *Risk, Uncertainty and Profit*. Chicago: University of Chicago Press.
Sarasvathy, S. (2001). What makes entrepreneurs entrepreneurial? University of Washington working paper series.
Shane, S. (2000). Prior knowledge and the discovery of entrepreneurial opportunities. *Organization Science*, 11 (4): 448–69.
Wiener, N. (1993). *Invention: The Care and Feeding of Ideas*. Cambridge, MA: MIT Press.

entrepreneurial orientation

G. T. Lumpkin and Gregory G. Dess

Entrepreneurial orientation (EO) is a term that addresses the mindset of firms engaged in the pursuit of new ventures and provides a useful framework for researching entrepreneurial activity. Many scholars have used the term to describe a fairly consistent set of related activities or processes (e.g., Ginsberg, 1985; Knight, 1997). Such processes incorporate a wide variety of activities that include planning, analysis, decision-making, and many aspects of the organization's culture, value system, and mission (Hart, 1992). Thus, an entrepreneurial orientation may be viewed as a firm-level strategy-making process that firms use to enact their organizational purpose, sustain their vision, and create competitive advantage(s). Research using the EO construct has focused primarily on firm-level phenomena. There is no inherent reason why the EO construct should not be used to assess individual-level entrepreneurial processes, especially among small firms where firm behavior tends to be a reflection of a single founder. However, the research instruments most commonly used to measure EO are firm-level scales and most prior research has focused at the organizational level of analysis (cf. Covin and Slevin, 1989).

Scholars have frequently investigated strategy making in terms of patterns of action or gestalts that are generalizable across many organizations (Rajagopalan, Rasheed, and Datta, 1993). EO represents a configuration of policies, practices, and processes that provide insights as to the basis of entrepreneurial decisions and actions. For example, Mintzberg (1973) suggested entrepreneurial, adaptive, and planning modes of strategy making, and later suggested a bargaining mode (Mintzberg, 1983). Miller and Friesen (1978) identified 11 strategy-making process dimensions that include, for example, integration, adaptiveness, expertise, innovation, and risk taking. Fredrickson (1986) suggested the dimensions of comprehensiveness, risk taking, proactiveness, rationality, and assertiveness.

The salient dimensions of EO have been derived from a review and integration of the strategy-making process and entrepreneurship literature (e.g., Covin and Slevin, 1991; Kanter,

1983; Miller, 1983; Miller and Friesen, 1978; Venkataraman, 1989). An early definition of entrepreneurial orientation was provided by Miller, who stated an entrepreneurial firm is one that "engages in product market innovation, undertakes somewhat risky ventures and is *first* to come up with 'proactive' innovations, beating competitors to the punch" (1983: 770). Based on Miller's conceptualization, three dimensions of EO have been identified and used consistently in the literature: innovativeness, risk taking, and proactiveness. Innovativeness is the predisposition to engage in creativity and experimentation through the introduction of new products/services, as well as technological leadership via R&D in new processes. Risk taking involves taking bold actions by venturing into the unknown, borrowing heavily, and/or committing significant resources to ventures in uncertain environments. Proactiveness is an opportunity-seeking, forward-looking perspective characterized by the introduction of new products and services ahead of the competition and acting in anticipation of future demand.

Lumpkin and Dess (1996) suggested that two additional dimensions were salient to entrepreneurial orientation. Drawing on Miller's (1983) definition and prior research (e.g., Burgelman, 1983; Hart, 1992; MacMillan and Day, 1987; Venkataraman, 1989), they identified competitive aggressiveness and autonomy as essential components of the entrepreneurial orientation construct. Entrepreneurial firms and start-ups are keenly concerned with opportunities and threats in the external environment because these factors may support or limit their success. The proactiveness component of EO captures the entrepreneurial response to opportunity, but research instruments based on Miller's (1983) definition omit measures of how entrepreneurial firms respond to threats. Competitive aggressiveness was added to reflect this aspect of EO. Competitive aggressiveness is the intensity of a firm's efforts to outperform rivals and is characterized by a strong offensive posture or aggressive responses to the actions of competitors. Research by Burgelman (1983) and Hart (1992) suggests entrepreneurial behavior is often generative and creative, involving the autonomous actions of organizational actors. For this reason, autonomy is thought to be an essential element of the EO construct. Autonomy is the independent action undertaken by entrepreneurial leaders or teams directed at bringing about a new venture and seeing it to fruition.

Building on prior research, Lumpkin and Dess (1996) suggested a framework to investigate the relationship between the dimensions of EO and firm performance, as well as the effect of organizational and environmental factors on the EO–performance relationship. Numerous studies have been conducted to investigate these factors, including the role of environment (e.g., Kreiser, Marino, and Weaver, 2002a; Zahra and Covin, 1995), organizational structure (e.g., Covin and Slevin, 1988; Miller, 1983), planning and control (e.g., Barringer and Bluedorn, 1999), individual differences (e.g., Becherer and Maurer, 1999), alliance usage (e.g., Dickson and Weaver, 1997), knowledge-based resources (e.g., Wiklund and Shepherd, 2003), and entrepreneurial management in international settings (e.g., Knight, 1997; Zahra and Garvis, 2000).

Many EO studies have focused on the entrepreneurial orientation–performance relationship (e.g., Covin and Slevin, 1989) and on the sustainability of the relationship between EO and performance (e.g., Wiklund, 1999). These studies have indicated that, in general, an entrepreneurial orientation is associated with strong performance. However, the relationship between EO and performance is often contingent on other environmental and/or organizational factors. For example, Covin and Slevin (1989) found that performance was related to the fit between EO, structure, and environmental variables: firms with high levels of EO were most effective if they had organic structures and functioned in hostile environments; firms in benign environments with mechanistic structures performed better if they had low EO. Entrepreneurial orientation may itself function as a moderator of performance relationships. For example, Wiklund and Shepherd (2003) found that the relationship between knowledge-based resources and performance was stronger among firms with higher levels of EO. Two studies that investigated the longitudinal nature of the EO–performance relationship reached similar conclusions: EO has a positive effect on firm financial performance and the strength of that

relationship increases over time (Wiklund, 1999; Zahra and Covin, 1995).

There has been some debate in the literature as to whether or not the dimensions of EO are independent or covary under certain conditions. Some have argued the entrepreneurial orientation construct is best viewed as a unidimensional concept (e.g., Covin and Slevin, 1989); others have argued the dimensions of EO may occur in different combinations (e.g., Lumpkin and Dess, 2001). In a rigorous structural equation analysis, Stetz et al. (2000) studied 865 healthcare executives and found that the dimensions of EO tended to vary independently rather than covary, and that as a predictor of firm growth the EO construct was more robust than unidimensional entrepreneurial constructs. A second study conducted by Kreiser, Marino, and Weaver (2002b) investigated the psychometric properties of EO data from six countries and reached a similar conclusion: the sub-dimensions of EO tend to vary independently of each other in many situations. Such findings suggest that unique combinations of EO provide more precise explanations of firm phenomena as well as greater insights into the EO–performance relationship.

The entrepreneurial orientation construct includes numerous promising and worthwhile research questions that warrant future research. First, scholars could explore what factors may enhance (or inhibit) the strength of the relationship between EO and firm performance. For example, under what conditions would otherwise strong cultures cause core rigidities (Hamel and Prahalad, 1996) and, subsequently, erode innovation and discourage risk taking? How might a leader's emotional intelligence (Goleman, 1998) improve an organization's willingness to take risks and engage in more proactive behaviors? And how do reward systems (e.g., behavioral based or outcome based) facilitate (or retard) such behaviors?

Second, researchers could also incorporate different perspectives on risk taking, given the increasing role of knowledge in the global economy. For example, firms that judiciously experiment with new products and processes may be able to subsequently turn initial failures into new resource combinations (McGrath, 1999), enabling them to create new "learning platforms"

(Grenadier and Weiss, 1997) for future value-creating endeavors. Capturing such dynamics and their outcomes involves a closer look at dependent variables that go beyond traditional short-term economic indicators.

Third, research endeavors should be directed at assessing and refining the EO construct itself. For example, Lyon, Lumpkin, and Dess (2000) have addressed the relative advantages and disadvantages associated with three alternate approaches: managerial perceptions, firm behaviors, and resource allocations. Ideally, when taken in combination, these approaches should enhance the reliability and validity of EO research.

Fourth, much can be learned by studying "best practices" of leading-edge organizations. Studies that focused on the relationship between EO and best practices could help researchers to inductively derive theory that can later be tested to confirm or disconfirm extant knowledge. Thus, the viability of descriptive and normative EO theory would be advanced.

Bibliography

Barringer, B. R. and Bluedorn, A. C. (1999). The relationship between corporate entrepreneurship and strategic management. *Strategic Management Journal*, 20: 421–44.

Becherer, R. C. and Maurer, J. G. (1999). The proactive personality disposition and entrepreneurial behavior among small company presidents. *Journal of Small Business Management*, 37: 28–36.

Burgelman, R. A. (1983). A process model of internal corporate venturing in the diversified major firm. *Administrative Science Quarterly*, 28: 223–44.

Covin, J. G. and Slevin, D. P. (1988). The influence of organization structure on the utility of an entrepreneurial top management style. *Journal of Management Studies*, 25: 217–34.

Covin, J. G. and Slevin, D. P. (1989). Strategic management of small firms in hostile and benign environments. *Strategic Management Journal*, 10: 75–87.

Covin, J. G. and Slevin, D. P. (1991). A conceptual model of entrepreneurship as firm behavior. *Entrepreneurship: Theory and Practice*, 16: 7–24.

Dickson, P. H. and Weaver, K. M. (1997). Environmental determinants and individual-level moderators of alliance use. *Academy of Management Journal*, 40: 404–25.

Fredrickson, J. W. (1986). The strategic decision process and organization structure. *Academy of Management Journal*, 11: 280–97.

Ginsberg, A. (1985). Measuring changes in entrepreneurial orientation following industry deregulation: The development of a diagnostic instrument. *Proceedings of the International Council of Small Business*, 50–7.

Goleman, D. (1998). What makes a leader? *Harvard Business Review*, 76: 92–105.

Grenadier, S. R. and Weiss, A. M. (1997). Investment in technological innovations: An option pricing approach. *Journal of Financial Economics*, 44: 397–416.

Hamel, G. and Prahalad, C. K. (1996). Competing in the new economy: Managing out of bounds. *Strategic Management Journal*, 17: 232–42.

Hart, S. (1992). An integrative framework for strategy-making processes. *Academy of Management Review*, 17: 327–51.

Kanter, R. M. (1983). *The Change Masters: Innovation and Entrepreneurship in the American Corporation*. New York: Simon and Schuster.

Knight, G. A. (1997). Cross-cultural reliability and validity of a scale to measure firm entrepreneurial orientation. *Journal of Business Venturing*, 12: 213–25.

Kreiser, P. M., Marino, L. D., and Weaver, K. M. (2002a). Reassessing the environment–EO link: The impact of environmental hostility on the dimensions of entrepreneurial orientation. *Best Paper Proceedings*, 2002 Academy of Management annual meeting, Denver, CO.

Kreiser, P. M., Marino, L. D., and Weaver, K. M. (2002b). Assessing the psychometric properties of the entrepreneurial orientation scale: A multi-country analysis. *Entrepreneurship: Theory and Practice*, 26: 71–95.

Lumpkin, G. T. and Dess, G. G. (1996). Clarifying the entrepreneurial orientation construct and linking it to performance. *Academy of Management Review*, 21: 135–72.

Lumpkin, G. T. and Dess, G. G. (2001). Linking two dimensions of entrepreneurial orientation to firm performance: The moderating role of environment and industry life cycle. *Journal of Business Venturing*, 16: 429–51.

Lyon, D. W., Lumpkin, G. T., and Dess, G. G. (2000). Enhancing entrepreneurial orientation research: Operationalizing and measuring a key strategic decision-making process. *Journal of Management*, 26: 1055–85.

MacMillan, I. C. and Day, D. L. (1987). Corporate ventures into industrial markets: Dynamics of aggressive entry. *Journal of Business Venturing*, 2: 29–39.

McGrath, R. G. (1999). Falling forward: Real options reasoning and entrepreneurial failure. *Academy of Management Review*, 24: 13–30.

Miller, D. (1983). The correlates of entrepreneurship in three types of firms. *Management Science*, 29: 770–91.

Miller, D. and Friesen, P. (1978). Archetypes of strategy formulation. *Management Science*, 24: 921–33.

Mintzberg, H. (1973). Strategy making in three modes. *California Management Review*, 16: 44–53.

Mintzberg, H. (1983). *Power In and Around Organizations*. Englewood Cliffs, NJ: Prentice-Hall.

Rajagopalan, N., Rasheed, A., and Datta, D. (1993). Strategic decision processes: Critical review and future directions. *Journal of Management*, 19: 349–84.

Stetz, P. E., Howell, R., Stewart, A., Blair, J. D., and Fottler, M. D. (2000). Multidimensionality of entrepreneurial firm-level processes: Do the dimensions covary? In *Frontiers of Entrepreneurship Research 2000*. Wellesley, MA: Babson College.

Venkataraman, N. (1989). Strategic orientation of business enterprises: The construct, dimensionality, and measurement. *Management Science*, 15 (8): 942–62.

Wiklund, J. (1999). The sustainability of the entrepreneurial orientation–performance relationship. *Entrepreneurship: Theory and Practice*, 24 (1): 37–48.

Wiklund, J. and Shepherd, D. (2003). Knowledge-based resources, entrepreneurial orientation, and the performance of small and medium-sized businesses. *Strategic Management Journal*, 24: 1307–14.

Zahra, S. A. and Covin, J. G. (1995). Contextual influences on the corporate entrepreneurship–performance relationship: A longitudinal analysis. *Journal of Business Venturing*, 10: 43–58.

Zahra, S. A. and Garvis, D. M. (2000). International corporate entrepreneurship and firm performance: The moderating effect of international environmental hostility. *Journal of Business Venturing*, 15: 469–92.

entrepreneurial reputations

Violina Rindova and Antoaneta Petkova

THE IMPORTANCE OF ENTREPRENEURIAL REPUTATIONS

Reputations have been identified as valuable intangible assets (Barney, 1991; Dierickx and Cool, 1989), because they influence the willingness of stakeholders to exchange resources with a given firm. Reputations influence stakeholders' willingness to exchange resources with a firm because they reflect collective perceptions about the ability of the firm to create value for various stakeholders (Rindova and Fombrun, 1999). Because most entrepreneurial settings are characterized by resource scarcity, entrepreneurial reputation is a particularly important asset that facilitates the growth and survival of a new venture (Aldrich, 2000). Even new ventures that are well funded by a sponsoring parent firm or strong financiers face the need to develop strong reputations because higher levels of re-source commitments by initial stakeholders are accompanied by higher expectations for economic returns. Therefore, building an entrepreneurial reputation early in the life of a new venture can significantly improve its chances for success.

The development of entrepreneurial reputations is associated with a number of unique challenges, not encountered by established firms in an industry (Aldrich, 2000). Reputations are an outcome of social interactions that take place in an organizational field, including competing firms, their customers and suppliers, and institutional intermediaries engaged in dissemination of information about firms (DiMaggio and Powell, 1983; Fombrun, 1996; Pollock and Rindova, 2003). In this environment, firms seek to attract the favor of stakeholders and gain access to the resources that these stakeholders control. Examples of strategic characteristics about which reputations convey information are the ability of a firm to produce high-quality products (Shapiro, 1983), its willingness to defend its competitive position against new entrants (Clark and Montgomery, 1998), and its interest in addressing the concerns of multiple stakeholders (Fombrun and Rindova, 2000).

Stakeholders in turn seek to identify firms that best meet their needs and expectations in order to achieve their own exchange goals. To do so, stakeholders observe and evaluate the actions of firms and the performance of their products (Weigelt and Camerer, 1988) and form perceptions of the firms' ability to create value. These perceptions define a firm's reputation (Rindova and Fombrun, 1999).

New ventures, however, tend to lack even public awareness of their existence and offerings (Aldrich and Fiol, 1994; Rao, 1994). They also have rather limited history and performance records to guide stakeholders' evaluations. Finally, in order to select a new venture as an exchange partner, stakeholders must be willing to trade products, services, and jobs that offer them relatively well-defined and understood means for achieving their exchange goals, with products, services, and jobs that may have poorly defined characteristics and unknown performance, but may offer a promise of better means to achieve the stakeholders' goals. Thus, entrepreneurial reputations are more likely to emphasize the value-creating *potential* of the novel products and opportunities associated with a new venture, rather than its performance history. Whereas reputations in general are based on extrapolations of the past, entrepreneurial reputations are based on assembling information cues that make it possible to envision the future.

Below, we outline three cognitive hurdles that new ventures must overcome in order to build their reputations: attracting attention, gaining legitimacy, and earning positive evaluations. Overcoming each of these hurdles leads to developing the three constituent elements of entrepreneurial reputations: prominence, legitimacy, and competitive prestige. We then discuss briefly the key resources through which new ventures provide stakeholders with information about their potential to create value: entrepreneurial human capital, social capital, and symbolic capital.

The Elements of Entrepreneurial Reputations

In order to attract potential stakeholders and enter exchange relationships with them, a new venture must overcome three major cognitive barriers. First, it must ensure that the potential stakeholders are aware of its existence, its activities, and the products and services it offers. Second, it must provide evidence that it is a legitimate organization – that is, that the new ways in which it seeks to satisfy stakeholder needs fit with existing norms and values in the organizational field. Third, the new venture must convince prospective stakeholders and other relevant publics that it can serve their interests and create value for them in ways superior to the already available alternatives offered by existing firms. Coping successfully with these three hurdles enables a new venture to build three distinct but interrelated elements of entrepreneurial reputations: prominence, legitimacy, and competitive prestige.

Prominence refers to the extent to which stakeholders are aware of the existence of the new venture; or in cognitive terms, the degree to which a new venture is available in their memory, so that they can readily recall information about it. Prominence is an important aspect of entrepreneurial reputations, not only

because it is practically impossible for stakeholders to exchange resources with a new enterprise if they do not even know of its existence, but also because the likelihood of them doing so increases with the prominence of the venture in their minds. Prominence is an initial step in building entrepreneurial reputations because only after the relevant publics are aware of the new venture's presence in the organizational field can they begin to form more specific impressions and evaluations of it (Rao, 1994).

After stakeholders have developed awareness of the new venture, they need to evaluate it, and they do so in two stages: they first must judge whether the new venture fits with the norms, values, and logics that exist in the organizational field (Aldrich and Fiol, 1994). These evaluations result in judgments of legitimacy, which are the second constituent element of entrepreneurial reputations (Lounsbury and Glynn, 2001). Finally, stakeholders evaluate the products and services of a new venture relative to existing standards of performance in the industry (Rindova and Fombrun, 1999) or to those of competing firms (Rao, 1994). These evaluations result in judgments of competitive superiority, which constitute the unique content of reputations as such – beliefs about the relative ability of firms to create value. Entrepreneurial reputations have the greatest value as intangible assets to new ventures when they combine all three elements. In the absence of prominence and legitimacy, the venture may appeal to a very limited set of stakeholders, whose support may be insufficient to ensure its survival and success.

The Drivers of Entrepreneurial Reputations

At first glance, all attempts to estimate a new venture's potential appear to be by necessity speculative in nature. Unlike established firms, for which stakeholders can rely on a proven track record, new ventures in general have very few tangible things to offer to stakeholders as evidence of their ability and potential. The founder of Hotmail, Sabeer Batia, expresses this problem when he states: "All we had was an idea" (Bronson, 1999: 85). However, in the new venture world, an idea and other intangible assets may have a high value if they make it possible for stakeholders to envision a previously invisible future. The idea, the relationships of the new venture, and the knowledge of its founders are such intangible assets, discussed next.

Symbolic capital. The idea, or the business concept about how an entrepreneur or a team of entrepreneurs ("founders" from here on) will exploit an entrepreneurial opportunity they have identified, is a key component of the symbolic capital of a new venture. The opportunity and the business concept to exploit it are at the heart of the entrepreneurial process. Entrepreneurial opportunities – defined as opportunities to create new goods, services, raw materials, and organizing methods and to sell them at greater than their production cost (Casson, 1982; Shane and Venkataraman, 2000) – vary in their quality. That is, different opportunities have different expected value (Shane and Venkataraman, 2000; Venkataraman, 1997). Some opportunities are perceived as more important or more exciting than others. For example, developing a cure for cancer is perceived as more important, and consequently more valuable an opportunity, than selling snacks to students (Shane and Venkataraman, 2000). Therefore, the quality of entrepreneurial opportunity contributes to the symbolic capital of the new venture.

Symbolic capital refers to the various meanings that stakeholders attach to the new venture. Whereas researchers have identified many types of capital to which a new venture has access, such as human, technological, financial, intellectual, social, and institutional capital (Lounsbury and Glynn, 2001), the symbolic capital associated with the business concept and the opportunity pursued by a new venture has not received much attention. Yet a compelling business concept and high-quality opportunity around which a new venture is formed can give it significant advantages in attracting public attention and achieving prominence.

Social capital. A second type of capital that is particularly relevant to the rapid accumulation of entrepreneurial reputations is the social capital of the new venture. Social capital is "the sum of the actual and potential resources . . . derived from the network of relationships" (Nahapiet and Ghoshal, 1998: 243) (*see* SOCIAL CAPITAL). Entrepreneurs rely extensively on their personal networks, including family, friends, and profes-

sional contacts, for material, financial, moral, and emotional support (Aldrich, 2000). These social relationships play a twofold role in the process of building entrepreneurial reputations. First, the people who know the founders personally are able to provide first-hand information and opinions regarding their personal and professional qualities and the viability of their venture. Second, outside observers can infer certain characteristics of the new venture by the quality of its social ties, because people tend to associate with others who have similar values and interests (Aldrich, 2000; Burt, 1982; Fischer, 1982; Marsden, 1987). Thus, affiliations of a new venture with prestigious financial backers, seasoned industry veterans, and large and established customers validate the potential of the venture signaled through its business concept and focal opportunity. They also provide legitimacy derived from the relative status of these affiliates, as high-status actors exert a disproportionate amount of influence on the choices of others (Rao, Davis, and Ward, 2000). New ventures with social ties to high-status partners have been found to perform better because their social ties provide them with a credible "stamp of approval" (Stuart, Huang, and Hybels, 1999).

Founders' human capital. Entrepreneurs possess different prior knowledge and experience that can be more or less useful for the new venture (Shane, 2000; Venkataraman, 1997). These varying levels of skills, training, and experience constitute entrepreneurial human capital (Becker, 1975; Davidsson and Honig, 2003; Gimeno et al., 1997; Mosakowski, 1998) (*see* ENTREPRENEURIAL HUMAN CAPITAL). Major sources of entrepreneurial human capital are formal education, informal training, work experience, general management experience, and especially previous start-up experience (Davidsson and Honig, 2003). Researchers distinguish between general human capital, which results from formal education and prior work experience and incorporates skills useful across a range of activities, and specific human capital, which is highly specific to the functioning of the venture, such as knowledge of industry customers and suppliers (Gimeno et al., 1997). The human capital of the founders provides important cues about the new venture's future prospects, because publics tend to believe strongly in the importance of leadership for the success or failure of any organizational form (Meindl, Ehrlich and Dukerich, 1985; Meindl and Ehrlich, 1987). The role of the entrepreneur's human capital for the public evaluations of the new venture is more pronounced than that of managers in established firms, because the effects of founders on organizational characteristics and performance are well documented (Boeker, 1989). Together, the symbolic, social capital, and human capital of the venture enable it to make credible promises that it will create value for its stakeholders, and thereby build its reputation more effectively.

Bibliography

Aldrich, H. (2000). *Organizations Evolving*. London: Sage.

Aldrich, H. and Fiol, M. (1994). Fools rush in? The institutional context of industry creation. *Academy of Management Review*, 19: 645–70.

Barney, J. B. (1991). Firm resources and sustained competitive advantage. *Journal of Management*, 17: 99–120.

Becker, G. S. (1975). *Human Capital*. New York: Columbia University Press.

Boeker, W. (1989). Strategic change: The effects of founding and history. *Academy of Management Journal*, 32: 489–515.

Bronson, P. (1999). *The Nudist on the Late Shift and Other True Tales of Silicon Valley*. New York: Random House.

Burt, R. S. (1982). *Toward a Structural Theory of Action*. New York: Academic Press.

Casson, M. (1982). *The Entrepreneur*. Totowa, NJ: Barnes and Noble.

Clark, B. H. and Montgomery, D. B. (1998). Deterrence, reputations, and competitive cognition. *Management Science*, 44: 62–82.

Davidsson, P. and Honig, B. (2003). The role of social and human capital among nascent entrepreneurs. *Journal of Business Venturing*, 18: 301–31.

Dierickx, I. and Cool, K. (1989). Asset stock accumulation and sustainability of competitive advantage. *Management Science*, 35: 1504–11.

DiMaggio, P. and Powell, W. (1983). The iron cage revisited: Institutional isomorphism and collective rationality in organizational fields. *American Sociological Review*, 48: 147–60.

Fischer, C. S. (1982). *To Dwell Among Friends*. Chicago: University of Chicago Press.

Fombrun, C. J. (1996). *Reputation: Realizing Value from the Corporate Image*. Boston, MA: Harvard Business School Press.

Fombrun, C. J. and Rindova, V. P. (2000). The road to transparency: Reputation management at Royal Dutch/Shell. In M. Schultz, M. J. Hatch, and M. H. Larsen (eds.), *The Expressive Organization*. New York: Oxford University Press.

Gimeno, J., Folta, T. B., Cooper, A. C., and Woo, C. Y. (1997). Survival of the fittest? Entrepreneurial human capital and the persistence of underperforming firms. *Administrative Science Quarterly*, 42: 750–83.

Lounsbury, M. and Glynn, M. A. (2001). Cultural entrepreneurship: Stories, legitimacy, and the acquisition of resources. *Strategic Management Journal*, 22: 545–64.

Marsden, P. V. (1987). Core discussion networks of Americans. *American Sociological Review*, 52: 122–31.

Meindl, J. R. and Ehrlich, S. B. (1987). The romance of leadership and the evaluation of organizational performance. *Academy of Management Journal*, 30: 91–109.

Meindl, J. R., Ehrlich, S. B., and Dukerich, J. M. (1985). The romance of leadership. *Administrative Science Quarterly*, 30: 78–102.

Mosakowski, E. (1998). Entrepreneurial resources, organizational choices, and competitive outcomes. *Organization Science*, 9: 625–43.

Nahapiet, J. and Ghoshal, S. (1998). Social capital, intellectual capital, and the organizational advantage. *Academy of Management Review*, 23: 242–66.

Pollock, T. and Rindova, V. (2003). Media legitimation effects in the market for initial public offerings. *Academy of Management Journal*, 46: 631–42.

Rao, H. (1994). The social construction of reputation: Certification contests, legitimation, and the survival of organizations in the American automobile industry: 1895–1912. *Strategic Management Journal*, 15: 29–44.

Rao, H., Davis, G. F., and Ward, A. (2000). Embeddedness, social identity and mobility: Why firms leave the Nasdaq and join the New York Stock Exchange. *Administrative Science Quarterly*, 45: 268–92.

Rindova, V. and Fombrun, C. (1999). Constructing competitive advantage: The role of firm–constituent interactions. *Strategic Management Journal*, 20: 691–710.

Shane, S. (2000). Prior knowledge and the discovery of entrepreneurial opportunities. *Organization Science*, 11: 448–69.

Shane, S. and Venkataraman, S. (2000). The promise of entrepreneurship as a field of research. *Academy of Management Review*, 25: 217–26.

Shapiro, C. (1983). Premiums for high quality products as returns to reputations. *Quarterly Journal of Economics*, 98: 659–80.

Stuart, T., Huang, H., and Hybels, R. (1999). Interorganizational endorsement and the performance of entrepreneurial ventures. *Administrative Science Quarterly*, 44: 315–49.

Venkataraman, S. (1997). The distinctive domain of entrepreneurship research. In J. Katz and R. Brockhaus (eds.), *Advances in Entrepreneurship, Firm Emergence, and Growth*. Greenwich, CT: JAI Press, 119–38.

Weigelt, K. and Camerer, C. (1988). Reputation and corporate strategy: A review of recent theory and applications. *Strategic Management Journal*, 9: 443–54.

entrepreneurial resources

Sharon A. Alvarez and Jay B. Barney

Resources are financial, physical, human, and organizational assets used by a firm to develop, manufacture, and deliver products or services to its customers (Barney, 1995).

Entrepreneurial resources are the tangible and intangible assets firms use to exploit competitive imperfections in markets. Examples of entrepreneurial resources include physical assets (e.g., a new technology), financial resources (e.g., capital from prior business endeavors), individual resources (e.g., a person's knowledge about a market imperfection or his/her cognitive capabilities), and organizational resources (e.g., teamwork and cooperation among several people working together to exploit a market imperfection).

Competitive imperfections in markets exist when information about technology, demand, or other determinants of competition in an industry are not widely understood by people or firms operating in that industry. Efforts to exploit these imperfections usually require the allocation of entrepreneurial resources. However, exploiting a market imperfection will only be a source of competitive advantage if the resources used to exploit that imperfection are valuable and rare and efficiently organized. Market imperfections can only be a source of sustained competitive advantage if the resources used to exploit them are valuable, rare, and costly to imitate and efficiently organized.

While all types of entrepreneurial resources can meet the criteria of valuable, rare, costly to imitate, and efficiently organized, those resources that are path dependent (as demonstrated by a resource's historical evolution), socially complex (e.g., organizational phenomena such as reputation, trust, and teamwork), or causally ambiguous (i.e., the uncertainty regarding the causes of efficiency differences) are most likely to be the source of sustained competitive advantage.

Certainly, there are organizational differences between resources that firms exploit to gain competitive advantage and resources that are used to exploit competitive imperfections. Questions examining the differences in how firms organize these resources to earn economic rents should prove to be fruitful ground for future research. Determining if firm performance differences are explained by resource differences, industry differences, differences in time, or by luck is another question worthy of scholarly inquiry. Finally, what is the relationship among resources and how do these relationships matter? Studying these and related issues should yield important insights about entrepreneurial resources and the role they play in ventures' success.

Bibliography

Barney, J. B. (1995). Looking inside for competitive advantage. *Academy of Management Executive*, 9 (4): 49–61.

entrepreneurial risk

Timothy B. Folta

Entrepreneurship has long been linked with the concept of risk. Scholars have viewed risk as fundamental to the entrepreneurial function, and the entrepreneur's ability to tolerate risk as central to the formation of new ventures. However, these views are not held by all, and there remains considerable debate about the relationship between risk and entrepreneurship. On a fundamental level, a precise definition of entrepreneurial risk has been elusive. This confusion may hamper discussions around the role of risk in entrepreneurship. In this essay, we set out to illuminate the discussion around entrepreneurial risk, beginning with some ideas about its definition.

A STARTING POINT FOR UNDERSTANDING ENTREPRENEURIAL RISK

Economists conceptualize risk as unanticipated and unpredictable movements in a variable of importance, typically income or revenue. The more volatile and unpredictable sources of income are, the riskier income is generally considered to be. From a statistical point of view, economic risk is generally measured as the variance of the probability distribution, or more appropriately, by the variance as conditioned on prior trends in the data. This latter correction adjusts for the situation where variance is predictable based on prior trends. (This advancement is the basis for the 2003 Nobel Prize in Economics won by Robert Engle.)

The concept of risk is central in early definitions of entrepreneurship. For example, Richard Cantillon (1680–1734) described the entrepreneur as someone who reduces risk for others by taking it on him or herself in the form of a fixed-price contract over time. The entrepreneur bears the risk caused by price fluctuations in consumer markets, while ensuring workers or suppliers by buying their products or labor services for resale before consumers have indicated how much they are willing to pay for them. If they guess right, they enjoy a surplus or profit; if not, they suffer a loss. H. K. Mangoldt (1824–68) brought the element of time into the equation of risk bearing, suggesting that the longer the productive process, the riskier would be the entrepreneurial function.

Frank Knight (1921) distinguished between risk and uncertainty as part of his analysis of profit and its origins. Knight adopted the reasoning that profit arises because people do not have perfect knowledge about the future. Whenever anything happens to make outcomes not match expectations, then the revenues from the goods will not equal costs, and profit may occur. The profits accrue to those parties willing to take on chance. In Knight's formulation, the economic implications of risk, which is measurable, and uncertainty, which is not, are decidedly different. Since risk can be quantified, entrepreneurs can make arrangements to "insure" themselves against it, but doing so will eliminate any profit potential.

We submit that it is worth considering under what conditions the distinction between risk and uncertainty is meaningful. This distinction between risk and uncertainty is somewhat artificial, since uncertainty represents a problem of "knowledge" of the relevant probabilities, not of their "existence." Moreover, one might argue that there are actually no probabilities to be "known" because probabilities of future events are really only "beliefs." Moreover, Knight's claim that risk should be inconsequential faces challenges on several fronts. Years after Knight's original treatise, it was pointed out that unsystematic or idiosyncratic risk is the type of risk that can be diversified away (Markowitz, 1952), so systematic risk is what should be pertinent to owners of assets. However, relative to the owners of corporations, entrepreneurs may find it difficult to diversify away risk that is unique to their venture, perhaps because of information problems or limited access to financial markets. Thus, it seems that entrepreneurs should be concerned about both (unsystematic and, in most cases, systematic) risk and uncertainty, as defined by Knight.

WHAT DO ENTREPRENEURS RISK?

The implication of the previous discussion is that the entrepreneur risks something in the event profits turn out worse than expected. This claim is not universally held. For example, Joseph Schumpeter did not view the entrepreneur as a risk bearer. In Schumpeter's view, the financial intermediary who lends the funds to the entrepreneur is the risk bearer. Some definitions of entrepreneurship are careful to point out that an entrepreneur need not own the resources of the firm, and hence, is not at risk of losing them (e.g., Stevenson et al., 1999, define entrepreneurship as the pursuit of opportunity without regard to resources currently controlled). At one time, one might have argued that an entrepreneur's reputation is "at risk," but many now view failure as a "badge of courage." Thus, one must be careful in identifying to what extent resources are "at risk."

In every case the entrepreneur risks the opportunity costs associated with starting the venture. These costs may be represented by the income the entrepreneur could have generated had he or she started another venture or chosen a wage earning position. These opportunity costs are represented by the individual's own discount rate and are the basis for the risk–return relationship in finance theory. The higher the discount rate (which is a function of systematic risk) underlying the venture opportunity, the higher are the expected returns the individual should demand. Since it is widely agreed that entrepreneurship is generally more risky than wage earning positions, one explanation for why individuals start ventures, and accept higher opportunity costs on average, is that they have higher expected returns than other income alternatives. Others have looked at the higher proportion of "failure" among smaller firms as evidence that these firms face more risk. However, we caution against this interpretation because failure seems to be a choice determined in part by each entrepreneur's unique threshold, or tolerance, for poor performance (Gimeno et al., 1997).

More recently, a stream of literature called real options theory has elaborated upon a different type of opportunity cost that is pertinent to the decision to start a venture. If starting a venture involves making sunk costs, then there are opportunity costs of committing to the venture. The entrepreneur cannot fully recoup the investment if things turn out poorly. In this theory, total risk defines opportunity costs, not merely systematic risk. The greater total risk, the greater the opportunity costs associated with starting a venture, which should lower the propensity for entrepreneurs to rush to start new ventures. Consistent with these expectations, O'Brien, Folta, and Johnson (2003) found that total risk lowered the likelihood of entrepreneurial entry. This perspective suggests that factors that raise the irreversibility of new venture creation should raise the riskiness of committing immediately to entrepreneurship.

OTHER EXPLANATIONS FOR HOW RISK IS LINKED WITH ENTREPRENEURSHIP

The high rates of entrepreneurial failure have led many researchers to question why we see such high rates of entry. Some have suggested that entrepreneurs are not only risk bearers, but also risk seekers (Begley and Boyd, 1987; McGrath, MacMillan, and Scheinberg, 1992).

This stands in contrast to managers of large organizations, who have been described as risk averse. Risk aversion is central to the positive relationship expected between risk and returns. In fact, few studies have shown statistically significant differences between entrepreneurs and managers in large organizations in their risk-taking propensity (Brockhaus, 1980; Low and MacMillan, 1988). Prospect theorists claim that risk-taking propensity may differ depending upon whether an individual is above or below some reference point (Kahneman and Tversky, 1984). Risky alternatives may be more acceptable when the decision-maker's economic situation is below the reference point. When this theory is applied to an entrepreneurial context it suggests that prospective entrepreneurs performing below aspiration levels may be more willing to initiate a venture than those above aspiration levels (Simon, Houghton, and Savelli, 2003, have found results consistent with the view that prospect theory explains entrepreneurial decision-making). This seems a promising area of research.

Rather than focusing on risk propensity, several scholars suggest that risk perception might explain why individuals start new ventures (Sitkin and Pablo, 1992; Palich and Bagby, 1995; Busenitz and Barney, 1997). It may be that entrepreneurs are more susceptible to biases and heuristics and are likely to perceive less risk in a given decision situation than are managers in large organizations. By being more willing to generalize from limited experience and by feeling overconfident that they will be able to master the major obstacles, entrepreneurs may conclude that a situation is simply less risky than would managers in large organizations. Cooper, Dunkelberg, and Woo (1998) found that 95 percent of entrepreneurs believe their venture will most probably succeed even though over half of all new ventures fail. Simon, Houghton, and Aquino (1999) found evidence that individuals start ventures because they do not perceive the risks involved and not because they knowingly accept high levels of risk.

CONCLUSION

We have considered that entrepreneurial risk is represented by an entrepreneur's inability to eliminate the stochastic nature of the environment. The existence of risk presents the opportunity for abnormal returns, but also the potential for losses. Let us be clear that increased risk propensity or decreased risk perceptions are neither necessary nor sufficient conditions for entrepreneurs to start ventures, but will certainly impact new venture formation.

Bibliography

Begley, T. M. and Boyd, D. P. (1987). Psychological characteristics associated with performance in entrepreneurial firms and smaller businesses. *Journal of Business Venturing*, 2: 79–93.

Brockhaus, R. H. (1980). Risk-taking propensity of entrepreneurs. *Academy of Management Journal*, 23: 509–20.

Busenitz, L. W. and Barney, J. B. (1997). Differences between entrepreneurs and managers in large organizations: Biases and heuristics in strategic decision-making. *Journal of Business Venturing*, 12: 9–30.

Cooper, A. C., Dunkelberg, W. C., and Woo, C. Y. (1988). Entrepreneurs' perceived chances of success. *Journal of Business Venturing*, 3: 97–108.

Gimeno, J., Folta, T. B., Cooper, A. C., and Woo, C. Y. (1997). Survival of the fittest? Entrepreneurial human capital and the persistence of underperforming firms. *Administrative Science Quarterly*, 42: 750–83.

Kahneman, D. and Tversky, A. (1984). Choices, values, and frames. *American Psychologist*, 39 (4): 341–50.

Knight, F. (1921). *Risk, Uncertainty, and Profit*. New York: Augustus Kelley.

Low, M. B. and MacMillan, I. C. (1988). Entrepreneurship: Past research and future challenges. *Journal of Management*, 14 (2): 139–61.

McGrath, R. G., MacMillan, I. C., and Scheinberg, S. (1992). Elitists, risk-takers, and rugged individualists? An exploratory analysis of cultural differences between entrepreneurs and non-entrepreneurs. *Journal of Business Venturing*, 7: 115–35.

Markowitz, H. M. (1952). The utility of wealth. *Journal of Political Economy*, 60: 151–8.

O'Brien, J. P., Folta, T. B., and Johnson, D. R. (2003). A real options perspective on entrepreneurial entry in the face of uncertainty. *Managerial and Decision Economics*, 24 (8): 515–33.

Palich, L. E. and Bagby, D. R. (1995). Using cognitive theory to explain entrepreneurial risk taking: Challenging conventional wisdom. *Journal of Business Venturing*, 10 (6): 425–38.

Simon, M., Houghton, S. M., and Aquino, K. (1999). Cognitive biases, risk perception, and venture formation: How individuals decide to start companies. *Journal of Business Venturing*, 15: 113–34.

Simon, M., Houghton, S. M., and Savelli, S. (2003). Out of the frying pan...? Why small business managers introduce high-risk products. *Journal of Business Venturing*, 18: 419–40.

Sitkin, S. B. and Pablo, A. L. (1992). Reconceptualizing the determinants of risk behavior. *Academy of Management Review*, 17 (1): 9–38.

Stevenson, H. H., Grousbeck, H. I., Roberts, M. J., and Bhide, A. V. (1999). *New Business Ventures and the Entrepreneur*, 5th edn. Boston, MA: Richard D. Irwin.

entrepreneurial service organizations

Robert C. Ford

While some might argue that all service organizations must be entrepreneurial to survive in an increasingly competitive global marketplace, there are some specific characteristics of entrepreneurial organizations that apply to service organizations as well.

Entrepreneurship encompasses acts of organizational creation, renewal, or innovation that occur within or outside an organization (Sharma and Chrisman, 1999). Entrepreneurial actions are the ways organizations implement entrepreneurship (*see* ENTREPRENEURSHIP). Ireland and his colleagues (Kuratko, Ireland, and Hornsby, 2001) define entrepreneurial actions as any newly fashioned behaviors through which companies exploit opportunities others have not noticed or aggressively pursued. "Novelty, in terms of new resources, customers, markets or a new combination of resources, customers or markets is the defining characteristic of entrepreneurial actions" (2001: 61). It seems reasonable to state entrepreneurial actions are taken by firms and individuals that have an entrepreneurial orientation (EO). Lumpkin and Dess (1996: 137), echoing Miller (1983) state: "The key dimensions that characterize an EO include a propensity to act autonomously, a willingness to innovate and take risks, and a tendency to be aggressive toward competitors and proactive relative to marketplace opportunities" (*see* ENTREPRENEURIAL ORIENTATION). Thus, an entrepreneurial service firm can be distinguished from a non-entrepreneurial service organization by the degree to which it takes entrepreneurial actions and displays an entrepreneurial orientation.

Distinguishing service organizations from other types of organizations is an equally challenging definitional issue. Most writers identify intangibility as the key feature that distinguishes a service from a product organization (Bowen and Ford, 2002). The fact that the service product is intangible has several important implications for the management and leadership of this type of organization. Producing an intangible product means that the customer and only the customer can define its quality and determine its value. It also means that services cannot be stored in inventory, are generally co-produced through some encounter between the customer and a service provider, and are simultaneously consumed and produced, making each service experience a different and unique product for each customer (Bowen and Ford, 2002; Zeithaml, Parasuraman, and Berry, 1985; Groonros, 2000; Lovelock, 2000).

A common definition of service is "an act or a performance offered by one party to another. Although the process may be tied to a physical product, the performance is essentially intangible and does not result in ownership of any of the factors of production" (Lovelock, 2000: 3). Because a service is consumed as it is produced (or performed), service organizations focus on the production process rather than a production outcome. This is a critical difference between services and manufacturing organizations. If you can't see the service product, then the act of producing it becomes the focus for defining how it is perceived in the customer's mind (Groonros, 2000). Perhaps the best way to define a service is to rely on Pine and Gilmore's (1999) distinction. They state: "experiences occur whenever a company intentionally uses services as the stage and goods as props to engage an individual. While commodities are fungible, goods tangible, and services intangible, experiences are memorable" (1999: 11–12). The variability in individual perceptions of experiences creates entrepreneurial opportunity.

Services are experienced holistically and consist of a service product (e.g., hamburger, rock concert), a service setting (e.g., physician's office, Olive Garden Restaurant), and a service delivery system (e.g., people, equipment, organization, and other systems that permit the delivery of the service product to the customer in the service setting) (Ford and Heaton, 2000). As these three elements collectively comprise and define the customer's experience, the variability in the ways they can be combined and managed creates entrepreneurial opportunity.

It should be noted that all services are not the same, as they can range from the monopolistic large electrical and public utility services to the entrepreneurial street corner entertainer. Thus, services can range from a capital-intensive category of organizations with high barriers to entry, like a public utility, to a limited or no-capital industry, like a website design service. Although all services produce an intangible experience, the degree to which that experience requires supporting tangible products, a suitable service setting, and delivery systems will vary widely across services.

Many writers have labored hard to distinguish among the types of services that exist. Lovelock and Yip (1996), for example, offer a classification scheme based on the type of processes used to create the service experience. They suggest services can be divided into people processing, possession processing, and information-based services. People processing offers tangible actions to the customer in person and require that the customer be actually at the "service factory." Examples include healthcare, transportation, and food and lodging services. Possession processing involves tangible actions to physical objects to improve their value to customers and include such services as auto repair, freight transportation, and warehousing. Information-based services depend on collecting, manipulating, interpreting, and transmitting information to create value. These services include accounting, education, Internet auctions, and consulting. Some believe that even these classifications are inadequate to completely cover the variety of services that exist. Maister (1983), for example, subdivides professional services into three types of client work: Brains (professional services requiring innovative and unique knowledge to solve complex problems, such as a defense attorney), Grey Hair (professional services that require successful experience in similar situations, such as a civil engineer), and Procedures (professional work that relies on well-established and efficient routines, such as a dentist).

Other writers offer typologies based on the degree to which the customer comes into contact with the organization to receive the service (Mills and Margulies, 1980; Chase, 1981; Schmenner, 1986). Thus, in this approach, a service can range from a pure service requiring customer presence (e.g., surgery, rock concert), to mixed services which require both customer contact and support facilities or back-of-house requirements (e.g., banks, restaurants), to quasi-manufacturing which require virtually no customer contact (e.g., distribution centers, repair shops, web-based services, customer service centers). Perhaps the simplest categorization is that offered by Albrecht and Zemke (1985) as "help me," "fix it," and "value added" services. The point is that there are multiple types of service organizations with many different types of structures, strategies, market environments, and production processes. Nonetheless, they share the characteristic of intangibility and all the derivative features that producing an intangible experience creates.

While it is increasingly difficult to find the point at which the traditional product-producing manufacturing organization crosses over into an experience-producing service organization, there are still major differences in how they are managed, organized, and staffed. Although entrepreneurial service organizations have not been widely studied as a distinct topic of empirical research and theoretical development (e.g., Davidsson and Wiklund, 2001), it is possible to suggest several key issues for both new and existing service organizations to address in seeking to gain the benefits of being entrepreneurial (Covin and Miles, 1999).

Entrepreneurship in both large and small organizations promotes the search for competitive advantages through product, process, and market innovations (Ireland et al., 2001). These authors go on to state: "These advantages are the product of proper positioning within the firms' industry; effective exploitation of idiosyncratic firm-specific resources, capabilities, and core competencies; and successful participation in unique networks or cooperative arrangements with other companies" (2001: 53). Since all entrepreneurial organizations seek ways to innovate to gain competitive advantage, services firms can look to their service product, service environment, and service delivery systems for opportunities to create an innovative niche.

The process for finding that innovative niche begins by identifying their current and potential customers' key drivers. If the organization's mission is to satisfy a niche in a large industry (e.g., to be a specialty restaurant chain, a local mortgage broker, or a neighborhood clinic), then it needs to identify the key drivers of the customers in that niche to find out what they are and how they can be met in a way that distinguishes this organization from competitors. The research literature identifies customer orientation as an important differentiation for entrepreneurial firms, and this would include service organizations as well (e.g., Agarwal, Erramilli, and Dev, 2003). What this means to the entrepreneurial service firm is that it should begin any strategic planning effort by identifying its present and hoped for customers' key drivers and then set itself and its processes up to meet them. While identifying customer key drivers sounds simple to do, average scores for service providers hover in the 60s and 70s, reported by the American Customer Satisfaction Index, suggesting that most service organizations are not doing very well in satisfying their customers. It also means considerable entrepreneurial opportunity.

The entrepreneurial service firm must find new ways to convince its present and future customers that its service product, environment, and delivery systems are somehow better able to meet their needs than any other available competitors in a chosen niche. A restaurant might do this with a novel "we guarantee you'll like our dinner or it's free" ad, by focusing only on some food that its customers tell it is desirable but currently unavailable in the marketplace, or some similar differentiating strategy that will establish a niche in the minds of its potential market.

Industry structure also has implications for entrepreneurial outcomes such as new entry success. Since heterogeneity is a characteristic of the service product, this offers the potential for unfilled market niches (Chrisman, Bauerschmidt, and Hofer, 1998). Panera Bread is a good example, as it fills a niche between the casual dining product and the fast food product. The company discovered an unmet customer need which created an innovative niche opportunity for a quick casual food restaurant. Their effort to fill that niche has been well rewarded.

Geographical location can also create niches for entrepreneurial service organizations. Providing a hot pizza is difficult when the production process is far away. Churches, retail stores, financial services, and even some healthcare services are selected on the basis of their location. Thus, the degree to which a geographic niche is unfilled with competing service offerings can have a bearing on entrepreneurial service organizations. These are only a few of the entrepreneurial opportunities that a careful assessment of the customer's key drivers can identify.

Successful service organizations display some key characteristics (Berry, 1999; Ford and Heaton, 2000; Bowen and Ford, 2002). They listen constantly to their customers, hire employees for attitude and train for skills, align their operating polices, procedures, human resources, and delivery systems with their service mission, continuously improve the service experience, create supportive environmental settings, quickly find and fairly fix service failures and problems, and actively respond to customer expectations, wants, needs, and behaviors. These key characteristics of successful service organizations strongly resemble those of entrepreneurial organizations, which is why many argue that successful service organizations are also entrepreneurial.

Bibliography

Agarwal, S., Erramilli, M. K., and Dev, C. S. (2003). Market orientation and performance in service firms: Role of innovation. *Journal of Services Marketing*, 17 (1): 68–82.

Albrecht, K. and Zemke, R. (1985). *Service America*. Homewood, IL: Dow Jones-Irwin.

Berry, L. (1999). *Discovering the Soul of Service*. New York: Free Press.

Bowen, J. and Ford, R. C. (2002). Managing service organizations: Does having a "thing" make a difference? *Journal of Management*, 28: 447–69.

Chase, R. B. (1981). The customer contact approach to services: Theoretical bases and practical extensions. *Operations Research*, 29: 698–706.

Chrisman, J. J., Bauerschmidt, A., and Hofer, C. W. (1998). The determinants of new venture performance: An extended model. *Entrepreneurship: Theory and Practice*, 22 (4): 5–28.

Covin, J. G. and Miles, M. P. (1999). Corporate entrepreneurship and the pursuit of competitive ad-

vantage. *Entreprenuership: Theory and Practice*, 23 (3): 47–63.

Davidsson, P. and Wiklund, J. (2001). Level of analysis in entrepreneurship research: Current research practice and suggestions for the future. *Entrepreneurship: Theory and Practice*, 25 (4): 81–99.

Ford, R. C. and Heaton, C. P. (2000). *Managing the Guest Experience in Hospitality Organizations*. Albany, NY: Delmar.

Groonros, C. (2000). *Service Management and Marketing*. Chichester: John Wiley and Sons.

Ireland, R. D., Hitt, M. A., Camp, S. M., and Sexton, D. L. (2001). Integrating entrepreneurship and strategic management actions to create firm wealth. *Academy of Management Executive*, 15 (1): 49–63.

Kuratko, D. F., Ireland, R. D., and Hornsby, J. S. (2001). Improving firms' performance through entrepreneurial actions. *Academy of Management Executive*, 15 (4): 61–72.

Lovelock, C. A. and Yip, G. S. (1996). Developing global strategies for service businesses. *California Management Review*, 38 (2): 64–86.

Lovelock, C. H. (2000). *Services Marketing*, 4th edn. Upper Saddle River, NJ: Prentice-Hall.

Lumpkin, G. T. and Dess, G. G. (1996). Clarifying the entrepreneurial orientation construct and linking it to performance. *Academy of Management Review*, 21: 135–72.

Maister, D. H. (1983). *Managing the Professional Service Firm*. New York: Free Press.

Miller, D. (1983). The correlates of entreprenuership in three types of firms. *Management Science*, 29: 770–91.

Mills, P. K. and Margulies, N. (1980). Toward a core typology of service organizations. *Academy of Management Review*, 5: 255–65.

Pine, B. J. and Gilmore, J. (1999). *The Experience Economy*, Boston, MA: HBS Press.

Schmenner, R. W. (1986). How can service businesses survive and prosper? *Sloan Management Review*, 27 (2): 21–32.

Sharma, P. and Chrisman, J. J. (1999). Toward a reconciliation of the definitional issues in the field of corporate entrepreneurship. *Entrepreneurship: Theory and Practice*, 23 (3): 11–28.

Zeithaml, V. A., Parasuraman, A., and Berry, L. A. (1985). Problems and strategies in services marketing. *Journal of Marketing*, 49 (1): 33–46.

entrepreneurial stories and legitimacy

Michael Lounsbury and Mary Ann Glynn

One of the most important problems for entrepreneurs involves gaining legitimacy among potential funders, suppliers, employees, and customers, as well as the general public. This problem is more acute to the extent that the entrepreneurial enterprise is novel and unique. Legitimacy, which flows from the widespread sociocultural support for a new venture, is crucial because it enables resource acquisition, the very development of a new entrepreneurial organization, and value creation. At the heart of attaining legitimacy is the ability to craft and tell a compelling story (Lounsbury and Glynn, 2001). Given that most start-ups lack proven track records, obvious asset value, and profitability, stories can provide needed accounts that explain, rationalize, and promote a new venture to reduce the uncertainty typically associated with entrepreneurship.

Despite the obvious importance of processes related to the attainment of legitimacy, attention to the dynamics of culture and symbolic activities such as storytelling has been limited in the entrepreneurship and strategy literatures (Thornton, 1999). This is partly because culture has been historically conceptualized as an all-determining normative force, allowing little theoretical space for agency. Over the past couple of decades, however, cultural sociologists have reconceptualized culture as a flexible set of tools that can be actively and strategically created and deployed by actors in their efforts to make sense of the world (e.g., Swidler, 1986). Reflecting this shift from a normative to a more cognitive approach to culture, Rao (1994: 41) argues that, in order to be successful, "entrepreneurs become skilled users of cultural tool kits rather than cultural dopes." Building on this more active conceptualization of culture, a focus on storytelling provides a useful direction for entrepreneurship researchers interested in the micro-mechanisms underlying new venture formation and establishment.

Stories make sense of an equivocal situation for both internal and external constituencies because they "selectively distill a complex jumble of otherwise ambiguous and contradictory activities, pronouncements, and impressions into a simplified and relatively coherent portrait" (Ashforth and Humphrey, 1997: 53). They are conventionally organized in three time-based structural components – beginning, middle, and end – with transitions and event sequences

propelled by plot lines and twists and shaped by defining characters (Bruner, 1990). In addition, any story consists of three basic elements: "a narrative subject in search of an object, a destinator (an extratextual force, the source of the subject's ideology), and a set of forces that either help or hinder the subject in acquiring the desired object" (Fiol, 1989: 279). Following this pattern, an entrepreneurial story might be structured accordingly: the *narrative subject* as the individual entrepreneur or the new venture; the *ultimate object or goal of the narrative* as a successful new enterprise, profitability, VC funding, or a positive reputation with potential stakeholders; and the *destinator* as the corporate and societal environment in which the narrative subject operates.

Entrepreneurial stories provide key data for venture capitalists and other institutional actors (such as investment banks, foundations, innovative organizations, etc.) who need to direct their attention to only the highest-potential opportunities in environments that are ambiguous and cognitively complex (Ocasio, 1997) to make future venture funding decisions (Camp and Sexton, 1992). Because many entrepreneurial ventures are unknown to external audiences, the creation of an appealing and coherent story may be one of the most crucial assets for a nascent enterprise. On this point, Aldrich and Fiol (1994: 652) contend: "Given the lack of externally validated arguments, [entrepreneurs] must draw on alternative forms of communication, such as narratives, to make a case that their ventures are compatible with more widely established sets of activities . . . narration works by suggestion and identification . . . express[ing] reasons to believe." Entrepreneurial stories, therefore, strive to make the unfamiliar familiar by framing the new venture (often through metaphor and analogy) in broader cultural terms that enable various actors to understand and assess the potential for a new venture to succeed.

More generally, stories, like other cultural artifacts, *function* to align an entrepreneur's underlying cultural mission, identity, and resources with that of key external constituents (Schein, 1992). A well-crafted story about entrepreneurial resources encapsulates the strategic goals and management of the new venture

(Ireland and Hitt, 1997) and indicates why a new venture merits investment and support. Once articulated, understood, and repeated, entrepreneurial stories become institutionalized accounts that provide both explanations of, and rationales for, entrepreneurial activity; in turn, such comprehensibility (or understandability) is the basis for legitimacy (Suchman, 1995).

Lounsbury and Glynn (2001) proposed two ways in which the content of entrepreneurial stories shapes and legitimates an entrepreneurial enterprise: (1) by emphasizing the distinctiveness of the new venture through a focus on identifying its unique characteristics, and (2) by stressing the normative appropriateness of the new venture by identifying its symbolic congruence with similar organizational forms and ideologies. The first type of story emphasizes the key attributes that are claimed to be central, distinctive, and enduring organizational characteristics (e.g., Albert and Whetten, 1985). This attribute-based approach to identity is perhaps most consistent with resource-based perspectives in the strategy literature, which exhort organizations to identify and exploit inimitable resources that can provide the basis for sustainable competitive advantage (Barney, 1991).

A second type of entrepreneurial story emphasizes relational aspects, or how a new venture can be located within already legitimated and distinct membership groups, defined by categories such as industry or sector (e.g., Elsbach and Kramer, 1996). This type of story shifts the locus of identity from the organizational level of the entrepreneurial venture to that of the inter-organizational, industry, or field level in which the new venture seeks to be perceived (e.g., Czarniawska and Wolff, 1998). Thus, the purpose is to cultivate an entrepreneurial identity that can align a new venture appropriately with extant institutionalized beliefs and practices from which legitimacy flows. These entrepreneurial stories often stress the positive features of the particular industry or product market segment to which they belong, rather than the novelty of their own enterprise.

While there has been very little research on entrepreneurial stories, legitimacy, and other cultural processes to date, attention to such issues will enable a deeper understanding of how resource acquisition and value creation ac-

tually occur as a result of entrepreneurship. One fruitful avenue for future research on entrepreneurial stories and legitimacy is to analyze how entrepreneurs balance the need for strategic distinctiveness against that of normative appropriateness (Glynn and Abzug, 1998) and other industry-level structural factors that may cause organizations to become more homogeneous. Do entrepreneurs and top managers seeking to shape the identity of their organizations strive for optimal distinctiveness by astutely assessing the degree to which an emphasis on sameness or distinctiveness will lead to the acquisition of resources and wealth creation? If so, under what conditions do entrepreneurial stories emphasize distinctiveness? Lounsbury and Glynn (2001) proposed that this will be more likely to occur in more mature industries that are already established as opposed to newly emerging product markets, but empirical research is needed. In general, the study of entrepreneurial stories and legitimacy is an exciting new area of research that has been relatively untapped and presents a munificent opportunity for scholars interested in the cultural drivers of economic action, as well as linkages between micro and macro processes.

Bibliography

Albert, S. and Whetten, D. A. (1985). Organizational identity. In B. M. Staw and L. L. Cummings (eds.), *Research in Organizational Behavior*, 7: 263–95: Greenwich, CT: JAI Press.

Aldrich, H. E. and Fiol, C. M. (1994). Fools rush in? The institutional context of industry creation. *Academy of Management Review*, 19: 645–70.

Ashforth, B. E. and Humphrey, R. H. (1997). The ubiquity and potency of labeling in organizations. *Organization Science*, 8: 43–58.

Barney, J. B. (1991). Firm resources and sustained competitive advantage. *Journal of Management*, 17: 99–120.

Bruner, J. (1990). *Acts of Meaning*. Cambridge, MA: Harvard University Press.

Camp, S. M. and Sexton, D. L. (1992). Trends in venture capital investment: Implications for high-technology firms. *Journal of Small Business Management*, 30: 11–19.

Czarniawska, B. and Wolff, R. (1998). Constructing new identities in established organization fields: Young universities in old Europe. *International Studies of Management and Organization*, 28: 32–56.

Elsbach, K. D. and Kramer, R. D. (1996). Members' responses to organizational identity threats:

Encountering and countering the *Business Week* rankings. *Administrative Science Quarterly*, 41: 442–76.

Fiol, C. M. (1989). A semiotic analysis of corporate language: Organizational boundaries and joint venturing. *Administrative Science Quarterly*, 34: 277–303.

Glynn, M. A. and Abzug, R. (1998). Isomorphism and competitive differentiation in the organizational name game. In J. A. C. Baum (ed.), *Advances in Strategic Management*, 15: 105–28.

Ireland, R. D. and Hitt, M. A. (1997). "Strategy-as-story": Clarifications and enhancements to Barry and Elmes' arguments. *Academy of Management Review*, 22: 844–7.

Lounsbury, M. and Glynn, M. A. (2001). Cultural entrepreneurship: Stories, legitimacy, and the acquisition of resources. *Strategic Management Journal*, 22: 545–64.

Ocasio, W. (1997). Towards an attention-based view of the firm. *Strategic Management Journal*, 18: 187–206.

Rao, H. (1994). The social construction of reputation: Certification contests, legitimation, and the survival of organizations in the American automobile industry, 1895–1912. *Strategic Management Journal*, 15: 29–44.

Schein, E. (1992). *Organizational Culture and Leadership*. San Francisco: Jossey-Bass.

Suchman, M. C. (1995). Managing legitimacy: Strategic and institutional approaches. *Academy of Management Review*, 20: 571–610.

Swidler, A. (1986). Culture in action: Symbols and strategies. *American Sociological Review*, 51: 273–86.

Thornton, P. H. (1999). The sociology of entrepreneurship. *Annual Review of Sociology*, 25: 19–46.

entrepreneurship

James J. Chrisman

Entrepreneurship refers to acts of organizational creation, renewal, or innovation that occur within, or independent of, an existing organization (Sharma and Chrisman, 1999: 17). Entrepreneurial activity that occurs within the boundaries of an existing organization is referred to as corporate entrepreneurship (*see* CORPORATE ENTREPRENEURSHIP). Independent entrepreneurship encompasses acts of organizational creation that are instigated by individuals acting independently of any association with an existing organization. The corollary term, entrepreneur (*see* ENTREPRENEUR), deals with the individuals who engage in independent or corporate entrepreneurship efforts.

The meaning of the term "entrepreneurship" has evolved and is currently subject to some debate (*see* HISTORY OF THE ACADEMIC STUDY OF ENTREPRENEURSHIP). McMullan and Long (1983), reviewing the development of the formal theoretical usages of the term since the early 1700s, identified three recurring themes: (1) the uncertainty and risk associated with entrepreneurial behaviors and activities, (2) the complementary competence required in organizing new economic activity for entrepreneurial success, and (3) innovative pursuit of potential opportunities. These themes are consistent with the contemporary view that the field of entrepreneurship should be devoted to studies of (1) why, when, and how people seek, discover, and pursue opportunities (*see* ENTREPRENEURIAL DISCOVERY; ENTREPRENEURIAL OPPORTUNITY), (2) why, when, and how different methods of organization and resource utilization are used for exploiting opportunities (*see* OPPORTUNITY EXPLOITATION), and (3) why, when, and how economic opportunities come into existence (Shane and Venkataraman, 2000).

In the current milieu, the debate has centered on whether the term should be reserved for activities that involve innovations (*see* INNOVATIONS) or should encompass all acts of organization creation, whether innovative or imitative (Sharma and Chrisman, 1999). On the one hand, Schumpeter (1934) argued that entrepreneurship upsets an existing equilibrium situation in an economy through the development of new combinations, which may involve new products or services, methods of production, markets, sources of supply, or industrial organization (*see* CREATIVE DESTRUCTION). On the other hand, according to Kirzner (1973) entrepreneurship promotes a movement by an economy toward an equilibrium position through entrepreneurial alertness (*see* ENTREPRENEURIAL ALERTNESS) to opportunities to exploit supply or demand asymmetries in existing markets that had gone unnoticed by industry participants due to imperfect information. Recognizing that these two arguments describe complementary rather than contradictory processes representing the ebbs and flows of economic activity over time, Cheah (1990) suggests that both theoretical perspectives should be taken into account in order to gain a full appreciation of the role of entrepreneurship in economic development.

Consistent with this viewpoint, Sharma and Chrisman (1999) have indicated that the study of entrepreneurship should be broad based and inclusive. In the context of developing a set of internally consistent definitions of the components of corporate entrepreneurship, their work suggests that different types of entrepreneurial activities can be identified, classified, and studied independently. Taking a similar tack, Bruyat and Julien (2000) argue entrepreneurship is about creating value (*see* CREATING VALUE) and the reciprocal impacts on individuals and environments that occur as a result of innovation or organizational creation. They propose that the extent to which the individual and the environment change as a result of the entrepreneurial process leads to different types of entrepreneurship, ranging from entrepreneurial reproduction, where neither the individual nor the environment change very much, to entrepreneurial venture, where the changes to each are profound.

Despite some theoretical debates, there is widespread consensus among scholars and practitioners on the importance of entrepreneurship for economic development. The work of Birch (1987) has been especially influential in demonstrating how new venture creation has led to job generation in the US economy. Birch has shown that start-ups are not evenly distributed across regions and that high-growth start-ups have disproportionate impacts. He suggests that a region's educational resources, labor force, government, infrastructure, and quality of life are especially important for fostering entrepreneurship.

By empirically demonstrating that entrepreneurship is neither trivial nor random in its incidence and impact, Birch's work has been significant in influencing the attitudes of public policy-makers who are in a position to positively, or negatively, alter the environment for entrepreneurship. His work has also contributed to a surge of scholarly interest in entrepreneurship, as evidenced by the subsequent rapid growth in research and educational programs devoted to the subject. On the other hand, Birch's findings have also fueled the debates summarized above, as not all entrepreneurial ventures are equal in their potential to contribute to the economy.

Much of the work on entrepreneurship deals with entrepreneurial behaviors and entrepreneurial decisions (Gartner, 1988) (*see* ENTREPRENEURIAL DECISIONS), the discovery and exploitation of opportunities (Shane and Venkataraman, 2000), and the acquisition, development, and deployment of the resources (*see* ENTREPRENEURIAL RESOURCES) necessary to translate an opportunity into a profitable business (Alvarez and Busenitz, 2001). These components are all essential to the study of entrepreneurship because organizational creation, renewal, and innovation are processes that are predicated on the identification and pursuit of opportunities that require resources not necessarily under the current control of an entrepreneur (Stevenson and Jarillo, 1990). Consequently, entrepreneurship can be viewed as a set of strategic decisions and actions (Chrisman, Bauerschmidt, and Hofer, 1998).

The strategic decisions and actions involved in entrepreneurship are different from the strategic decisions and actions of mature, stable organizations, however (*see* STRATEGIC ENTREPRENEURSHIP). First, the opportunity being pursued is new. At a minimum, the opportunity is new to the individual or the organization; at the extreme, the opportunity is one never before recognized or even anticipated as a value-creating possibility. The uncertainty involved in forecasting the size, nature, and evolution of an opportunity makes its pursuit very risky (*see* ENTREPRENEURIAL RISK). To be successful in such a high risk situation requires either, separately or in combination, superior cognitive abilities on the part of an entrepreneur, access to information not readily available to others, or a great deal of luck (Shane and Venkataraman, 2000).

Second, an established organization already has tangible and intangible resources available to pursue opportunities, and at least some appreciation of the types of resources that must be developed to replenish its existing inventory. By contrast, entrepreneurship involves estimating the amounts of human, physical, and financial resources that will be required to innovate or organize, without the benefit of history. Often, it is the lack of sufficient tangible resources such as money or equipment that provides the greatest obstacle to the survival of an entrepreneurial enterprise in the short term (Chrisman, Bauerschmidt, and Hofer, 1998). Entrepreneurs also must anticipate the types of resources required to satisfy customer needs in the present and future and figure out how to deploy those resources in a way that is unique and cannot be easily imitated or circumvented by alternative means. It is largely the ability to develop and deploy intangible resources, particularly knowledge (*see* KNOWLEDGE-BASED ASSETS IN ENTREPRENEURIAL VENTURES), that spells the difference between average and superior entrepreneurial outcomes (Chrisman, Bauerschmidt, and Hofer, 1998). The difficulty in making and implementing strategic decisions regarding resources and opportunities has led some to argue that sustainable competitive advantage (*see* COMPETITIVE ADVANTAGE) in entrepreneurship consists of the ability of an entrepreneur to recognize opportunity, organize resources, and create superior heterogeneous outputs (Alvarez and Busenitz, 2001).

The importance of entrepreneurship as a strategic process perhaps explains why the majority of investors, particularly venture capitalists (*see* VENTURE CAPITAL), require a business plan (*see* BUSINESS PLAN) before they will invest in an entrepreneurial venture. However, the tasks involved in entrepreneurship do not end with making strategic choices. Entrepreneurs must investigate the nature of the competitive environment, develop and produce the product or service to be sold, determine the legal structure for the business, select a location, buy or rent equipment, hire employees, purchase a business license, obtain inventory and supplies, choose a marketing approach, and deal with a whole host of additional necessary administrative and operational concerns. Success in entrepreneurship is therefore primarily a function of the decisions made by an entrepreneur on the strategic, administrative, and operational issues involved in innovation, organizational creation, or renewal.

See also *entrepreneurial growth; entrepreneurial leadership*

Bibliography

Alvarez, S. A. and Busenitz, L. W. (2001). The entrepreneurship of resource-based theory. *Journal of Management*, 27: 755–75.

Birch, D. (1987). *Job Creation in America*. New York: Free Press.

Bruyat, C. and Julien, P.-A. (2000). Defining the field of research in entrepreneurship. *Journal of Business Venturing*, 16: 165–80.

Cheah, H.-B. (1990). Schumpeterian and Austrian entrepreneurship: Unity within duality. *Journal of Business Venturing*, 5: 341–7.

Chrisman, J. J., Bauerschmidt, A., and Hofer, C. W. (1998). The determinants of new venture performance: An extended model. *Entrepreneurship: Theory and Practice*, 23 (1): 5–29.

Gartner, W. B. (1988). "Who is an entrepreneur?" is the wrong question. *American Journal of Small Business*, 12 (4): 11–32.

Kirzner, I. M. (1973). *Competitive Entrepreneurship*. Chicago: University of Chicago Press.

McMullan, W. E. and Long, W. (1983). The meaning of entrepreneurship. *American Journal of Small Business*, (2): 47–56.

Schumpeter, J. A. (1934). *The Theory of Economic Development*. Cambridge, MA: Harvard University Press.

Shane, S. and Venkataraman, S. (2000). The promise of entrepreneurship as a field of research. *Academy of Management Review*, 25: 217–26.

Sharma, P. and Chrisman, J. J. (1999). Toward a reconciliation of the definitional issues in the field of corporate entrepreneurship. *Entrepreneurship: Theory and Practice*, 23 (3): 11–27.

Stevenson, H. H. and Jarillo, J. C. (1990). A paradigm of entrepreneurship: Entrepreneurial management. *Strategic Management Journal*, 11 (winter): 17–27.

ethics in entrepreneurship

Jeffrey S. Harrison

Ethics represent a very challenging topic to study in any field, since there is not even consensus on what the term means. To simplify this discussion, I am going to associate ethics with a form of social morality, recognizing that the specific definitions of morality will vary depending on the societal context. When I use the term "ethical," I am referring to attitudes, behaviors, and outcomes that most members of a particular society would consider ethical. Also, in an effort to discuss the intersection of ethics with entrepreneurship in an abbreviated format, I am going to focus on entrepreneurship only as it pertains to creation of a new business entity to provide a new or existing good or service to a new or existing market. I will first discuss some of the ethical implications of entrepreneurial activities from a societal perspective, followed by an examination of work that has examined the ethics of entrepreneurs themselves.

For many reasons, entrepreneurship is a central public policy issue in most countries (Brenkert, 2002). It has been linked to the creation of millions of jobs and new products and services. These products and services have altered the way people work and live, allowing them to perform tasks and enjoy life in ways that were previously inconceivable. In addition, entrepreneurship is associated with the concept of self-determination by providing opportunities for people to own and operate businesses. All of this has led to greater efficiency and the creation of wealth. From a Western capitalist perspective, these are great things. However, not all societies view wealth creation in the same positive light. For example, in spite of recent advances in China with regard to support of entrepreneurial activity, the communist mindset tends to be much more concerned about the distribution of this wealth. Chinese leaders "tolerate" the concentration of wealth and power in the hands of entrepreneurs because they understand the connection between entrepreneurship and the overall wealth of a country (Brown, 2002).

Varying levels of entrepreneurship across countries provides evidence that some social orders are more encouraging to entrepreneurship than others (Brenkert, 2002). Obviously, the existence of venture capital is a huge determinant of such variance. However, the legal system is also a key factor. In general, the less encumbered a citizenry is with legal restrictions, laws, and regulations pertaining to business dealings, the more likely that entrepreneurship will take place.

Another interesting development in this stream of thinking is the role that entrepreneurship plays in reducing inequities among organizational stakeholders. Venkataraman (2002) calls these inequities "value anomalies." For example, an employee may add much more value to an organization than what is received in return. In these situations, if society allows it, the employee may sever ties with the organization to pursue a separate venture and thus become an entrepreneur. Venkataraman (2002) also suggests that major shifts in technologies can lead to numerous value anomalies, which may build up until they result in sweeping changes to organizations and industries. One example of this phenomenon is the large numbers of "computer nerds" of the late twentieth century who became owners or co-owners of their own companies (Harrison, 2002). Many of them previously worked for large corporations, where their talents were underutilized and under-rewarded. In essence, wealth was redistributed to them as sweeping changes took place in technologies and the resulting organizational forms. The absence of a social order that facilitates entrepreneurship would have stifled these equilibrating processes.

Nonetheless, these arguments in favor of a society unencumbered by legal restrictions to entrepreneurship, taken to the extreme, can be dangerous. The fact is that people may engage in entrepreneurship for good or bad reasons (Brenkert, 2002). For example, an illegal drug dealer may peddle narcotics to teenagers in an attempt to create wealth. Most people from any culture would agree that this is a bad thing for society. Laws are enacted to protect against such activities which, in one sense, also stifles entrepreneurship. The problem is that there is not a reliable connection between law and ethics. For example, some companies buy prescription medicines in Canada and then sell them illegally in the United States. One of their primary targets is older retired people who can't afford to buy the higher-priced drugs in the United States. In many ways, these entrepreneurs are engaged in the same sorts of activities, albeit the outcomes are quite different. Governments have to find a balance between protecting their citizens and facilitating entrepreneurial behaviors.

With regard to promoting fairness or moral practices, corporations tend to be more open to public inspection than entrepreneurial firms (Mitchell, 2002). More information is disclosed to the public as a result of legal requirements.

Also, entrepreneurial ventures tend not to be subject to the same level of laws, rules, and regulations that protect society and its individual citizens. Furthermore, governance practices tend to be feudal/political rather than democratic in a smaller, entrepreneurial business. This means that there are fewer stakeholders that have legitimacy or power in the organization, with most of the power resting in the entrepreneur. This situation means that the ethical and moral conduct of the organization as an entity is largely determined by the ethical and moral standards of the entrepreneur. Consequently, another critical issue is whether entrepreneurs tend to be more or less ethical than other types of managers.

People who become entrepreneurs tend to be unconventional thinkers. As mavericks and risk takers, they break away from many social norms. Consequently, it is reasonable to think that their ethics could be different from other types of managers. Indeed, Teal and Carroll (1999) found evidence that entrepreneurs exhibit moral reasoning skills at a higher level than either middle-level managers or the general adult population. Working with the defining issues test developed by Rest (1979), they discovered that entrepreneurs were more likely to think independently and reject social norms. In fact, almost none of their entrepreneurs exhibited moral reasoning at the lowest levels. In another study that compared the ethical standards of managers with entrepreneurs, Bucar (2001) found that more entrepreneurs believed it was unethical to use company services, supplies, or time in non-company activities. Also, a larger percentage of entrepreneurs felt that it was wrong to take longer than necessary to do a job, to authorize subordinates to violate company policy, or to hire competitors to learn trade secrets.

Not surprisingly, personal ethics also vary by country. Bucar, Glas, and Hisrich (2003) discovered some striking differences among entrepreneurs and managers in Slovenia, the US, and Russia. For example, 91.7 percent of the Slovenian entrepreneurs in their sample felt that it was wrong to take extra personal time during lunch hours and breaks, compared to 80 percent for US entrepreneurs and 69.8 percent for Russian entrepreneurs. For managers, the percentages were 92.6 percent in Slovenia and 56.8 percent in the US (Russian managers were not included). As might be expected, only 49.7 percent of Russian entrepreneurs believed it was wrong to give gifts in exchange for preferential treatment, compared with 81 percent of Slovenian entrepreneurs and 84.8 percent of American entrepreneurs. Managers in each country were similar in percentages to their entrepreneur counterparts.

To summarize, entrepreneurship is a central issue to policy-makers of nations throughout the world. Although the wealth-creating benefits of entrepreneurial activities are widely extolled, serious societal concerns exist regarding distribution of wealth and protection of citizens against potential abuses. Successful entrepreneurs sometimes build great wealth and power in society, and entrepreneurial firms tend not to be subject to the same oversight as corporations. Consequently, the ethical behavior of an entrepreneurial firm largely depends on the ethics of the entrepreneur. Fortunately, by most measures, entrepreneurs tend to have higher ethical standards and moral reasoning than other types of managers. As a caveat to this statement, we should remember that some entrepreneurs, such as drug dealers, engage in unethical business activities. The subjects that have been sampled in this stream of research reflect only a portion of the larger population of entrepreneurs.

Bibliography

Brenkert, G. G. (2002). Entrepreneurship, ethics and the good society. *Ethics and Entrepreneurship*. Ruffin Series No. 3, 5–44. Society for Business Ethics, Charlottesville, VA.

Brown, B. (2002). Entrepreneurship and ethics in the Chinese context. *Ethics and Entrepreneurship*. Ruffin Series No. 3, 219–30. Society for Business Ethics, Charlottesville, VA.

Bucar, B. (2001). Ethics of business managers vs. entrepreneurs. *Developmental Entrepreneurship*, 6 (1): 1–21.

Bucar, B., Glas, M., and Hisrich, R. D. (2003). Ethics and entrepreneurs: An international comparative study. *Journal of Business Venturing*, 18: 261–81.

Harrison, J. S. (2002). A stakeholder perspective of entrepreneurial activity: Beyond normative theory. *Ethics and Entrepreneurship*. Ruffin Series No. 3, 5–44. Society for Business Ethics, Charlottesville, VA.

Mitchell, R. K. (2002). Entrepreneurship and stakeholder theory: Comment on Ruffin lecture 2. *Ethics and*

Entrepreneurship. Ruffin Series No. 3, 175–96. Society for Business Ethics, Charlottesville, VA.

Rest, J. R. (1979). *Development in Judging Moral Issues*. Minneapolis: University of Minnesota Press.

Teal, E. J. and Carroll, A. B. (1999). Moral reasoning skills: Are entrepreneurs different? *Journal of Business Ethics*, 19: 229–40.

Venkataraman, S. (2002). Stakeholder value equilibration and the entrepreneurial process. *Ethics and Entrepreneurship*. Ruffin Series No. 3, 45–58. Society for Business Ethics, Charlottesville, VA.

executive succession in entrepreneurial business

Lloyd P. Steier

Executive succession represents a significant transition within a business wherein an incumbent leader passes on the authority and responsibility for the operation of the firm to a successor. As leaders greatly influence firm strategy and performance, succession is a most important aspect of long-term survival and success (Miller, 1993; Lee, Lim, and Lim, 2003). For entrepreneurial businesses, next to overcoming the "liabilities of newness" (Stinchombe, 1965) encountered at start-up, succession of the Founder-CEO (Wasserman, 2003) is the most critical event relative to survival. In essence, this transition largely determines whether the business will continue beyond the life of its founder. On a more general level, many researchers have observed that every succession event is potentially a precarious time for firms, as executives and organizational members mutually adjust to new strategies, roles, routines, and relationships (Haveman, 1993).

There are a number of factors and events that precipitate executive succession in entrepreneurial businesses. At the personal level, these factors include age, changing interests, good or bad performance, illness, or death. At the organizational level, Wasserman (2003: 152) found two events that typically influence succession: "the completion of product development and the raising of a new round of financing." Each of these events signals the need for a new set of management skills. Wasserman further observed that, paradoxically, it is the achievement of "critical milestones" in entrepreneurial business

that "actually causes the chance of Founder-CEO succession to rise dramatically."

THE CHALLENGES OF EXECUTIVE SUCCESSION IN DIFFERENT TYPES OF ENTREPRENEURIAL BUSINESSES

The challenges of executive succession are both considerable and varied. As entrepreneurial businesses can be defined in multiple ways, it is useful to discuss succession challenges within the context of varied definitions or "archetypes" (Miller, 1983).

Entrepreneurs, acting as founders, create new organizations. A common definition of entrepreneurship contends that entrepreneurs, acting as founders, create new organizations (Gartner, 1988). Initial succession marks a significant event in the life of a business because it is a transition to a professionally or family managed firm. From this perspective, entrepreneurial businesses are new firms created and run by owner-managers; succession represents the boundary or signpost wherein a transition is made from entrepreneurship to another stage.

Entrepreneurial businesses are often founded by charismatic leaders. This type of leadership presents the challenge of what Max Weber described as "institutionalizing" charisma (Davis, 1968; Haveman and Khaire, 2004). A further related challenge is transferring knowledge – both explicit and tacit – from the incumbent to the successor (Le Breton-Miller, Miller, and Steier, 2004).

Founder-CEOs (Wasserman, 2003) typically have four qualities that distinguish them from other CEOs: a greater emotional attachment to their firms, a stronger ownership position, greater control, and greater ability to remain in – or influence – a firm after they have given up control. These qualities present a further set of challenges relative to executive succession. Most notably they tend to provide the desire and the means to keep the business in the family. Although that might be the stated intent, sometimes a founder's identity is so intertwined with the business they are unable to complete, or even confront, succession in a meaningful way. Nepotism further complicates the process – particularly if it is excessive. Although nepotism is much maligned as providing a foundation for an inferior form of business organization (e.g., Max Weber's notion of bureaucracy), in reality it exists widely and can be a source of business advantage. According to Bellow (2003), nepotism is a natural human tendency widely practiced throughout history. He further argues it needs to be acknowledged, understood, praised, and celebrated. In a similar vein, Lee, Lim, and Lim (2003) propose that it is not nepotism that drives the appointments of relatives in business as much as an economic rationale which attempts to reduce the risk associated with engaging outside agents. Sometimes family members make the best candidates to replace an incumbent CEO, particularly when the succession process is handled properly. Thus, in matters of executive succession, the challenge for family businesses is to recognize the natural tendency towards excessive nepotism (the rigors of the marketplace are not kind to incompetent heirs) while being mindful of the advantages that it provides.

Entrepreneurial businesses create something new and innovative. A second definition of entrepreneurial businesses posits that they innovate and "create something new, something different; they change or transmute values" (Drucker, 1985: 22). This definition subscribes to Schumpeterian notions that entrepreneurial firms are engaged in new activities that result in new combinations of means of production. According to Schumpeter (1934), entrepreneurial firms can be identified by strategic behavior that would include any of the following: the introduction of new goods or services, opening new markets, opening new sources of supply, and industrial reorganization. This notion of entrepreneurship assumes that innovative activity – not age, size, or founder characteristics – is the most relevant factor. Within this context, Aldrich (1999: 80) makes a useful distinction between "reproducer" and "innovator" organizations. He defines reproducer organizations as "those organizations started in an established population whose routines and competencies vary only minimally, if at all, from those of existing organizations," whereas innovative organizations are "those organizations started by entrepreneurs whose routines and competencies vary significantly from those of existing organizations." In effect, reproducers have an existing roadmap of roles and routines to follow; innovators do not. In matters of executive succession, innovative firms often illustrate an interesting paradox. For some of these firms, sustainable competitive advantage is derived from having "heterogeneous and idiosyncratic" resources and capabilities that cannot be easily imitated by others (Hitt et al., 2001: 482). The "know how" or "recipes" residing within the leader can be one of these resources. Thus the very source of competitive advantage can suddenly become a disadvantage if the hard-to-imitate resources and capabilities reside primarily within the leader and are not appropriately reproduced in the succession process. In cases where a firm's roles, routines, and recipes are highly idiosyncratic, insiders or family members often make suitable successors simply because they have had the most appropriate apprenticeship. However, it is important to recognize that there is a huge difference between replicating existing roles and routines and inventing new ones. Firms that derive their competitive advantage from continuously inventing and implementing new roles and routines may need to search more widely before an appropriate successor is found.

Entrepreneurial businesses are growth oriented. A third definition of entrepreneurial businesses is that they have an orientation towards growth (Wasserman, 2003). As they grow, they encounter a well-known cycle of "evolution and revolution" (Greiner, 1972) wherein they proceed through predictable stages with an accompanying set of new crises. These crises require a new set of skills from their leaders that must be either learned by the incumbent or acquired through executive succession. Individual action must be accompanied by delegation and control; innovative activity must become institutionalized within the organization. Common transition challenges that must be met by founding entrepreneurs in growing firms include moving from doing, to managing, to managing managers. Thus, in growth-oriented firms, it is often not enough to simply clone the existing CEO; required skills must be identified and accessed.

IMPORTANT STAGES IN THE EXECUTIVE
SUCCESSION PROCESS

There is general agreement that executive succession should be a process, not an event. Although numerous researchers have used a varied terminology to describe this process (Dyck et al., 2002; Miller, Steier, and Le Breton-Miller, 2003; Le Breton-Miller, Miller, and Steier, 2004; Sharma, Chrisman, and Chua, 2003), executive succession in entrepreneurial businesses can be characterized as having several discernable stages.

Anticipating the need for a successor.   The precept of key stakeholders accepting the need for change before meaningful change can occur (well developed in the change literature) clearly applies to matters of executive succession. Unwillingness to confront retirement is merely one of the issues at this stage; others include recognizing and accepting the need for a new skill set.

Anticipating strategic direction and needs of the organization.   An organization needs to have reasonable clarity about the nature of its business, products/services, markets, and competitive strategy. The selection of a new CEO must be compatible with an organization's intended direction.

Identifying suitable candidates.   As already suggested, activities within a firm, such as replacing a charismatic leader, achievement of certain milestones, or a new round of financing, all dictate unique strategic imperatives requiring differing skill sets of the CEO. Candidate selection must match strategic intent.

Acquiring the appropriate skill set.   Depending on the strategic direction and succession availability, a firm may choose to go "outside" or "inside" the firm when choosing a successor. Some firms elect to choose a new outside CEO who possesses a set of skills the firm cannot easily acquire. For example, firms that raise additional financing through an initial public offering (IPO) find it helpful to recruit someone with IPO experience. Other firms, particularly those with idiosyncratic roles and routines, choose to recruit and develop insiders (Le Breton-Miller et al., 2004).

Passing the baton.   The relay race, wherein the actual passing of a baton is critical for team success, is a commonly used metaphor in executive succession. In essence, incumbents and potential successors must choreograph a harmonious transfer of power and responsibilities (Dyck et al., 2002).

Post-succession activities.   Retired CEOs of entrepreneurial firms often continue to influence the business after they have given up control (Wasserman, 2003). Although ex-CEOs represent a wonderful resource repository, factors such as charisma, strong emotional attachment to the firm, and unresolved identity issues can lead to unwelcome meddling. Firms need to strive to adopt governance mechanisms that optimize the predecessor and incumbent CEO relationship.

CONCLUSION

In matters of succession, entrepreneurial businesses face unique challenges. First, the charismatic leadership evident in many entrepreneurial businesses is hard to duplicate. Second, entrepreneurial firms tend not to have established roles, routines, and networks to the same degree as mature firms. Third, entrepreneurial businesses often exhibit idiosyncratic roles and routines that are hard to replicate. Fourth, owner-founder firms have the option of passing on the stewardship to a family member; nepotism, albeit much maligned, presents some advantages for family firms, along with its own unique challenges. Fifth, some entrepreneurial firms have neither the time nor the resources to develop an internal managerial talent pool. Sixth, entrepreneurial businesses with a strong orientation towards growth typically encounter new crises as they grow.

Entrepreneurial businesses also manifest at least three distinctly different organizational forms, each with its own accompanying set of succession challenges. New businesses created by owner-founders face the challenge of institutionalizing charisma, as well as transferring explicit and tacit knowledge from the incumbent CEO. Innovative businesses face the challenge of reproducing idiosyncratic roles and routines. Growth-oriented firms must access new managerial skills that are not easily found within the firm. Research suggests there is no "one best" candidate to assume control and, depending on a firm's needs, suitable successors may be found among family members, personnel within the firm, or outsiders. Finally, succession is usefully viewed as a process involving a series of stages.

Bibliography

Aldrich, H. (1999). *Organizations Evolving*. London: Sage.

Bellow, A. (2003). *In Praise of Nepotism: A Natural History*. New York: Doubleday.

Davis, S. M. (1968). Entrepreneurial succession. *Administrative Science Quarterly*, 13: 402–16.

Drucker, P. (1985). *Innovation and Entrepreneurship*. New York: Harper and Row.

Dyck, B., Mauws, M., Starke, F. A., and Mischke, G. A. (2002). Passing the baton: The importance of sequence, timing, technique, and communication in executive succession. *Journal of Business Venturing*, 17: 143–62.

Gartner, W. B., (1988). Who is an entrepreneur? Is the wrong question, *American Journal of Small Business*, 12: 11–32.

Greiner, L. E. (1972). Evolution and revolution as organizations grow. *Harvard Business Review*, 50: 37–47.

Haveman, H. A. (1993). Ghosts of managers past: Managerial succession and organizational mortality. *Academy of Management Journal*, 36: 864–81.

Haveman, H. A. and Khaire, M. V. (2004). Survival beyond succession? The contingent impact of founder succession on organizational failure. *Journal of Business Venturing*, in press.

Hitt, M. A., Ireland, R. D., Camp, S. M., and Sexton, D. L. (2001). Strategic entrepreneurship: Entrepreneurial strategies for wealth creation. *Strategic Management Journal*, 22: 479–91.

Le Breton-Miller, I., Miller, D., and Steier, L. (2004). Towards an integrative model of effective FOB succession. *Entrepreneurship: Theory and Practice*, in press.

Lee, K. S., Lim, G. H., and Lim, W. S. (2003). Family business succession: Appropriation risk and choice of successor. *Academy of Management Review*, 28: 657–66.

Miller, D. (1983). The correlates of entrepreneurship in three kinds of firms. *Management Science*, 29: 770–91.

Miller, D. (1993). Some organizational consequences of CEO succession. *Academy of Management Journal*, 36: 644–59.

Miller, D., Steier, L., and Le Breton-Miller, I. (2003). Lost in time: Intergenerational succession, change, and failure in family business. *Journal of Business Venturing*, 18: 513–31.

Schumpeter, J. A. (1934). *The Theory of Economic Development*. Cambridge, MA: Harvard University Press.

Sharma, P., Chrisman, J. J., and Chua, J. H. (2003). Predictors of satisfaction with the succession process in family firms. *Journal of Business Venturing*, 18: 667–87.

Stinchcombe, A. L. (1965). Social structure and organizations. In J. G. March (ed.), *Handbook of Organizations*, 142–93. New York: Rand McNally.

Wasserman, N. (2003). Founder-CEO succession and the paradox of entrepreneurial success. *Organization Science*, 14: 149–72.

F

family business

Frank Hoy

Serious academic attention toward family business is recent, yet the origins are obscure. The editor of *Family Business Review* asserted in 2003 that family business was only twenty years old as a subject of scholarly study (Astrachan, 2003). He based his argument on a special issue of the journal *Organization Dynamics* that appeared in 1983. Others might cite Léon Danco as the seminal figure in the field. Danco's book, *Beyond Survival* (1975) stimulated attention toward attributes of family firms that were distinct from standard curricula in business college degree programs. A strong argument could be made for an article that has become a classic in the scholarly literature on family firms, "Transferring power in the family business" by Barnes and Hershon, which appeared in the *Harvard Business Review* in 1976. Published in a journal read by both practitioners and academics, this article continues to be frequently cited in the family business literature.

In addition to these contributions, two other factors played important roles in family business gaining a foothold at universities:

- Family business programs have proliferated at universities. The University of Pennsylvania formed the first one in 1979. The second was created at Oregon State University in 1985. Today, there are more than one hundred in the United States, plus programs in at least ten other countries. These institutes, forums, and centers are typically organized to provide continuing education and consulting to family owned firms. In doing so, they provide faculty with access to data for research and publishing.

- The Family Firm Institute (FFI) was founded in 1986 as a nexus for those concerned with family enterprises. The FFI is an international professional membership organization that provides interdisciplinary education and networking opportunities for family business advisors, consultants, educators, and researchers. The diverse membership of FFI includes consultants, attorneys, accountants, therapists, financial advisors, academics, and others who have family owned firms as their clientele. In 1988, FFI launched *Family Business Review*, the only scholarly journal devoted to family business. Through *FBR*, researchers have an outlet for the findings of their family enterprise investigations.

A major issue in assessing the quality, trends, and contributions of family business research has been the lack of a generally accepted definition of family business. This problem is not unique to this field, but is shared with entrepreneurship and many behavioral sciences.

DEFINITIONS

In an exhaustive literature review, Sharma, Chrisman, and Chua (1996) found 34 distinct definitions of the term "family business." They vary on such dimensions as ownership, management, employment, relationships, interaction, and generational involvement. Regarding the last, one of the debates among those conducting research is whether family participation must be multi-generational in order to qualify. In the inaugural issue of *Family Business Review*, the editors announced a policy of not defining the term, but requiring authors to state specifically their operational definition when submitting a paper for consideration. Thus, readers will know what a family business is for any given study, but variation across articles may reduce the ability to generalize or aggregate findings.

Just as the term "entrepreneurship" has become a domain label under which multiple subjects are encompassed (e.g., angel investors, global start-ups, intrapreneurship, small business, venture capital, etc.), family business is not merely a defined entity. Multiple and inter-relating disciplines make up the body of knowledge in family business.

BODY OF KNOWLEDGE

The FFI created a Body of Knowledge Task Force in 1995 and designated it a permanent committee in 1997. The mission of the committee is "to identify and integrate existing and emerging knowledge about family businesses" from and for the various disciplines represented in the membership of the Institute (Family Firm Institute, 2003: 1). The contents of this body of knowledge may constitute a proxy for the domain of family business. Acknowledging the complexity and diversity of the field, the committee identified four major content areas with which a family business expert should have familiarity:

- Behavioral science
- Finance
- Law
- Management science

Sharma, Chrisman, and Chua published their annotated bibliography, mentioned above, in 1996. Drawing from the American Business Index – Global, they observed that only 188 family business-related articles were published between 1971 and 1985, but for 1986 to 1995 they could document 680 articles. The preponderance of the studies they reviewed fell within a strategic management framework. The editors classified the literature into six strategy categories: goals and objectives, strategy formulation and content, strategy implementation and design, strategic evaluation and control, general management and ownership issues, and organizational evolution and change. The general management and ownership issues category contains the bulk of the research on succession, which Sharma, Chrisman, and Chua found to

represent approximately 20 percent of the entire family business literature. They labeled their second major framework for classification "family influence on the business."

Dyer and Sánchez (1998) presented a retrospective of the research that had appeared in the first decade of *Family Business Review*. They found that the scholarly articles were dominated by management professors. Of the 226 academic-based authors who were listed over the 10-year period, 174 were in management departments. This dominance occurred despite the intent by the journal and its parent, the Family Firm Institute, to be multidisciplinary. The most frequent topics addressed in the articles were:

- Interpersonal family dynamics
- Succession
- Interpersonal business dynamics
- Business performance and growth

Within these various disciplines are topics that fall within the domain of entrepreneurship.

FAMILY BUSINESS AND ENTREPRENEURSHIP

The Entrepreneurship Division of the Academy of Management incorporated the study and teaching of family business in its original domain statement. The fields, however, do not completely overlap. Family business is predominantly focused on the firm and its survival from generation to generation. It is concerned with the healthy functioning of both the enterprise and the family unit. Financially, the focus is on wealth retention. With entrepreneurship, attention is given to pre-venture activities: opportunity recognition, start-up capital, feasibility assessment. Innovation and early stage survival issues take precedence. The focus is on wealth creation and harvesting. Subjects such as psychological counseling and estate planning are rarely found in the entrepreneurship literature.

An early attempt to link family business and entrepreneurship was offered by Hoy and Verser (1994). Working from Gartner's (1990) effort to identify elements of the entrepreneurship domain, they proposed a set of continua on which entrepreneurship topics and family business topics were clearly delineated on each end, but merged in the center.

More recently, the *Journal of Business Venturing* produced two special issues on family business. The first resulted from a conference held in Edmonton, co-sponsored by the University of Alberta and the University of Calgary in 2001. The organizers of the conference (Chrisman, Chua, and Steier, 2003) contended that theories can be applied to the nexus of entrepreneurship and family business. They based their argument on four observations from prior research:

1 Many, if not a majority, of new ventures are created with family involvement.
2 Entrepreneurship is a special case of strategic management and the formation of family firms demonstrates the confluence of economic and non-economic considerations that influence strategic decisions.
3 Family business entrepreneurs seek to build businesses that are also family institutions.
4 The appointment of an entrepreneurial leader may be the key to successful family firm succession.

The conference brought together experts in various academic fields to examine whether family firms are in any ways different from non-family firms, and, if so, whether these differences lead to competitive advantages or disadvantages.

A second set of papers from the Edmonton conference appeared in *Entrepreneurship: Theory and Practice* (Chua, Chrisman, and Steier, 2003). In these, the authors wrestled with definitional issues, but the issue's major contribution was to examine negative economic consequences of family involvement through the lens of agency cost theory and to contrast that perspective with the benefits suggested by the resource-based view. The subsequent issue of the *Journal of Business Venturing*, while developed independently of their work, is a natural extension of their theory building, by attempting to find connections between family business and entrepreneurship research (Rogoff and Heck, 2003). The editors contend that research in the two fields followed parallel tracks, with three areas of commonality: (1) a focus on the business; (2) examination of traditional business dimensions such as strategy, management, production, labor, and

performance; and (3) investigation of organizational stages and transitions.

When the three issues are taken together, the emergence of prospective research streams in the overlapping domains becomes evident. A few potentially productive directions of flow follow:

● Family systems theory has had limited impact on family business research because of the emphasis on the business to the exclusion of the family. Changing definitions and compositions of "family" in North America may be having dramatic effects on business formation, growth, and survival that systems theory may help scholars to understand and predict.
● New applications of the resource-based view of the firm and agency cost theory are helping to explain the tension that exists between rational decision-making and altruism in financing family business creation and survival.
● Succession, the dominant theme of family business literature, is being redefined at the nexus with entrepreneurship, with evidence suggesting that the successor's role is not necessarily to bring professional management skills to the firm, but to infuse an organization in mature or declining stages with an innovative spark or entrepreneurial vigor.

CONCLUSION

Traditionally, management education has attempted to instruct students in applying logic and engaging in rational decision-making. The encroachment of family business programs in schools of business, combined with research studies that demonstrate the impact of family relationships on company performance, forces reconsideration of widely accepted theories and models. In particular, entrepreneurship scholars are incorporating family concepts and issues into their studies. Graduates who enter entrepreneurial careers are likely to draw on family members for financing, labor, advice, networking, and other associated activities. The fledgling connections of the fields are more likely to expand than to be severed.

Bibliography

Astrachan, J. H. (2003). Commentary on the special issue: The emergence of a field. *Journal of Business Venturing*, 18: 567–72.

Barnes, L. H. and Hershon, S. A. (1976). Transferring power in the family business. *Harvard Business Review*, 53 (4): 105–14.

Chrisman, J. J., Chua, J. H., and Steier, L. P. (2003). An introduction to theories of family business. *Journal of Business Venturing*, 18: 441–8.

Chua, J. H., Chrisman, J. J., and Steier, L. P. (2003). Extending the theoretical horizons of family business research. *Entrepreneurship: Theory and Practice*, 27: 331–8.

Danco, L. (1975). *Beyond Survival: A Business Owner's Guide for Success*. Cleveland, OH: University Press.

Dyer, W. G. and Sánchez, M. (1998). Current state of family business theory and practice as reflected in *Family Business Review* 1988–1997. *Family Business Review*, 11: 287–96.

Family Firm Institute (2003). *The Body of Knowledge (BOK) Book*. Boston, MA: Family Firm Institute.

Gartner, W. B. (1990). What are we talking about when we are talking about entrepreneurship? *Journal of Business Venturing*, 5: 15–28.

Hoy, F. and Verser, T. G. (1994). Emerging business, emerging field: Entrepreneurship and the family firm. *Entrepreneurship: Theory and Practice*, 19: 9–23.

Rogoff, E. G. and Heck, R. K. Z. (2003). Evolving research in entrepreneurship and family business: Recognizing family as the oxygen that feeds the fire of entrepreneurship. *Journal of Business Venturing*, 18: 559–66.

Sharma, P., Chrisman, J. J., and Chua, J. H. (eds.) (1996). *A Review and Annotated Bibliography of Family Business Studies*. Boston, MA: Kluwer Academic Publishers.

franchising

Steven C. Michael

Franchising, where independent businesses operate under a shared trademark using a common production process, is an organizational form used primarily by service businesses. Franchising is big business in the economy at large, carrying 10 percent of US retail trade and services. Franchising is also commonly used as a method of international entrepreneurship; a recent survey identified over 1 million franchisees worldwide.

Historically, franchising was introduced in the United States in the early twentieth century by manufacturers in order to secure local distribution of their product. Franchise chains formed at that time still dominate automobile and gasoline retailing and soft drink and beer distribution. This type of franchising is called product franchising. A second type, business format franchising, arose in the 1950s by entrepreneurs in services industries and is the subject of this article. Franchising is an important method for entrepreneurs who develop new concepts and products in services to assemble resources efficiently, to grow the firm rapidly, and to manage it effectively.

HOW FRANCHISING WORKS

The mechanics of business format franchising are as follows. A franchise is a legal contract between the owner of a production process and a trademark (the franchisor, such as McDonald's) and a local business person (franchisee) to sell products or services under the franchisor's trademark, employing a production process developed by the franchisor. When a franchise contract is signed, the franchisee pays a lump sum, a franchise fee. After signing the contract, the franchisor gives the franchisee services needed to open the unit, including training and blueprints for the production process, and in some cases support for site selection or construction management. The franchisee typically makes all necessary investments in land, building, and equipment to open the particular site.

After opening, the franchisor provides periodic inspection of the franchise (to ensure operating standards are being followed), access to trademarks, and marketing services (such as advertising and new product development). In return for these services, the franchisee pays a royalty on sales (typically ranging between 1–10 percent) and a royalty for marketing expenses (from 0–6 percent), commonly called the advertising fee. Generally, franchisees do not sell products of the franchisor (although important exceptions exist); the franchisor is compensated for the trademark and its management. The franchise chain is composed of units franchised to local operators and units owned by the franchisor. Both types operate the same production process and sell under the same trademark, but most franchise chains are primarily composed of franchised units.

As an organizational form, franchising has a large and visible presence in consumer industries such as restaurants, lodging, auto repair, real estate, hair styling, and specialty retailing, where it has captured typically 30–40 percent of sales. Business services where franchising is prominent include temporary employment, commercial cleaning, printing and copying, tax preparation, and accounting services. Recent areas of growth include home healthcare, business signage, and child development and education. Moreover, franchising's share of sales ranges from 71 percent of the printing and copying market to 0.5 percent of the accounting market. But the wide range of shares indicates the importance of industry-specific factors in the choice of organizational form. Product differentiation in these service and trading businesses is large, grounded in the physical dispersion and localized monopolies of units and in the heterogeneity of customers' tastes.

WHY FRANCHISING?

Strategically, franchising is an organizational form chosen by entrepreneurs in order to compete in certain industries. Services entrepreneurs choose franchising in order to solve the problem of agency or the problem of resource scarcity. The problem of agency occurs when one person works for another; the agent sometimes pursues her own interest at the expense of the principal. For example, employees (agents) typically do not work as hard as their employer (principal) would like. When operating a chain of dispersed service outlets, each outlet typically requires intensive on-site supervision. Franchising makes the local supervisor the owner of the local business, granting to the supervisor-franchisee the profits after all expenses have been paid. Requiring site managers to invest their own capital and giving them profits after costs induces the franchisee-manager to put forth more effort in supervision than would a corporate employee-manager. Through franchising, greater operational efficiency is obtained, and the agency problem is mitigated.

The problem of resource scarcity notes that service entrepreneurs face constraints to growth. The entrepreneur requires financial capital for

rollout of the successful business concept across the nation. (Lacking physical assets or sophisticated technology, service firms face particular difficulties in financing.) The entrepreneur also requires information regarding desirable locations for the business, as well as information regarding sources of labor supply. Finally, the entrepreneur requires site managers to implement the proven business concept at dispersed locations. Franchising gives access to all three of these resources rapidly through the use of franchisees, who provide their own capital, their own knowledge of geographic locations and labor markets, and their own managerial labor to the chain. The two theories, agency and resource scarcity, are complementary, particularly if resource scarcity is taken to explain a short-run decision while agency explains the persistence of franchising.

CONSEQUENCES OF USING FRANCHISING

By using franchisees' capital (rather than bankers'), by using franchisees' geographic knowledge (rather than consultants'), and by encouraging franchisees to self-select for management (rather than engaging in a hiring process), franchising is widely regarded to facilitate rapid growth by entrepreneurs. Services typically lack intellectual property protection, so rapid growth is often the only way to secure first mover advantage. In particular, services such as retailing and restaurants typically must be delivered at a particular place, so preemption of valuable real estate may be possible. Also, the first entrepreneur in service and retail trade may shape customer preferences for the hamburger, the motel, or the copy shop in directions that benefit the first mover (e.g., two all-beef patties must have a particular "special sauce" in order to be desirable). A premium is then created on rapid expansion of geographic sites. More sites allow the preemption of more real estate, and more sites also allow for a broader base of customers to experience the product in order to shape their preferences.

The gains of faster growth and first mover advantage come at a cost, however. Franchise chains are created by legal contracts, not employment relationships. As a result, franchisees are much more independent than employees, and therefore the franchisor has less control than a fully owned chain. Each franchisee is free to set his own pricing, for example, making chain-wide promotion difficult.

In addition to problems of coordination, the sharing of the trademark across independent entities creates the risk of free-riding. The power of the franchise chain is that it shares a trademark across multiple units, allowing customers to link consumption experiences in time and space. That trademark requires investment in intangible but costly items such as advertising and quality control, for which costs are specific to one franchisee but benefits are shared across franchisees. For example, a billboard erected by one franchisee may induce a customer to stop at a unit of the chain owned by another franchisee. The potential for free-riding is created due to this shared trademark.

To claim that free-riding *can* occur is not the same as claiming that free-riding *does* occur. Franchisors are aware of the risk of free-riding and take a number of managerial actions to reduce or mitigate the problem. Despite these efforts, research has shown that free-riding does occur; franchise chains have lower quality and less advertising than owned chains (chains that do not employ franchising at all). The failure to control quality is at least in part due to the difficulties of termination. Termination of the franchise relationship is the primary sanction available to the franchisor, but it is a blunt instrument that can only be used with the supervision of the court.

The individuals who purchase franchises (franchisees) are entrepreneurs of a different sort. While not innovators, they do bear risk and they do bring a novel product bearing a trademark to a particular location or customer group. In general, failure rates for franchisees are similar or a little lower than failure rates for independent entrepreneurs in services. Returns, however, are generally higher because of the participation in the franchise chain. Therefore, buying a franchise is often a good choice for some entrepreneurs.

CONCLUSION

Franchising is best viewed as a resource assembly method that enables the entrepreneur in service industries to assemble necessary resources to quickly exploit opportunity. The entrepreneur develops an innovation in retail trade or services, and turns to franchising to develop resources quickly in order to gather persons, sites, and money needed for expansion. Rapid expansion is necessary in order to secure desirable real estate and desirable mind space against potential imitators. Franchising also provides an ongoing supply of motivated managers for dispersed operations. In a world where resources are scarce, whether managerial, informational, or financial, franchising as a method of rapid expansion becomes a crucial strategic decision.

For a guide to the business details of franchising, Bond and Bond (annual) issue a list of franchises and an overview for potential franchisees. The most integrative academic article addressing agency and competitive effects is Caves and Murphy (1976). For a discussion of the two reasons for franchising, see Combs and Ketchen (1999). For a discussion of the potential for rapid growth, see Shane (1996) and Michael (2003). For a discussion of the problems of free-riding, see Michael (2000).

Bibliography

Bond, R. E. and Bond, C. E. (annual). *The Source Book of Franchising Opportunities*. Homewood, IL: Dow Jones-Irwin.
Caves, R. E. and Murphy, W. F. (1976). Franchising: Firms, markets, and intangible assets. *Southern Economic Journal*, 42: 572–86.
Combs, J. G. and Ketchen, D. J. (1999). Can capital scarcity help agency theory explain franchising? A test of the capital scarcity hypothesis. *Academy of Management Journal*, 42: 196–207.
Michael, S. C. (2000). The effect of organizational form on quality: The case of franchising. *Journal of Economic Behavior and Organization*, 43: 295–318.
Michael, S. C. (2003). First mover advantage through franchising. *Journal of Business Venturing*, 18: 61–80.
Shane, S. (1996). Hybrid organizational arrangements and their implications for firm growth and survival: A study of new franchisors. *Academy of Management Journal*, 39: 216–34.

G

geographic location and regional variation in entrepreneurship

Entrepreneurial activity does not exist within a vacuum; rather, it is activity which is firmly rooted in the context in which it is being undertaken. Ventures are created and grown and succeed or fail within specific geographic contexts that may be more or less munificent along a number of dimensions. These dimensions include risk capital, skilled labor, technical and scientific knowledge, specialized suppliers, supportive cultural norms and values, and social capital/networks. The idea that the munificence of the geographic location of a venture matters is supported by findings that the level of relevant activity occurring within the venture's geographic location complements the venture's on-going R&D (Zucker, Darby, and Brewer, 1998), increases its ability to develop new products (Deeds, DeCarolis, and Coombs, 1999), and makes the venture more attractive to investors (DeCarolis and Deeds, 1999). Each of these findings highlights critical benefits that a geographic location can provide to entrepreneurial ventures. However, research has also documented declining and even negative effects of concentration on venture research productivity (Deeds, DeCarolis, and Coombs, 1999) and the rate of venture IPOs (Stuart and Sorenson, 2003). It appears that competition for resources within a highly concentrated geography reduces ventures' ability to create new products or access the resources required to become a public company.

Research shows that the rate, scope, and success of entrepreneurial activity vary across regions. Silicon Valley has achieved international renown as a hot-bed of entrepreneurial activity, but metropolitan areas as diverse as Seattle, San Diego, Washington DC, Atlanta, Austin, Minneapolis, and Boston have also achieved notoriety as hot beds of entrepreneurship. Alternatively, cities such as Cleveland, St. Louis, Buffalo, Detroit, Houston, Birmingham, and others have such low levels of entrepreneurial activity and success that fostering entrepreneurship has become a major focus of policymakers in these regions. The remainder of this essay explores both what we know about the roots of regional variation in entrepreneurial activity and what we do not know, by examining several streams of literature, including agglomeration economics, social networks and social capital, cultural norms and values, and amenities, culture, and bohemians.

The tendency for ventures in an industry to cluster has been noted in economics for decades. Marshall's troika of benefits – labor pooling, specialized suppliers, and knowledge spillovers – underpins most of the research in this stream. The basic idea is that as ventures with similar needs and pursuits cluster in a specific geographic location, competitive benefits accrue to those ventures because of a larger pool of labor with the skill base required. This provides ventures with more flexibility to adjust their labor base to market demands and improves their ability to recruit skilled labor. An active job market, which provides numerous alternative employers to potential hires, may be particularly important to new ventures, given their high risk of failure. Highly skilled employees are unlikely to uproot their lives to move to a region where there are few alternative employers. Thus, geographic areas with clusters of new ventures are likely to have higher rates of formation, growth, and success because they have access to a superior labor force.

Ventures in a geographic cluster benefit from specialized suppliers of the inputs needed by entrepreneurial ventures: risk capital, legal know-how, experienced value-added investors, and even landlords familiar with the needs and requirements of new ventures. The clustering of venture capitalists and suppliers of risk capital, advice, and contacts has been well documented. What is less well documented is the specialization of the suppliers of legal services, consultants, educational institutions, and landlords. As a simple example of the benefits of specialized suppliers, landlords familiar with the needs and challenges of new ventures in areas such as Silicon Valley frequently waive deposits or tenant improvement fees, in exchange for warrants, options, or future payments. This immediately lowers the cash outflow of the venture, allowing it to focus more of its resources on the important early stage process of product or service development.

Perhaps the best-researched benefits of clustering are knowledge spillovers. The localization of knowledge transfer is well documented. There is strong evidence that firms and universities tend to acquire new knowledge from within their own region (Jaffe, Trajtenberg, and Henderson, 1993). There is also evidence that alliances and supply contracts are localized (von Hippel, 1988), as are social networks (Rogers and Larsen, 1984). Research has also found that industries in which new knowledge is critical have a greater propensity to cluster than other industries (Audretsch and Stephan, 1996).

Geographic proximity of organizations with similar interests and expertise promotes the natural exchange of ideas through both formal and informal networks (Deeds, DeCarolis, and Coombs, 1999; Saxenian, 1994) and creates opportunities to capture knowledge spillovers. Knowledge spillovers have been credited for the relationship between venture proximity to major sources of scientific research and venture productivity (Zucker, Darby, and Armstrong, 1998). A locally bounded network has advantages in both costs and ease of knowledge transfer. Bounding the network locally restricts the search for partners and in turn decreases search costs, as well as travel costs and communication costs. Each specific geographic location generally has a common set of cultural norms and values, practices and terminology which serve to facilitate the flow of information between parties (Saxenian, 1994). Geographic proximity also reduces the costs and increases the frequency of personal interactions that create social relations and enhances trust among the participants in a network (Porter, 1998).

The assumption that localized knowledge spillovers are freely available to ventures has come under question (Zucker, Darby, and Brewer, 1998). Locating in the right area may not be sufficient to benefit from the region's knowledge; rather, tapping knowledge external to the venture requires the venture to establish a network of relationships with the sources of knowledge. Knowledge may not be freely available; knowledge may be available primarily through network connections between ventures and the sources of knowledge (i.e., scientists, university departments, research institutes, etc.). Given the importance of knowledge acquisition in the entrepreneurial process, the munificence of a geographic location is likely to influence the amount of entrepreneurial activity, size, and scope of the ventures created, and their rate of success and failure.

Recently, work on geography and entrepreneurial activity has expanded beyond the boundaries of the work of Marshall to consider both regional culture and the attractiveness of the region as a place to live and work. Busenitz, Gomez, and Spencer (2000) developed and validated a three-construct profile of a country's institutional profile for entrepreneurship. Their constructs of the regulatory, cognitive, and normative characteristics of a country provide a basis for examining the effects of various institutional arrangements within a country (perhaps even a region) on entrepreneurial activity. The regulatory dimension considers the legal and governmental aspects that affect the costs and risks of entrepreneurship. The cognitive dimension is an attempt to assess the knowledge and skills possessed by the people in a region or a country about the establishment and operation of a new business. Finally, the normative dimension is an attempt to assess the region's cultural support for entrepreneurship by looking at the level of admiration for entrepreneurs, as well as the value placed on innovation, risk taking, and creativity. While validated, these measures provide an opportunity for serious research into the role of cultural and institutional arrangements in regional variation in entrepreneurship. This is an area that is ripe for additional research, with the potential to have an important effect on public policy.

Recently, significant work in the field of economic geography has focused on the quality of a region's labor pool, and the requirements for creating, attracting, and maintaining high quality/skilled labor in a region. For example, work by Florida (2002) on diversity and "Bohemians" argues that tolerance of diversity is critical to the attraction and retention of knowledge workers at the center of today's entrepreneurial economy. While still evolving, this stream of research indicates that a tolerant and diverse region with significant amenities will attract the type of creative labor force and provide the type of cultural values that support entrepreneurial activity.

Regional variation in entrepreneurship is a complex phenomenon and difficult to explain. Beginning with the work of Marshall (1920), economists and more recently management scholars, economic geographers, and sociologists have all begun to examine this regional variation. While we are a long way from explaining the variation, Marshall's troika of labor pooling, specialized suppliers, and knowledge spillovers remains the basis for much of what we know. The more current areas of research, such as culture, social networks, diversity, and amenities, do not refute Marshall's ideas, but rather extend our understanding of how areas develop a regional advantage in the quality of the skilled labor pool and the mechanisms by which knowledge spillovers are captured. Future research is likely to entail longitudinal studies on the interplay between regional characteristics and entrepreneurial outcomes that examine not only the relationship between regional characteristics and entrepreneurial activity, but also explore the causal relationships among these variables.

Bibliography

Audretsch, D. B. and Stephan, P. E. (1996). Company–scientist location links: The case of biotechnology. *American Economic Review*, 86: 641–52.

Busenitz, L., Gomez, C., and Spencer, J. W. (2000). Country institutional profiles: Unlocking entrepreneurial phenomena. *Academy of Management Journal*, 43: 994–1003.

DeCarolis, D. and Deeds, D. L. (1999). The impact of stocks and flows of organizational knowledge on firm performance: An empirical investigation of the biotechnology industry. *Strategic Management Journal*, 20: 953–68.

Deeds, D. L., DeCarolis, D., and Coombs, J. E. (1997). The impact of timing and firm capabilities on the amount of capital raised in an initial public offering: Evidence from the biotechnology industry. *Journal of Business Venturing*, 12: 31–46.

Deeds, D. L., DeCarolis, D., and Coombs, J. E. (1999). Dynamic capabilities and new product development in high-technology ventures: An empirical analysis of new biotechnology firms. *Journal of Business Venturing*, 15: 211–29.

Florida, R. (2002). Bohemia and economic geography. *Journal of Economic Geography*, 2: 55–71.

Jaffe, A. B., Trajtenberg, M., and Henderson, R. (1993). Geographic localization of knowledge spillovers as evidenced by patent citations. *Quarterly Journal of Economics*, 108: 577–98.

Krugman, P. (1991). *Geography and Trade*. Cambridge, MA: MIT Press.

Marshall, A. (1920). *Industry and Trade*. London: Macmillan.

Porter, M. E. (1998). Clusters and the new economics of competition. *Harvard Business Review*, 76 (6): 77–90.

Rogers, E. M. and Larsen, J. K. (1984). *Silicon Valley Fever: Growth of High-Technology Culture*. New York: Basic Books.

Saxenian, A. (1994). *Culture and Competition in Silicon Valley and Route 128*. Cambridge, MA: Harvard University Press.

Stuart, T. and Sorenson, O. (2003). The geography of opportunity: Spatial heterogeneity in founding rates and the performance of biotechnology firms. *Research Policy*, 32 (2): 229–53.

von Hippel, E. (1988). *The Sources of Innovation*. New York: Oxford University Press.

Zucker, L. G., Darby, M. R., and Armstrong, J. (1998). Geographically localized knowledge: Spillovers or markets? *Economic Inquiry*, 36: 65–86.

Zucker, L. G., Darby, M. R., and Brewer, M. B. (1998). Intellectual human capital and the birth of US biotechnology enterprises. *American Economic Review*, 88: 290–306.

H

habitual entrepreneurs

Deniz Ucbasaran, Paul Westhead, and Mike Wright

Entrepreneurial behavior is increasingly recognized as heterogeneous. One notable source of heterogeneity is based on variations in the level of experience among entrepreneurs. This has led to the distinction between experienced ("habitual") entrepreneurs and first-time ("novice") entrepreneurs, and among habitual entrepreneurs, "serial" and "portfolio" entrepreneurs.

DEFINING NOVICE, HABITUAL, SERIAL, AND PORTFOLIO ENTREPRENEURS

Ownership rights are crucial for undertaking entrepreneurship, as they allow the entrepreneur to make decisions about the coordination of resources that will generate entrepreneurial profits. Entrepreneurship does not only involve the creation of an enterprise. Thus, we can distinguish novice and habitual entrepreneurs as follows. *Novice entrepreneurs* represent individuals who have no prior experience of owning a business, but currently have a majority equity stake in a single independent business, or a minority stake among a team, which they have either established, purchased, or inherited.

Defining habitual entrepreneurs is a conceptually difficult task and there is no generally accepted definition. Building on earlier work, Westhead et al. (2003) define *habitual entrepreneurs* to include individuals who have or have had a minority and/or majority equity stake in two or more businesses which were established, purchased, and/or inherited.

Among habitual entrepreneurs, two subtypes have been distinguished which depend on whether business ownership experience was acquired sequentially or concurrently. *Serial entrepreneurs* are individuals who have sold/closed at least one business in which they had a minority or majority ownership stake and currently have a minority or majority ownership stake in a single independent business that has been either established, purchased, or inherited. In contrast, *portfolio entrepreneurs* are individuals who currently have minority and/or majority ownership stakes in two or more independent businesses that have either been established, purchased, and/or inherited.

AMOUNT OF HABITUAL ENTREPRENEURSHIP

Studies conducted in the UK suggest that 12–44 percent of respondents in private firms are habitual entrepreneurs. This wide spread in the UK may be attributed to differences in definitions and samples used. Some studies report figures relating to specific regions within the UK, while others report figures relating to representative samples in Great Britain. Where representative samples are used, the figures tend to oscillate around 37 percent, but tend to focus on habitual founders of firms alone. A survey in Great Britain found that serial and portfolio entrepreneurs respectively owned 25 percent and 12 percent of independent firms (Westhead and Wright, 1998). Evidence from the USA, Australia, and Malaysia suggests that 51 percent, 49 percent, and 38 percent of respondents, respectively, are habitual entrepreneurs. Detected differences may in part be due to definitional and sample variations. They may also be due to infrastructural and cultural variations, such as how active the capital market in each country is, government policies (e.g., towards failed businesses and entrepreneurs), and attitudes towards entrepreneurship and risk.

CONCEPTS

Human capital theory offers a fertile ground for understanding the differences between entrepreneurs in terms of their business ownership experience. Entrepreneurial experience may be viewed as a contributor to an entrepreneur's human capital (Gimeno et al., 1997; Ucbasaran et al., 2003). In particular, business ownership experience is a component of entrepreneurship-specific human capital (i.e., largely applicable to the entrepreneurship domain). Business ownership experience may provide entrepreneurs with access to a variety of resources that can be utilized in identifying and exploiting subsequent opportunities, such as first-hand knowledge of how to start or purchase a business; additional managerial experience; an enhanced reputation (if successful); better access to financial capital (and potentially on better terms); and broader social capital (i.e., networks). The development of subsequent businesses owned by habitual entrepreneurs can therefore be enhanced by overcoming the liabilities of newness and attaining developmental milestones quicker, relative to novice entrepreneurs (Starr and Bygrave, 1991). As a result of their experience, habitual entrepreneurs can develop broader and more diverse human capital than their novice counterparts.

Human capital includes cognitive characteristics. The interrelationship between cognition and experience provides a basis for understanding how business ownership experience can shape an entrepreneur's human capital (Ucbasaran et al., 2003). Expert information processing theory suggests that differences in the cognition of "experts" and "novices" can be partly attributed to their levels of experience. "Experts" are viewed as having more extensive and elaborate knowledge structures than "novices." Further, "experts" are able to manipulate incoming information into recognizable patterns (i.e., unify disparate information), and then match the information to appropriate actions. This ability reduces the burden of cognitive processing, which can allow the "expert" to concentrate on novel or unique material. Habitual entrepreneurs may be more reliant on information processing resembling that of an "expert." Also, they may display a stronger reliance on entrepreneurial cognition, which is the result of a combination of schematic factors (i.e., perception of greater chances of success, more behavioural control, and greater reliance on decision-making shortcuts) and often based on the use of heuristics in decision-making. While business ownership is associated with several assets, it can also be associated with a number of liabilities, such as hubris and denial of mistakes made. Denial involves attributing mistakes to external reasons when they should be attributed to the entrepreneur. Habitual entrepreneurs who have learned from previous failures and successes generally avoid decision-making biases (e.g., hubris and insufficient adjustments resulting in the repetition of past errors).

The distinction between serial and portfolio entrepreneurs can be analyzed in terms of two career anchors; that is, the pattern of self-perceived talents, motives, and values which serve to guide, constrain, stabilize, and integrate the person's career. The first anchor is that of autonomy/independence, which represents a desire for freedom from rules and the control of others. The second is the entrepreneurship anchor, which focuses on the creation of something new, involving the motivation to overcome obstacles, the willingness to run risks, and the desire for personal prominence in whatever is accomplished (Schein, 1985). Individuals associated with the autonomy anchor tend to be involved in ventures one at a time (like serial entrepreneurs), whereas those associated with an entrepreneurship anchor tend to be involved in multiple ventures simultaneously (like portfolio entrepreneurs) (Katz, 1994). Consequently, their respective career anchors may explain differences between serial and portfolio entrepreneurs.

Rosa (1998) explored the process of business cluster formation by portfolio entrepreneurs and suggested that there may be a blurring between the boundaries of serial and portfolio entrepreneurs, as the latter may exit from some of their businesses, introducing a "serial" dimension to their behavior. Furthermore, Wright, Robbie, and Ennew (1997) identified heterogeneity among serial entrepreneurs in terms of their motivations and the methods used to develop their ventures. Among novice entrepreneurs there may be a need to distinguish between one-time entrepreneurs and those that will move on to becoming habitual entrepreneurs. Considering an entrepreneur who has been involved in a venture for 20 years as a novice just because they have only owned a single business may be inappropriate.

Evidence

Several studies have found differences between novice and habitual entrepreneurs in terms of their demographic and background characteristics (e.g., age, education, gender, parental background) (Birley and Westhead, 1993; Kolvereid and Bullvåg, 1993). Serial and portfolio entrepreneurs have been found to differ in terms of their motivations and background characteristics (Westhead and Wright, 1998) and business gestation practices (Alsos and Kolvereid, 1998).

Central findings from the most recent and comprehensive study by Westhead et al. (2003) are that portfolio entrepreneurs are more likely than serial or novice entrepreneurs to seek personal wealth from business ownership, to perceive themselves as having higher organizing ability and the ability to identify good opportunities, to use a wide range of information sources in searching for opportunities, to have more equity partners (i.e., team members), to recruit the most talented people, and to use more external finance. Serial entrepreneurs were more likely than portfolio entrepreneurs to rely more on previous contacts in searching for opportunities, to see themselves as having technical or functional expertise, and to have failed to spot any opportunities within the last five years.

Few studies have found that the businesses owned by habitual entrepreneurs outperform their novice counterparts. This may be because business ownership has both liabilities, such as hubris and denial (Starr and Bygrave, 1991), as well as assets. This suggests that among habitual entrepreneurs there is a need to distinguish between expert habitual entrepreneurs and experienced habitual entrepreneurs. The former may be viewed as having the ability to reflect on and learn from their experiences, while this is not the case for the latter. Based on a sample of Scottish firms, Westhead et al. (2003) found that portfolio entrepreneurs outperformed both novice

and serial entrepreneurs in terms of sales and employment growth.

Implications

Public policy has generally focused on supporting the supply of novice entrepreneurs. Recognition of the contributions made by habitual entrepreneurs suggests that rather than provision of blanket support to all types of entrepreneurs, regardless of need and ability, policymakers and practitioners should support the specific needs of habitual entrepreneurs, as well as novice entrepreneurs. To broaden the entrepreneurial pool and increase the future stocks of serial and portfolio entrepreneurs, novice entrepreneurs could be encouraged to acquire some of the skills accumulated by successful habitual entrepreneurs, particularly portfolio entrepreneurs.

Bibliography

Alsos, G. A. and Kolvereid, L. (1998). The business gestation process of novice, serial, and parallel business founders. *Entrepreneurship: Theory and Practice*, 22: 101–14.

Birley, S. and Westhead, P. (1993). A comparison of new businesses established by "novice" and "habitual" founders in Great Britain. *International Small Business Journal*, 12: 38–60.

Gimeno, J., Folta, T. B., Cooper, A. C., and Woo, C. Y. (1997). Survival of the fittest? Entrepreneurial human capital and the persistence of underperforming firms. *Administrative Science Quarterly*, 42: 750–83.

Katz, J. A. (1994). Modeling entrepreneurial career progressions: Concepts and considerations. *Entrepreneurship: Theory and Practice*, 19: 23–39.

Kolvereid, L. and Bullvåg, E. (1993). Novices versus experienced founders: An exploratory investigation. In S. Birley, I. MacMillan, and S. Subramony (eds.), *Entrepreneurship Research: Global Perspectives*. Amsterdam: Elsevier Science Publishers, 275–85.

Rosa, P. (1998). Entrepreneurial processes of business cluster formation and growth by "habitual" entrepreneurs. *Entrepreneurship: Theory and Practice*, 22: 43–61.

Schein, E. H. (1978). *Career Dynamics: Matching Individual and Organizational Needs*. Reading, MA: Addison-Wesley.

Schein, E. H. (1985). *Career Anchors: Discovering Your Real Values*. San Diego, CA: University Associates.

Starr, J. and Bygrave, W. (1991). The assets and liabilities of prior start-up experience: An exploratory study of multiple venture entrepreneurs. In N. C. Churchill, W. D. Bygrave, J. G. Covin, D. L. Sexton,

D. P. Slevin, K. H. Vesper, and W. E. Wetzel (eds.), *Frontiers of Entrepreneurship Research 1991*. Wellesley, MA: Babson College, 213–27.

Ucbasaran, D., Wright, M., Westhead, P., and Busenitz, L. (2003). The impact of entrepreneurial experience on opportunity identification and exploitation: Habitual and novice entrepreneurs. In J. A. Katz and D. A. Shepherd (eds.), *Cognitive Approaches to Entrepreneurship*: *Advances in Entrepreneurship, Firm Emergence, and Growth*, 6: 231–63.

Westhead, P. and Wright, M. (1998). Novice, portfolio, and serial founders: Are they different? *Journal of Business Venturing*, 13: 173–204.

Westhead, P., Ucbasaran, D., Wright, M., and Martin, F. (2003). Habitual entrepreneurs in Scotland: Characteristics, search processes, learning, and performance – Summary Report. Glasgow: Scottish Enterprise.

Wright, M., Robbie, K., and Ennew, C. (1997). Venture capitalists and serial entrepreneurs. *Journal of Business Venturing*, 12: 227–49.

harvesting the entrepreneurial venture

J. William Petty

INTRODUCTION

Harvesting is the final phase in the entrepreneurial value creation process, which includes building, growing, and harvesting. Harvesting is the process entrepreneurs and investors use to exit a business and liquidate their investment in a firm. While all three phases are important pieces of the entrepreneurial process, many entrepreneurs who fail to execute a successful harvest do not realize the full benefits of their years of labor.

Harvesting is the means for capturing or unlocking value, reducing risk, and creating exit options. It is about more than money, as it also involves personal and non-financial considerations. As a consequence, even upon realizing an acceptable monetary value for the firm, an entrepreneur who is not prepared for the lifestyle transition that accompanies the harvest may come away disappointed with the overall outcome. Thus, crafting a harvest strategy is as essential to the entrepreneur's personal success as it is to his or her financial success. The message to the entrepreneur is this: the time to develop an effective harvest strategy is now, not later.

As a firm moves toward the harvest, two questions regarding value are of primary importance. First, are the current owners/managers creating value? You can harvest only what you have created. Value is created when a firm's return on invested capital is greater than the investors' opportunity cost of funds, which relates both to the firm's operating profit margins and its efficient use of total capital invested. Second, could a new set of owners create more value than the current owners? If so, then the firm would have greater value in the hands of new owners. Growing a venture to the point of diminishing returns and then selling it to others who can carry it to the next level is a proven way to create value. How this incremental value will be shared between the old and the new owners depends largely on who wants the deal the most or who has the most leverage.

We will now look at the harvest options available to the entrepreneur. We then offer recommendations for avoiding problem areas in the harvest process.

HARVESTING OPTIONS: HOW DO WE CAPTURE THE VALUE CREATED?

There are three commonly used ways to harvest an investment: (1) selling the firm, (2) releasing the firm's free cash flows to its owners, or (3) offering stock to the public through an initial public offering (IPO).

Option 1: Selling the firm. Unquestionably, selling the firm is far and away the most common approach for entrepreneurs and investors to execute the harvest. The issues arising from the sale of a firm – like any harvest strategy – involve questions of how to value the firm as well as how to structure the deal. When selling a firm, the entrepreneur, for all practical purposes, has one of three choices: strategic sales, financial sales, and employee sales. The strategic buyer is interested in synergies, the financial buyer is interested in existing business cash flows, and the employee buyer is interested in preserving employment.

Strategic sale

From the seller's perspective, the key point in a strategic acquisition is that the value strategic buyers place on the business depends on the synergies that the buyers think they can create.

Since the value of the business to the buyers derives from both its stand-alone characteristics and its synergies, strategic buyers often pay a higher price than purely financial buyers, who value the business only as a stand-alone entity.

Financial sale

Financial buyers, unlike strategic buyers, look primarily to a firm's stand-alone cash-generating potential as the source of value. Often, the source of value the financial buyer hopes to tap relates to stimulating future sales growth, reducing costs, or both. This fact has an important implication for the owner of the firm being purchased. The buyer often will make changes in the firm's operations that translate into higher pressures on the firm's personnel and may result in decisions that the original owner was unwilling or unable to make, which frequently levies a high cost on the firm's employees.

Employee stock ownership plans

ESOPs are a way for a firm to be sold either in part or in total to its employees. A wide variety of companies have used these plans for many reasons. As a method of selling an entrepreneurial company, though, an ESOP appears to be the last resort, behind strategic and financial sales.

Option 2: Releasing the firm's free cash flows. The second harvesting strategy involves the orderly withdrawal of the owner's investment. The withdrawal process might be immediate if the owner simply sells off the assets of the firm and ceases business operations. However, for a value-creating firm – one that earns attractive rates of return for its investors – such would not make economic sense. The mere fact that a firm is earning rates of return that exceed the investors' opportunity cost of funds indicates that the company is worth more as a going concern than a dead one. Thus, we would not want to rationalize the company; instead, we could simply not continue to grow the business, and in so doing increase the "free cash flows" that can be returned to the investors.

In a firm's early years, all its cash flow is usually devoted to growing the firm. As a consequence, the firm's free cash flow during this period is zero or even negative, requiring its owners to seek outside cash to finance its growth. As the firm matures and the opportunity to grow the business declines, sizable free cash flows frequently become available to its owners. Rather than reinvesting all the cash flows in the company, the owners can begin to withdraw the cash, thus harvesting their investment. If they do so, only the amount of cash that is necessary to maintain current markets is retained and reinvested; thus, there would be little if any effort to grow the present markets or expand into new markets.

Harvesting by withdrawing the firm's cash outflow has two primary advantages: the owners can retain control of the firm while they harvest their investment, and they do not have to seek out a buyer or incur the expenses entailed in consummating a sale. There are disadvantages, however. Reducing reinvestment when the firm faces valuable growth opportunities results in lost value creation; it could leave the firm unable to sustain its competitive advantage while the owners are harvesting the venture. If so, the end result may be an unintended reduction in harvestable value, compared with the potential value of the firm as a long-term going concern. There may also be tax disadvantages to an orderly liquidation compared with other harvest methods. Finally, for the entrepreneur who is simply tired of day-to-day operations, siphoning off the free cash flows over time may require too much patience. Unless other people in the firm are qualified to manage it, this strategy may be doomed to failure.

Option 3: The IPO. Many entrepreneurs look to the prospect of an IPO as the "holy grail" of their career. However, in reality, an IPO is used primarily as a way to raise additional equity capital to finance company growth, and only secondarily as a way to harvest the owner's investment.

The IPO process may be one of the most exhilarating – but frustrating and exhausting – experiences of an entrepreneur's life. Managers frequently discover that they do not like being exposed to the variability of public capital markets and to the prying questions of public-market investors.

From the entrepreneur's perspective, it is necessary to consider the shift in power that occurs during the IPO process. When the chain of events begins, the company's management is in control. They can dictate whether or not to go public and who the investment banker will be. After the prospectus has been prepared and the road show is under way, however, the firm's management, including the entrepreneur, is no longer the primary decision-maker. The investment banker is now in control. Finally, the marketplace, in concert with the investment banker, begins to take over, and ultimately it is the market that dictates the final outcome. This process can be disconcerting to the entrepreneur if all does not go as expected.

In addition to the issue of who controls the events and decisions in the IPO process, it is important that the entrepreneur understand the investment banker's motivations in the process. Who is the investor banker's primary customer here? Clearly, the issuing firm is rewarding the underwriter for its services through the fees paid and participation in the deal. But the investment banker is also selling the securities to its customers, who typically will be involved in future deals. As a result, the investment banker may have a tendency to favor the buyers of the firm's stock more than the firm that is going public. The entrepreneur just needs to be aware of the potential conflict.

DEVELOPING AN EFFECTIVE HARVEST STRATEGY

Based on in-depth interviews with entrepreneurs, investors, and investment bankers located across the US who have been part of one or more company exits, we offer the following suggestions to avoid problems in exiting the venture (for the complete study, see Petty, Martin, and Kensinger, 1999).

When designing the terms of the harvest, cash is king.   Other things being equal, cash is generally preferred over stock and other forms of remuneration.

Anticipate the harvest.   Investors are always concerned about how to exit, and entrepreneurs need to have a similar mindset. Peter Hermann, general partner at Heritage Partners, a private equity investment group, notes: "People generally stumble into the exit and don't plan for it." However, for Hermann, "The exit strategy begins when the money goes in." Jack Kearney, formally at Rauscher, Pierce, and Refsnes, indicates that an exit strategy should be anticipated in advance, unless "the entrepreneur expects to die in the CEO chair. The worst of all worlds is to realize, for health or other reasons, that you have to sell the company right now" (Petty, Martin, and Kensinger, 1999: 55).

Having an exit plan in place is also important, because the window of opportunity can open and close quickly. The opportunity to exit is triggered by the arrival of a willing and able buyer, not just an interested seller. From the perspective of an IPO, hot markets may offer very attractive opportunities.

Having bought businesses does not prepare you for selling your company.   Entrepreneurs who have been involved in the acquisition of other firms are still ill-prepared for the strains and stresses associated with selling their own businesses. A buyer can be quite unemotional and detached, while a seller is likely to be much more concerned about non-financial considerations.

Get good advice.   Entrepreneurs learn to operate their businesses through experience gained in repeated day-to-day activities. However, they may engage in a harvest transaction only once in a lifetime. Thus, they have a real need for good advice, both from experienced professionals and from entrepreneurs who have personally been through a harvest. Jack Furst at Hicks, Muse, Tate, and Furst believes that advisors can give entrepreneurs a reality check. He contends that, without independent advice, entrepreneurs frequently fall prey to thinking they want to sell unconditionally, when in fact they really want to sell only if an unrealistically high price is offered.

It is also wise for an entrepreneur to talk to other entrepreneurs who have sold a firm or taken it public. Professional advice is vital, but entrepreneurs stress the importance of talking with someone who has exited a company.

Most of all, understand what you want.   For an entrepreneur, exiting a business that has been an integral part of life for a long time can be a very emotional experience. When an entrepreneur invests a substantial part of his or her working life in growing a business, a real sense of loss may accompany the harvest. Thus, entrepreneurs should think very carefully about their motives for exiting and what they plan to do after the exit. Entrepreneurs who exit their investment frequently have great expectations about what life is going to be like with a lot of liquidity, something many of them have never known. The exit does provide the long-sought liquidity, but some entrepreneurs find managing money – in contrast to operating their own company – less rewarding than they had expected.

Entrepreneurs may also become disillusioned when they come to understand more fully how their sense of personal identity was intertwined with their business. Peter Hermann states: "Seller's remorse is definitely a major issue for a number of entrepreneurs. Search your soul and make a list of what you want to achieve with the exit."

SUMMARY

Harvesting is the means entrepreneurs and investors use to exit a business and, ideally, unlock the value of their investment in the firm. It is more than merely selling and leaving a business. It involves capturing value (cash flows), reducing risk, and creating future options.

There are three basic ways to exit an investment in a privately owned company: (1) selling the firm, (2) releasing the firm's cash flows to its owners, or (3) offering stock either to the public markets or to private investors.

The following advice is offered to any entrepreneur wanting to harvest a business investment:

- Cash is king.
- Anticipate the harvest.
- Selling a firm is not the same as buying.
- Entrepreneurs have a real need for good advice, both from experienced professionals and from those who have personally been through an exit.
- Be careful what you wish for – you may get it. So understand what is important before harvesting your personal and financial investment in your company.

Bibliography

Petty, J. W., Martin, J., and Kensinger, J. (1999). *Harvesting Investments in Private Companies*. Newark, NJ: Financial Executive Research Foundation.

history of the academic study of entrepreneurship

Arnold C. Cooper

There have been entrepreneurs throughout human history. However, entrepreneurship, as an academic field of study, is quite young. The first course in entrepreneurship was apparently offered at the Harvard Business School in 1947 by Myles Mace. Early courses often dealt primarily with small business management. It was many years before business schools began to offer courses focusing upon entrepreneurship.

The first conference on small businesses and their problems was held at St. Gallen University in Switzerland in 1948 and has been held every other year since then. The predecessor organization of ICSB, the National Council for Small Business Management Development, grew from a conference on small business management development held at the University of Colorado in 1956. Many of the early leaders were with the US Small Business Administration. The organization had a strong orientation toward small business education and included many university educators involved in service or outreach programs. The name of the organization was changed to the International Council for Small Business in 1977.

The first academic conference on entrepreneurship research was at Purdue in the fall of 1970. It brought together 12 researchers to report upon their studies of technical entrepreneurship in various parts of the country.

Within the Academy of Management, Karl Vesper held an organizational meeting in 1974 for those interested in forming an Interest Group on Entrepreneurship. The Interest Group was formed as a part of the Division of Business Policy and Planning. The Entrepreneurship Interest Group did not achieve full status as the Entrepreneurship Division of the Academy of Management until 1987.

What was termed the First International Conference on Entrepreneurship Research was held in Toronto in 1973; it brought together primarily Canadian and American researchers. There was an effort during that period to organize a new professional organization of professors interested in the field. It was called SERA, the Society for Entrepreneurship Research and

Application. There was a mailing list of 42 members. However, it never progressed very far. The International Symposium of Entrepreneurship and Enterprise Development (ISEED) was held in Cincinnati in 1975. This one-time conference was a very ambitious undertaking, with an international steering committee and many sponsors and cooperating agencies. It involved more than 230 participants from all over the world, who gathered for the four-day conference. Many were with government agencies which sponsored programs to encourage entrepreneurship, and they reported upon their experiences.

A number of interesting developments occurred at Babson. The Academy of Distinguished Entrepreneurs was established in 1978 to recognize "world-class" entrepreneurs. This became the prototype of other programs to recognize entrepreneurs, including the Ernst and Young "Entrepreneur of the Year Awards," the NFIB "Best in America" contest, and a number of local and regional programs intended to celebrate entrepreneurs and their achievements. The Babson Research Conference was started in 1981. Karl Vesper and Jack Hornaday organized the first conference, which involved the presentation of 39 papers. It was established from the beginning as a working conference, with a required paper as the ticket for admission for all of the participants. The Price-Babson College Fellows Program, directed at experienced business people who were interested in teaching entrepreneurship, started in 1984.

The Small Business Institute Program (SBI) was started in 1972 at Texas Tech University. This program, sponsored by the Small Business Administration, provided support to universities which set up courses in which students consulted with small businesses. This program got off to a fast start and by 1976 there were 398 universities participating. The professional organization, SBIDA, was organized to bring involved faculty together. Although SBA no longer funds this program, variations of it can be found on many campuses and SBIDA continues as an organization binding together faculty who share interests in students learning through consulting.

The first of the "State of the Art" conferences was held at Baylor in 1980. A number of researchers were invited to summarize what was known and not known on particular topics. There were five subsequent conferences, which were held about every three to five years. These were organized primarily by Don Sexton and each resulted in a book.

When scholars first began to try to publish articles on entrepreneurship there were few outlets. The *Journal of Small Business Management* started in 1963 under the auspices of the National Council for Small Business and became the official publication of the successor organization, ICSB, in 1977. The *American Journal of Small Business* was started about 1976; in 1988, under the leadership of Ray Bagby, its name was changed to *Entrepreneurship: Theory and Practice.* The *Journal of Business Venturing* was started in 1985 by Ian MacMillan under the sponsorship of New York University and the Wharton School. *Entrepreneurship and Regional Development* was started in 1989.

In reviewing these developments, it is clear that many of the journals we read and conferences we attend were started in the last 20 years, only about half of a professional's working life. This is indeed a young field.

Not only is this field young, but it has also been relatively small in number of full-time faculty. Although there has been a great growth in total courses, the number of people devoting their full energies to teaching and research in the area has continued to be limited. Many of the courses are taught by non-tenure track faculty, often on a part-time basis. These are often fine teachers, but their other commitments are such that they are usually not involved in developing the intellectual capital of the field. Even where tenure track faculty are involved, they often teach and do work in other areas in addition to entrepreneurship. Furthermore, many entrepreneurship faculty are of an applied bent, good at relating to practicing managers, but sometimes less inclined toward research. The upshot of all of this is that the number of full-time faculty, particularly young faculty, doing research in the field has been relatively small.

The current condition of entrepreneurship reflects tremendous growth in almost all dimensions of the field. The number of major universities with entrepreneurship courses (according to the periodic surveys by Karl Vesper) has increased from fewer than 10 in 1967, to 105 in 1975, 173 in 1980, 250 in 1984, and 370 in 1993. Since the first MBA entrepreneurship major was offered at the University of Southern California in 1972, many undergraduate and MBA programs have added sets of courses and majors. More recently, it was reported that there are more than 2,200 courses at 1,600 colleges and universities (Brush et al., 2003).

The number of English language journals has grown to 44. Conferences are now so numerous that it is difficult to keep track of them. There are 277 chaired professorships in the field. More than 100 universities have established Entrepreneurship Centers (Brush et al., 2003). These serve as focal points for research, for outreach, for student enrichment, and for fundraising.

Public interest in entrepreneurship is quite high. Magazines such as *INC* (started in 1979) and *Entrepreneur* (started in 1977) attract both subscribers and advertisers. Articles in the general business press attract widespread readership. Not only are there articles about how to be an entrepreneur, there are also articles "about" entrepreneurs. The evolution of entrepreneurs to the role of folk heroes is a remarkable development. *USA Today* surveyed young people, asking that if they could devote one year to any occupation, which would they choose. For the women, 47 percent chose entrepreneur, more than tour guide or novelist. For the young men, 38 percent chose entrepreneur, even more than professional athlete. A Gallup poll reported that over 90 percent of Americans would approve if either a daughter or son attempted to start a small business.

This widespread interest in entrepreneurship reflects what is happening in society. A few years ago, *Fortune* magazine estimated that the average young person entering the job market would have ten different jobs with five different organizations before retirement. Old industries decline and well-known corporate names disappear. Many young people recognize that they must take responsibility for their own careers. Even if they expect to start with larger firms and hope to stay with them, conditions can change. Those who have developed entrepreneurial skills will be better prepared for a constantly changing world and they may also have more interesting options in the future. In addition, it is increasingly clear that many of the careers offering the greatest rewards and excitement are in entrepreneurial firms.

Whether the academic study of entrepreneurship will continue to grow will depend upon student interest, the value of research and writing in the field, and the continued support of foundations, government agencies, and universities. The record over recent years suggests that this is still a developing field which is likely to have even greater impact in the future.

Bibliography

Brush, C. G., Duhaime, I. M., Gartner, W. B., Stewart, A., Katz, J. A., Hitt, M. A., Alvarez, S. A., Meyer, G. D., and Venkataraman, S. (2003). Doctoral education in the field of entrepreneurship. *Journal of Management*, 29 (3): 309–32.

human resources

Robert L. Heneman and Judith W. Tansky

Recent research has shown that human capital (rather than financial capital or other tangible resources) is the major issue with which entrepreneurs must cope to grow profitably (Heneman, Tansky, and Camp, 2000). Brush, Greene, and Hart (2001) argued that the development and composition of initial resources are vital to the success of a new venture. However, entrepreneurs often overlook or underestimate the importance of initial resource investments. In fact, Brush, Greene, and Hart (2001) point out that a substantial number of new ventures fail each year because of ineffective management, human failings, or the inability of the firm to attract and maintain qualified personnel. This perspective is consistent with Penrose's (1959) argument that managing human resources is a critical variable in the growth of emerging firms. In addition to entrepreneurial ventures, we know that small firms are important to the US economy. In 2002, for example, 99.7 percent of the 5,652,544 companies in the United States had fewer than 500 employees (USSBA, 2002).

Long ago, Tead and Metcalf (1933) acknowledged that human resource management decisions were becoming increasingly complex and that line managers did not have the time or expertise to deal with laws and regulations. In their discussion of resource choices that entrepreneurs must make, Brush, Greene, and Hart (2001) recognized that human resources are complex and often intangible, making them difficult to identify and measure. In start-up ventures, the entrepreneur must assemble and attract the necessary people to combine with various other resources to ensure the firm's survival and its subsequent growth. On the other hand, in existing entrepreneurial firms, be they high-growth or small firms, managing human capital requires careful matching of people to jobs and to the organization to positively affect some important measures of organizational effectiveness. Attendance, retention performance, satisfaction, safety and health, cost minimization, and customer service are examples of organizational effectiveness measures on which human capital has a direct effect.

Regardless of the type of entrepreneurial firm (e.g., a start-up venture, a fast-growth enterprise, or a stable entrepreneurial venture), entrepreneurs or a managerial team must make a variety of decisions about the acquisition, development, and effective deployment of human capital. These human resource decisions can be grouped into the following categories: (1) staffing, which includes recruiting talent, hiring, and branding the image of the company to attract and retain the best people; (2) training and developing people; (3) rewarding people, together with compensation and benefits; (4) employee relations, including mental and physical well-being at work and non-related problems that affect job performance; and (5) organizational development or the decisions that are made to guarantee that the entrepreneurial venture or firm successfully evolves over time in terms of structure, process, and people.

Although research has been limited in this area, some best practices to achieve growth in entrepreneurial ventures have been identified (Tansky and Heneman, in press; Heneman, Tansky, and Camp, 2000; Heneman and Tansky, 2002). When examining best practices, we should note that the firm's growth stage is based on the arguments that organizations evolve in a consistent and predictable manner (Hanks et al., 1993). As firms move through the

various stages of growth, several problems must be addressed. Unique management skills, priorities, and structures are required to effectively manage the factors associated with the firm's stages of growth. Firms can also be examined based on size measured by number of employees. Best practices include the following:

- Human capital should be emphasized over social capital (e.g., social networks) and organizational capital (e.g., policies and procedures), regardless of the firm's growth stage.
- Maintenance activities related to human resources (e.g., payroll administration, complying with employment regulations, and dealing with labor/union issues) are a necessary, but not sufficient, condition for organizational effectiveness.
- Visionary human resource practices (e.g., training and development, setting competitive compensation levels, maintaining productivity, and managing morale) are more likely to contribute to entrepreneurial growth than are maintenance activities.
- Regardless of size or growth stage, the venture's human resource practices must be aligned with the firm's culture and strategy.
- The vision of the CEO/founder must be clearly communicated to employees.
- Learning and growth opportunities are needed to develop high-potential employees who can perform multiple roles during start-up of the firm and high-growth.

Research supports these best practices. Heneman and Tansky (2002), for example, found that in start-up ventures, entrepreneurs normally perform the duties associated with human resources. However, further growth leads to hiring consultants to perform some of the functions. With still additional growth, a human resource department may be added for efficiency and to support the unique capabilities the entrepreneurial venture has developed. Eventually, time-consuming services such as payroll and benefits may be outsourced. In both start-up ventures and high-growth entrepreneurial firms, Heneman and Tansky (2002) also discovered that (1) an emphasis is placed on hiring the right people and training and developing current employees; (2) very few formalized systems exist at the time of the venture's launch; (3) it is more likely that employees will go out of their way to help new employees learn their jobs; (4) employees are more relationship oriented and work together for the firm's benefit; (5) it is more likely that profit sharing, stock options, and pay rises based on individual performance will be offered to employees; (6) employees are more likely to shape their own job description.

Other issues also affect human resource practices in entrepreneurial ventures. For example, entrepreneurs must be prepared to help their venture contend with external shocks that can affect the management of people (Jacoby, 2003). As an example, when the business cycle is on an upturn, labor often becomes scarce. Human resource professionals are needed to apply the best available techniques to attract and retain talent for the entrepreneurial venture. As another example, laws and regulations concerning the management of human resources in organizations have proliferated over the past fifty years (Kauffman, 1997). Staff assistance may be needed to verify that the venture is complying with all relevant laws and regulations.

In summary, human resource concerns have been identified by CEOs/founders as the most crucial issue affecting the growth of entrepreneurial ventures. The need for human resource staff assistance is particularly acute when the economy is in an upswing and when new laws and regulations are passed. Organizational outcomes influenced by human resource decisions include attendance, retention, performance, satisfaction, safety and health, cost minimization, and customer service. Best human resource practices for entrepreneurial firms include the careful alignment of human resource decisions with the vision of the CEO/founder and the venture's strategy and culture.

Bibliography

Brush, C. G., Greene, P. G., and Hart, M. M. (2001). From initial idea to unique advantage: The entrepreneurial challenge of constructing a resource base. *Academy of Management Executive*, 15 (1): 64–80.

Hanks, S. H., Watson, C. J., Jansen, E., and Chandler, G. N. (1993). Tightening the life cycle construct: A taxonomic study of growth-stage configurations in high-technology organizations. *Entrepreneurship: Theory and Practice*, 18 (2): 5–29.

Heneman, R. L. and Tansky, J. W. (2002). Human resource management models for entrepreneurial firms: Existing knowledge and new directions. In J. Katz and T. Welbourne (eds.), *Advances in Entrepreneurship, Firm Emergence, and Growth, Vol. 5: Human Resource Management in Emerging Firms.* Greenwich, CT: JAI Press.

Heneman, R. L., Tansky, J. W., and Camp, S. M. (2000). Human resource practices in small and medium-size enterprises: Unanswered questions and future research perspectives. *Entrepreneurship: Theory and Practice*, 25 (1): 1–16.

Jacoby, S. M. (2003). A century of human resource management. In B. C. Kauffman, R. A. Beaumont, and R. B. Helfgott (eds.), *Industrial Relations and Human Resources and Beyond.* Armonk, NY: M. E. Sharpe.

Kauffman, B. E. (1997). *Government Regulation of the Employment Relationship.* Madison, WI: Industrial Relations Research Association.

Penrose, E. T. (1959). *The Theory of the Growth of the Firm.* Oxford: Blackwell.

Tansky, J. A. and Heneman, R. L. (in press). Introduction to the special issue on human resource management in SMEs: A call for more research. *Human Resource Management Journal.*

Tead, H. and Metcalf, H. (1933). *Personnel Administration.* New York: McGraw-Hill.

United States Small Business Administration Office of Advocacy (USSBA) (2002). *Statistics About Business Size (Including Small Businesses) from the US Census Bureau.* www.sba.gov.

I

incubators

Donald O. Neubaum and Zhe Zhang

Incubators refer to economic development tools and programs designed to promote and accelerate the growth of entrepreneurial companies through the provision of a variety of services and resources (Barrow, 2001). Incubators help new ventures overcome the liabilities of newness by offering start-up firms many benefits not available to the typical new venture. These benefits include flexible, low-cost office or lab rental space, access to sources of capital, and a number of business and support services, such as a secretarial pool or administrative staff, shipping, receiving, and copying services, and human resource, finance, legal, information technology, and accounting services. Members of incubators can also benefit from the flow of skills and resources across multiple members within the incubator's network or ventures. Business expertise, however, is perhaps the most valuable resource incubators provide, as they can offer consulting services and help incubatees develop business and marketing strategies. Given that nearly 60 percent of all new businesses fail within four years of start-up, mostly due to insufficient financing and a lack of managerial expertise, incubators can assist new ventures through their infancy with the intent of nurturing them to the point they can become self-sustaining (Sherman, 1999).

Through their collective arrangement, incubator firms can gain access to higher quality and lower cost business and professional services than they would be able to garner on their own. During start-up, new venture managers can invest half of their time on administrative chores which can be more quickly and efficiently managed within the incubator (Hansen et al., 2000).

To help fund their operations and offset the costs of the services and space provided, incubators may charge reduced fees, take a portion of the venture's revenues, or even acquire an equity stake (usually 20–40 percent) in their incubatees, although the latter practice is far more prevalent among for-profit incubators.

The first incubator was created in 1959 outside Buffalo, NY, by Joseph Manusco, who bought a dilapidated 850,000 square foot Massey Ferguson factory (Barrow, 2001). Within a year, Manusco was renting space to approximately 20 small companies, one of which was a company that incubated chickens, which is how the name "incubator" was created. By 1980, 12 incubators existed within the United States; that number rose to over 950 by 2003 (with about a third of these being for-profit) with another 3,000 worldwide (only about one-tenth being for profit).

According to the National Business Incubation Association (NBIA, 2003), incubators can be broadly classified into three categories. The first, technology incubators (also called technology innovation centers and/or science parks), include incubators which are established with the primary purpose of commercializing new technologies or creating new innovation opportunities. These facilities are often affiliated with research universities that wish to transfer technologies developed in academic labs into commercial uses, or with major corporations that feel the need to create an external venture to "spin-in" or "spin-off" businesses which might not be completely compatible with the parent firm's existing businesses or technologies. Technology incubators also help corporations provide incentives to their more entrepreneurially oriented employees. About 40 percent of incubators are technology focused.

The second type of incubators are empowerment or microenterprise incubators, which account for less than 5 percent of incubators. These incubators are typically created by state and local governments to address socioeconomic issues, like creating jobs, growing or diversifying the economic base of a community, or revitalizing neighborhoods.

The third type, mixed use incubators, which account for nearly half of all incubators, are mostly concerned with fostering new businesses of all kinds. Some of these mixed use incubators might focus on specific industries or niches, like biotechnology, information technology, or Internet start-ups.

Despite their differing goals and objectives, evidence suggests that incubators can be effective. Typically, incubator ventures graduate to self-sustaining, stand-alone status after two and a half years, with the vast majority of these graduates (87 percent) remaining in business. The NBIA reports that their member incubators generate $45 in local revenue taxes for every $1 of public subsidy they receive and that North American incubators have created over half a million jobs since 1980. In 2001, approximately 35,000 North American incubator companies existed.

Early incubators were typically not-for-profit and emphasized economic development goals. In recent years, that trend has changed, as the prevalence of for-profits incubators, or "business accelerators," has increased, many designed based on the experience of venture capitalists. The explosion and wealth creation of many "dot.coms" fueled the rapid expansion of these accelerators, which have the goal of fast-tracking a new venture toward an IPO or developing the new venture into an attractive acquisition target which allows the investing accelerator to reap substantial profits. Accelerators are generally highly involved in the planning and operations of the ventures under their control. During the 1980s, other for-profit models, labeled "EcoNets," "MetaCompanies," or "Internet keiretsus," flourished. EcoNets are aggressive incubators which retain control of the ventures after start-up and orchestrate their network of hatchlings while trying to capitalize on the synergistic benefits of a diversified portfolio of businesses. MetaCompanies combine the characteristics of an incubator, a venture capitalist

firm, and a diversified operating company, but tend to focus on a more narrow line of business than their EcoNet counterparts. Many for-profit incubators and accelerators have struggled, and even failed, due to the infrequency of liquidity events (i.e., IPOs or acquisitions) that leads to financial difficulties, as well as their over-reliance on information technology ventures which failed when the dot.com bubble burst (Johnsrud, Theis, and Bezerra, 2003). Many of those accelerators that survived have been forced to diversify their portfolios and develop more traditional revenue streams, such as collecting fees for service, to remain solvent.

Several studies have examined the best practices of incubators. For example, one study found that in addition to offering a wide variety of services, high-performing incubators either had a strong relationship with a research university, or a medical or research laboratory, or was located in a metropolitan area with ample access to technology-based companies and high-quality business service firms (Tornatzky, Sherman, and Adkins, 2003). Hansen and his colleagues (2000) suggest that "networked incubators," which deliberately foster partnerships among the start-ups and facilitate rather than control the entrepreneurial spirit of the incubatees, provide the model for incubator effectiveness. According to the NBIA (2003), model business incubators should not only be concerned with contributing to the economic community by maximizing the launch of successful companies, but should also consider themselves "a dynamic model of a sustainable, efficient business operation." The latter is achieved by developing a realistic and financially solid plan, recruiting skilled talent to manage the incubator, developing a committed board of directors, building the collective resources, offerings, and capabilities of the incubator, weaving the incubator firms into the local economic community, fostering mutually beneficial relationships between the ventures within the incubator, and practicing continuous improvement to provide better services to future prospective businesses.

Bibliography

Barrow, C. (2001). *Incubators: A Realist's Guide to the World's New Business Accelerators*. New York: Wiley.

Hansen, M. T., Chesbrough, H. W., Nohria, N., and Sull, D. N. (2000). Network incubators: Hothouses of the new economy. *Harvard Business Review*, September–October: 74–84.

Johnsrud, C. S., Theis, R. P., and Bezerra, M. (2003). Business incubation: Emerging trends for profitability and economic development in the US, Central Asia, and the Middle East. Washington, DC: US Department of Commerce Technology Administration.

National Business Incubation Association (2003). http://www.nbia.org.

Sherman, H. D. (1999). Assessing the intervention effectiveness of business incubation programs on new business start-up. *Journal of Developmental Entrepreneurship*, 4: 117–13.

Tornatzky, L., Sherman, H., and Adkins, D. (2003). A national benchmarking analysis of technology business incubator performance and practices. Washington, DC: US Department of Commerce Technology Administration.

incumbents' advantage

Frank T. Rothaermel

Most academics and practitioners highlight the advantages enjoyed by new entrants (Foster, 1986; Christensen, 1997). New entrants are often viewed as initiating a Schumpeterian process of creative destruction (*see* CREATIVE DE-STRUCTION), frequently replacing industry incumbents and rising to dominance. Yet there are many examples of incumbents who successfully weather waves of radical change in a wide range of industries, including computing and the life sciences (Hill and Rothaermel, 2003). Thus, entrepreneurs and entrepreneurship scholars need to be aware of the advantages enjoyed by incumbents that may retard entrepreneurial success.

The pioneering work of Schumpeter (1934, 1942) is not clear on whether incumbents or new entrants are likely to succeed in commercializing innovation, because it suggests that both – new entrants and incumbents – can have the upper hand when innovation occurs. Schumpeter attributed the incumbents' advantage to monopoly power that allows for limited competition and scale advantages in access to capital and R&D funding, among other advantages. Later work in industrial organization economics, emphasizing differential economic incentives, clarified that incumbents are likely to be successful when an innovation is *incremental*, while new entrants are favored when an innovation is *radical* (Tirole, 1998) (*see* RADICAL INNOVATIONS).

More recent theoretical work has highlighted the importance of complementary assets in determining whether incumbents or new entrants are more likely to profit from an innovation (Teece, 1986). The commercialization of an innovation "requires that the know-how in question be utilized in conjunction with other capabilities or assets. Services such as marketing, competitive manufacturing, and after-sales support are almost always needed. These services are obtained from complementary assets, which are specialized" (Teece, 1986: 288). Examples include the commercialization of the CAT scanner or soft-drink innovations like diet cola, where the innovators (EMI and RC Cola) lost to incumbents (GE Medical Systems and Pepsi, Coke) due to a lack of specialized complementary assets.

Following Teece (1986), we suggest that the *type* of complementary assets necessary to commercialize an innovation is likely to be paramount in determining the performance consequences for incumbent firms. In particular, we argue that incumbents are advantageously positioned when the complementary assets needed to commercialize an innovation are specialized or co-specialized to the innovation. Specialized complementary assets exhibit unilateral dependence between the innovation and the complementary assets, while co-specialized complementary assets are characterized by a bilateral dependence. A stellar reputation for quality and service in hospital equipment is considered a specialized complementary asset, while specialized repair facilities for Mazda's rotary engine would be a co-specialized complementary asset. We use the term *specialized complementary assets* to denote both specialized and co-specialized complementary assets.

Recent empirical research has shown that incumbents even benefit from radical innovation through leveraging specialized complementary assets. Tripsas (1997), in her longitudinal study documenting multiple waves of innovation in the typesetting industry, showed that incumbents who were able to leverage specialized complementary assets like manufacturing capabilities, proprietary font libraries, or a sales and service network, continued to thrive in the face of radical technological innovation, time and time again. Rothaermel (2001a) also provided some evidence for the notion that incumbent pharmaceutical firms were able to leverage their complementary assets in downstream value chain activities, such as clinical trial and regulatory management as well as drug distribution, through interfirm cooperation with new entrants. This alliance strategy has not only yielded superior firm performance for some incumbents, but also improved the overall industry performance of incumbents as a group, because they were able to extract significant innovation rents despite the fact that the innovation was introduced by new entrants (Rothaermel, 2001b). The key to continued superior incumbent performance in both the typesetting and pharmaceutical industries was specialized complementary assets held by incumbents. These assets are frequently *non-technological* in nature and are built over long periods of time.

Thus, complementary assets needed to commercialize an innovation ought to be of particular interest to entrepreneurs and entrepreneurship scholars. Hill (1997) posited that new entrants should go it alone if they have the required complementary assets and barriers to entry are high. When new entrants lack complementary assets, they should enter into a cooperative arrangement with an incumbent firm. New entrants may be able to obtain complementary assets in strategic factor markets (Barney, 1986), and if they are priced below their rent-generating potential, new entrants are well positioned to extract the profits from innovating (*see* COM-PETITIVE ADVANTAGE). Taken together, innovation is the *sine qua non* of entrepreneurship. Yet incumbents enjoy many advantages that have a direct bearing on whether entrepreneurial ventures will succeed or fail. This fact offers abundant research opportunities to enhance our understanding of entrepreneurship and to more accurately inform practice.

Bibliography

Barney, J. B. (1986). Strategic factor markets: Expectations, luck, and business strategy. *Management Science*, 32: 1231–41.
Christensen, C. M. (1997). *The Innovator's Dilemma: When New Technologies Cause Great Firms to Fail.* Boston, MA: Harvard Business School Press.
Foster, R. N. (1986). *Innovation: The Attacker's Advantage.* New York: Summit Books.
Hill, C. W. L. (1997). Establishing a standard: Competitive strategy and technology standards in winner-take-all industries. *Academy of Management Executive*, 11: 7–25.
Hill, C. W. L. and Rothaermel, F. T. (2003). The performance of incumbent firms in the face of radical technological innovation. *Academy of Management Review*, 28: 257–74.
Rothaermel, F. T. (2001a). Incumbent's advantage through exploiting complementary assets via interfirm cooperation. *Strategic Management Journal*, 22: 687–99.
Rothaermel, F. T. (2001b). Complementary assets, strategic alliances, and the incumbent's advantage: An empirical study of industry and firm effects in the biopharmaceutical industry. *Research Policy*, 30: 1235–51.
Schumpeter, J. A. (1934). *The Theory of Economic Development.* Cambridge, MA: Harvard University Press.
Schumpeter, J. A. (1942). *Capitalism, Socialism and Democracy.* New York: Harper and Row.
Teece, D. J. (1986). Profiting from technological innovation: Implications for integration, collaboration, licensing, and public policy. *Research Policy*, 15: 285–305.
Tirole, J. (1998). *The Theory of Industrial Organization.* Cambridge, MA: MIT Press.
Tripsas, M. (1997). Unraveling the process of creative destruction: Complementary assets and incumbent survival in the typesetter industry. *Strategic Management Journal*, 18: 119–42.

initial public offerings and new ventures

S. Trevis Certo

Initial public offerings (IPOs) transition privately held new ventures into the arena of public trading. Firms have undertaken IPOs in over thirty countries, but the majority of IPO research involves firms in the United States (for a review of IPO research in international settings, see Ritter, 1998). In the US, privately held firms are typically owned by a small number of investors (*see* ENTREPRENEUR; BUSINESS ANGEL NETWORK; VENTURE CAPITAL) and are not required to file financial statements with the Securities and Exchange Commission (SEC).

While IPOs are usually associated with new ventures, it is important to note that they also apply to spin-offs (*see* SPIN-OFFS), reverse leveraged buyouts, and closed-end mutual funds. The majority of IPO researchers, however, typically exclude such IPOs from analysis. Research indicates that entrepreneurs serve as CEO for approximately 50 percent of IPO firms, with the remainder led by "professional" managers (Certo et al., 2001).

Undertaking an IPO (also known as "going public") transitions the private firm into a publicly traded company. With this new status of being publicly traded, shares of the IPO firm's stock are listed on a stock exchange (e.g., New York Stock Exchange) and investors are able to buy and sell shares of the company's stock through stockbrokers. In addition, the SEC requires publicly traded companies to abide by certain rules and regulations, such as the requirement that such firms must file audited financial statements.

IPOs have become a rather popular financing tool; between 1980 and 2001 over 6,200 firms raised nearly $500 billion through IPOs in the United States (Ritter and Welch, 2002). Research suggests a number of reasons for which firms undertake IPOs (Rock, 1986). First, an IPO helps the firm raise new capital. By issuing new shares to the public, the firm brings in new capital to invest in new technologies, manufacturing facilities, employees, etc. Second, the IPO helps the firm's initial investors to diversify their investments in the firm. Specifically, executives and investors in some firms use the IPO as an opportunity to sell existing shares; presumably these investors are able to use the proceeds from such sales to invest in other types of investment vehicles. In this sense, many venture capitalists view IPOs as a primary exit strategy. Third, firms undertake IPOs to gain organizational legitimacy (Certo, 2003). Existing as a publicly traded firm may establish credibility among key stakeholders such as customers, suppliers, and employees.

Owners and executives of firms going public adhere to a standardized IPO process (for a detailed description of the IPO process, see Ellis, Michaely, and O'Hara, 1999). The first step in this process usually involves enlisting the assistance of a lead investment banker (investment bankers are also referred to as underwriters). With the assistance of the underwriter, executives begin to draft the registration statement. The registration statement, which must be filed with the SEC, details the company's strategy, top executives, and financial statements. The investment banker then uses this registration statement to market the firm to potential investors. The investment banker also arranges for road shows, which involve presentations by the company's top executives to potential investors, such as mutual and pension fund managers. After these road shows, the investment banker gauges demand for the offering by querying potential investors with respect to their desires to purchase shares in the company; this process is referred to as "book building" (for an excellent description of book building, see Cornelli and Goldreich, 2001). Based on these queries, investment bankers determine the final price at which shares of the company will sell to the public. This final price is known as the IPO's offer price.

Empirical research has determined two trends with respect to the performance of IPO firms. The first trend involves the consistent underpricing of IPOs, and the second trend concerns the consistent long-term underperformance of IPO firms. The following sections detail research examining these two trends.

UNDERPRICING

Research suggests that on the first day of public trading, the share prices of IPO firms regularly close at prices that exceed their offer prices. This phenomenon is referred to as underpricing. A fictional example of XYZ, Inc.'s IPO will illustrate how underpricing occurs. Suppose that underwriters established an offer price of $10 per share for XYZ. At the end of the first day of trading, though, shares of XYZ closed at $13 per share. In this example, the firm raised $10 for each share of equity sold to the public. The closing price of $13 indicates, however, that the price set by investment bankers was less than the price determined by the stock market at the end of the first day of trading; this is known as IPO underpricing.

Underpricing produces consequences for both IPO firms and investors. Continuing the example of XYZ, Inc., executives of XYZ received $10 (offer price) for each share of stock sold to new investors. If the investment banker had priced the shares efficiently, however, executives of XYZ would have received $13 for each share sold to new investors. In other words, efficient pricing would have enabled executives to receive an extra $3 per share to invest in new technologies, equipment, employees, etc. Instead, this extra $3 is captured by the initial investors, who purchased shares of XYZ for $10 and witnessed the price increase to $13 by the end of the first day of trading. Because the IPO firm does not capture this value, some commentators have referred to underpricing as "leaving money on the table" (e.g., Ritter and Welch, 2002) and questioned the efficiency of the IPO pricing process (Lowry and Schwert, 2004).

Empirical work by Ritter and Welch (2002) indicates that underpricing represents an economically significant phenomenon that appears to vary with overall investor attitudes. In the 1980s, for example, shares of IPO firms were underpriced by 7.4 percent on average; underpricing during this period resulted in approximately $5.4 billion dollars being left on the table. In just 1999 and 2000, though, shares of IPO firms were underpriced by 65 percent on average, which resulted in over $65 billion being left on the table. Despite the prevalence of this market anomaly, relatively little is known with respect to the determinants of underpricing (Daily et al., 2003).

THE LONG-RUN PERFORMANCE OF IPO FIRMS

Another trend associated with the performance of IPO firms involves the relative underperformance of firms in the years immediately following their IPOs. Ritter and Welch (2002) reported that the average firm going public between 1980 and 2001 trailed the general stock market by over 23 percent in the three years following its IPO. Complementing this finding, Jain and Kini (2000) analyzed a sample of firms undertaking IPOs between 1977 and 1990 and found that only about 75 percent of these firms continued to operate independently as public corporations within five years after their IPOs. In other words, more than 25 percent of these firms failed to maintain their status as publicly traded companies within five years of their IPOs.

As compared to the underpricing literature, there exists a less substantial stream of research examining the long-run underperformance of IPO firms. Jain and Kini (2000), for example, found that firms backed by venture capitalists were more likely to survive than firms not backed by a venture capitalist. Mikkelson, Partch, and Shah (1997) found that larger IPO firms enjoyed higher levels of operating performance as compared to smaller IPO firms.

Although difficult to measure, overconfidence might also represent a potential explanation for the long-run underperformance of IPO firms. Specifically, it could be that both entrepreneurs and investors are overly optimistic at the time of the IPO. Such overconfidence could lead entrepreneurs to invest IPO proceeds in projects that are unlikely to reap benefits and investors to invest their capital in IPO firms with questionable growth prospects.

CONCLUSION

Going public will continue to represent a popular financing strategy for entrepreneurs and venture capitalists as they attempt to advance their firms. The substantial body of research examining IPO firms notwithstanding, there exist several additional areas for further exploration. Future research, for example, could further examine the pricing of IPOs. While extant research focuses primarily on prospectuses to examine IPO pricing, future research might involve collecting primary data from investment bankers, entrepreneurs, and venture capitalists. Understanding how these important stakeholders perceive IPO firms might help in explaining IPO prices.

Complementing this research on IPO pricing, additional examinations of the long-run performance of IPO firms are warranted. Specifically, future research could examine how changes within the firm help to circumvent long-run performance problems. Changes in top management team structures, for example, might help firms to adapt to the rigors of public trading. Similarly, changes in diversification levels, financial structures, strategies, and compensation systems might also influence long-run performance. Studies examining these issues would surely benefit scholars in multiple disciplines who continue to explore the IPO process.

Bibliography

Certo, S. T. (2003). Influencing IPO investors with prestige: Signaling with board structures. *Academy of Management Review*, 28: 432–46.

Certo, S. T., Covin, J., Daily, C. M., and Dalton, D. R. (2001). Wealth and the effects of founder management among IPO-stage new ventures. *Strategic Management Journal*, 22: 641–58.

Cornelli, F. and Goldreich, D. (2001). Book building and strategic allocation. *Journal of Finance*, 56: 2337–69.

Daily, C. M., Certo, S. T., Dalton, D. R., and Roengpitya, R. (2003). IPO underpricing: A meta-analysis and research synthesis. *Entrepreneurship: Theory and Practice*, 27 (3): 271–95.

Ellis, K., Michaely, R., and O'Hara, M. (1999). A guide to the initial public offering process. *Corporate Finance Review*, 3: 14–18.

Jain, B. A. and Kini, O. (2000). Does the presence of venture capitalists improve the survival profile of IPO firms? *Journal of Business Finance and Accounting*, 27: 1139–76.

Lowry, M. and Schwert, G. W. (2004). Is the IPO pricing process efficient? *Journal of Financial Economics* (in press).

Mikkelson, W. H., Partch, M. M., and Shah, K. (1997). Ownership and operating performance of companies that go public. *Journal of Financial Economics*, 44: 281–307.

Ritter, J. R. (1998). Initial public offerings. *Contemporary Finance Digest*, 2: 5–30.

Ritter, J. R. and Welch, I. (2002). A review of IPO activity, pricing, and allocations. *Journal of Finance*, 57: 1795–828.

Rock, K. (1986). Why new issues are underpriced. *Journal of Financial Economics*, 15: 187–212.

innovations

Gautam Ahuja and PuayKhoon Toh

Technological innovations are commercialized inventions, where inventions refer to the development of a new idea or an act of creation (Hitt, Hoskisson, and Nixon, 1993). Innovations can take the form of new products, new uses for existing products, and new devices, designs, services, methods of production, or systems of arrangements. Technological innovations can thus come in many different forms: a new computer chip (device), a new ergonomic design for chairs (design), allowing for issue of electronic air-tickets through Internet websites (service), a new desalination technology to obtain fresh water (methods of production), and a new arrangement of the production line that improves quality control (system of arrangements). Because innovations are end products of successful inventions, the two constructs ("innovations" and "inventions") are often perceived to be synonymous. However, one should recognize that the same invention could be commercialized in different forms, hence appearing as different innovations. For example, a new invention in the art of coffee-making can be embodied in the form of a new coffee-maker machine that incorporates this new principle, or it can be a new procedure for making the coffee – a specific and explicit method of combining coffee beans and hot water, leading to the transformation of such raw materials into the beverage, without a specific product that incorporates this procedure.

The key component to an innovation is the "newness" or novelty in the underlying invention, the improvement(s) that it entails over the existing pool of knowledge in its field. It is through the ability to improve on current knowledge and better satisfy consumer needs that an invention creates value, and hence justifies its commercialization. The value of the innovation represents the extent of the improvement and the value that users of the innovation place on such improvements. Hence, while the extent of "newness" in the invention might be high, such novelty does not necessarily translate into a high-value innovation, unless this novelty adds commensurate value to users.

Innovations can also refer to novelties in organization design or practice. For instance, M-form and matrix structures are illustrations of organizational design innovations. Similarly, total quality management is an illustration of an organizational practice innovation.

There are various dimensions along which innovations have been classified, namely: (1) radical vs. incremental (Abernathy and Utterback, 1978) (*see* RADICAL INNOVATIONS); (2) competence-destroying vs. competence-enhancing (Tushman and Anderson,

1986); (3) architectural vs. modular (Henderson and Clark, 1990); (4) disruptive vs. sustaining (Christensen, 1997; Adner, 2002) (*see* DISRUP-TIVE INNOVATIONS); and (5) product vs. process. Most of the above innovation types have been studied in the realm of technologies. Classifications (1), (2), and (4) are based on the *effects* of innovations, whereas classifications (3) and (5) are based on the *nature* of the innovations.

The various typologies are discussed briefly below:

1   A radical innovation is one where the extent of novelty is high, in terms of either performance on a set of attributes (or price performance) or if it represents a major change or a breakaway from the previous technological trajectory. It is often associated with terms like "breakthrough inventions" (Ahuja and Lampert, 2001) and discontinuous innovation (Tushman and Anderson, 1986).

2   To the extent that the radical innovation creates a discontinuity in the original technological trajectory, it can also be competence-destroying, if it renders previous know-how irrelevant as it pushes the technological frontier towards one defined along a new trajectory. For example, the arrival of PC technology in effect reduces the value of word processor and typewriter technologies and makes irrelevant the production competencies that typewriter producers built up over the years. On the other hand, an incremental innovation is one that represents minor improvements over existing technologies and know-how. The novelty embedded in such innovation is less. Such innovation often tends to enhance or preserve the value of existing knowledge and products (hence it may be competence enhancing), and does not create a major breakthrough; nor does it cause any large discontinuities in the existing technological trajectory.

3   The architectural/modular dimension of innovation represents an almost orthogonal dimension to that of radical/incremental, and draws on the concept of recombination. To the extent that innovations arise from the recombination of existing knowledge components, architectural innovations can have "radical" effects despite not using any radic-

ally new knowledge components. Architectural innovations embody mainly the knowledge of how to recombine existing elements, and a radical architectural innovation is one that is radical in its method of recombining existing elements. Modular innovations, on the other hand, represent improvements in the knowledge embedded in the individual components. Henderson and Clark (1990) give the example of the room fan: the modular components are the blade, the motor, the blade guard, and control system, etc., and the architectural knowledge is the know-how of putting the various components together to create moving air.

4   An innovation is disruptive if it disrupts the original technological trajectory and displaces the mainstream technology – oddly, not with a superior technology, but rather with what is at least initially an inferior one (Christensen, 1997). The disruptive innovation, while having poorer performance on some dimensions, is able to satisfy the main needs of the mainstream consumers at lower cost and hence takes over the market, while the original technology is too focused on the needs of the most sophisticated consumers and misses the chance of meeting the growing demand for a product with a different value proposition.

5   Innovations can also be classified according to the nature or form in which the innovation resides. Innovations taking the form of a new object, device, design, or service are called product innovations, and innovations taking the form of a new arrangement or method are called process innovations. An alternate distinction between product and process innovations has also been suggested (Scherer, 1984; Cohen and Klepper, 1996). Process innovations are those that are used in the industry in which they are created, while product inventions are those that are used in an industry different from the one in which they are created.

Innovations are often measured using counts of patents, new products, or new processes. A patent, by definition, represents a unique and novel element of knowledge, and gives the inventor the exclusive rights to the invention.

Such legal protection of intellectual property rights provides an incentive for inventors to file patents for their patentable inventions. If the value of the invention exceeds the cost of patenting, then the inventor will prefer to file for a patent. Hence, patents are perceived as good indicators of innovations of at least some economic significance. However, patents are naturally not complete measures of all innovations, as some inventors might choose to keep the invention secret (and hence not file for a patent), or some innovations may not be patentable (e.g., when the novelty of the innovation cannot be made explicit). Finally, patents vary considerably in their economic value, and many patents have very little economic value. Industries also differ considerably in the efficacy of patents at protecting innovations and hence are characterized by widely varying propensities to patent inventions.

Similarly, product and process count measures of innovation present some strengths. They represent a more "advanced" indicator of innovation in that the innovation has been extended from the patent stage to a market or usage stage. However, such data are generally difficult to collect and demarcating new products and processes can be complex.

Bibliography

Abernathy, W. J. and Utterback, J. (1978). Patterns of industrial innovation. *Technology Review*, June–July: 40–7.

Adner, R. (2002). When are technologies disruptive? A demand-based view of the emergence of competition. *Strategic Management Journal*, 23: 667–88.

Ahuja, G. and Lampert, C. M. (2001). Entrepreneurship in the large corporation: A longitudinal study of how established firms create breakthrough inventions. *Strategic Management Journal*, 22: 521–43.

Christensen, C. M. (1997). *The Innovator's Dilemma*. Boston, MA: Harvard Business School Press.

Cohen, W. M. and Klepper, S. (1996). Firm size and the nature of innovation within industries: The case of process and product R&D. *Review of Economics and Statistics*, 78 (2): 232–43.

Dosi, G. (1982). Technological paradigms and technological trajectories. *Research Policy*, 11: 147–62.

Henderson, R. M. and Clark, K. B. (1990) Architectural innovation: The reconfiguration of existing product technologies and the failure of established firms. *Administrative Science Quarterly*, 35 (1): 9–30.

Hitt, M., Hoskisson, R., and Nixon, R. D. (1993). A mid-range theory of interfunctional integration, its antecedents and outcomes. *Journal of Engineering and Technology Management*, 10 (1, 2): 161–85.

Levinthal, D. A. and March, J. G. (1993). The myopia of leaning. *Strategic Management Journal* 14 (winter special issue): 95–112.

Scherer, F. M. (1984). Using linked patent and R&D data to measure interindustry technology flows. In Z. Griliches (ed.), *R&D, Patents, and Productivity*. Chicago: University of Chicago Press, for the National Bureau of Economic Research.

Tushman, M. L. and Anderson, P. (1986). Technological discontinuities and organizational environments. *Administrative Science Quarterly*, 31: 436–65.

internal venturing

Shaker A. Zahra and JiFeng Yu

Corporate venturing (CV) refers to the process by which an organization enters a new domestic or foreign market. This process enables established organizations to create and use products or process innovations to target new markets (Venkataraman, MacMillan, and McGrath, 1992). These activities could be external (e.g., alliances, corporate venture capital and acquisitions) or internal. Internal venturing activities stimulate and promote entrepreneurial activities within a company's ongoing operations. Some refer to internal venturing as "internal entrepreneurship," "intra-corporate entrepreneurship," or "internal corporate entrepreneurship" (for a review, see Schollhammer, 1982). The theoretical domain and importance of these activities have evolved over the past two decades, reflecting the changes that have occurred in the business environment and managerial practice.

EVOLUTION OF THE INTERNAL VENTURING CONCEPT

Earlier writings on internal venturing have highlighted formally sanctioned organizational activities intended to stimulate innovation in a firm's operations (Schollhammer, 1982). Some of these activities are opportunistic in nature, exploiting transient opportunities in the firm's existing markets or operations. Internal venturing activities may be incubative, focusing on creating a setting in which new ideas or initiatives are explored, supported, evaluated, and institution-alized. Some incubative activities require the creation of autonomous business units that de-velop new business concepts and practices (Zahra, 1991, 1996).

Burgelman's (1983a, 1983b, 1984) research was a milestone in the study of internal ventur-ing. It separated formally induced (i.e., formally sanctioned) from autonomous (informal) efforts aimed at creating strategic options for the firm through entrepreneurship. Pinchott (1985) later observed that employees and middle managers often initiate informal projects that increase in-novation, allowing their companies to enter market arenas. Employees initiate these auto-nomous activities even when formal systems do not exist to create the momentum for change. Bootlegging and skunkworks are popular infor-mal approaches to internal venturing. While formal and autonomous venturing activities may collide, they often complement one another. The role of senior management centers on creat-ing the mechanisms that induce and strategically exploit complementarity among various formal and informal initiatives. Therefore, by the mid-1990s, several corporations had initiated mul-tiple programs to encourage internal venturing by facilitating the coexistence of formal and in-formal activities.

APPROACHES TO INTERNAL VENTURING

Companies vary considerably in their ap-proaches to internal venturing. Some companies simply assign this task to a senior manager of an existing unit, such as R&D. Other companies create a task force or a cross-functional team that champions these activities and reports on their progress to the firm's top management. Other companies have created autonomous units whose sole responsibility is to create the context, process, and systems that foster and sustain internal venturing. For example, in 1996, Nortel Networks created a "business ven-tures group" with a mandate to "identify, culti-vate and incubate possible stand-alone internal ventures" (O'Connor and Maslyn, 2002: 2). The group has an advisory board that seeks input from everyone in the company. The ventures' group provides a hospitable place where new business concepts are identified and screened against preset criteria. Once successfully

screened, a business proposal is developed and refined. Promising proposals are then presented to the business venture group's advisory board. Ideas that meet organizational and strategic cri-teria are approved for investment and given the time to develop. Upon evaluation of their pro-gress, final recommendations about the fate of these projects are made. Projects could be spun-in (for internal development), spun-out exter-nally, licensed, or terminated. Throughout these various activities, the business venture group is expected to work with the company's various business units and keep senior managers informed.

SUCCESSFUL RECIPES FOR INTERNAL VENTURING

Success in internal venturing requires strategic clarity about the firm's direction, competencies, and objectives. It is necessary also to recognize the limitations of formal innovation systems that might exist within the organization and accept the possibility that employees, at all levels, can contribute to the firm's ability to innovate and take risks. Internal venturing programs also re-quire successful and sometimes forceful cham-pions to sell innovative business ideas to senior managers. Champions connect the outcomes of the internal venturing process to the firm's vari-ous existing units, creating a basis for synergy in sharing the firm's assets. These programs re-quire a longer time horizon to succeed, which requires sustained organizational support. Stra-tegic control systems that appreciate the explor-atory nature of the firm's internal venturing activities are also needed to safeguard against a short-term orientation in managing these activ-ities. The success of these programs also requires resolving conflicts and communication issues that arise between venture groups and existing units. Champions devote considerable energy to linking various organizational units and ensuring that new initiatives are connected to the strategic vision of the organization.

IMPORTANCE OF INTERNAL VENTURING

Internal venturing activities foster innovations of different types (Baden-Fuller, 1995) by creat-ing a setting in which new ideas receive political and organizational support. Internal venturing units also provide a safe environment in which

new ideas are tested and refined before presenting them to operating units or senior managers.
These activities can promote organizational
learning and the acquisition of valuable new
knowledge (Zahra, Nielsen, and Bogner, 1999).
This learning can be organizational (how to
structure things), strategic (how and where to
compete), or technological. Internal venturing
also makes use of different knowledge bases
that exist within the firm, generating the requisite combinative knowledge that becomes the
foundation of competitive advantage. By linking
diverse bodies of knowledge, internal venturing
units also create a setting in which various organizational members from different divisions
interact, share their experiences, and learn.
This sharing becomes a foundation for joint
innovative activities crossing divisional boundaries. Organizational learning also serves to
create new competencies, allowing the firm to
redefine its strategic arena differently and compete in ways that give supremacy over its rivals.
Understandably, some research reveals that internal venturing is conducive to higher profitability and growth (Zahra, 1991). Another
benefit of internal venturing is providing a
forum that fosters employee innovativeness,
which can improve productivity. When employees feel safe to innovate, they are likely to experiment with new combinations of resources,
providing a basis for differentiation that creates
competitive advantage.

Bibliography

Baden-Fuller, C. (1995). Strategic innovation, corporate
entrepreneurship and matching outside-in to inside-
out approaches to strategy research. *British Journal of
Management*, 6 (special issue): S3–S16.
Burgelman, R. A. (1983a). A process model of internal
corporate venturing in the diversified major firm. *Administrative Science Quarterly*, 28: 223–44.
Burgelman, R. A. (1983b). A model of the interaction
of strategic behavior, corporate contest, and the concept of strategy. *Academy of Management Review*, 8:
61–70.
Burgelman, R. A. (1984). Managing the internal corporate
venturing process. *Sloan Management Review*, winter:
33–48.
O'Connor, G. C. and Maslyn, W. T. (2002). *Nortel Network's Business Ventures Group*. Troy, NY: Lally School
of Management and Technology, Rensselaer Polytechnic Institute.

Pinchott, G. (1985). *Intrapreneuring*. New York: Harper
and Row.
Schollhammer, H. (1982). Internal corporate entrepren-
eurship. In C. A. Kent, D. L. Sexton, and K. H. Vesper
(eds.), *Encyclopedia of Entrepreneurship*. Englewood
Cliffs, NJ: Prentice-Hall, 209–29.
Venkataraman, S., MacMillan, I. C., and McGrath, R. C.
(1992). Progress in research on corporate venturing. In
D. L. Sexton and J. D. Kasarda (eds.), *The State of the
Art of Entrepreneurship*. Boston, MA: PWS-Kent,
487–519.
Zahra, S. A. (1991). Predictors and financial outcomes of
corporate entrepreneurship: An exploratory study.
Journal of Business Venturing, 6: 259–85.
Zahra, S. A. (1996). Governance, ownership, and corporate entrepreneurship: The moderating impact of
industry technological opportunities. *Academy of Management Journal*, 39: 1713–35.
Zahra, S., Nielsen, A., and Bogner, W. (1999). Corporate
entrepreneurship, knowledge and competence development. *Entrepreneurship: Theory and Practice*, 23:
169–89.

international entrepreneurship

Benjamin M. Oviatt and Patricia P. McDougall

We define international entrepreneurship as the
discovery, enactment, evaluation, and exploitation of opportunities – across national borders –
to create future goods and services (McDougall
and Oviatt, forthcoming). The scholarly study
of international entrepreneurship attempts to
answer questions about how, by whom, and
with what effects those opportunities are acted
upon. It includes two branches: (1) the study of
entrepreneurial activity that itself crosses
national borders and (2) the comparison of domestic entrepreneurial activities in multiple
countries.

The definition is a deliberate effort to blend
the foci of entrepreneurship and international
business, and we believe a full understanding of
the definition requires an appreciation of its
evolution. Furthermore, we believe understanding is also aided by examples of well-conducted
research from both branches of study in international entrepreneurship.

In their comprehensive review of international entrepreneurship, Zahra and George
(2002) noted that the first known reference to
the term "international entrepreneurship" was

in a three-page article by Morrow (1988), in which the author showed the impact of technological advances and increased cultural awareness in making once remote markets accessible to established companies and new ventures. The following year, McDougall's (1989) study comparing domestic and international new ventures marked the beginning of academic study specifically positioned as international entrepreneurship research. She narrowly defined international entrepreneurship as "the development of international new ventures or start-ups that, from their inception, engage in international business" (1989: 388).

At the 1992 Academy of Management meetings, a commissioned task force held a special session entitled "What does international entrepreneurship mean to division members?" The general consensus of the membership was that the definition of international entrepreneurship needed to be broad and its multidimensionality should be encouraged (Giamartino, McDougall, and Bird, 1993).

While most of the early work in international entrepreneurship emanated from entrepreneurship scholars, Wright and Ricks (1994) highlighted it as a newly emerging research direction for international business scholars, which was noteworthy since international business researchers at that time focused almost exclusively on established companies. Their definition also drew attention to the need to include a comparative focus.

More recently, McDougall and Oviatt proposed a new definition of international entrepreneurship in a Special Research Forum in the *Academy of Management Journal*, noting that firm size or age were not defining characteristics: "International entrepreneurship is a combination of innovative, proactive, and risk-seeking behavior that crosses national borders and is intended to create value in organizations" (2000: 903).

Highlighting the fact that the bulk of international entrepreneurship research has focused on the internationalization of new ventures, Zahra and George (2002) sought to emphasize the role of established firms in international entrepreneurship. They defined international entrepreneurship as "the process of creatively discovering and exploiting opportunities that lie outside a firm's domestic markets in the pursuit of competitive advantage" (2002: 261). Thus, Zahra and George more explicitly included corporate entrepreneurship.

As noted by Young, Dimitratos, and Dana (2003) in the inaugural issue of the *Journal of International Entrepreneurship*, a journal dedicated exclusively to the study of this growing field, regular "soul-searching" on the boundaries of international entrepreneurship is not unique. They noted that during the last decade significant discussions in international business have taken place, with definitions ranging from "transactions that cross national boundaries" (Rugman and Hodgetts, 1995: 4) to "a multi-level economic exchange process" (Toyne, 1997: 37). Within entrepreneurship, a definitional debate has plagued the field since its infancy (see, for example, Gartner, 1988; Venkataraman, 1997; Shane and Venkataraman, 2000). Building on the definition of entrepreneurship recently proposed by Shane and Venkataraman (2000), we have reformulated our definition of international entrepreneurship to the definition set forth in the first sentence of this essay. As the fields of entrepreneurship and international business continue to evolve, we expect the definition of international entrepreneurship will also evolve.

Two examples of international entrepreneurship, one from each branch of inquiry, may improve the reader's understanding and may even stimulate additional research. An example of the study of cross-border entrepreneurial behavior is Zahra, Ireland, and Hitt's (2000) empirical study of the relationships between international expansion, technological learning, and new venture performance. The research was conducted on a sample of 321 independent and corporate ventures that were (1) six years old or younger, (2) headquartered in the United States, (3) competing in a dozen high-technology industries, and (4) deriving an average of 17 percent of their sales from foreign sources. Thus, the sample focused on firms exploiting relatively new and likely innovative opportunities across national borders, thereby fitting our definition of international entrepreneurship.

The study took into account a variety of variables using many rich data sources, including mailed surveys, archival data, telephone contacts, and emailed responses. The results were complex and cannot be fully explained here, but evidence was found that new ventures that diversify internationally might sacrifice speed in international expansion for breadth and depth in technological learning. Deeper technological learning was associated with the use of high-control entry modes, such as acquisition and establishment of new ventures. Proactive knowledge–integration efforts, such as analysis of new information by cross-functional teams and consultants, were associated with greater depth and breadth of technological learning in international new ventures. Technological learning was also shown to be positively linked to new venture performance. Readers wanting to know more are encouraged to read the entire article. It was recognized as the best article published in the *Academy of Management Journal* in 2000.

The Global Entrepreneurship Monitor (Reynolds et al., 2002) is a rich example of the comparative branch of international entrepreneurship. The study is published each year in the fall, and in its fourth year entrepreneurial activity in 37 countries was compared on a variety of dimensions. Teams of researchers in the countries gathered data on economic and social conditions, conducted interviews of many experts, administered surveys to those experts, and surveyed representative samples of the national populations. Thus, the data and the teams gathering them were highly international, and the objective was to compare entrepreneurial activities in many countries. Therefore, it clearly represents the international study of entrepreneurship.

Each year, the Global Entrepreneurship Monitor finds wide differences in the level of entrepreneurial activity from country to country, shows that variation in national economic growth rates is associated with those differences, and explores explanatory factors. Even more valuable, because the Global Entrepreneurship Monitor evaluates these issues from year to year, it can show longitudinal dynamics in entrepreneurial behavior around the world.

The domain of international entrepreneurship provides abundant opportunities for further scholarly inquiry. For scholars focusing on entrepreneurial activity that crosses national borders, we propose two very broad research questions: What effects do fluctuating international economic conditions have on the amount, speed, direction, and mode of cross-border transactions by entrepreneurial firms? What factors cause entrepreneurial firms to withdraw from international activity, and once withdrawal occurs, what stimulates entrepreneurial firms to increase their level of internationalization? Within the comparative branch of international entrepreneurship, we are particularly intrigued with the evidence of the positive association between entrepreneurial activity and improved national living standards. Therefore, it becomes important to determine the most effective and efficient way of encouraging entrepreneurship in nations where entrepreneurial activity is weak.

With 15 years of research inquiry, international entrepreneurship has grown to adolescence. As an adolescent discipline, we expect researchers will continue to explore the boundaries of the field and further seek to elucidate why international entrepreneurship should be regarded as a distinct area of scholarly investigation. The field is rich with possibility and opportunity (Acs, Dana, and Jones, 2003) and offers significant collaborative challenges as it, by definition, benefits from the work of scholars in multiple countries and the expertise of scholars in multiple disciplines.

Bibliography

Acs, Z., Dana, L.-P., and Jones, M. V. (2003). Toward new horizons: The internationalization of entrepreneurship. *Journal of International Entrepreneurship*, 1: 5–12.
Gartner, W. B. (1988). "Who is an entrepreneur?" is the wrong question. *American Journal of Small Business*, 12: 11–32.
Giamartino, G. A., McDougall, P. P., and Bird, B. J. (1993). International entrepreneurship: The state of the field. *Entrepreneurship: Theory and Practice*, 18: 37–41.
McDougall, P. P. (1989). International versus domestic entrepreneurship: New venture strategic behavior and industry structure. *Journal of Business Venturing*, 4: 387–99.
McDougall, P. P. and Oviatt, B. M. (2000). International entrepreneurship: The intersection of two research paths. *Academy of Management Journal*, 43: 902–8.
McDougall, P. P. and Oviatt, B. M. (forthcoming). Some fundamental issues in international entrepreneurship. *Entrepreneurship: Theory and Practice*.

Morrow, J. F. (1988). International entrepreneurship: A new growth opportunity. *New Management*, 3: 59–61.

Reynolds, P. D., Bygrave, W. D., Autio, E., Cox, L. W., and Hay, W. (2002). *Global Entrepreneurship Monitor*. Kansas City: E. M. Kauffman Foundation.

Rugman, A. M. and Hodgetts, R. M. (1995). *International Business: A Strategic Management Approach*. New York: McGraw-Hill.

Shane, S. and Venkataraman, S. (2000). The promise of entrepreneurship as a field of research. *Academy of Management Review*, 25: 217–26.

Toyne, B. (1997). The conceptual frontiers of international business. In I. Islam and W. Shepherd (eds.), *Current Issues in International Business*. Cheltenham: Edward Elgar, 35–59.

Venkataraman, S. (1997). The distinctive domain of entrepreneurship research. In J. A. Katz (ed.), *Advances in Entrepreneurship, Firm Emergence, and Growth*, Vol. 3. Greenwich, CT: JAI Press, 119–38.

Wright, R. W. and Ricks, D. A. (1994). Trends in international business research: Twenty-five years later. *Journal of International Business Studies*, 25: 687–701.

Young, S., Dimitratos, P., and Dana, L.-P. (2003). International entrepreneurship research: What scope for international business theories? *Journal of International Entrepreneurship*, 1: 31–42.

Zahra, S. A. and George, G. (2002). International entrepreneurship: The current status of the field and future research agenda. In M. A. Hitt, R. D. Ireland, S. M. Camp, and D. L. Sexton (eds.), *Strategic Entrepreneurship: Creating a New Mindset*. Oxford: Blackwell.

Zahra, S. A., Ireland, R. D., and Hitt, M. A. (2000). International expansion by new venture firms: International diversity, mode of market entry, technological learning and performance. *Academy of Management Journal*, 43: 925–50.

knowledge life cycles and entrepreneurial ventures

Andrew C. Inkpen

Knowledge is the lifeblood of all organizations and especially for entrepreneurs. All new ventures originally begin as an idea about an opportunity for new goods, services, managerial practices, or markets. For an entrepreneurial idea to be transformed into a real commercial venture, knowledge must be created. Increasingly, the creation of organizational knowledge is becoming a managerial priority for all organizations. New knowledge provides the basis for organizational renewal and sustainable competitive advantage and is at the heart of the creative process embodied in entrepreneurship. In this essay I examine knowledge, its life cycles, and its relationship with entrepreneurial ventures. I begin with a discussion of knowledge types and then consider how knowledge evolves in the firm and in a broader environmental context. I then discuss knowledge life cycles from two perspectives: (1) the transformation of knowledge from idea through product development and organizational knowledge-sharing within an organization or new venture; and (2) the evolution of the individual idea from a single firm to a larger network and ultimately to commoditization as a public good. I conclude with several suggestions for future research.

Types of Organizational Knowledge

Knowledge can be defined as information that is laden with experience, judgment, intuition, and value (Nonaka and Takeuchi, 1995). Because the nature of knowledge will influence the volume and type of entrepreneurial opportunities (Eckhardt and Shane, 2003), a starting point in understanding knowledge life cycles is a consid-

eration of knowledge types. I begin with the distinction between tacit and explicit knowledge. Polanyi (1962) defined tacit knowledge as knowledge that is non-verbalizable, intuitive, and unarticulated. Spender (1996a) suggested tacit knowledge could be understood best as knowledge that has not yet been abstracted from practice. It is knowledge that has been transformed into habit and made traditional in the sense that it becomes "the way things are done around here" (Spender, 1996b). Tacit knowledge is highly context specific and has a personal quality, which makes it difficult to formalize and communicate (Nonaka, 1994). Explicit knowledge can be transmitted in formal, systematic language and may include explicit facts, axiomatic propositions, and symbols (Kogut and Zander, 1992). It can be codified or articulated in manuals, computer programs, training tools, and so on.

The distinction between explicit and tacit should not be viewed as a dichotomy, but rather as a spectrum with the two knowledge types at either end. Winter (1987) identified other taxonomic dimensions of knowledge, including complex vs. simple, not teachable vs. teachable, and not observable in use vs. observable in use. Similarly, although the distinction between tacit and explicit is important, it does not allow us to consider any gray areas between completely tacit and completely explicit knowledge. Knowledge types, therefore, must be classified on a continuum that ranges from explicit knowledge embodied in specific products and processes to tacit knowledge acquired through experience and use and embodied in individual cognition and organization routines.

Nonaka and Takeuchi (1995) suggested that a key challenge for organizations is the conversion of tacit knowledge to explicit knowledge. I would argue that the conversion of abstract tacit knowledge into commercial viability is the essence of entrepreneurial knowledge creation. Knowledge that is tacit and highly personal has little commercial value until it can be converted into explicit knowledge and embodied in real products and services that other organizational members can understand. However, such a conversion process exposes the knowledge to the hazard of imitation by other firms. Zander and Kogut (1995) discussed the trade-off between the need to share and transfer knowledge internally and the risk of exposing the knowledge to imitation. For the entrepreneur to create a viable new venture, the conversion of new knowledge and its protection are dual and sometimes competing objectives.

Recognizing that firms' idiosyncratic knowledge consists mostly of tacit, difficult to imitate knowledge, Spender (1996b) developed a more comprehensive typology of organizational knowledge, encompassing individual and social levels. Whereas individuals have knowledge that is practical, communities have knowledge that constitutes the socialization and social activities of the individuals within them. Individuals constantly acquire knowledge, share it with their organizational community and, thus, increase the collective store of knowledge while maintaining a common individual knowledge with their co-workers.

In Spender's (1996b) typology, explicit knowledge stored in databanks, standard operating procedures, manuals, and so on is referred to as objectified knowledge. Tacit knowledge is separated into three subtypes: conscious, automatic, and collective. Individual tacit knowledge can be either conscious or automatic. Automatic knowledge is implicit knowledge that "happens by itself" and is often taken for granted. Conscious knowledge may be codified, perhaps as a set of notes, and is potentially available to other people. Collective knowledge is tacit knowledge of a social or communal nature. For the entrepreneur, converting individual tacit knowledge to collective knowledge is a critical step because it means the knowledge then exists in more than the mind of the innovator.

Finally, knowledge can be viewed in terms of its content. Dess et al. (2003) identified three types of knowledge content: technical, integrative, and exploitative. Technical knowledge is specialized in nature and is concerned with the properties of specific activities. Integrative knowledge is a product of how a firm has learned to combine its unique resources and capabilities to create value. Exploitative knowledge expands as the firm learns how to creatively find value-creating ways to exploit technical and integrative knowledge sets.

KNOWLEDGE LIFE CYCLES

Birkinshaw and Sheehan (2002) proposed a knowledge life cycle with four stages: creation, mobilization, diffusion, and commoditization. Knowledge creation starts as an idea that is highly tacit, difficult to articulate to others, and often conceived to address a specific problem. As the creator of the knowledge further develops the idea, perhaps sharing it with colleagues, the knowledge begins the transition from tacit conscious to tacit collective. This transition represents the mobilization stage. Knowledge becomes known to others, who are then in a position to challenge, critique, and modify the ideas. As the knowledge gets supplemented with new ideas and becomes more explicit, diffusion beyond a small circle of individuals and organizations begins to occur. In the diffusion stage, the knowledge becomes widely known in the relevant marketplace. In the final commoditization stage, the knowledge becomes a public good, which means the organizational challenge is how to manage knowledge that is already well known and broadly diffused.

The Birkinshaw and Sheehan model conceptually overlaps with Nonaka and Takeuchi's (1995) spiral of knowledge creation. The crucial difference is that Nonaka and Takeuchi focus on knowledge within the firm and how innovation occurs. Birkinshaw and Sheehan (2002) addressed the life cycle from creation, to innovation, to knowledge as a public good. In Nonaka and Takeuchi's model, the key underlying process in knowledge creation and innovation is the interaction between tacit and explicit knowledge. As Nonaka and Takeuchi (1995) make clear, the tacit knowledge of individuals is the basis of organizational knowledge creation. Organizations cannot create knowledge without individuals, but unless individual knowledge is shared with other individuals and groups, the knowledge will have a limited impact on organizational effectiveness. Hence, organizational knowledge creation should be viewed as a process whereby the knowledge held by individuals is amplified and internalized as part of an organization's knowledge base (Nonaka, 1994).

As knowledge is transformed from an individual to a collective state, organizational knowledge is created (Nonaka and Takeuchi, 1995). The transformation occurs in a dynamic process involving various organizational levels and carriers of knowledge. Specific learning processes are at work at each level. At the individual level, the critical process is interpreting and sense making; at the group level it is integrating; and at the organization level it is integrating and institutionalizing (Inkpen and Crossan, 1995). To capture the dynamic movement of knowledge across the levels, Nonaka (1994) developed the concept of a spiral of knowledge creation. In the spiral, knowledge moves upward in an organization, starting at the individual level, moving to the group level, and then up to the firm level. As the knowledge spirals upward in the organization, it may be enriched and amplified as individuals interact with each other and with their organizations.

The Organizational Knowledge Cycle

From the previous section, it can be seen that there are two distinct knowledge cycles of relevance for the entrepreneur. The first is that which occurs within a specific organization. In the organizational life cycle, knowledge starts as an idea within the mind of an innovator about an opportunity. For that opportunity to be exploited, the knowledge must spiral upward in an organization, which may result in a new internal venture or a form of corporate entrepreneurship. Regardless of the organizational outcome, the key process is that of the spiral from individual idea to a new venture and innovative outcome. In Nonaka and Takeuchi's (1995) framework, various enabling conditions create the antecedents for the knowledge spiral. The antecedents include organizational intention, individual autonomy, fluctuation and creative chaos, redundancy, and requisite variety. When the conditions are present, organizational knowledge creation can occur.

Nonaka and Takeuchi's (1995) theoretical model was a major advance in the knowledge management area because it incorporated novel theoretical ideas with valid examples of innovation, such as Matsushita's Home Bakery. The interplay between tacit and explicit knowledge is the key underlying process in their model. Designing organizations to enhance creativity requires an appreciation for organizational knowledge evolution. Although heavily focused on Japanese firms, Nonaka and Takeuchi's five phases of knowledge creation provide a template for understanding how knowledge moves from idea through product development and organizational knowledge sharing. The five phases are: sharing tacit knowledge, creating concepts, justifying concepts, building an archetype, and cross-leveling of knowledge. It is not difficult to see that these phases conceptually overlap with organizing models of new venture activity, which involve stages such as entrepreneurial identification, discovery, and exploitation of entrepreneurial opportunities. Indeed, one could argue that the new venture creation process is essentially a process of knowledge creation. Until an original innovative idea is made explicit and transformed through a dynamic process into organizational knowledge that can be transmitted and articulated, the idea's value will be limited. As the idea is transformed, a new venture may be created and exploitation becomes possible.

Knowledge and its Evolution from Idea to Public Good

The Birkinshaw and Sheehan (2002) life cycle traces the evolution of the individual idea from a single firm to a broader industry population and ultimately to commoditization as a public good. They use the example of quality management to illustrate the evolution of a body of knowledge over the life cycle. This broader life cycle mirrors the life cycle of entrepreneurial opportunities (Eckhardt and Shane, 2003). When entrepreneurs exploit opportunities, they transfer knowledge to others about the opportunity, how it works, and how it can be implemented. In doing so, knowledge diffuses to potential imitators, which can erode the value of the opportunity. Alternatively, the entrepreneur may impose or create barriers to imitation, via patents, knowledge protection devices, or secrecy.

There are entrepreneurial opportunities at each stage of the broad knowledge life cycle. However, as Birkinshaw and Sheehan (2002) argued, companies cannot realistically expect to be active in all the stages. Thus, firms and entrepreneurs seeking new opportunities must understand the knowledge life cycle associated with their innovative ideas. Conventional wisdom suggests that ideas grounded in public knowledge will have entered the commoditization stage, limiting opportunities for creating sustainable competitive advantage. On the contrary, although knowledge may have entered the commoditization stage, there will always be new opportunities associated with that knowledge. Commoditized knowledge offers opportunities to recombine and extend knowledge in new value-creating activities. For example, in the international wine industry, the science of making wine is an ancient technology and one that would surely be classified as a commodity. While there have been a few technical innovations in recent years in the wine industry, the most valuable innovations have occurred in downstream areas such as branding, labeling, and advertising. Innovations in these areas have resulted in major new wine industry competitors emerging from countries such as Australia and Chile. Entrepreneurs have capitalized on the willingness of Old World wine producers to accept commoditization as the natural order of the industry.

Moreover, knowledge life cycles can be renewed, as the wine industry example illustrates. As wine industry knowledge became collectively known and commoditized, creative wine industry firms adapted to the environment and spawned a new knowledge life cycle around innovations in areas such as labeling, advertising, Internet sales, and so on. Thus, rather than viewing the knowledge life cycle as an evolution with an endpoint, it should be viewed as a series of stages that continues to spawn new entrepreneurial opportunities along the life cycle.

The Knowledge Life Cycle as an Evolutionary Perspective

Various scholars have called for an evolutionary approach to the study of entrepreneurship. The idea of evolution means that the concepts will evolve over time and in so doing impact other concepts. For example, Aldrich and Martinez (2001) argued that an evolutionary approach should study the creation of organizations, the way in which entrepreneurs adapt and use organizational resources, the circumstances under which new ventures survive and prosper, and the manner in which successful ventures are imitated and perpetuated by other entrepreneurs. Knowledge life cycles, both within the firm and within broader society, should be an integral element in such an evolutionary approach. Since entrepreneurs exploit opportunities and create knowledge, the origin and evolution of entrepreneurial knowledge should play a key role in entrepreneurship research and practice.

In addition, the network in which knowledge gets created has an important role in shaping how knowledge evolves. Networks also evolve and their evolution will be correlated with knowledge life cycles. The knowledge that entrepreneurs acquire and exploit often comes from within a network of existing and future producers, supporting organizations, and a labor market. The configuration of a network structure determines the pattern of linkages among network members. Elements of configuration such as hierarchy, density, and connectivity affect the flexibility and ease of knowledge exchange through their impact on the extent of contact and accessibility among network members (Krackhardt, 1992). The structural, cognitive, and relational dimensions of an internal firm network will influence the movement of knowledge from creation to diffusion within a firm. Once knowledge is diffused beyond the firm, in its path to eventual commoditization, various networks and the social context in which firms are embedded will impact the knowledge evolution.

Conclusion

Generating, capturing, and leveraging knowledge, as the key to competitive success, is a notion that is widely accepted. New knowledge, and especially knowledge from outside the firm, can be an important stimulus for change and organizational improvement. Since unique knowledge is the most valuable capital of entrepreneurs, understanding the link between knowledge life cycles and new ventures should be a primary area of study in the field of entrepreneurship. This short essay touches on some of the underlying conceptual issues involving knowledge life cycles, entrepreneurship, and new ventures. Future research could address a variety of interesting issues, such as: What is the life cycle of knowledge as it is transferred from one new venture to the next? At what stage in the organizational knowledge life cycle should a new venture transfer knowledge to potential customers and how does this transfer impact the ability of the entrepreneur to establish legitimacy? What are the managerial processes that support or hinder the movement of knowledge from tacit idea to explicit new product? Can the knowledge life cycle be effectively managed in a manner that supports new venture value creation? Do different knowledge life cycle stages play a greater or lesser role in contributing to new venture success? What role do organizational processes and control play in facilitating the spiral of knowledge from idea to exploited opportunity? How does knowledge move through regional knowledge networks and what are the key stages where the knowledge interacts with entrepreneurs and other network members?

Bibliography

Aldrich, H. E. and Martinez, M. A. (2001). Many are called but few are chosen: An evolutionary perspective for the study of entrepreneurship. *Entrepreneurship: Theory and Practice*, 25: 21–56.

Birkinshaw, J. and Sheehan, T. (2002). Managing the knowledge life cycle. *Sloan Management Review*, fall: 75–83.

Dess, G. G., Ireland, R. D., Zahra, S. A., Floyd, S. W., Janney, J. J., and Lane, P. J. (2003). Emerging issues in corporate entrepreneurship. *Journal of Management*, 29: 351–79.

Eckhardt, J. T. and Shane, S. A. (2003). Opportunities and entrepreneurship. *Journal of Management*, 29: 333–49.

Inkpen, A. C. and Crossan, M. M. (1995). Believing is seeing: Joint ventures and organizational learning. *Journal of Management Studies*, 32: 595–618.

Kogut, B. and Zander, U. (1992). Knowledge of the firm, combinative capabilities, and the replication of technology. *Organization Science*, 3: 383–97.

Krackhardt, D. (1992). The strength of strong ties. In N. Nohria and R. G. Eccles (eds.), *Networks and Organizations: Structure, Form and Action*. Boston, MA: Harvard Business School Press, 216–39.

Nonaka, I. (1994). A dynamic theory of organizational knowledge. *Organization Science*, 5: 14–37.

Nonaka, I. and Takeuchi, H. (1995). *The Knowledge-Creating Company: How Japanese Companies Create the Dynamics of Innovation*. New York: Oxford University Press.

Polanyi, M. (1962). *Personal Knowledge: Towards a Post-Critical Philosophy*. Chicago: University of Chicago Press.

Spender, J. C. (1996a). Organizational knowledge, learning, and memory: Three concepts in search of a theory. *Journal of Organizational Change*, 9: 63–78.

Spender, J. C. (1996b). Making knowledge the basis of a dynamic theory of the firm. *Strategic Management Journal* (special issue): 45–62.

Winter, S. G. (1987). Knowledge and competence as strategic assets. In D. Teece (ed.), *The Competitive Challenge*. Cambridge, MA: Ballinger Publishing, 159–84.

Zander, U. and Kogut, B. (1995). Knowledge and the speed of transfer and imitation of organizational capabilities: An empirical test. *Organization Science*, 6: 76–92.

knowledge-based assets in entrepreneurial ventures

Anjali Bakhru and Robert M. Grant

The vigor and dynamism of developing research in entrepreneurship during the past decade owes much to the increased fusion of the fields of entrepreneurship, strategic management, organizational evolution, and organizational ecology. The most important contributions of strategic management have been ideas associated with resource-based and knowledge-based approaches to the firm. The role of resources in general, and knowledge in particular, has been important in the origins of entrepreneurial activity and in influencing the performance and early development of start-up businesses. In addition, emphasis on the role of knowledge assets in entrepreneurship has provided closer links with the macro-level study of entrepreneurial activity undertaken by economic and social geographers and economic historians (see, for example, Saxenian, 1994; Acs, 2000). These studies have placed emphasis on the role of localized concentrations of scientific and technical knowledge (Zucker, Darby and Brewer, 1998), on information through social networks (Aldrich and Zimmer, 1986), and the role of venture capitalists in supplying know-how – as well as the financing of entrepreneurial activity (Freeman, 1986). Our focus is on the micro-level literature, particularly upon the sources of individual entrepreneurs' knowledge and the processes through which new enterprises convert individual knowledge into organizational capabilities.

At the root of the knowledge-based view is the characterization of the firm as a repository of knowledge (Kogut and Zander, 1992). In the case of new start-up enterprises, knowledge resides primarily within the individual members of the firm – the younger the firm, the more important is individual knowledge relative to organizational knowledge. The founders of new firms have histories (Helfat and Lieberman, 2001); typically, it is their prior work experience that is the primary source of the knowledge that is critical both to the decision to found a new enterprise and to the initial performance of their new venture. The distinction between venture creation and venture performance is an important one. We argue that the value of prior experience relates primarily to creating the new venture and ensuring that it becomes operational. However, the greatest challenge facing the new enterprise is survival. Research across sectors and across countries shows that mortality rates among new enterprises are very high. This is notably the case in new industries, where high rates of entry are matched by high rates of failure – especially among start-up firms (Carroll et al., 1996). The challenge of survival is especially great in a new industry because survival requires constant adaptation to the rapid rate of evolution of the industry environment. Despite considerable research into the biographical characteristics of entrepreneurs and the performance of the business ventures they found – including the effects of education, managerial experience, and prior entrepreneurial experience (e.g., Sandberg and Hofer, 1987), the result of the research lacks consistency and robustness. It seems likely that the knowledge of the entrepreneur – as determined by prior experiences – is influential in the decision to found an enterprise, in the characteristics of that enterprise, and in its initial success. However, longer term, it is the enterprise's ability to develop and deploy its knowledge base that becomes much more important for survival and growth.

In terms of the knowledge base of individual entrepreneurs, prior work experience offers entrepreneurs two types of knowledge that are crucial to the founding and subsequent survival of their new ventures: (1) the ability to recognize business opportunities, and (2) the organizational and managerial know-how for establishing and developing a new enterprise. The prior work experience of founders is relevant to both categories of knowledge, although other sources of knowledge are potentially relevant to the first category. First, research has shown that business opportunities are likely to have been identified and formalized based on an individual's previous work experience (Shane, 2000), although the ability to recognize business opportunities could have been informed by other types of prior experience gained through educational experience or social contact, for example. Second, while the role of the prior experience of founders is shown to be important in the early performance of a new venture (Stuart and Abetti, 1990), it is increasingly being cited in relation to its effect on venture creation, where our focus here is on the knowledge gained through prior work experience that is relevant to the managerial challenge of developing and establishing a new venture. Recent research more specifically links the prior managerial experience of founders to a capability-based perspective. Among the *Inc. 500* high-growth start-ups, Romanelli and Schoonhoven (2001: 47) show "a very close association between the expertise and experience of the founders and the kinds of organizations they created." Alvarez and Busenitz (2001) state that the role of entrepreneurs can be considered in resource terms. The "entrepreneurial resource" can be considered in terms of (1) entrepreneurial recognition, or the recognition and seeking of business opportunities, and (2) the ability to combine and organize resources. Having recognized a business opportunity, an entrepreneur is further able to combine and coordinate resources within the new venture, where these resources comprise the tangible (physical, financial), intangible (brand), and human resources that are essential to ensuring that the new venture is operational. In other words, a key component of managerial knowledge is a manager's prior experience of creating and developing routines and capabilities.

Central to the challenge of new venture creation is the challenge of developing the routines and capabilities that are essential to making the venture fully operational. Research has highlighted the importance of the managerial role in relation to the selection and evolution of capabilities: the importance of the top management team's influence on the evolution of the firm's capability set (Levinthal, 1995; Kazanjian and Rao, 1999), and how managerial input in the selection and development of capabilities can differ greatly across firms (Amit and Schoemaker, 1993). However, it is with respect to the nature of the managerial task that we can better understand the role of managerial knowledge in the creation of routines and capabilities.

The managerial challenge can be considered to comprise the development of the underlying operational and technical routines that are specific to functional areas (i.e., component routines), as well as the structure of which they are a part (i.e., the architectural routines that integrate component routines both within and across functional areas). While the value of prior experience relates to the tacit knowledge (knowing how) and the explicit knowledge (knowing about) that entrepreneurs bring with them, it is argued that the relative value of the types of knowledge that the entrepreneur possesses is better understood in relation to the capability-based challenge. The managerial knowledge required for developing routines and capabilities can be considered to comprise two elements: the requisite component knowledge underlying specific routines, as well as the architectural knowledge critical for the integration of routines and capabilities.

Kirzner (1979) makes a distinction between entrepreneurial knowledge and the knowledge expert, suggesting that it is the entrepreneur who hires the latter. Alvarez and Busenitz (2001) similarly distinguish between the specific knowledge of the expert (such as technological expertise) and the entrepreneur's knowledge. While the entrepreneur may have specialized knowledge, it is with regard to the tacit, generalized knowledge of how to organize specialized knowledge that is the entrepreneur's critical intangible resource.

Recent empirical research on capability development in new online ventures provides further support for the value of the entrepreneur's architectural knowledge assets (Bakhru, 2003). A dis-

tinction is made between the role of prior experience at different layers in the managerial hierarchy. The importance of the prior organizational experience of the top or senior management team relates to their ability to develop the overall blueprint for the creation of capabilities within online operations, or "capability blueprint," where this refers to the overall structure or architecture of the firm's capability set, including consideration of the main tasks or processes of which these core functions comprise. In contrast, it is the next layer of management that is more directly responsible for the creation of organizational routines. The relevance of their prior organizational experience relates to the "technical" knowledge considered vital to creating specific functional and operational routines.

It is argued that a key resource in new ventures are the knowledge assets that entrepreneurs bring with them. While the role of entrepreneurs can be considered in relation to business opportunity recognition, the critical role of the entrepreneur is in creating the venture and ensuring that it is operational. As such, value lies in the architectural knowledge assets of the entrepreneur that are essential for the integration of routines and capabilities and that are, in turn, derived from the tacit, generalized knowledge that is a product of the entrepreneur's prior work experience.

Bibliography

Acs, Z. J. (2000). *Innovation and the Growth of Cities*. Cheltenham: Edward Elgar.

Aldrich, H. E. and Zimmer, C. (1986). Entrepreneurship through social networks. In D. L. Sexton and R. W. Smilor (eds.), *The Art and Science of Entrepreneurship*. Cambridge, MA: Ballinger, 3–23.

Alvarez, S. A. and Busenitz, L. W. (2001). The entrepreneurship of resource-based theory. *Journal of Management*, 27: 755–75.

Amit, R. and Schoemaker, P. J. (1993). Strategic assets and organizational rent. *Strategic Management Journal*, 14: 33–46.

Bakhru, A. (2003). Competitive advantage in new markets: The case of online business. Unpublished doctoral thesis, Cass Business School, City University, London.

Carroll, G. R., Bigelow, L. S., Seidel, M.-D., and Tsai, B. (1996). The fates of *de novo* and *de alio* producers in the American automobile industry, 1885–1981. *Strategic Management Journal*, 17 (summer special issue): 117–37.

Freeman, J. (1986). Entrepreneurs as organizational products: Semiconductor firms and venture capital firms. In G. Libecap (ed.), *Advances in the Study of Entrepreneurship, Innovation, and Economic Growth*. Greenwich, CT: JAI Press.

Helfat, C. E. and Lieberman, M. (2001). The birth of capabilities: Market entry and the importance of pre-history. Paper presented at the Academy of Management Annual Meeting, Washington, DC.

Kazanjian, R. K. and Rao, H. (1999). Research note: The creation of capabilities in new ventures – a longitudinal study. *Organization Studies*, 20 (1): 125–42.

Kirzner, I. (1979). *Perception, Opportunity, and Profit*. Chicago: University of Chicago Press.

Kogut, B. and Zander, U. (1992). Knowledge of the firm, combinative capabilities, and the replication of technology. *Organization Science*, 3: 383–97.

Levinthal, D. (1995). Strategic management and the exploration of diversity. In C. A. Montgomery (ed.), *Resource-Based and Evolutionary Theories of the Firm: Towards a Synthesis*. Boston, MA: Kluwer Academic Publishers.

Romanelli, E. and Schoonhoven, C. B. (2001). The local origins of new firms. In C. B. Schoonhoven and E. Romanelli (eds.), *The Entrepreneurship Dynamic*. Stanford, CA: Stanford University Press, 40–67.

Sandberg, W. R. and Hofer, C. W. (1987). Improving new venture performance: The role of strategy, industry, structure, and the entrepreneur. *Journal of Business Venturing*, 2: 5–28.

Saxenian, A. (1994). *Regional Advantage: Culture and Competition in Silicon Valley and Route 128*. Cambridge, MA: Harvard University Press.

Shane, S. (2000). Prior knowledge and the discovery of entrepreneurial opportunities. *Strategic Management Journal*, 11: 448–69.

Stuart, R. W. and Abetti, P. A. (1990). Impact of entrepreneurial and management experience on early performance. *Journal of Business Venturing*, 5 (3): 151–62.

Zucker, L. G., Darby, M. R., and Brewer, M. B. (1998). Intellectual human capital and the birth of US biotechnology enterprises. *American Economic Review*, 88: 290–306.

L

liability of newness

Claudia Bird Schoonhoven

The origin of the phrase "liability of newness" can be traced to Arthur Stinchcombe's article on social structure and organizations, published in 1965. In this article Stinchcombe argues that poorly understood conditions are responsible for the comparative death rates of new and old organizations and particularly for why a higher proportion of new organizations appear to fail than older ones. Stinchcombe's implicit definition of the liability of newness is that new organizations face a constellation of problems associated with their newly founded status which renders them particularly prone to failure. Stinchcombe argues that four main problems comprise the liability of newness and that social conditions at the time of founding affect the degree of liability a new firm faces.

First, new organizations – especially *new types* of organizations – generally involve the creation and learning of new roles. Some organizational roles must be invented *de nouveau* – and regardless, all roles require learning by the new organization's members. Initially, new organizations must contend with employees' generalized skills acquired prior to the new firm's founding until sufficient time has passed for employees to learn and efficiently execute their new roles. Essentially, a new firm must invest time, either explicitly or implicitly, in educating its new employees to execute their responsibilities. In an older organization, by contrast, position incumbents can efficiently transmit to their successors organization-specific skills required for the smooth execution of a role, including otherwise implicit knowledge such as dealing with sources of tension and conflict.

Second, the process of inventing and learning new roles is costly because of the time required for invention and learning. The creation of a new role requires negotiation with others in the organization to agree that the role and its responsibilities are appropriate. As a consequence, role creation and its negotiation involve uncertainty, interpersonal conflict, and temporary organizational inefficiencies. Therefore, this process involves trial and error as new employees invent and refine their new roles. Much is taken for granted in organizations and generalized skills brought from a prior organization may require substantial customizing for use in the new organization, depending on the other roles also being created and customized for the new context. In a larger well-established organization, several coordinated positions may, in combination, execute a given function – say perhaps the many different jobs in a financial accounting department. In a new organization, *the* accountant must define and execute the entire set of tasks, including how to systematically extract the relevant data from others in an efficient manner – some of whom may not understand that the accountant expects them to deliver accurate and timely data. Thus, the "creation of new roles" really involves the creation of a new system of roles, responsibilities, and relationships between positions in the new organization.

Third, new organizations rely heavily on "social relations among strangers," a famous Stinchcombe phrase. When a new organization is founded, the new employees are typically strangers to one another, with no job history in common. Interpersonal trust is initially very low among strangers; as a consequence, relationships between co-workers in a new organization are precarious. Can you depend on others to execute their role responsibilities in a timely manner at a tolerable level of competence? Embedded in the phrase "social relations among strangers" is the understanding that in some cultures responsibilities to others, like family and friends, override obligations to relative strangers, even in the same work organization. Initially, low loyalty to the employment contract is likely to exist, and thus the commitment of a new hire to the new organization is also precarious. The degree to which the "social relations among strangers" liability is problematic for a new organization depends upon whether the external social structure emphasizes differences in the relative trustworthiness of strangers when compared to kin and friends. As a consequence, the culture in which a new organization is embedded can mediate or exacerbate this source of newness liabilities.

Stinchcombe's fourth and last dimension of the liability of newness involves the difficulties that new organizations face in establishing relationships with other organizations, especially potential customers and suppliers. Whereas older organizations have built stable ties with their customers and suppliers over time, including knowing whom to call for action, new organizations must start from scratch to build stable relationships with external organizations. The stronger the ties between existing organizations (i.e., competitors and their customers), the more difficult it will be for the new organization to establish initial ties to outside firms.

Beyond these four described by Stinchcombe, yet another dimension of the liability of newness exists. New organizations established for the purpose of creating new knowledge face an additional liability, the liability of innovation. New firms founded in science-based industries are especially prone to this threat to their survival. The time required to create the requisite knowledge for new products or services in new firms is uncertain. It is difficult to predict when the first working prototype will be complete and furthermore when revenue from the sales of those products on the market will be realized. The inability to predict time to prototype completion and first market sales may require that the new organization exist months longer than expected while paying for salaries and materials without revenues to support the expenses. As a consequence, new organizations attempting to

create highly innovative products often take longer to achieve their first revenues (Schoonhoven, Eisenhardt, and Lyman, 1990). The longer the new firm must exist without a stable revenue stream, the higher the likelihood it will fail to survive.

To summarize, the liability of newness hinges on Stinchcombe's assessment of internal organizational relationships, as well as relations with the external environment. Trust among members helps create an efficient organization, but it requires time to develop. Similarly, creating and refining roles, relationships, and routines, establishing relationships with other organizations, and learning about the external environment all take time. Once these patterned relationships are established, however, a social structure supporting the new organization's survival chances has been created.

Research on the Liabilities of Newness

An indicator of the pervasive impact of Stinchcombe's original article is that it has been cited approximately 863 times since 1965. Initially, those who built on Stinchcombe's insights were primarily organization theorists doing research on the relationship between social structure and organizations, writ large. For example, in the late 1960s, studies focused on utopian communities (Kanter, 1968), the evolution of organization environments (Terreberry, 1968), and the context of organization structures. However, these early papers did not focus on entrepreneurship or new firms *per se*.

Throughout the 1970s and 1990s a research base emerged conceptualized as the creation of new firms. In these works, the liabilities of newness, proxied as age of firm, were studied in conjunction with firm survival. Early research in the organization ecology tradition found support for Stinchcombe's argument that death rates of young organizations exceed those of older ones. For example, Carroll (1983) demonstrated this pattern of outcomes in a study of 63 diverse kinds of organizations. Freeman, Carroll, and Hannan (1983) found similar patterns for labor unions, semiconductor firms, and San Francisco newspaper publishers. More generally, these research findings are referred to as "negative age dependent mortality or death rates." For reviews of the multitude of studies that have reported this pattern, see Aldrich and Marsden (1988), Singh and Lumsden (1990), and Hannan et al. (1998).

It should be noted, however, that some research shows that mortality rates do not always decline monotonically after founding. That is, the life chances of organizations do not always improve with age. Referred to as the "liability of adolescence," some have found that death rates sometimes increase for a brief early portion of the life span before declining over the remainder of the typical life span (e.g., Fichman and Levinthal, 1991). Others speak of the "liability of obsolescence." In this case, increasing organizational age is argued to increase the mortality rate, primarily because organizations become locked on strategies and structures more appropriate for earlier years of their existence – those conditions which are now obsolete. This "lock" is sometimes referred to as structural inertia, where it becomes increasingly difficult for older organizations to adapt sufficiently to a changing environment. Lastly, there is some research on the "liability of senescence." Somewhat akin to early descriptions of bureaucracy, the accumulation of rules, routines, and structures (i.e., red tape) renders an older organization less efficient and thus older organizations in these cases have higher mortality rates (Barron, West, and Hannan, 1994).

As these latter variations on "age liabilities" suggest, the relationship between organizational age and death rates is more complicated than it might appear. Complications might arise especially if unmeasured heterogeneity exists. It has been shown to generate spurious negative age dependence (Tuma and Hannan, 1984), which in the case of research on the liabilities of newness can be confounding. An important source of unmeasured heterogeneity is the variable of organizational size, which was not controlled in some early studies of organizational age and mortality. Because organizations tend to grow with age, variation in size might account for observed low death rates of older organizations. We conclude that this issue is far from being resolved. For information on the joint effects of organizational age and size on death rates, see Hannan et al. (1998) and Hannan and Carroll (2000: 319–22), who conclude that several technical and substantive matters need clarification

before the joint effects of age and size on organizational death rates can be clearly understood. In summary, organizational size likely should be controlled in the study of organizational age, ensuring that size is measured repeatedly over the life span of the organizations examined.

ENTREPRENEURIAL ACTIONS TO AMELIORATE THE LIABILITIES OF NEWNESS

Given what we know, what are practical actions entrepreneurs can take to minimize or ameliorate their own new ventures' liabilities of newness? Recall that internally the liabilities of newness focus on new people, the new organization, and the creation of new technology. New organizations should not attempt to reinvent existing or older organizational practices; rather, they should import standard solutions for common problems faced by organizations in the industry. Common ways of organizing the accounting and customer service units exist within most industries, and thus adopting these procedures rather than inventing *de novo* routines is efficient for the new venture. This argument also suggests hiring industry-experienced veterans already familiar with the routine functions needed for the new venture; their knowledge can substantially facilitate the organization and operations in early days of the new organization.

Part of the problem in creating and negotiating new roles is that some employees may take the limits of their perceived responsibilities seriously. Because many problems a new firm faces are novel to it and thus not included in anyone's job description *per se*, problems may go unattended because no one perceives them as her or his responsibility. New firms require employees who can take initiative when new problems are encountered and who accept responsibility for getting work done perhaps beyond the perceived scope of their responsibilities. A high initiative and responsibility-taking workforce has a better chance of collectively resolving a new firm's problems than those who operate from the perspective of narrow job descriptions.

Founders and members of the top management team have a substantial effect on the life chances of a new venture. Creating a top management team with substantial heterogeneity has survival advantages for new ventures. For example, variation in years of experience in the industry, in technical expertise, education, and age all combine to create a top management with a mix of talents and viewpoints that advantage a new firm (Eisenhardt and Schoonhoven, 1989, 1990). Similarly, cutting edge, relatively young engineers led by industry-experienced technical veterans enhance the new firm's ability to get its innovative products to market. In addition to top management team heterogeneity new ventures would do well to obtain some non-stranger top managers who have had previous joint work experience with one another and who have had at least three years of industry experience variation.

We also know that top management teams that seek modest innovation in their first products have advantages over those that seek to create highly innovative products. The liability of innovation is substantially reduced when firms tackle first products that can be created by building on existing knowledge rather than those derived from the creation of substantial new knowledge. Highly novel products consume R&D time and other resources and thus risk depleting the financial resources of a new company before the first product begins to produce stable revenues (Schoonhoven, Eisenhardt, and Lyman, 1990: 198).

Stinchcombe argued that external social conditions at the time of birth have an important effect on new venture survival. External newness liabilities focus on a new venture's paucity of relationships with other organizations, especially those that may eventually develop a vested interest in the success of the new venture, such as potential investors. Schoonhoven and Eisenhardt (1992: 217) defined an incubator region as a confluence of industry-specific resources contained within a circumscribed geographic area that may be mobilized to create and sustain new ventures in a given industry. A multidimensional concept, rich incubator regions contain a substantial number of existing same-industry firms, a stock of industry-savvy investors, armed with substantial capital for new venture investment, a stock of industry-trained technical experts and production workers, and service firms that specialize in supporting the focal industry. These researchers found that new ventures established in incubator regions low in

industry-specific resources had a significantly higher risk of death at an early age (Schoonhoven and Eisenhardt, 1992: 240). This research supports the following conclusion: to reduce liabilities of newness, technology-based entrepreneurs should locate their new firms in regions dense with industry-specific resources such as industry suppliers, risk capital investors experienced with their industry, and industry-experienced managers and production workers.

In summary, substantial research supports Stinchcombe's (1965) early theorizing about the liabilities of newness, and specifically that new firms have a higher likelihood of failure than older firms. Additional research on new firms has shown that entrepreneurs may take practical actions to help reduce their ventures' newness liabilities and as a consequence, enhance the likelihood of their new ventures' survival.

Bibliography

Aldrich, H. E. and Marsden, P. V. (1988). Environments and organizations. In N. Smelser (ed.), *Handbook of Sociology*. Beverly Hills, CA: Sage, 361–92.

Barron, D. N., West, E., and Hannan, M. T. (1994). A time to grow and a time to die: Growth and mortality of credit unions in New York, 1914–1990. *American Journal of Sociology*, 100: 381–421.

Carroll, G. (1983). A stochastic model of organizational mortality: Review and reanalysis. *Social Science Research*, 12: 303–29.

Eisenhardt, K. M. and Schoonhoven, C. B. (1990). Organizational growth: Linking founding team, strategy, environment, and growth among US semiconductor ventures, 1977–1988. *Administrative Science Quarterly*, 35: 504–29.

Fichman, M. and Levinthal, D. A. (1991). Honeymoons and the liability of adolescence: A new perspective on duration dependence in social and organizational relationships. *Academy of Management Review*, 16: 442–68.

Freeman, J., Carroll, G. R., and Hannan, M. T. (1983). The liability of newness: Age dependence in organizational death rates. *American Sociological Review*, 48: 692–710.

Hannan, M. T. (1998). Rethinking age dependence in organizational mortality: Logical formalizations. *American Journal of Sociology*, 104: 85–123.

Hannan, M. T. and Carroll, G. R. (2000). *The Demography of Corporations and Industries*. Princeton, NJ: Princeton University Press.

Hannan, M. T., Carroll, G. R., Dobrev, S. D., Han, J., and Torres, J. C. (1998). Organizational mortality in European and American automobile industries, Part I: Revisiting the effects of age and size. *European Sociological Review*, 14: 279–302.

Kanter, R. M. (1968). Commitment mechanisms in utopian communities. *American Sociological Review*, 33 (4): 499–551.

Schoonhoven, C. B. and Eisenhardt, K. M. (1989). *The Incubator Region on the Creation and Survival of New Semiconductor Ventures in the US 1978–1986*. Washington, DC: US Department of Commerce, National Technical Information Service.

Schoonhoven, C. B. and Eisenhardt, K. M. (1992). Regions as industrial incubators of technology-based ventures. In E. S. Mills and J. F. McDonald (eds.), *Sources of Metropolitan Growth*. New Brunswick, NJ: Center for Urban Policy Research.

Schoonhoven, C. B., Eisenhardt, K. M., and Lyman, K. (1990). Speeding products to market: Waiting time to first product introduction in new firms. *Administrative Science Quarterly*, 35: 177–207.

Singh, J. and Lumsden, C. J. (1990). Theory and research in organizational ecology. *Annual Review of Sociology*, 16: 161–95.

Stinchcombe, A. L. (1965). Social structure and organizations. In J. G. March (ed.), *Handbook of Organizations*. Chicago: Rand McNally, 142–93.

Terreberry, S. (1968). The evolution of organizational environments. *Administrative Science Quarterly*, 12 (4): 590–613.

Tuma, N. B. and Hannan, M. T. (1984). *Social Dynamics: Models and Methods*. Orlando, FL: Academic Press.

location effects on entrepreneurial ventures

Joseph E. Coombs

To what extent does a regional environment affect a new venture's success? If a firm simply locates in a region rich in the knowledge that it needs to succeed, will it increase its chance of success or does the venture need to directly involve itself through collaboration with the local knowledge creators in order to benefit? How does location affect the flow of financial resources into a venture? These are important questions that must be answered to meet Schumpeter's challenge to investigate the conditions that create opportunities for, support, and impede entrepreneurial activity (Schumpeter, 1942, 1991).

Economists have recognized for decades that firms in the same industry tend to cluster geographically. This phenomenon has been observed in the Texas lodging industry (Chung and Kalnins, 2001), the Manhattan hotel industry (Baum and Haveman, 1997; Baum and Mezias, 1992), the biotechnology industry (DeCarolis and Deeds, 1999; Deeds, DeCarolis, and Coombs, 2000; Stuart and Sorenson, 2003; Zucker, Darby, and Armstrong, 1998), footwear production (Sorenson and Audia, 2000), Internet software and equipment (Zacharakis, Shepherd, and Coombs, 2003), and computers (Saxenian, 1994), as well as textiles, leather goods, furniture, ceramic tiles, and automobile production (Sorenson and Audia, 2000). This observation has led to a stream of research devoted to agglomeration economies. This economic explanation for observed clustering activity emphasizes the benefits of locating one's firm within a geographic center of production. These benefits include decreased transportation costs, proximity to raw materials, and access to a labor force with unique skills (Acs, FitzRoy, and Smith, 1999; Sorenson and Audia, 2000). In particular, Krugman (1991a, 1991b) and Marshall (1920) have suggested three factors that foster the creation of industry clusters: a pooled market for specialized labor, the development of specialized intermediate goods industries, and knowledge spillovers. Arthur (1990) provides a second model of regional development described as self-reinforcing expertise, in which geographic variance in technical progress exists because regions with innovative activity develop specialized resources critical to the next phase of innovation. In each of these models, knowledge spillovers play a particularly important role. By locating in a geographic cluster of similar ventures, a venture is able to take advantage of knowledge spillovers from competitors and from other institutions. In the biotechnology industry, research universities are an example of an institution that can be the source of knowledge spillovers beneficial to the ventures in the local geographic cluster (Acs, Audretsch, and Feldman, 1992, 1994; Audretsch and Stephan, 1996; Jaffe, 1989; Jaffe, Trajtenberg, and Henderson, 1993; Mansfield, 1995; Zucker, Darby, and Brewer, 1998).

THE INFLUENCE OF INCREASING CLUSTER CONCENTRATION

While there is considerable evidence as to the benefits of being located among a cluster of similar ventures, researchers have recently noted that as clusters become more concentrated, increased competition for inputs, in particular labor, adversely affects new ventures (Deeds, DeCarolis, and Coombs, 2000; Folta, Cooper, and Baik, 2003; Hannan and Freeman, 1977; Pouder and St. John, 1996; Shaver and Flyer, 2000; Sorenson and Audia, 2000; Stuart and Sorenson, 2003). Organization ecology and sociology, in particular, inform us that competition within geographically local organization populations is more intense than outside these concentrated locations (Carroll and Wade, 1991; Hannan and Carroll, 1992). Empirical evidence tends to support this perspective. For example, Sorenson and Audia (2000) reported that shoe manufacturing plants in or near large concentrations of shoe producers are significantly more likely to fail than more isolated plants. Stuart and Sorenson (2003) established a negative relationship between biotechnology cluster density and time to initial public offering. Baum and Mezias (1992) showed that in the Manhattan hotel industry establishments that were similar in location, price, and physical size reduced each other's survival probabilities. Deeds, DeCarolis, and Coombs (2000) demonstrated that lower geographic concentration levels supported new product development in the biotechnology industry, but increased geographic concentration overtaxed local resource stocks and negatively affected individual ventures' new product development capabilities. Further, Shaver and Flyer (2000), following their study of the location choices of foreign Greenfield investments in US manufacturing industries, put forth the view that ventures with the best technologies, human capital, training programs, and employees have an incentive to locate away from industry clusters. They suggested it is ventures with lesser technologies, human capital, training programs, suppliers, or distributors that benefit most from being located in clusters, as they can gain access to resources from ventures endowed with the best technologies, human capital, training programs, suppliers, or distributors.

Ventures with an abundance of the best resources thus provide resources to ventures with lesser resources, but receive little in return and thus have an incentive to avoid clusters. Thus, agglomeration economics and organizational ecology provide competing views on the benefits of industry clusters. Recent work by Zucker, Darby, and Brewer (1998) on the biotechnology industry suggests a possible mediating influence at work between industry cluster characteristics and venture performance.

KNOWLEDGE SPILLOVERS OR MARKETS FOR INFORMATION?

Zucker, Darby, and Armstrong (1998) questioned the assumption that localized knowledge spillovers are freely available to ventures and that ventures have the necessary capabilities to recognize and assimilate these spillovers. Rather than being freely available, localized knowledge may be available primarily through identifiable market exchanges made between local ventures and the sources of local knowledge (i.e., scientists, university departments, research institutes, etc.). The empirical evidence supports this position. Zucker, Darby, and Armstrong (1998) reported that the significant influence of location (as measured by the number of star biotechnology scientists in a firm's geographic location) on research productivity (measured as products in development) disappears when the star scientist variable is broken down into those with direct venture links and those without. Thus, the level of connectedness to one's cluster mediates the relationship between simply being located in the cluster and venture performance. This research suggests an important role for networks within geographic clusters. Sorenson and Audia (2000) provided recent evidence that social networks' importance goes far beyond facilitating knowledge transfer.

Sorenson and Audia (2000) hypothesized that heterogeneity in entrepreneurial opportunities maintains geographic clustering well past the point at which concentration begins to negatively affect venture performance. The rationale behind this intriguing insight is that entrepreneurs need contact with existing ventures in the industry. These contacts provide the entrepreneur with tacit knowledge of the industry, important social ties, and self-confidence that collectively make it possible for them to mobilize the resources required to start a new venture. Geographic clusters provide substantial opportunities for repeated contacts and thus may provide an advantage not available to entrepreneurs outside of the cluster. This could explain why we can observe higher founding rates in geographic clusters, yet also observe higher death rates.

LOOKING TO THE FUTURE

Researchers should move beyond the advantages and disadvantages of clusters and focus instead on firm-level and individual-level characteristics that make operating within or outside clusters more advantageous to new ventures. Zucker, Darby, and Armstrong (1998) presented evidence that firms connected to specific sources of knowledge (i.e., star scientists) benefit more from this connection than from merely being located within a biotechnology cluster. Sorenson and Audia (2000) also suggested that personal networks within clusters allow entrepreneurs to benefit from the cluster even when the cluster itself is in decline. An interesting avenue for future research is the influence of social networks on an entrepreneur's success when located inside or outside a cluster. Further, is it beneficial for an entrepreneur outside of a cluster to have a social network that includes individuals within an industry cluster? Lastly, there is evidence that geographic cluster effects fade over time, but only very slowly (Jaffe, Trajtenberg, and Henderson, 1993). Research may further investigate why geographic clusters tend to persist and the conditions under which clusters can evolve to support new industries.

Bibliography

Acs, Z. J., Audretsch, D. B., and Feldman, M. P. (1992). Real effects of academic research: Comment. *American Economic Review*, 82: 363–7.

Acs, Z. J., Audretsch, D. B., and Feldman, M. P. (1994). R&D spillovers and recipient firm size. *Review of Economics and Statistics*, 76: 336–40.

Acs, Z. J., FitzRoy, F. R., and Smith, I. (1999). High-technology employment, wages, and university R&D spillovers: Evidence from US cities. *Economics of Innovation and New Technology*, 8 (1–2): 57–78.

Arthur, B. W. (1990). Positive feedbacks in the economy. *Scientific American*, February: 92–9.

Audretsch, D. B. and Stephan, P. E. (1996). Company–scientist location links: The case of biotechnology. *American Economic Review*, 86: 641–52.

Baum, J. and Haveman, H. (1997.) Love thy neighbor? Differentiation and agglomeration in the Manhattan hotel industry, 1898–1990. *Administrative Science Quarterly*, 42: 304–39.

Baum, J. and Mezias, S. (1992). Localized competition and organizational failure in the Manhattan hotel industry, 1898–1990. *Administrative Science Quarterly*, 37: 580–604.

Carroll, G. R. and Wade, J. B. (1991). Density dependence in the organizational evolution of the American brewing industry across different levels of analysis. *Social Science Research*, 20: 271–302.

Chung, W. and Kalnins, A. (2001). Agglomeration effects and performance: A test of the Texas lodging industry. *Strategic Management Journal*, 22: 969–88.

DeCarolis, D. M. and Deeds, D. L. (1999). The impact of stocks and flows of organizational knowledge on firm performance: An empirical investigation of the biotechnology industry. *Strategic Management Journal*, 20: 953–68.

Deeds, D. L., DeCarolis, D., and Coombs, J. E. (2000). Dynamic capabilities and new product development in high-technology ventures: An empirical analysis of new biotechnology firms. *Journal of Business Venturing*, 15: 211–29.

Folta, T. B., Cooper, A. C., and Baik, Y. (2003). Returns to cluster size for biotechnology firms. Working paper, Purdue University.

Hannan, M. T. and Carroll, G. R. (1992). *Dynamics of Organizational Populations*. New York: Oxford University Press.

Hannan, M. T. and Freeman, J. (1977). The population ecology of organizations. *American Journal of Sociology*, 82: 929–64.

Jaffe, A. B. (1989). Real effects of academic research. *American Economic Review*, 79: 957–70.

Jaffe, A. B., Trajtenberg, M., and Henderson, R. (1993). Geographic localization of knowledge spillovers as evidenced by patent citations. *Quarterly Journal of Economics*, 108: 577–98.

Krugman, P. (1991a). *Geography and Trade*. Cambridge, MA: MIT Press.

Krugman, P. (1991b). Increasing returns and economic geography. *Journal of Political Economy*, 99: 483–99.

Mansfield, E. (1995). Academic research underlying industrial innovation: Sources, characteristics, and financing. *Review of Economics and Statistics*, 77: 55–65.

Marshall, A. (1920). *Industry and Trade*. London: Macmillan.

Pouder, R. and St. John, C. H. (1996). Hot spots and blind spots: Geographical clusters of firms and innovation. *Academy of Management Review*, 21: 1192–225.

Saxenian, A. (1994). *Culture and Competition in Silicon Valley and Route 128*. Cambridge, MA: Harvard University Press.

Schumpeter, J. A. (1942). *Capitalism, Socialism, and Democracy*. New York: Harper and Row.

Schumpeter, J. A. (1991). Comments on a plan for the study of entrepreneurship. In R. Swedberg (ed.), *The Economics and Sociology of Capitalism*. Princeton, NJ: Princeton University Press.

Shaver, J. M. and Flyer, F. (2000). Agglomeration economies, firm heterogeneity, and foreign direct investment in the United States. *Strategic Management Journal*, 21: 1175–93.

Sorenson, O. and Audia, P. G. (2000). The social structure of entrepreneurial activity: Geographic concentration of footwear production in the United States, 1940–1989. *American Journal of Sociology*, 106: 424–62.

Stuart, T. and Sorenson, O. (2003). The geography of opportunity: Spatial heterogeneity in founding rates and the performance of biotechnology firms. *Research Policy*, 32: 229–53.

Zacharakis, A. L., Shepherd, D. A., and Coombs, J. E. (2003). The development of venture-capital-backed Internet companies: An ecosystem perspective. *Journal of Business Venturing*, 18: 217–31.

Zucker, L. G., Darby, M. R., and Armstrong, J. (1998). Geographically localized knowledge: Spillovers or markets? *Economic Inquiry*, 36: 65–86.

Zucker, L. G., Darby, M. R., and Brewer, M. B. (1998). Intellectual human capital and the birth of US biotechnology enterprises. *American Economic Review*, 88: 290–306.

management buy-outs

Mike Wright and Andrew Burrows

From highly leveraged transactions involving listed companies in the US in the early 1980s, buy-outs have become an international phenomenon. In Europe, the UK, France, and the Netherlands in particular have seen considerable buy-out activity. Buy-outs were an important feature of the privatization of state assets during the transition from communism to the market in Central and Eastern Europe, while the need for major restructuring in Japan and Korea has given an impetus to buy-outs in the Far East.

DEFINITIONS

Management buy-outs (MBOs) involve the acquisition by incumbent management of the business where they are employed, with the purchase price being mainly met by a private equity/venture capital firm providing significant amounts of equity and/or banks providing debt. Management buy-ins (MBIs) are a similar form of transaction, but differ in that the entrepreneurs leading the transaction come from outside the company. A hybrid buy-in/management buy-out (BIMBO) combines the benefits of existing internal management and the contribution of external entrepreneurs; these transactions have developed to address the shortcomings of pure MBIs, where asymmetric information problems faced by outsiders contributed to significantly higher failure rates than for MBOs.

Leveraged buy-outs (LBOs) are typically led by specialist financiers whose executives take direct equity holdings in the acquired corporation, but with the vast majority of the funding for the purchase being in the form of debt. Incumbent management may play a marginal role in putting the transaction together and in

equity holding and may even be replaced. If the managers are heavily involved, the transaction may be termed a leveraged management buy-out (LMBO). Similar to LBOs, investor buy-outs (IBOs) have developed where private equity groups initiate and lead the transaction, but with the degree of leverage being substantially less. Other variants include MEBOs, where management and employees both provide equity. The initial buy-out transaction may be used as a platform for further acquisitions, a so-called buy-and-build or leveraged-build-up strategy. Such deals are typically aimed at consolidating fragmented industries.

CONCEPTUAL ISSUES

Traditionally, buy-outs have been viewed as involving enterprises in mature cash-generative industries with few opportunities to invest free cash flow. The stereotypical cases have concerned listed companies where an agency problem exists between diffuse shareholders and management holding little equity in the business. In these cases, efficiency gains were available from taking the corporation private and introducing a buy-out structure involving increased equity incentives for management; the pressures of servicing high leverage and active involvement by private equity investors through board membership contributed to the resolution of agency cost problems arising from the separation of ownership and control.

Typically, the purchase price in a buy-out is met by a small amount of funds provided by management and the rest a mix of external private equity and bank debt. In smaller transactions, management may obtain a significant majority of the equity. A major problem may be asymmetric information between incumbent management and the private equity provider concerning the current position of the business and its future prospects. This problem may create differences in valuation of the business and hence differing views about the size of each party's equity stake. The use of convertible and redeemable stock can help resolve this problem by making the size of each party's equity stake dependent on the outcome of projections. If performance targets are met, the redemption of redeemable shares enables managers to increase their equity stake. If targets are not met, convertible shares become straightforward common stock, thus increasing the stake of the private equity firm and enabling it to achieve its target rate of return. Private equity firms are also likely to insist on various conditions in the shareholders' agreement that constrain management's behavior and which may give them powers of control under certain conditions. Debt may be provided through various forms of senior debt secured on assets, subordinated (mezzanine) debt linked to cash flow, and in very large transactions high yield and securitized debt. Covenants attached to the provision of debt also involve close monitoring relationships between banks and their buy-out clients. Breaches of these covenants are typically an early warning signal of problems, giving time for corrective action to be taken rather than a signal to put a company into bankruptcy proceedings.

Although the taking private of whole listed corporations has involved very high profile transactions, numerically this kind of deal accounts for a small minority of most buy-out markets. Recent evidence also indicates that the rationale for and type of public to private buy-outs is changing, to focus more on cases where relatively small corporations face the problems of illiquid markets for their shares and where top managers already have significant equity holdings.

Internationally, the most common sources of buy-outs are divestitures from large corporations. Most divestitures are from domestic corporations, but a significant number of transactions arise as restructuring corporations find it attractive to dispose of overseas divisions that may pose greater control problems than domestic activities. Divestitures as buy-outs tend to involve activities that do not have a trading rela-

tionship with the parent company. However, a significant minority of buy-outs involve substantial levels of trading with the parent. The attraction of buy-outs in these circumstances lies in the ability to adopt more appropriate incentives for managers than is possible within a group structure. For the parent, pressure to perform may be exerted on management through asymmetries of interdependence, where the buy-out is more dependent on the parent than vice versa. For the divisional management, the buy-out offers the scope to pursue external growth opportunities that were constrained within a group structure. In Japan, pressures to restructure heavily indebted keiretsus are producing an increasing stream of buy-outs where management can realize growth opportunities (Wright, Kitamura, and Hoskisson, 2003). Buy-outs also offer considerable scope for the privatization of state-owned activities, as they introduce important incentive and control mechanisms that are absent under public ownership (Wright et al., 2000).

Family businesses facing succession problems also provide a major source of buy-out opportunities, especially in European countries where industry is dominated by large numbers of private businesses. Buy-outs can be attractive to founders as they maintain the independence of the firm as well as potential tax advantages in some countries. Buy-outs of family businesses are often viewed as avoiding the agency problems involved in buy-outs of listed firms or divisions. However, important asymmetries of information may exist in favor of either the vendor or the incumbent management. These information asymmetries may be influenced by the extent of involvement of the vendors in the running of the business before the buy-out, their intentions regarding future involvement, as well as the negotiating stance adopted; that is, whether it is cooperative, competitive, coordinative, or command oriented (Howorth, Westhead, and Wright, 2004). The interplay of these factors influences whether the transfer process is successful and whether the price paid is deemed, *ex post*, to have been a fair one.

Management in buy-outs may not merely respond to greater incentives. Rather, managers may have an entrepreneurial mindset that enables them to perceive entrepreneurial opportunities but which cannot be realized within the existing ownership and control structure (Wright et al., 2000; Wright, Hoskisson, and Busenitz, 2001). Bureaucratic control systems may make it difficult for management in divisions to convince the head office of the attractiveness of potential opportunities in new markets where there is little concrete information.

PERFORMANCE

Most studies of post buy-out performance changes have concerned the short period after the transaction and generally identify substantial improvements in profitability two or three years after the buy-out compared to cash flow and productivity measures one year prior to buy-out (Jensen, 1993). Improved working capital management and productivity are important sources of improved performance. Evidence indicates that at the plant level, buy-outs underperform comparable non-buy-outs in terms of total factor productivity before buy-out, but significantly outperform them following the change in ownership. Productivity improvements are often associated with substantial downsizing of the enterprises concerned, with subsequent re-employment being at below comparable industry levels.

Improvements in performance may also be down, based on innovative behavior by management teams. Significant increases in new product development as well as more effective use of R&D expenditures are found to occur post-buy out, especially in smaller venture-backed transactions, which the entrepreneurs concerned believe would not otherwise have happened (Wright, Thompson, and Robbie, 1992; Zahra, 1995).

EXITS

Buy-outs have sometimes been argued to be short-lived, highly leveraged transactions led by leveraged buy-out associations that are little more than a disguised form of asset stripping. Evidence shows that buy-outs have a heterogeneous life cycle: some last a short time, while others retain the buy-out form for considerable periods. While about half of larger buy-outs are sold or floated on a stock market within four years, the majority last well above seven years. Larger transactions are found to change their

ownership form again significantly sooner than smaller buy-outs.

The principal factors influencing the longevity of a buy-out relate to the objectives and needs of the parties involved – owner-managers, financiers, and the company itself (Wright et al., 1994). The extent and form of exit from buy-outs and buy-ins are also influenced at least to some degree by the cyclical nature of stock and takeover market conditions. When these exit routes are problematical, yet financiers with limited-life closed end funds need to realize their gains, new forms of exit may be sought. An important option in these conditions is the secondary buy-out or buy-in, involving a sale from one private equity firm to another. In such circumstances, the incoming private equity firm needs to be convinced that the reasons for sale are genuine and that it can identify prospects for further upside gains.

FUTURE RESEARCH

Buy-outs have become a more common feature of the economic landscape, both in multiple sectors and countries where they are found. Although buy-outs have become an international phenomenon, quantitative research across countries in particular is limited. Increasing practitioner attention is turning towards entrepreneurial aspects of buy-outs, as generating gains purely from downsizing becomes more difficult to achieve. From an academic point of view, greater interest in entrepreneurial concerns is emerging as the limitations of agency-based theories in explaining the wide scope of buy-outs become recognized.

Bibliography

Howorth, C., Westhead, P., and Wright, M. (2004). Information asymmetry and opportunism: A study of management buy-outs and buy-ins. *Journal of Business Venturing*, forthcoming.
Jensen, M. C. (1993). The modern industrial revolution, exit, and the failure of internal control systems. *Journal of Finance*, 48: 831–80.
Wright, M., Hoskisson, R. E., and Busenitz, L. W. (2001). Firm rebirth: Buyouts as facilitators of strategic growth and entrepreneurship. *Academy of Management Executive*, 15 (1): 111–25.
Wright, M., Hoskisson, R. E., Busenitz, L. W., and Dial, J. (2000). Entrepreneurial growth through privatiza-

tion: The upside of management buyouts. *Academy of Management Review*, 25: 591–601.

Wright, M., Kitamura, M., and Hoskisson, R. E. (2003). Management buy-outs and restructuring Japanese corporations. *Long Range Planning*, 36 (4): 355–74.

Wright, M., Robbie, K., Thompson, S., and Starkey, K. (1994). Longevity and the life cycle of management buy-outs. *Strategic Management Journal*, 15: 215–28.

Wright, M., Thompson, S., and Robbie, K. (1992). Venture capital and management-led leveraged buy-outs: The European perspective. *Journal of Business Venturing*, 7: 47–71.

Zahra, S. A. (1995). Corporate entrepreneurship and financial performance: The case of management leveraged buyouts. *Journal of Business Venturing*, 10: 225–47.

market disequilibrium

Thomas J. Dean

It is common for entrepreneurship scholars to point to states of disequilibria as the fundamental source of entrepreneurial opportunities. As such, the concept is central to our understanding of the nature of entrepreneurship, the sources of entrepreneurial profit, and the role entrepreneurs play in the economic system. Explicating the concept of market disequilibrium requires an understanding of its antonym, the concept of equilibrium.

First, there is no singular application of the concept of equilibrium. Rather, equilibrium is better understood as a general modeling approach that is applied to multiple questions and contexts. Thus, equilibrium analysis in the field of economics is a tool used to analyze a variety of economic problems. Most relevant to the understanding of entrepreneurship and entrepreneurial opportunity are microeconomists' perspectives on equilibrium. Within the field of microeconomics, equilibrium generally refers to the price and quantity at which a given market is in balance (supply equals demand). In other words, equilibrium exists at the intersection of the upward sloping demand curve and downward sloping supply curve. Partial equilibrium results when a single market achieves equilibrium, while general equilibrium occurs when several interrelated markets achieve equilibrium simultaneously. Thus, general equilibrium models may gauge the extent to which an economy as a whole has achieved an equilibrium state. Furthermore, under the assumptions of competitive markets, such states have been mathematically proven to maximize social welfare (defined as Pareto efficient).

Regardless of its application, it is critical to understand that time is a central dimension in the concept of equilibrium. Reference to equilibrium typically suggests the condition of a system at a point in time. Thus, equilibrium is a state, rather than a process. Yet equilibrium analysis is a dynamic tool in two respects. First, a state of equilibrium implies that the system under consideration has reached temporal stability. In other words, barring external influences on the system components, the system has reached a stasis whereby it will continue in its present operation indefinitely. Second, time is relevant to equilibrium because systems normally require some time to achieve the static state referred to as equilibrium. In other words, it is typically over some period wherein action and reaction cycles evolve to a balanced state whereby the dynamics of the interaction no longer change.

Both the resource-based view (RBV) of the firm (Barney, 1991; Wernerfelt, 1984) and game theory provide examples of equilibrium models wherein time is a critical element. RBV attempts to explain the persistence of economic profit at equilibrium. The basic premise is that all economic profits should disappear with competition over time unless barriers to the movement of factors to production exist (Barney, 1986). Thus, RBV suggests that, with the passage of time and the actions and reactions of competitors, profits will be competed away, unless something obstructs the competitive process (i.e., valuable resources that are rare, inimitable, and non-substitutable). Furthermore, the basic question of RBV is whether such a profit can persist indefinitely (in stasis or equilibrium) once the interaction of the various system elements has been completed.

The time required for a system to reach an equilibrium state varies substantially by the nature of the system. In chemical and physical systems, equilibrium may be achieved in nanoseconds. In economic systems, however, achieving equilibrium may take years, decades, or perhaps even centuries, as economic actions and reactions require some time to complete. Economists refer to the period of interactions in which the system is moving toward the equilibrium state as the lag. Lags result because it often takes substantial time for economic information to be transferred to various agents, and for these agents to react to the information and implement appropriate economic actions. Realistically, some markets have the potential to equilibrate more quickly than others. For example, financial markets are often assumed to be efficient relative to certain factor markets.

With some exceptions, equilibrium analysis ignores the processes occurring during such lags, focusing instead on the final outcome of the interactions between economic agents. Thus, equilibrium analysis often recognizes the role of entrepreneurship but usually neglects to examine it. Furthermore, such analysis often assumes that markets equilibrate quickly and are therefore relatively uninteresting from an analytical standpoint. In short, the assumption of rapid market equilibration results in a de-emphasis of the equilibration process in favor of examination of the end-state it produces. In contrast, research in entrepreneurship is particularly interested in the process of market equilibration and, by extension, states of market disequilibrium.

Our consideration of the nature of market equilibrium suggests that the concept of market disequilibrium represents a market condition wherein stasis has not been reached in the interactions between economic players. What is important in this definition is that it focuses upon a market condition that exists at a given point in time. In other words, like equilibrium, market disequilibrium describes a state in the market. But perhaps most importantly, this state is necessarily temporary, as, by definition, it is not at equilibrium. Thus, disequilibrium implies eventual transformation in the nature of the economic system over time, from a state of disequilibrium to either a state of equilibrium or alternative state of disequilibrium. Moreover, it is this market movement, or the drivers for movement, in the market, that is of particular interest to the study of entrepreneurship.

Researchers have often addressed the role of entrepreneurship in the movement of markets toward or away from the condition of disequilib-

rium. Schumpeter (1934) viewed entrepreneurs as disequilibrators who, through the process of creative destruction, introduce spontaneous and discontinuous change and thereby disturb the current state of the market. In contrast, Austrian economists (Kirzner, 1973, 1997) and others (Leibenstein, 1968, 1979; Schultz, 1975; Dean and Meyer, 1996) view the entrepreneurial process as fundamentally equilibrating as the actions of entrepreneurs move markets closer to a state of perfection. In this view, the market gaps and imperfections inherent to states of disequilibrium represent profit opportunities that are eliminated through entrepreneurial action. Disequilibrium is created by exogenous changes in technologies, tastes and preferences, sources of supply, and other factors. As such, the entrepreneur is more of an arbitrageur who discovers previously unknown changes in market conditions (Kirzner, 1973, 1997; Knight, 1921; Mises, 1949). The dichotomy between views of the entrepreneur as equilibrator versus entrepreneur as disequilibrator remains one of the fundamental paradoxes of the field, which, with some exception (Cheah, 1990), remains unexplored. The solution to this paradox likely rests in the separation of the disequilibrating and equilibrating roles of entrepreneurial actors, as it is possible that the act of implementing an entrepreneurial venture may have both equilibrating and disequilibrating influences.

Numerous authors, especially those who view entrepreneurs as market equilibrators, have associated the existence of disequilibrium states with opportunity for profit and/or entrepreneurship (Kirzner, 1997; Leinbenstein, 1968; Dean and Meyer, 1996; Shane and Venkataraman, 2000). Kirzner (1973, 1997), for example, refers to profit opportunities engendered in the errors and ignorance of market participants. Leibenstein (1968, 1979) discusses market imperfections that increase the scope for entrepreneurial activity, while Knight (1921) emphasizes entrepreneurial opportunities in dynamic, uncertain markets. More recently, Eckhardt and Shane (2003) emphasize the role of information asymmetries and exogenous shocks, while Dean and McMullen (2002) discuss conditions of market failure as the source of economic opportunity. Characterizing the nature and causes of disequilibrium states may be particularly productive for the study of entre-preneurship, as review of the economic literature suggests that some of the most fruitful conclu-sions from equilibrium analysis result from the study of departures therefrom.

Entrepreneurship researchers have also sug-gested that market systems, especially those with extended adjustment lags, are susceptible to con-tinual external disruption, which effectively prevents attainment of an equilibrium state. Be-cause an equilibrium state obtains from the ful-fillment of initial system conditions, any alteration to these conditions prevents the attain-ment of that state and reestablishes the trajectory of the system. Many believe the lag is so long and external changes so continual that the market is better conceptualized as a dynamic learning pro-cess subject to continual external influence, dis-ruption, and altered convergence. Indeed, this is perhaps a more realistic conception of the market. Of course, this conception is contradict-ory to economists' emphasis on an ideal but perhaps unobtainable equilibrium state. In short, markets likely remain in states of disequi-librium, implying the continual scope for entre-preneurial action.

Our exploration into market disequilibrium suggests that the concept plays a central role in the understanding of the nature of entrepreneur-ship and its function in the economic system. Whether we believe that entrepreneurs create or exploit disequilibrium conditions, it is clear that entrepreneurs alter market conditions and market conditions motivate entrepreneurial action. Central questions of the field revolve around the disequilibrium concept and include the nature of disequilibrium, the economic op-portunities inherent therein, the means of ex-ploiting such states, and the effect of the entrepreneur on market conditions and social welfare.

Bibliography

Barney, J. B. (1986). Strategic factor markets: Expecta-tions, luck, and business strategy. *Management Science*, 32 (10): 1231–41.

Barney, J. B. (1991). Firm resources and sustained com-petitive advantage. *Journal of Management*, 17: 99–120.

Cheah, H. (1990). Schumpeterian and Austrian entre-preneurship: Unity within duality. *Journal of Business Venturing*, 5: 341–7.

Dean, T. J. and McMullen, J. (2002). Market failure and entrepreneurial opportunity. Academy of Management Best Paper Proceedings.

Dean, T. J. and Meyer, G. D. (1996). Industry environ-ments and new venture formations in US manufactur-ing: A conceptual and empirical analysis of demand determinants. *Journal of Business Venturing*, 11 (2): 107–32.

Eckhardt, J. T. and Shane, S. A. (2003). Opportunities and entrepreneurship. *Journal of Management*, 29 (3): 333–49.

Kirzner, I. M. (1973). *Competition and Entrepreneurship*. Chicago: University of Chicago Press.

Kirzner, I. M. (1997). Entrepreneurial discovery and the competitive market process: An Austrian approach. *Journal of Economic Literature*, 35: 60–85.

Knight, F. H. (1921). *Risk, Uncertainty, and Profit*. Boston, MA: Houghton Mifflin.

Leibenstein, H. (1968). Entrepreneurship and develop-ment. *American Economic Review*, 58: 72–83.

Leibenstein, H. (1979). The general x-efficiency para-digm and the role of the entrepreneur. In M. J. Rizzo (ed.), *Time, Uncertainty, and Disequilibrium*. Lexington, MA: D. C. Heath, 127–39.

Mises, L. (1949). *Human Action: A Treatise on Economics*. Chicago: Henry Regnery.

Shane, S. and Venkataraman, S. (2000). The promise of entrepreneurship as a field of research. *Academy of Management Review*, 26 (1): 217–26.

Schultz, T. W. (1975). The value of the ability to deal with disequilibrium. *Journal of Economic Literature*, 13 (2): 827–46.

Schumpeter, J. (1934). *The Theory of Economic Develop-ment*. Cambridge, MA: Harvard University Press.

Wernerfelt, B. (1984). A resource-based view of the firm. *Strategic Management Journal*, 5: 171–80.

minority entrepreneurship

Patricia G. Greene

CONCEPT

Minority entrepreneurship is a broad concept, the use of which is largely situation dependent. However, in its most specific usage it refers to the creation and growth of businesses by non-majority individuals. The topic is one of interest around the world and is often linked to broader, more macro questions related to various issues such as migration, assimilation, and level of eco-nomic achievement. Immigrant-owned business and ethnic entrepreneurship are related areas of research with overlapping but not identical approaches to concept, theory, and method (Greene, 1997). Immigrant-owned business is defined according to the individual's mode of entry into a geographic region. There are no other inherent assumptions about the owner(s), the creation process, or levels of community involvement. Ethnic entrepreneurship refers to those individuals with common nationalities or migration experiences, combining both individual and community levels of analysis to examine their entrepreneurial behaviors through shared connections and interactions (Waldinger, Aldrich, and Ward, 1990).

DEFINITION

The Small Business Administration adopted the specific term "minority enterprise" in 1969 as part of the US government's approach to increase the number and revenue-generating potential of black-owned businesses. The term replaced "socially disadvantaged" or "economically disadvantaged," which were used to launch the 8(a) program designed to increase the level of federal purchases made from these businesses. The programs were also dedicated to improving the provision of both direct and guaranteed loans as well as federal contract set-asides. Other terms that have been used include Disadvantaged Business Enterprise (DBE), Historically Underutilized Business (HUB), and Small Disadvantaged Business (SDB).

While occasionally the term "minority business owner" also includes a consideration of gender (thereby classifying women as a minority category), most often the defining dimensions are based upon "race" and/or ethnicity. While a debate is underway regarding racial and ethnic categories, the US census currently consolidates economic reporting on minority businesses as including black, Hispanic, Asian Pacific, and Native American. There is an additional requirement that at least 51 percent of the business be owned and operated by at least one member of a minority group. However, the ownership definition does vary by group. The National Suppliers Development Council viewed the 51 percent ownership requirement as constraining the entrepreneurial growth of these businesses by limiting sources of additional funding to debt or the equity investment of other minority owners. This group therefore changed its definition to allow for as low as 30 percent minority ownership.

MEASUREMENT

The US conducts large-scale national data collection efforts to better understand the US economy, with the underlying benefit of learning about the phenomenon of minority entrepreneurship, including the impact of these businesses upon the national economy. Data collection is the responsibility of the US Census Bureau. Both the Public Use Microdata Samples (PUMS), drawn from the decennial census, and the Survey of Income and Program Participation (SIPP), drawn from a special series of national panels, include data on minority-owned businesses. However, the most complete representation is derived from the surveys of the federal economic census. The census uses the governmental definition of 51 percent ownership. In previous years, the Characteristics of Business Owners (CBO) and the Survey of Minority Owned Businesses (SMOBE) were used to build an aggregate description of the state of minority-owned businesses in the US. The latest data available are from the 1997 survey and show that approximately 3 million firms, representing about 15 percent of all US firms, are minority owned (US SBA, 1999). The growth rates of these firms are notable: minority-owned firms grew at 30 percent while non-minority firms grew at 4 percent. The firms generated approximately $591 billion in revenues. Of these, 615,222 had employees and created 4.5 million jobs with an aggregate payroll of approximately $96 billion (US SBA, 2002). The data collected for the 2002 economic census will be reported as the Survey of Business Owners and Self-Employed Persons (SBO) 2002.

The Panel Study of Entrepreneurial Dynamics (PSED) is a national data collection effort driven by a theoretical focus upon nascent entrepreneurs – those in the start-up process. The program was supported through a consortium of schools, foundations, and government organizations and included two National Science Foundation grants (Carter et al., 1998; Greene et al., 1999). Findings include propensity rates for specific population groups showing that minority business owners are more likely to be in the process of starting a business than are white men. Resulting theoretical explanations focus upon issues of human and social capital, more limited access to opportunity structures, and less beneficial social networks to assist the start-up process (Reynolds, 2000).

Descriptive studies using the large-scale US federal databases have been the foundation of much work to ground the phenomena in statistics (see Bates, 1997, for a complete review). Theoretical explanations underlying any of the dimensions in question are more limited and often focus upon differences between majority and minority entrepreneurs and their businesses. Others emphasize types of entrepreneurial behaviors as a means of economic survival. The most specific theoretical framework builds upon the concept of ethnic entrepreneurship to propose a "truncated middleman minority theory" that recognizes the artificial detour taken by African Americans due to external influences of slavery and long-term discrimination (Butler, 1991). This detour is seen to have prematurely cut off a large proportion of the entrepreneurial tradition among African Americans.

RESEARCH AREAS

The primary issues in this general research area can be summarized under two questions. First, why are minority-owned businesses underrepresented in the overall population of small businesses? Second, why do existing minority-owned businesses tend to stay smaller than their majority-owned counterparts? Means of exploring these issues include research questions on demographics and resources of the owner(s) and the business, the start-up process, business outcomes, economic development, labor market issues, and opportunity structures. Results from these studies will be useful to entrepreneurs, resource providers, educators, and policy-makers.

Bibliography

Bates, T. (1997). *Race, Self-Employment, and Upward Mobility: An Illusive American Dream*. Baltimore, MD: Johns Hopkins University Press.

Butler, J. S. (1991). *Entrepreneurship and Self-Help among Black Americans: A Reconsideration of Race and Economics*. New York: State University of New York Press.

Carter, N., Brush, C., Aldrich, A., Greene, P., and Katz, J. (1998). The influence of founder's gender in business start-ups. National Science Foundation. Grant 9809841.

Greene, P. G. (1997). A call for conceptual clarity. Comments on Bates: Why are firms owned by Asian immigrants lagging behind black-owned businesses? *National Journal of Sociology*, 10 (2): 49–55.

Greene, P. G., Carter, N., Reynolds, P., Aldrich, H., and Stearns, T. (1999). The influence of founder's race in the start-up process. National Science Foundation. Grant 9905255.

Reynolds, P. D. (2000). National panel study of US business start-ups: Background and methodology. In J. A. Katz (ed.), *Advances in Entrepreneurship, Firm Emergence, and Growth*, Vol. 4. Stamford, CT: JAI Press, 153–227.

US Small Business Administration, Office of Advocacy (1999). *Minority Business*. Washington, DC.

US Small Business Administration, Office of Advocacy (2002). *Minorities in Business, 2001*. Washington, DC.

Waldinger, R., Aldrich, H., Ward, R., and associates (1990). *Ethnic Entrepreneurs*. Newbury Park, CA: Sage.

N

nascent entrepreneur

Nancy M. Carter

The term "nascent entrepreneur" has been added to the literature in the past ten years as researchers focused greater attention on understanding the earliest stages of organization emergence (Carter et al., 2003). Studies showing that new businesses provide profound social and economic benefits stimulated researchers and policy-makers to learn more about how new businesses come into existence, how many were being formed, at what rate, and information on the individuals who were starting the businesses. Previous research had relied on retrospective reports of entrepreneurs who already had their businesses established to relate how the entrepreneurial career choice was made, the processes of early creation and launch, and why some start-up efforts were successful while others were discontinued. Concern about the validity of the reminiscences of new firm owners to reflect organization emergence led to efforts to study nascent entrepreneurs – individuals who were actively involved in business start-up activities.

Identifying individuals actively engaged in the creation of new organizations is not a trivial issue. It is both time consuming and expensive. Because a business is not yet tangible, typical sampling frames for studying new firms – like business registries or census data – are not useful for locating or determining exactly who is a nascent entrepreneur. Simply put, "nascent entrepreneur" refers to individuals, or teams of individuals, who are initiating activities intended to culminate in the start-up of a new business. These individuals come from two potential sources: the population at large and existing businesses. Individuals in the population who decide to start a new business are referred to as "independent nascent entrepreneurs." Those starting a new business or new venture for their employer as part of a current job assignment are referred to as "corporate nascent entrepreneurs." Both groups are referred to as nascent entrepreneurs and undertake a series of activities to enact a new business, including the assembly of resources using social networks.

The process of organization emergence (see figure 1) involves four stages: (1) start-up intentions; (2) gestation; (3) infancy; and (4) adolescence; and four transition points: (1) conception; (2) discontinuance; (3) firm birth; and (4) firm growth. All of these stages and transitions are affected by the social, political, and economic context where emergence is occurring. Nascent entrepreneurs are the primary actors in the first two stages and the first three transition points in the model.

The first stage of organization emergence represents the stock of all individuals with an intention to start a new business and who act on that intention. During this stage of emergence, the question is about what qualifies an individual as a nascent entrepreneur and whether these individuals are different from others in the general or business firm populations.

Researchers have applied numerous criteria for determining who is a nascent entrepreneur, ranging from requiring only that individuals have given serious thought to starting a business (Usbasaran, Westhead, and Wright, 2001), to requiring that individuals satisfy a series of progressive conditions before qualifying (Reynolds and White, 1997). The Panel Study of Entrepreneurial Dynamics (PSED), a multi-university initiative to study firm emergence, applied one of the most comprehensive sets of qualifying criteria (Gartner et al., 2004). The collaborative project specified three conditions

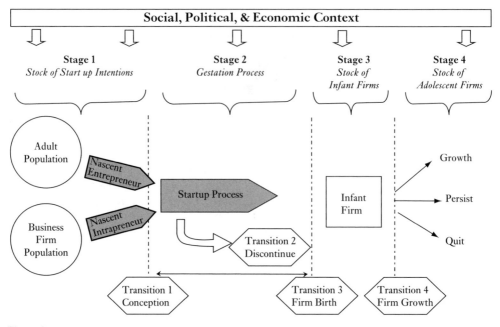

Figure 1
Source: adapted from Reynolds et al. (2004)

that a nascent entrepreneur must meet: (1) participation; (2) current involvement; and (3) ownership; and a further refining condition: (4) autonomy. To meet the first two criteria, individuals had to report that they were actively trying, either alone or with others, to start a new business and that at least some of their start-up activities had occurred during the past 12 months. Recognizing that there is an upper limit to the level of activity before the entrepreneurial effort transitions from nascency to an infant new business, the PSED specified that any initiative that had achieved more than 3 months of positive cash flow that covered expenses and salaries for the owner/manager was an infant business. Individuals who had developed their start-up effort to that extent were disqualified as nascent entrepreneurs.

PSED respondents who demonstrated that their involvement in the start-up process qualified as active involvement were then required to demonstrate further commitment to the start-up through the investment of money. The investment of time, while necessary, was not sufficient

by itself. Because ownership was defined as full or partial ownership, it was possible that in some instances another business – non-persons – might have majority control of the new initiative. To be designated as an "autonomous nascent entrepreneur," the PSED specified that a start-up initiative could involve no more than 49 percent ownership by other businesses. This refinement of the definition ensured that a nascent entrepreneur, or a team of nascent entrepreneurs, controlled the creation effort.

Once an individual qualifies as a nascent entrepreneur, organization conception is said to have occurred and the nascent entrepreneur transitions into the second stage of the emergence process: gestation. During the gestation stage, nascent entrepreneurs are seen as the architects of the start-up and who engage in assembling and investing resources to create new products, identify new customers, or acquire new skills and knowledge in an effort to establish the new business. Questions of interest to researchers about the gestation stage focus on determining how nascent entrepreneurs go about the process of starting the business. For example, how many and what types of resources are invested? How are these resources accumulated? What are the characteristics of individuals involved in the start-up process? How long does it take to get the business up and running, or before the nascent entrepreneur gets discouraged and gives up?

Nascent entrepreneurs transition out of the gestation stage either when they succeed in getting the business established, or when they give up and abandon the start-up effort. These two transitions are represented in figure 1 as firm birth and discontinuance.

VARIATION WITHIN THE POPULATION

From a population ecology perspective, nascent entrepreneurs' intentions and activities and the contexts of their start-ups constitute a major source of organizational variation (Aldrich, 1999). Other criteria for defining what qualifies an individual as a nascent entrepreneur provide additional explanations for the population variation. For example, is the nascent entrepreneur a novice entrepreneur (individuals with no prior business start-up experience); a habitual entrepreneur in the process of starting yet another new business (individuals with prior start-up experience); a serial entrepreneur (involved with several start-up experiences, shutting down one before starting the other); or a portfolio entrepreneur (operates an existing business they started while beginning efforts to create this new initiative) (Usbasaran, Westhead, and Wright, 2001)? Criteria that contrast organizational forms (e.g., franchising, family firms, management buy-outs or buy-ins) also illustrate that the nascent entrepreneur category is not homogeneous.

Finally, it is important to recognize that although many people start a business entirely on their own, others begin with a team, making the enterprise a collective effort from the beginning. When a team of individuals initiates the start-up, should additional, or different, criteria be imposed to designate who is a nascent entrepreneur? Much of the literature on start-up teams assumes that team formation represents a deliberate choice by a lead entrepreneur (Davidsson and Honig, 2003). Implicit in these discussions is the assumption that a team is normally planned,

rather than emergent. Ruef, Aldrich, and Carter (2003), however, showed that other factors play a role in start-up team formation, such as the existence of previous relations between founders. Their findings reveal that about half of all start-ups in the US begin as team-led ventures and that prior social relations among the team members have a pronounced effect on the team's composition. More than 70 percent of the teams they studied were comprised of family members, 53 percent were being started by spouses/partners, and another 18 percent involved other family members. Because these team members are bound by social, psychological, and emotional ties, do all of the individuals qualify as nascent entrepreneurs, or are differentiating criteria needed for tracking team-based initiatives?

Identifying and locating nascent entrepreneurs is neither easy nor inexpensive. Because these individuals are responsible for such a significant social and economic phenomenon, efforts to determine who they are and to track their start-up processes is an investment well spent.

Bibliography

Aldrich, H. (1999). *Organizations Evolving*. London: Sage.

Carter, N. M., Gartner, W. B., Shaver, K. G., and Gatewood, E. J. (2003). The career reasons of nascent entrepreneurs. *Journal of Business Venturing*, 18: 13–40.

Davidsson, P. and Honig, B. (2003). The role of social and human capital among nascent entrepreneurs. *Journal of Business Venturing*, 18: 301–31.

Gartner, W. B., Shaver, K. G., Carter, N. M., and Reynolds, P. D. (2004). *Handbook of Entrepreneurial Dynamics: The Process of Business Creation in Contemporary America*. San Francisco, CA: Sage.

Reynolds, P. D. and White, S. B. (1997). *The Entrepreneurial Process*. Westport, CT: Quorum Books.

Reynolds, P. D., Carter, N. M., Gartner, W. B., and Greene, P. G. (2004). The prevalence of nascent entrepreneurs in the United States: Evidence from the panel study of entrepreneurial dynamics. *Small Business Economics* (forthcoming).

Ruef, M., Aldrich, H., and Carter, N. M. (2003). The structure of founding teams: Homophily, strong ties, and isolation among US entrepreneurs. *American Sociological Review*, 68: 195–224.

Usbasaran, D., Westhead, P., and Wright, M. (2001). The focus of entrepreneurial research: Contextual and process issues. *Entrepreneurship: Theory and Practice*, 25 (4): 57–80.

navigating uncertainty: from scenarios to flexible options

Paul J. H. Schoemaker

Any entrepreneur knows that uncertainty is not the enemy but the source of new rent-creating opportunities. As the nineteenth-century British banker Nathan Rothschild observed: "Great fortunes are made when the cannonballs are falling in the harbor, not when the violins play in the ballroom." To unlock these opportunities, however, requires a very different approach to strategy and implementation than what is taught in MBA programs or practiced in large companies today. Entrepreneurs need to be experts at *navigating uncertainty* and turning it into strategic advantage (Christensen, 1997; Foster, 1986; Hamel and Prahalad, 1994). Seldom will a business plan play out as originally envisioned. The challenge is to navigate the currents of uncertainty the way a surfer negotiates the breaking waves of the ocean. Agility, talent, intuition, and dedication alone, however, may not be enough. Academic research has amply shown how poorly people deal with risk and uncertainty when left to their own devices (Gilovich, Griffin, and Kahneman, 2002; Kahneman, Slovic, and Tversky, 1982; MacCrimmon and Wehrung, 1986; Schoemaker, 2002).

The successful entrepreneur must know (1) how to develop and analyze multiple external scenarios, (2) craft nimble strategies with just the right amount of flexibility and commitment, (3) implement the selected strategies using a dynamic-options approach, and (4) make real-time adjustments through dynamic monitoring. As Louis Pasteur noted: "Chance only favors the prepared mind." The key challenge is how to prepare the entrepreneurial mind to profit from chance. Prussian General Helmuth von Moltke observed: "No plan survives contact with the enemy." As those in the venture capital industry know well, most business plans will likewise be changed considerably in the first few years once reality starts to interfere. Hence, a successful business plan must possess robust as well as flexible components as part of the overall strategy. Figure 1 summarizes one approach – which is developed further below, based on Schoemaker (2002) – that can accomplish this

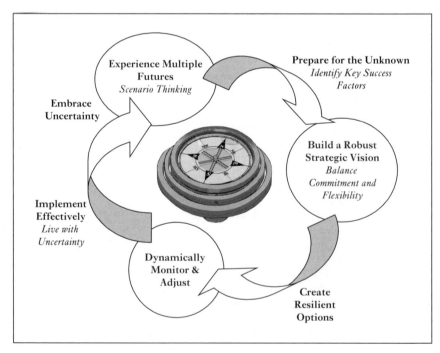

Figure 1   Strategic compass

challenging goal. For other, largely complementary approaches to navigating uncertainty, see Courtney (2001) or De Meyer, Loch, and Pich (2002).

DEVELOP MULTIPLE SCENARIOS

Scenario planning is an effective tool for helping entrepreneurs make sense of the complex world they face. The basic idea is used to capture the full range of future uncertainties by means of a few compelling stories that describe very different external conditions the organization may face. Scenarios focus on macro and industry uncertainties – those issues the firm cannot control and must live with one way or another. Scenario planning is as much an art as a science. Numerous articles and books describe the basic philosophy; the underlying methodology itself is not difficult to grasp (Fahey and Randall, 1998; Ringland, 1998; Schoemaker, 1991, 1993; Van der Heijden, 1996). What matters most is to have high quality inputs and then to reduce all these insights into a limited number of internally consistent scenarios that collectively cover a wide range. In more sophisticated applications, the scenarios can be elaborated using system dynamic simulations (Sterman, 2000).

The main benefit of scenario planning is that the new enterprise is forced to rehearse a plausible future before it actually occurs, so as to be better prepared for specific surprises it may confront. A second major benefit is that entrepreneurs can explore new strategic opportunities that are suggested by the scenarios. For example, a recession scenario versus a high growth or technological breakthrough scenario may prompt very different strategic options. Good scenarios stimulate proactive strategies. A third benefit is that scenario planning can productively challenge managers' most deeply held assumptions about the world (Mason and Mitroff, 1981). Scenarios can help surface the critical assumptions entrepreneurs make. As they used to say at Royal Dutch/Shell – one of the acknowledged pioneers in this area – scenario analysis is not so much about planning as about changing mindsets (Schoemaker and Van der Heijden, 1992).

DEVELOP A FLEXIBLE STRATEGY

Many scenario-planning processes fail because managers jump directly from the scenarios into specific actions, without taking time to develop strategies that exhibit the appropriate level of flexibility. Even though entrepreneurs may generally acknowledge that the world is highly uncertain, they often lock the organization into rigid commitments. Just consider how many entrepreneurs overcommitted, near the height of the dot.com bubble, to marketing plans, leases, employment agreements, etc. that they later regretted. This mistake can be avoided by designing an appropriate level of flexibility into all those plans and strategies that are not robust across the various possible scenarios. Many scholars have emphasized the importance of maintaining strategic flexibility (Bahrami, 1992; Beinhocker, 1999; Ghemawat, 1991).

The basic approach to developing a flexible strategy is simple. First, the entrepreneur should list the strategies required to succeed in one of several scenarios. Then, a similar list should be developed for each of the other scenarios. Second, the entrepreneur should highlight those strategies that are common to every scenario. These are "no-brainers." The entrepreneur can go ahead and commit strongly to these "no-regrets" strategies since they are needed in every scenario. Third, the entrepreneur should rank the remaining strategies in terms of how robust or fragile they are across scenarios. A strategy that makes sense in just one scenario is less robust (i.e., more fragile) than one that is suitable for, say, two scenarios. Fourth, the entrepreneur should invest stagewise in these fragile strategies (insofar as is possible) and conduct a financial analysis of each investment that includes a real-options perspective rather than just a static net-present-value (NPV) approach (Courtney, 2001).

REAL-OPTIONS THINKING

The basic idea behind real-options thinking is to make small commitments when uncertainty is high, wait until more is learned about which way the world moves, and then either increase the investment (if the option is in the money) or pull the plug (if it is out of the money). To do this systematically, the entrepreneur may wish to construct a decision tree (Raiffa, 1968) for each investment such that it is clearly indicated (1) where the key uncertainties are that will be resolved within the life of the project and

(2) what possible downstream actions the entrepreneur might take depending on how each uncertainty plays out. Once a strategic investment is examined this way, it often makes sense to proceed with a small commitment when a purely static NPV analysis would perhaps argue against the project all together. Options analysis seeks to identify all post-decisional points of flexibility and then impute an explicit value for any new information that may be learned after the initial commitment has been made. The essence of this approach is to pursue a staged investment strategy whenever uncertainty is high, rather than take an all-or-nothing bet (see Hamilton, 2000, for a good strategic overview).

In addition to staging strategic options to exploit the value of flexibility and new information, there are other ways to manage uncertainty that extend beyond the project itself. First of all, any investment should be viewed in the context of the complete portfolio of investments made rather than in isolation. Second, there are various techniques that may allow the entrepreneur to shift the distribution of returns around its mean (at a price). These include traditional insurance options, as well as such financial techniques as contingent contracts, hedges, or other forms of risk sharing. In addition, it is important to create sufficient organizational agility and flexibility – through early detection and fluid decision-making – so that strategies can be quickly adjusted as the fog of the future lifts. Indeed, such quick footedness is usually viewed as an important advantage that good entrepreneurs have over larger, more inert organizations (Eisenhardt and Brown, 1998; Senge, 1990).

Monitor in Real Time

The last step in our model entails dynamic monitoring and timely adjustment. It does little good to buy an option on the future and then let it expire due to neglect when it is in fact in the money. With financial call options, an investor only has to monitor the price of the stock and the expiration date of the option. When dealing with real options, the monitoring system will typically be much more complex. Sales trends, customer behavior, economic indicators, as well as competitive moves, may all be factors that affect the embedded options, probabilities, or cash flows

represented in the decision tree. Ideally, the entrepreneur will need a tailored dashboard for each strategic investment so that it can be determined, in real time, when to exercise downstream contingency plans.

There are multiple ways to monitor a scenario-based strategy. One company set up an elaborate war room, so that it could visually depict and monitor the main drivers for each scenario. Once critical threshold values are crossed, a trigger may be sent for action. Another company organized online discussion groups where managers post messages (such as newspaper clippings or factoids) about the external environment, with editorial commentary about possible implications for the firm. Still others establish committees that review the current strategy on a regular basis. Only the entrepreneur can determine what type of monitoring system will work best in any particular situation.

Conclusion

The model sketched and diagrammed in figure 1 draws on the research frontiers of decision sciences, organization theory, strategy, and cognitive psychology. It seeks to integrate the most practical contributions these various fields have made to navigating uncertainty. One only needs to follow the daily news to appreciate the risks of being unprepared for change. And yet the rewards for actively pursuing new opportunities are greater than ever before. More than any other capability, developing personal (human capital) as well as organizational skills in seizing initiatives in shifting or unpredictable circumstances will remain the key to entrepreneurial success.

Bibliography

Bahrami, H. (1992). The emerging flexible organization: Perspectives from Silicon Valley. *California Management Review*, 34 (4): 33–52.
Beinhocker, E. D. (1999). Robust adaptive strategies. *Sloan Management Review*, 95–106.
Christensen, C. (1997). *The Innovator's Dilemma*. Boston, MA: Harvard Business School Press.
Courtney, H. (2001). *20/20 Foresight*. Boston, MA: Harvard Business School Press.
De Meyer, A., Loch, C. H., and Pich, M. T. (2002). Managing project uncertainty: From variations to chaos. *Sloan Management Review*, 43 (2): 60–7.

Eisenhardt, K. and Brown, S. (1998). *Competing on the Edge: Strategy as Structured Chaos*. Boston, MA: Harvard Business School Press.

Fahey, L. and Randall, R. (eds.) (1998). *Learning from the Future*. New York: Wiley.

Foster, R. (1986). *Innovation: The Attacker's Advantage*. New York: Summit Books.

Ghemawat, P. (1991). *Commitment: The Dynamic of Strategy*. New York: Free Press.

Gilovich, T., Griffin, D., and Kahneman, D. (2002). *Heuristics and Biases: The Psychology of Intuitive Judgment*. Cambridge: Cambridge University Press.

Hamel, G. and Prahalad, C. K. (1994). *Competing for the Future*. Boston, MA: Harvard Business School Press.

Hamilton, W. F. (2000). Managing real options. In G. S. Day and P. J. H. Schoemaker (eds.), *Wharton on Managing Emerging Technologies*. New York: Wiley.

Kahneman, D., Slovic, P., and Tversky, A. (eds.) (1982). *Judgment Under Uncertainty: Heuristics and Biases*. Cambridge: Cambridge University Press.

MacCrimmon, K. R. and Wehrung, D. A. (1986). *Taking Risks: The Management of Uncertainty*. New York: Free Press.

Mason, R. O. and Mitroff, I. L. (1981). *Challenging Strategic Planning Assumptions*. New York: Wiley.

Raiffa, H. (1968). *Decision Analysis: Introductory Lectures on Choices Under Uncertainty*. Reading, MA: Addison-Wesley.

Ringland, G. (1998). *Scenario Planning*. New York: Wiley.

Schoemaker, P. J. H. (1991). When and how to use scenario planning: A heuristic approach with illustration. *Journal of Forecasting*, 10: 549–64.

Schoemaker, P. J. H. (1993). Multiple scenario developing: Its conceptual and behavioral basis. *Strategic Management Journal*, 14: 193–213.

Schoemaker, P. J. H. (2002). *Profiting from Uncertainty: Strategies for Succeeding No Matter What the Future Brings*. New York: Free Press.

Schoemaker, P. J. H. and Van der Heijden, K. A. J. M. (1992). Integrating scenarios into strategic planning at Royal Dutch/Shell. *Planning Review*, 20: 41–6.

Senge, P. (1990). The leader's new work: Building a learning organization. *Sloan Management Review*, 7–23.

Sterman, J. D. (2000). *Business Dynamics: Systems Thinking and Modeling for a Complex World*. New York: McGraw-Hill/Irwin.

Van der Heijden, K. (1996). *Scenarios: The Art of Strategic Conversation*. New York: Wiley.

O

opportunity exploitation

Johan Wiklund

DEFINITION

Opportunity exploitation refers to activities conducted in order to gain economic returns from the discovery of a potential entrepreneurial opportunity. It involves the decision to act upon a perceived opportunity and the associated behaviors aimed at realizing the value of the opportunity. During opportunity exploitation people acquire and organize requisite resources and competencies to develop a product or service and take it to an existing or new market.

THE DECISION TO EXPLOIT AN OPPORTUNITY

Not all opportunities being perceived are acted upon. The marshaling of resources is associated with costs and the outcomes of an attempt to exploit a perceived entrepreneurial opportunity are uncertain. Therefore, deciding on whether or not to exploit an opportunity involves weighing the potential value of the opportunity against the costs of exploiting it, and comparing this to the outcomes of other possible courses of action. Two factors influence whether or not individuals choose to exploit discovered opportunities: the nature of the opportunity and the nature of the individual (Shane and Venkataraman, 2000). Opportunity exploitation will be more costly for individuals with less resource endowments who need to acquire the resources necessary for exploitation than for those who already possess substantial human, social, and financial capital. However, these resources can be valuable also for pursuing other courses of action. Therefore, individuals with access to more resources are better able to exploit oppor-

tunities, but may have incentives for not choosing to do so. In addition, people make different conjectures about how appropriate an opportunity is, depending on prior experience and psychological characteristics such as their belief in their ability to exploit the opportunity (i.e., their self-efficacy).

The degree of innovativeness of the opportunity also influences the likelihood of exploitation. Attempting to exploit innovative opportunities of a path-breaking nature entails substantial uncertainty because it is impossible to know the chances of success. Imitative opportunities, largely replicating what already exists, may be risky, but it is possible to have an idea of the chances of succeeding. While the potential returns of innovative opportunities may be greater, people are generally skeptical of entrepreneurial endeavors where the chances of success are unknowable. Therefore, assuming risk aversion, exploitation of innovative opportunities is less likely than exploitation of imitative opportunities.

ORGANIZATIONAL MODE OF EXPLOITATION

In principle, it is possible to identify two organizational modes for exploiting opportunities. The first is through the start-up of a new firm and the other is to exploit opportunities within the framework of an existing firm. The choice between these organizational modes is influenced by the resources needed to pursue the opportunity. If these resources are embedded within the resources of an existing firm, the internal mode is more likely. Existing firms often have access to know-how, financial capital, and other resources valuable to opportunity exploitation. On the other hand, these firms may be unwilling to devote those to initiatives that are not in line with current business. If there are no relationships between the resources needed for the new opportunity and the resources of an existing firm, the start-up mode is more likely. In other words, incremental and competence-enhancing opportunities, which rely on existing resources and competencies, are more likely to be pursued by incumbent firms, while radical and competence-destroying opportunities more likely will be pursued by new entrants (Tushman and Anderson, 1986). In addition, the situation and incentives of individuals discovering opportunities, such as employment status and the possibility of appropriating the value of exploiting the opportunity, influence the choice of mode.

THE OPPORTUNITY EXPLOITATION PROCESS

Several different models describing the process of opportunity exploitation have been developed. In particular, the start-up mode of organizing has been described. One important insight from these empirical studies is that the discovery and exploitation processes are intimately entwined and that the opportunity as first conceived may change during the exploitation process as a result of learning about the market and about the possibility of delivering the product or service.

These studies have also found that it is far from a linear process, and that the behaviors, their sequencing and pacing, differ across exploitation processes. To deal with the multitude of processes, typologies have been suggested (e.g., Bhave, 1994; Sarasvathy, 2001). Research findings suggest exploitation processes can be classified depending on whether an innovative or an imitative opportunity is pursued. Different types of strategies, knowledge, and behaviors appear important depending on which type of opportunity is pursued. Carefully planned processes can be contrasted with adaptive exploitation processes. The former are characterized by projections of the future and incremental behaviors following predetermined patterns. The latter are associated with adaptive trial-and-error strategies where the outcomes of previous behaviors guide the behaviors conducted in the future. The decision to exploit an opportunity can be triggered by the discovery of a potential opportunity, but such a decision (e.g., by starting an independent business) may also pre-

cede opportunity discovery – thus, exploitation processes will differ.

SUCCESS AND FAILURE

The capability of appropriately acquiring and organizing resources for opportunity exploitation largely resides in the know-how of individual entrepreneurs, embedded in their human and social capital. Research suggests that specific decision-making strategies based on heuristics enable individuals to come up with innovative solutions in complex and uncertain situations (Alvarez and Busenitz, 2001). For example, using heuristics can involve significant thought leaps leading to innovative ideas in situations where information is scarce. Further, information acquired from social networks helps reduce uncertainty about, and assists in acquiring other resources necessary for, opportunity exploitation.

In the process of exploiting a new opportunity, resources are shifted from their existing uses and put to new use. This entails uncertainty, because the productivity of existing resource combinations is known, while the productivity of a new combination is unknown (Moran and Ghoshal, 1999). Once a new opportunity has been pursued and reaches some success, the specific resource combination pursued becomes explicit and knowable to competitors, and the uncertainty associated with it drops dramatically. To sustain a competitive advantage, initial exploiters must create barriers, such as first-mover advantages or intellectual property protection, or start exploiting new opportunities.

Many attempts to exploit opportunities fail, as evidenced by high rates of abandoned efforts to create new ventures and high failure rates among newly founded ventures. These failures can be attributed to entrepreneurs pursuing opportunities that, in fact, are not lucrative, or poor understanding of opportunities that may well be lucrative, or poor execution of the exploitation of opportunities. The causes of failure are not easily teased out and conflicting views in the literature largely depend on how opportunities are conceptualized and studied. However, it is safe to say that many failures occur because of poorly executed exploitation, irrespective of the characteristics of the opportunity or how well it was understood.

Bibliography

Alvarez, S. A. and Busenitz, L. W. (2001). The entrepreneurship of resource-based theory. *Journal of Management*, 27: 755–75.

Bhave, M. P. (1994). A process model of entrepreneurial venture creation. *Journal of Business Venturing*, 9: 223–42.

Moran, P. and Ghoshal, S. (1999). Markets, firms, and the process of economic development. *Academy of Management Review*, 24 (3): 390–412.

Sarasvathy, S. D. (2001). Causation and effectuation: Toward a theoretical shift from economic inevitability to entrepreneurial contingency. *Academy of Management Review*, 26: 243–63.

Shane, S. A. and Venkataraman, S. (2000). The promise of entrepreneurship as a field of research. *Academy of Management Review*, 25: 217–26.

Tushman, M. L. and Anderson, P. (1986). Technological discontinuities and organizational environments. *Administrative Science Quarterly*, 31: 439–65.

outsourcing

David Lei

Outsourcing refers to the strategic decision to utilize other firms to perform value-creating activities (primary and/or support) once conducted in-house (Bettis, Bradley, and Hamel, 1992; Lei and Hitt, 1996; Porter, 1985). Firms often rely on outsourcing as a vehicle to reduce the fixed costs of their operations and to exit less promising businesses, as well as to become more agile and responsive to their customers' needs. Yet the decision to outsource has potentially profound consequences for a firm's long-term competitiveness and technological leadership, particularly if it involves core activities that emanate from highly tacit, firm-specific sources of knowledge and core competencies that enhance causal ambiguity (Badaracco, 1991; Lei, Hitt, and Bettis, 1996; Reed and DeFillippi, 1990).

NATURE OF OUTSOURCING

In its most general sense, outsourcing enables a firm to substitute fixed costs with recurring variable costs for key inputs. Additionally, by furthering its reliance on suppliers, a firm also raises its transaction and coordination costs while narrowing the scope of its internal activities. A firm can choose the degree to which it relies on outsourcing to manage its current cost structure. At one extreme, a firm can outsource almost all of its value-adding activities and operate in a virtual format whereby it coordinates the information and value flows among its web of designers, suppliers, distributors, and other economic entities. At the other extreme, a firm may decide to perform most, if not all, of its activities in-house to maximize control over the full extent of its value chain. The vast majority of firms, however, engage in varying degrees of outsourcing whereby external suppliers play some role in providing an important input to the firm's value proposition (e.g., product and/or service).

Outsourcing approaches can vary in the extent of formalization, asset exchanges, level of managerial interaction, and procedural standardization that they involve. In some situations, outsourcing could represent a highly formalized process that requires close interaction among managers, extensive co-management or transfer of assets, and a high degree of procedural/process standardization to ensure product/service quality and/or new process investment/improvement (e.g., recent moves in the automobile industry with first-tier suppliers). In these relationships, there is tight-coupling between the firm and its supplier(s) that is required to share and jointly manage the risks of such endeavors (Takeishi, 2001). In other cases, outsourcing may involve much less interaction among managers, but instead culminate in a series of arm's-length contracts and asset exchanges to ensure that key economic objectives are attained (e.g., delivery, cost, quality in healthcare). These outsourcing relationships rely on well-established guidelines and parameters to provide the necessary context and structure (embedded coordination) that support a more loosely coupled approach among firms and their suppliers (Sanchez and Mahoney, 1996; Weick, 1989).

FORMS OF OUTSOURCING

The most prototypical form of outsourcing relationships relies on an arm's-length approach to negotiating and working with external suppliers. The objective is to reduce the host firm's internal fixed cost base by engaging multiple providers in order to minimize the potential risks of opportunism. More intricate forms of outsourcing rely on close personal relationships to build stronger relational and network-based advantages. Closer ties may enable both parties to gain important resource-based advantages, such as access to knowledge, proprietary capabilities, and other intangible assets or resources (Gulati, 1999; Helfat, 2000; Peteraf, 1993; Priem and Butler, 2001). Likewise, closer ties build the social capital necessary to provide a degree of self-sustaining governance of the outsourcing relationship through shared norms, thus conferring some degree of relational advantage (Dyer and Singh, 1998; Uzzi, 1997). Over time, additional resource benefits may accrue to either the outsourcing firm or its supplier by virtue of its position within a potentially expanding network of firms (Gnyawali and Madhavan, 2001).

Perhaps the most sophisticated form of outsourcing is the notion of the extended network. In this configuration, a firm seeks to complement its internal resources with that of new capabilities that are either sourced or even absorbed from a network of cooperating and competing firms to reap external economies of scale and scope (Gulati, Nohria, and Zaheer, 2000; Lei, 2003; Zahra and George, 2002). The economic logic of the extended network stems from the growing web-like configuration of multiple firms becoming increasingly specialized along a core value-creating activity. Yet "co-opetition" (Brandenburger and Nalebuff, 1996) shapes the underlying strategic context of outsourcing as relationships developed throughout the network could possibly provide important channels or conduits to key resources possessed by other interconnected firms. To the extent that an outsourcing firm may be able to "bridge" ties (McEvily and Zaheer, 1999) from one supplier to another, it could exploit the centrality of its network position to enhance its resource access (Brass and Burkhardt, 1992). Moreover, highly dense or interconnected, extended networks can accelerate faster information, knowledge, and physical flows as firms begin to share increasingly similar coordination mechanisms. These interconnections facilitate the rise of modular product designs (Sanchez and Mahoney, 1996) and even corporate organization designs that enable different suppliers to compete for network position (Lei, Hitt, and Goldhar, 1996; Schilling, 2000). Increasing density,

and the social ties that result, could limit direct forms of interfirm competition within the network (Gynawali and Madhavan, 2001), but amplify the tendency towards competence-based competition (Hamel, 1991), whereby firms seek to outlearn each other in creating new, distinctive resources and capabilities (Lei, 2003).

COOPERATION, COMPETITION, AND FUTURE GROWTH

Outsourcing reduces the boundaries between firms, thereby increasing both sequential and reciprocal interdependence (Thompson, 1967). Thus, outsourcing generates significant coordination issues, particularly concerning knowledge sharing, joint investment costs, rising strategic dependency on suppliers, "hollowing out," and the coordination of managers and personnel from different firms. Outsourcing strategies compel firms to balance cooperation with competition. Knowledge flows (particularly tacit skills) can unintentionally strengthen future competitors, particularly if underlying technologies are applicable across numerous products (Lei, Hitt, and Bettis, 1996), and require firms to discern their suppliers' long-term intentions (Bettis, Bradley, and Hamel, 1992). Such "co-opetition" is particularly difficult to manage in highly extended supplier networks, especially in high-velocity competitive environments. Carefully managed, selective outsourcing can help firms preserve resources needed to learn new skills and capabilities to sustain core businesses; however, financial incentives in many firms may result in excessive outsourcing to reduce short-term costs at the expense of long-term competitiveness. In particular, initial outsourcing of lower value-added components, services, or activities may trigger escalating dependence, in which the firm begins to rely on a partner or supplier to provide an ever-higher level of competence, skill, or technology. Thus, firms should adopt a measured approach towards outsourcing, and gauge its potential impact on effects on learning and building its core competencies. From a perspective of competence-based competition, the growth of outsourcing and extended supplier networks will require managers to compete on two parallel dimensions of competitive advantage: cost improvement and interfirm learning.

Outsourcing and Entrepreneurship

A carefully balanced approach to outsourcing can promote the efficient use of capital and lay the foundation for focused growth. In particular, outsourcing plays a key part in many younger entrepreneurial firms' business plans, as management must channel all existing resources to conceive and realize a distinctive value proposition. For example, many small firms that have successfully designed cutting-edge technology products and services have relied on larger suppliers and partners to gain access to state-of-the-art manufacturing and distribution facilities. Some recent entrepreneurial start-up firms in Silicon Valley have utilized a virtual organization design from their inception, whereby all non-core functions and activities are outsourced to preserve agility in fast-changing markets. Many emerging semiconductor firms are sometimes collectively known as the "fabulous fabless," since they focus exclusively on cultivating highly tacit design-based skills, while outsourcing the engineering and manufacturing of the finished chips to larger, foundry-based firms. Nevertheless, larger established firms can also selectively use outsourcing in a similar manner to sharpen their focus on core businesses and activities. By freeing up capital that was once tied up in highly mature or declining businesses, outsourcing may enable established firms to invest in new activities, skills, or competencies that facilitate entry into new markets.

Bibliography

Badaracco, J. L. (1991). *The Knowledge Link: How Firms Compete through Strategic Alliances*. Boston, MA: Harvard Business School Press.

Bettis, R., Bradley, S., and Hamel, G. (1992). Outsourcing and industrial decline. *Academy of Management Executive*, 6: 7–22.

Brandenburger, A. M. and Nalebuff, B. J. (1996). *Co-opetition*. New York: Doubleday.

Brass, D. J. and Burkhardt, M. E. (1992). Centrality and power in organizations. In N. Nohria and R. Eccles (eds.), *Networks and Organizations: Structure, Form and Action*. New York: McGraw-Hill, 191–215.

Dyer, J. H. and Singh, H. (1998). The relational view: Cooperative strategy and sources of interorganizational competitive advantage. *Academy of Management Review*, 23: 660–79.

Gulati, R. (1999). Network location and learning: The influence of network resources and firm capabilities on alliance formation. *Strategic Management Journal*, 20: 397–420.

Gulati, R., Nohria, N., and Zaheer, A. (2000). Strategic networks. *Strategic Management Journal*, 21: 203–16.

Gnyawali, D. R. and Madhavan, R. (2001). Cooperative networks and competitive dynamics: A structural embeddedness perspective. *Academy of Management Review*, 26: 431–45.

Hamel, G. (1991). Competition for competence and inter-partner learning within international alliances. *Strategic Management Journal*, 12: 83–103.

Helfat, C. E. (2000). The evolution of capabilities. *Strategic Management Journal*, 21: 955–9.

Lei, D. (2003). Competition, cooperation, and learning: The new dynamics of strategy and organization design for the innovation net. *International Journal of Technology Management*, 26: 694–716.

Lei, D. and Hitt, M. A. (1996). Strategic restructuring and outsourcing: The effects of mergers and acquisitions and LBOs on building firm skills and capabilities. *Journal of Management*, 21: 835–59.

Lei, D., Hitt, M. A., and Bettis, R. A. (1996). Dynamic core competencies through meta-learning and strategic context. *Journal of Management*, 22: 549–69.

Lei, D., Hitt, M. A., and Goldhar, J. D. (1996). Advanced manufacturing technology: Organization design and strategic flexibility. *Organization Studies*, 17: 501–23.

McEvily, B. and Zaheer, A. (1999). Bridging ties: A source of firm heterogeneity in competitive capabilities. *Strategic Management Journal*, 20: 1133–56.

Peteraf, M. A. (1993). The cornerstones of competitive advantage: A resource-based view. *Strategic Management Journal*, 14: 179–91.

Porter, M. E. (1985). *Competitive Advantage*. New York: Free Press.

Priem, R. L. and Butler, J. E. (2001). Is the resource-based "view" a useful perspective for strategic management research? *Academy of Management Review*, 26: 26–40.

Reed, R. and DeFillippi, R. J. (1990). Causal ambiguity, barriers to imitation, and sustainable competitive advantage. *Academy of Management Review*, 15: 88–102.

Sanchez, R. and Mahoney, J. (1996). Modularity, flexibility, and knowledge management in product and organizational design. *Strategic Management Journal*, 17: 63–76.

Schilling, M. A. (2000). Toward a general modular systems theory and its application to interfirm product modularity. *Academy of Management Review*, 25: 312–34.

Takeishi, A. (2001). Bridging inter-and intra-firm boundaries: Management of supplier involvement in automobile product development. *Strategic Management Journal*, 22: 404–34.

Thompson, J. D. (1967). *Organizations in Action*. New York: McGraw-Hill.

Uzzi, B. (1997). Social structure and competition in inter-firm networks: The paradox of embeddedness. *Administrative Science Quarterly*, 42: 35–67.

Weick, K. E. (1989). *The Social Psychology of Organizing*. Reading, MA: Addison-Wesley.

Zahra, S. A. and George, G. (2002). Absorptive capacity: A review, reconceptualization, and extension. *Academy of Management Review*, 27: 185–203.

outsourcing in entrepreneurial ventures

Abdul A. Rasheed and K. Matthew Gilley

Managers of entrepreneurial ventures are increasingly turning to outsourcing to enhance their firms' effectiveness. While there are many intuitively appealing arguments for outsourcing as a means to increase organizational performance, there are few empirical studies of the topic. Moreover, these studies have primarily focused on large, established organizations. Thus, the outsourcing practices of entrepreneurial ventures, as well as the performance effects of those practices, are not widely understood. What is clear, however, is that outsourcing allows entrepreneurial firms to narrowly focus their scarce resources on what they do best, while leaving the remaining tasks to outside firms.

Defining Outsourcing

Outsourcing involves the procurement of physical and/or service inputs from outside organizations and can be divided into two categories: *core* outsourcing and *peripheral* outsourcing (Gilley and Rasheed, 2000). Core outsourcing refers to the outsourcing of strategically relevant, core activities, whereas peripheral outsourcing involves non-core activities having little potential to convey a long-run competitive advantage.

Outsourcing represents the fundamental decision to reject the internalization of an activity and may arise in two ways. First, outsourcing may involve the *substitution* of market transactions for internal activities. This occurs when an organization ceases performing an activity in-house and shifts it to an outside supplier. Second, outsourcing may arise through *abstention*. That is, a firm may decide never to engage

in a given activity, thus abstaining from it altogether. This latter form is especially relevant for new entrepreneurial ventures making internalization decisions for the first time. In deciding which resources and capabilities to assemble internally, new ventures must determine from which activities to abstain and upon which activities to focus their limited managerial and financial resources. As such, abstention-related outsourcing decisions are key strategic decisions for new entrepreneurial ventures.

Theoretical Perspectives

Multiple theoretical perspectives are useful to the study of outsourcing by entrepreneurial ventures. Some of these perspectives are briefly presented below.

The resource-based view. New entrepreneurial ventures must make numerous choices as to which activities to internalize and which to outsource. Given limited resources and pressures to have a product or service ready for the market in the shortest possible time, most new ventures do not have the luxury of internalizing more than a very limited set of activities. Essentially, the decision to engage in outsourcing by entrepreneurial ventures hinges on which resources and capabilities to build internally and which to access through outsourcing agreements.

The resource-based view (RBV) of the firm is valuable to managers of entrepreneurial ventures facing outsourcing decisions and trying to determine which resources and activities to develop internally. RBV focuses on resource heterogeneity among firms and seeks to explain competitive success on the basis of resource characteristics possessed by firms (Barney, 1991).

Brush, Greene, and Hart (2001) applied RBV to the study of new venture creation. They suggest that attracting resources to a new venture is the greatest challenge faced by entrepreneurs. To be successful, new ventures should be able to attract a set of human, social, financial, physical, technological, and organizational resources and combine them in ways that are valuable, unique, and difficult to imitate. Given that most new ventures tend to operate with limited resources, the key is to accurately specify which resources and activities are critical to the venture's success and to internalize those. The challenge, then, is to identify the resource and competence bundles that are most likely to yield a sustainable competitive advantage and focus on developing those in-house, while outsourcing the rest. Indeed, the complex network of inter-organizational outsourcing relationships established by managers of entrepreneurial ventures constitutes a resource critical to the venture's viability. Of paramount importance to entrepreneurial ventures is the management of the activities that have been internalized. As the firm grows, it is imperative to conduct periodic evaluations of the activities that were internalized at inception. Such evaluations may lead to further outsourcing by substitution, so that the firm can continue to focus on its core competencies.

Several organizations have outsourced with great success. For instance, much of Nike's initial success was due to a clear decision to outsource the manufacturing function and to combine the venture's limited resources in a unique and inimitable fashion. The Topsy Tail Company, a Dallas-based firm focusing on hair care items and fashion accessories, generated approximately $80 million in annual revenues with just three employees. Topsy Tail's management did this through abstention-based outsourcing by focusing from the company's inception on a very narrow set of tasks, while outsourcing manufacturing and order fulfillment to outside specialists. Both Nike and Topsy Tail determined that resources and activities yielding the greatest potential for competitive advantage were to be internalized, while lower value-adding activities were to be outsourced.

Transaction cost theory. The classic approach to transactions costs (Williamson, 1975) suggests that if the transactions costs associated with procuring a product or service from outside the firm are lower than the coordination costs associated with internalizing the activity, it is preferable to source it from outside. However, for entrepreneurial ventures considering abstention-related outsourcing, the costs of internalization are difficult to determine accurately. Many of these are intangible, such as the reduction of managerial focus caused by internalizing more activities. This should tilt the scales in favor of outsourcing

for many entrepreneurial ventures, especially upon start-up.

Institutional theory. Institutional theory seeks to explain organizational isomorphism, which is the tendency towards increasing homogeneity of organizational forms and practices within an industry, through mimetic, coercive, and normative processes. Ang and Cummings (1997) studied information system (IS) outsourcing in banking and found that federal regulator influence (coercive and normative) and peer influence (mimetic) affected IS outsourcing. They found that smaller firms (banks in this case) engage in more IS outsourcing. The conclusion is that institutional pressures may be stronger for smaller firms. Extrapolating these results to the new venture context, it seems reasonable that new ventures, due to their limited resources as well as pressures from their peers, venture capitalists, and banks, are more likely to resort to outsourcing than older, larger, more well-established firms.

ANTECEDENTS AND OUTCOMES OF OUTSOURCING

Recently, researchers have examined a number of contextual factors that affect the relationship between outsourcing and performance, as well as factors considered to be important motivators of the decision to outsource. Some of this research is discussed below.

Business-level strategy. Gilley and Rasheed (2000) found that the effects of outsourcing are not the same for firms pursuing different business-level strategies. Studying small and medium-sized manufacturing firms, they found that peripheral outsourcing has a positive effect on performance for cost leaders. Similarly, a positive relationship was found between core outsourcing and performance for firms pursuing an innovative differentiation strategy. Thus, it seems that financial success is predicated on matching outsourcing strategy and business-level strategy for small and medium-sized enterprises.

Environmental dynamism. Environmental dynamism refers to the rate of unpredictable environmental change. Gilley, McGee, and Rasheed (2004) found that higher levels of perceived

on the consumer's computer system (Lesavich, 2001). While business method patents can provide some protection from imitation, they offer only minimal defense, since many common business practices already employed in a number of industrial sectors are largely associated with automated computer processes and/or work in conjunction with the Internet. Thus, to achieve sustainable competitive advantage from business methods, entrepreneurs and entrepreneurial ventures might be better served to focus more attention to exploiting tacit knowledge exchanges, since these are generally more difficult for competitors to fully understand, assimilate, and enact.

PATENT PROTECTION AND COMPETITIVE ADVANTAGE

Since innovation is one of the primary foci for entrepreneurs and entrepreneurial ventures, exploiting, leveraging, and protecting one's technologies, products, processes, and intellectual property is one of the entrepreneur's fundamental concerns. Beyond the satisfaction of customers' needs and/or the efficiencies of operations that a patented innovation can generate, patents offer several additional ways to create competitive advantage. First, a patent can be a very effective barrier to entry. Polaroid Corporation won a patent infringement lawsuit against Eastman Kodak Company that forced Kodak out of the instant photography market. In addition, Kodak had to pay Polaroid more than $909 million in damages for patent infringement. Second, a patent can be the basis for stimulating both horizontal and vertical strategic alliances between the patent holder and other firms. Third, a patent can be used to generate royalty income, sometimes in the millions and hundreds of millions of dollars, through licensing to a third party. Fourth, patents can be used as leverage in the negotiations of an acquisition, sale of a business, or appropriation of start-up capital. Fifth, patents can be sold or auctioned to generate additional funds. This was the case when Exponential Technology Inc. auctioned off 45 pending and issued patents for more than $5 million that was used to pay off some of the firm's outstanding debt (Picarille, 1997). Sixth, a patent can be used as support for launching a

counter-claim during a firm's pending patent infringement suit. The giant chipmaker Intel Corporation filed such a counter-claim against Digital Equipment Corporation, alleging that Digital infringed on 14 of Intel's patents when designing the Alpha processor. Three months earlier, Digital had filed a suit claiming that Intel had infringed on 10 of its patents when constructing the Pentium, Pentium Pro, and Pentium II (Picarille, 1997).

PATENT PROTECTION ISSUES

While patents can help firms achieve their objectives and provide the potential to develop a competitive advantage, procuring a patent can be a formidable task, particularly for entrepreneurs and entrepreneurial ventures with limited time, resources, and little experience in these matters. We cite several reasons for this. First, the filing of a patent can be a complicated, laborious, and time-consuming process. To begin, an inventor must convince USPTO that their invention is an original idea. This normally requires that a thorough patent search be conducted prior to filing a formal patent application. Moreover, USPTO usually takes approximately two years to award a patent, while patents for high-technology inventions can take longer. This long duration in obtaining a patent can defeat the purpose of securing intellectual property protection, particularly in fast-cycle industries where obsolescence is incessant. Delays in procuring a patent can also pose serious problems in securing funding for entrepreneurial start-ups. Take, for example, the case of Teseda Corporation, a two-year-old start-up firm that developed an integrated circuit tester. Teseda Corporation based much of its support for a third round of funding on the upcoming patent award for its innovation. However, backlogs at USPTO in awarding patents put in question whether the needed funding would come in time (Roberts, 2003).

Second, patents can be expensive even if a patent attorney is not retained, since patent application fees range from $380–770, issuing fees range from $480–1,300, and maintenance fees range from $910–3,220. The time and costs required to procure a patent can be particularly debilitating to an entrepreneur or start-up entrepreneurial venture since the available time and financial resources are often stretched thin and cannot be diverted from focusing on central facets of the enterprise.

Third, a patent may not always be an effective recourse to protect intellectual property. An individual inventor when threatened with a lawsuit that could prove financially devastating to the business may have to settle out of court in order to ensure survival of the business. To this point, Diametrics Medical had devised a technology that was estimated to create $3 billion revenue in the medical equipment market. However, a Fortune 100 conglomerate, Pittsburgh Paint Glass, sued Diametrics for patent infringement and theft of trade secrets. Because this lawsuit could have threatened the firm's existence, Diametrics settled the lawsuit for $5.25 million so it could continue to operate (Welles, 1994).

CONCLUSION

Patents can assist firms of all sizes by serving as an effective barrier to entry and source of revenue, competitive advantage, and value creation. Patents can be essential to entrepreneurs and entrepreneurial ventures in protecting new technologies, new products, intellectual property, and first-mover advantages. However, securing a patent can prove to be a daunting task for some entrepreneurs, since many entrepreneurs and entrepreneurial ventures cannot afford the time and money to procure patent protection. Paradoxically, large, more established firms are often better equipped to procure patent protection, since they may have more financial, organizational, and human resources, including patent attorneys, who are knowledgeable in patent procurement and who can handle the complex administrative issues surrounding securing a patent.

Bibliography

Lesavich, S. (2001). Are all business method patents "one-click" away from vulnerability? *Intellectual Property and Technology Law Journal*, 13 (6): 1–5.
Picarille, L. (1997). Patents promise protection and profits. *Computer Reseller News*, 754: 3–8.
Roberts, B. (2003). Patent applications pile up. *Electronics Business*, 29 (10): 21.
Welles, E. (1994). Blood feud. *Inc.*, 16 (12): 60.

patterns of entrepreneurship development

S. Michael Camp

Ever since Schumpeter first described entrepreneurship as the introduction of new resource configurations, researchers have striven to understand the entrepreneurship development process. For this summary, entrepreneurship development is defined as the process of creating and advancing new ventures to an effective and mature state. The study of new venture development has been organized around the core domains first delineated in Gartner's (1985) governing framework: (1) the acquisition and assembly of firm-level resources (i.e., the behavioral process); (2) the cognitive motivations and decision-making processes of the founding entrepreneur(s); (3) the supportive qualities of the contextual environment; and (4) the strategic, structural, and performance characteristics of the new venture(s). Since the last domain has been the primary area of study in strategic management, the focus of this summary will be on the patterns observed in the first three domains.

PATTERNS IN THE BEHAVIORAL PROCESSES OF NEW VENTURE DEVELOPMENT

Webster (1976) published one of the earliest conceptual models of the new venture creation process in the first issue of the *Academy of Management Review*. Building from the theoretical foundation of the life cycle of the firm, Webster's model included a five-stage sequence beginning with pre-venture conceptualization and extending through venture termination. Several years later, Block and MacMillan (1985) relied on the foundations of milestone planning to propose a more comprehensive model that included ten stages: (1) concept and product testing; (2) prototyping; (3) first financing; (4) completion of initial plant tests; (5) market testing; (6) production start-up; (7) first sale; (8) first competitive action; (9) first redesign; and (10) first significant price change. Though Block and MacMillan's model provided more detail than other models being developed at the time, it was limited in that it applied primarily to technology-based, product manufacturing firms.

Bhave (1994) empirically demonstrated new venture development to be an iterative, non-linear, feedback-driven, cognitive and physical process. Based on his findings, Bhave proposed a new model that applied to different types of new ventures, and its enhanced applicability set the stage for future research. His model included the following steps: (1) opportunity recognition; (2) set-up of production technology; (3) organization creation; (4) product development; (5) market entry; and (6) market feedback.

For ease of analysis, Bhave grouped these steps into three overarching stages: (1) the opportunity stage, (2) the organization creation stage, and (3) the exchange stage. These three stages comprise the current overarching framework for the behavioral perspective of the new venture development process.

The opportunity stage is where the entrepreneur's idea for a new venture is first conceptualized and its feasibility initially assessed. Research at the opportunity stage has mostly concentrated on opportunity recognition (Venkataraman, 1997; Kirzner, 1973), information search (McGrath, 1999; Cooper, Folta, and Woo, 1995; Kaish and Gilad, 1991), and product/prototype development (Bhave, 1994). The organization creation stage, often referred to as the implementation stage, is where the enterprising effort shifts to the acquisition and assembly of firm-level resources. Research at this second stage has focused on resource acquisition (Greene and Brown, 1997; Teece, Pisano, and Shuen, 1997), networking (Low and MacMillan, 1988; Johannisson et al., 1994), and firm structure and strategy (i.e., resource deployment) (Chandler and Hanks, 1994; Mosakowski, 1993). The exchange stage begins at market entry and is comprised of early supply chain transactions. This stage, often labeled the evaluation stage, represents the first market-based test of the entrepreneur's vision for the new venture. Research at this stage has focused on entrepreneurial orientation (Miller and Friesen, 1982; Covin and Slevin, 1989; Lumpkin and Dess, 1996) and new venture performance (Birley and Westhead, 1990; Chandler and Hanks, 1993; Cooper, 1993).

PATTERNS IN THE COGNITIVE PROCESSES IN NEW VENTURE DEVELOPMENT

Despite the difficulties in conducting cognitive research, several patterns have emerged in the study of the cognitive processes in new venture creation. Shaver and Scott (1991) were among

the first to challenge the field of entrepreneurship in this important area of study. They argued that an entrepreneur's cognitive representations of the world influenced the new venture creation process. They challenged researchers to consider the orienting dispositions, motivational principles, personal motives, and the antecedents of choice of lead entrepreneurs. Their call set the stage for several significant conceptual and empirical studies throughout the next decade. In response, Kamm and Nurick (1993) provided one of the first staged decision-making models that demonstrated how differences in the strategy, structure, and performance of new ventures were determined by unique motivations and cognitions of the lead entrepreneur during the formation process.

In an attempt to explain why some individuals were entrepreneurial while others, under similar circumstances, were not, Learned (1993) proposed several cognitive dimensions leading up to the decision to launch a new venture. The first dimension focused on the entrepreneur's *propensity* to launch a new business. Learned (1993) noted that not all individuals have the necessary propensity to create a new venture, arguing that an individual's psychological traits combine with specific life experiences to provide entrepreneurial potential. Despite the level of entrepreneurial propensity, Learned (1993) also suggested that a person's *intention* to launch a new business determines his or her behavior. He suggested that certain situations interact with specific person-level variables to bring about start-up efforts. Furthermore, Learned (1993) recognized that among those individuals who possess the propensity and the intention to launch a new business, the *sense-making process* will differentiate between those who fail and those who succeed. He asserted that those who are unable to identify and properly configure the necessary resources will abandon the effort before the new venture is actually launched.

Since Learned's propositions, an individual's propensity, intentions, and mental competency have been the focus of much of the research into the cognitive aspects of new venture development. More recently, Simon, Houghton, and Aquino (2000) empirically confirmed Learned's proposition concerning failure. They studied how entrepreneurs cope with the risks associated with start-up decisions and found that belief in the *law of small numbers* and the *illusion of control* lowered an entrepreneur's perception of the riskiness of a new venture. The authors argued that such biases, while enhancing the likelihood of launching a new venture, may impede its performance.

PATTERNS IN ENVIRONMENTAL FACTORS CONDUCIVE TO NEW VENTURE DEVELOPMENT

Van de Ven (1993) argued that the study of entrepreneurship development had been limited by its focus on the characteristics and behaviors of individual entrepreneurs and by its treatment of the social, economic, and political infrastructure for entrepreneurship as externalities. Gnyawali and Fogel (1994) further asserted that, despite an increase in the number of studies, researchers had not compiled an integrated framework for studying the environmental conditions conducive to entrepreneurship. Gnyawali and Fogel provided a framework comprised of several dimensions of the environment linked to the core elements of new venture development. Specific emphasis was given to the role of environmental conditions in developing enterprising *opportunities* and enhancing the entrepreneur's *propensity for* and *ability to* create ventures.

Research on environmental conditions for new venture development has primarily derived from the theoretical foundations of resource dependence and population ecology. Resource dependence suggests that new ventures use market transactions to acquire the resources they cannot generate internally. Population ecology asserts that, in order to survive over time, new firms must adapt to their market environments, environments that are in part constrained by resource availability. Using these theoretical foundations, researchers have consistently demonstrated the strong relationship between environmental resource conditions and new venture creation (Specht, 1993; Reynolds, Storey, and Westhead, 1994), survival (Romanelli, 1989), and strategy (Zahra, 1996).

The environmental resources most often studied in new venture development include: (1) the entrepreneurial assets of financial, human, and technology capital; (2) cultural capital (i.e., community values, attitudes, and beliefs); and, more recently, (3) social capital. Starr and Fondas (1993) used the organizational socialization perspective to describe how entrepreneurs adapt their attitudes and behaviors in response to *socializing agents* and *contextual pressures*. Their approach provided additional explanations for why some individuals are more successful than others at creating new ventures. Stuart and Sorenson (2003) studied the tendency of related businesses to *cluster* in physical space. They argued that industries cluster in part because it is difficult for new ventures to mobilize critical resources when they are not physically located near those resources. The authors therefore suggested that opportunities for new venture development mirror the distribution of essential resources.

CONTINGENCIES THAT INFLUENCE NEW VENTURE DEVELOPMENT PATTERNS

Despite emerging patterns, there are a number of contingent factors that have been found to influence the new venture development process and which provide fruitful areas for future research. Four of the more significant contingencies are the gender of the lead entrepreneur, the corporate environment, industry structure, and the cultural context.

Differences in the performance of male- and female-led enterprises have been well documented. Businesses started by women are typically smaller and grow slower than do businesses started by men. Female entrepreneurs also tend to congregate in service and retail trades, while males tend to concentrate in manufacturing and construction trades (Ljunggren and Kolvereid, 1996). Researchers contend that these differences are in part explained by differences in the cognitive and behavioral processes men and women employ in firm creation (Bird and Brush, 2002).

Researchers have also studied the new venture development process within existing organizations (McGrath, Venkataraman, and MacMillan, 1994; Hitt et al., 1999; Russell, 1999). Research on corporate venturing has focused on the disadvantages of bureaucracy and inflexibility and the advantages of resource capacity. Also, research on the differences in resource capacity and accessibility between industries has revealed significant differences in new venture formation process by industry. Vander-Werf (1993) demonstrated that the information asymmetries in new industries make them particularly favorable for the creation of new ventures.

Finally, when studying cross-cultural differences in entrepreneurship, it is clear that some cultures produce many more new ventures than others. Busenitz and Lau (1996) showed that differences in the rate of new venture development between cultures could be explained by the values, norms, and beliefs people held about themselves as entrepreneurs. These factors provide a rich opportunity for enhancing the understanding of new venture development.

Bibliography

Bhave, M. P. (1994). A process model of entrepreneurial venture creation. *Journal of Business Venturing*, 9: 223–42.

Bird, B. and Brush, C. (2002). A gendered perspective on organizational creation. *Entrepreneurship: Theory and Practice*, 26 (3): 41–65.

Birley, S. J. and Westhead, P. (1990). Growth and performance contrasts between types of small firms. *Strategic Management Journal*, 11: 535–57.

Block, Z. and MacMillan, I. C. (1985). Milestones for successful venture planning. *Harvard Business Review*, 63 (5): 184–9.

Busenitz, L. W. and Lau, C. (1996). A cross-cultural cognitive model of new venture creation. *Entrepreneurship: Theory and Practice*, 20 (4): 25–39.

Chandler, G. and Hanks, S. H. (1993). Measuring the performance of emerging businesses: A validation study. *Journal of Business Venturing*, 8: 391–408.

Chandler, G. and Hanks, S. H. (1994). Market attractiveness, resource-based capabilities, venture strategies, and venture performance. *Journal of Business Venturing*, 9: 331–49.

Cooper, A. C. (1993). Challenges in predicting new firm performance. *Journal of Business Venturing*, 8: 241–53.

Cooper, A. C., Folta, T. B., and Woo, C. (1995). Entrepreneurial information search. *Journal of Business Venturing*, 10: 107–20.

Covin, J. G. and Slevin, D. P. (1989). Strategic management of small firms in hostile and benign environments. *Strategic Management Journal*, 10: 75–87.

Gartner, W. B. (1985). A conceptual framework for describing the phenomenon of new venture creation. *Academy of Management Review*, 10: 696–705.

Greene, P. G. and Brown, T. E. (1997). Resource needs and the dynamic capitalism typology. *Journal of Business Venturing*, 12: 161–73.

Gnyawali, D. R. and Fogel, D. S. (1994). Environments for entrepreneurship development: Key dimensions and research implications. *Entrepreneurship: Theory and Practice*, 18 (4): 43–62.

Hitt, M. A., Nixon, R. D., Hoskisson, R. E., and Kochhar, R. (1999). Corporate entrepreneurship and cross-functional fertilization: Activation, process, and disintegration of a new product design team. *Entrepreneurship: Theory and Practice*, 23 (2): 145–67.

Johannisson, B., Alexanderson, O., Nowicki, K., and Senneseth, K. (1994). Beyond anarchy and organization: Entrepreneurs in contextual networks. *Entrepreneurship and Regional Development*, 6: 329–56.

Kaish, S. and Gilad, B. (1991). Characteristics of opportunities search of entrepreneurs versus executives: Sources, interests, general alertness. *Journal of Business Venturing*, 6: 45–61.

Kamm, J. B. and Nurick, A. J. (1993). The stages of team venture formation: A decision-making model. *Entrepreneurship: Theory and Practice*, 17 (2): 17–27.

Kirzner, I. (1973). *Competition and Entrepreneurship*. Chicago: University of Chicago Press.

Learned, K. E. (1993). What happened before the organization? A model of organization formation. *Entrepreneurship: Theory and Practice*, 17 (1): 39–48.

Ljunggren, E. and Kolvereid, L. (1996). New business formation: Does gender make a difference? *Women in Management Review*, 11 (4): 3–12.

Low, M. B. and MacMillan, I. C. (1988). Entrepreneurship: Past research and future challenges. *Journal of Management*, 35: 139–61.

Lumpkin, G. T. and Dess, G. G. (1996). Clarifying the entrepreneurial orientation construct and linking it to performance. *Academy of Management Review*, 21: 135–72.

McGrath, R. G. (1999). Falling forward: Real options reasoning and entrepreneurial failure. *Academy of Management Review*, 24: 13–30.

McGrath, R. G., Venkataraman, S., and MacMillan, I. C. (1994). The advantage chain: Antecedents to rents from internal corporate ventures. *Journal of Business Venturing*, 9: 351–69.

Miller, D. and Friesen, P. H. (1982). Innovation in conservative and entrepreneurial firms: Two models of strategic momentum. *Strategic Management Journal*, 3: 1–25.

Mosakowski, E. (1993). A resource-based perspective on the dynamic strategy–performance relationship: An empirical examination of the focus and differentiation strategies in entrepreneurial firms. *Journal of Management*, 19: 819–39.

Reynolds, P. D., Storey, D. J., and Westhead, P. (1994). Cross-national comparisons of the variation in new firm formation rates. *Regional Studies*, 28: 443–56.

Romanelli, E. B. (1989). Environments and strategies of organization start-up: Effects on early survival. *Administrative Science Quarterly*, 34: 369–87.

Russell, R. D. (1999). Developing a process model of intrapreneurial systems: A cognitive mapping approach. *Entrepreneurship: Theory and Practice*, 23 (1): 65–84.

Shaver, K. G. and Scott, L. R. (1991). Person, process, choice: The psychology of new venture creation. *Entrepreneurship: Theory and Practice*, 16 (2): 23–46.

Simon, M., Houghton, S. M., and Aquino, K. (2000). Cognitive biases, risk perception, and venture formation: How individuals decide to start companies. *Journal of Business Venturing*, 15: 113–34.

Specht, P. H. (1993). Munificence and carrying capacity of the environment and organizational formation. *Entrepreneurship: Theory and Practice*, 17 (1): 77–86.

Starr, J. A. and Fondas, N. (1993). A model of entrepreneurial socialization and organization formation. *Entrepreneurship: Theory and Practice*, 17 (1): 67–76.

Stuart, T. and Sorenson, O. (2003). The geography of opportunity: Spatial heterogeneity in founding rates and the performance of biotechnology firms. *Research Policy*, 32 (2): 229–53.

Teece, D. J., Pisano, G., and Shuen, A. (1997). Dynamic capabilities and strategic management. *Strategic Management Journal*, 18: 509–33.

Van de Ven, A. H. (1993). The development of an infrastructure for entrepreneurship. *Journal of Business Venturing*, 8: 211–30.

VanderWerf, P. A. (1993). A model of venture creation in new industries. *Entrepreneurship: Theory and Practice*, 17 (2): 39–47.

Venkataraman, S. (1997). The distinctive domain of entrepreneurship research. In J. A. Katz (ed.), *Advances in Entrepreneurship, Firm Emergence and Growth*. Greenwich, CT: JAI Press, III: 139–202.

Webster, F. A. (1976). A model for new venture initiation – a discourse on rapacity and the independent entrepreneur. *Academy of Management Review*, 1: 26–37.

Zahra, S. A. (1996). Technology strategy and financial performance: Examining the moderating role of the firm's competitive environment. *Journal of Business Venturing*, 11: 189–219.

product innovation and entrepreneurship

K. Mark Weaver

INTRODUCTION

Attempting to understand innovation can lead us on a search of epic proportions. A 2004 web search on AOL entering the word "innovation" produced 462,000 pages of entries. Innovation, it seems, is truly a topic of interest for non-profit, governmental, and business organizations. To bring some order to this information, we examine the following topics: (1) definitional issues, (2) innovation as a process, (3) management of innovation, and (4) innovation from a people perspective. The goal is to provide guidelines and tools to increase organizational success.

DEFINING THE CORE CONCEPT

Related concepts must be studied to define innovation. Innovation, creativity, and invention all bring to mind new ideas, change, and opportunity. The common use of these three terms in an almost interchangeable fashion can result in confusion about what is being discussed. Consider creativity, for example. Creativity can be defined as the search for a new concept, decision, or discovery and is an essential but not sufficient part of a definition of innovation. Invention is the use of the idea to create a new product or process. Heap (1989) suggests innovation can best be distinguished from invention by focusing on the process of implementing a new invention, rather than the creation of the invention. Udell (1990) suggests innovation is a process linked to and dependent upon creativity (the generation of ideas) and invention (the conversion of ideas to a value-adding good) that results in a series of activities culminating in a product/process being accepted in the marketplace. This process view of innovation highlights the thesis that defining innovation must consider both creativity and invention as parts of the overall process. As shown in figure 1, ideas lead to invention, to evaluation, to refinement, and finally to implementation. This model leads us to consider alternative ways of defining innovation.

Although innovation has been defined in numerous ways, two approaches are used to highlight the core elements of a definition. First, innovation is "the development of new ideas by people who over time engage in transactions with others in an institutional context" (Van de Ven, 1986). This approach uses the ideas to represent products, processes, or services that create value. While useful, it may be slightly cumbersome, adding confusion over how it is different from creativity and invention. A second, more useful definition comes from

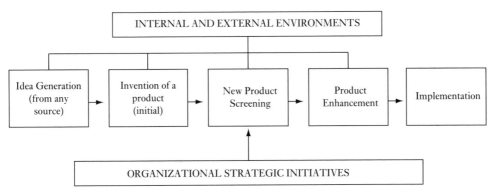

Figure 1 Creativity, Invention, and Innovation Model

the Innovation Network website and is "people creating value though the implementation of new ideas" (Wycoff, 2004). This approach focuses on people (often groups), the strategic process of adding value (not just newness), and implementation in a process model of innovation. This definition allows us to consider innovation as a complete system or process that consists of behavioral aspects (people and groups), a screening process, and outcomes. With this approach we consider products/processes where continuums and models can be developed to track and evaluate what is occurring.

To discuss alternative approaches to the innovation process, two key innovation classification schemes must be discussed. In a recent *Fast Company* article (Wycoff, 2004: 119), Christensen is quoted as using "disruptive" and "sustaining" as innovation categories as a way to capture the essence of innovations. The Boston Consulting Group (Andrews and King, 2003) uses "incremental" and "radical" terminology for essentially the same thing. Joyce Wycoff (2004), founder of the Innovation Network, suggests less loaded words could be useful and proposes a "spectrum of innovation" idea that includes improving, evolving, and game-changing terms to reduce resistance to the existing terminology. These approaches at defining the concept lead us to look at how innovation is implemented and managed.

INNOVATION AS A PROCESS

Definitions, new typologies, and processes to facilitate innovation must also consider why innovation is so difficult to create and to imple-

ment. Tushman and O'Reilly (1997) suggest that success is a potential killer of innovation because of organizational inertia and the constant use of incremental rather than more game-changing innovations. They term this a "tyranny of success" and use examples of product class winners who lost ground because of inertia. IBM (personal computers), Goodyear (tires), Zenith (televisions), Volkswagen (automobiles), Ampex (video recorders), Sears (retailing), and Fuji and Xerox (photocopiers) are examples of firms suffering from a "tyranny of success." These examples demonstrate that all types of industries are subject to this phenomenon. Tushman and O'Reilly make a strong case that to avoid this fate, innovative organizations must support taking chances and tolerating mistakes. In addition, firms must focus on groups for implementation and encourage a need for speed and a sense of urgency as new norms in the innovative organization.

Like Wycoff (2004), Tushman and O'Reilly (1997) support the stream of innovation model for success. They define it as "those multiple types of innovation through which a firm can simultaneously reap the benefits of periodic incremental changes as well as shape the pace and direction of breakthrough innovations and subsequent industry standards" (1997: 166). These views of innovation as typologies, processes, and streams suggest that some paradoxes (such as a cost versus investment outlook in innovation efforts, results related to tactical or a strategic long-term vision, and a balance of incremental and disruptive/radical/game-changing innovations) exist in innovative organizations (see

Avlonitis, Papastathopoulou, and Gounaris, 2001, for additional reviews of these types of typologies, processes, and streams).

Tushman and O'Reilly (1997: 166) propose "managing ambidextrously" as a solution to these paradoxes. As shown in figure 2, ambidextrous organizations build in the paradoxes and possible contradictions based on *time* – how they operate today compared to how they operate in the future – by maintaining entrepreneurial units and supporting all types of innovation. Tushman and O'Reilly (1997: 167) use Sony and the Walkman product as an instructive example. From one basic platform, Sony generated 30 incremental versions, then expanded to

4 platforms and over 160 versions that integrated the incremental and more radical changes over a 10-year period that permitted them to extend a mature technology. This suggests that the stream of innovation model has merit. However, innovation must also be effectively managed.

MANAGING INNOVATION

Nolan (1989) suggests "managing innovation" is an idea that makes this streaming approach work. He defines managing innovation as "creating the environment where innovative behavior is encouraged and rewarded." In addition, Heap (1989) and McCormick (2001) use this

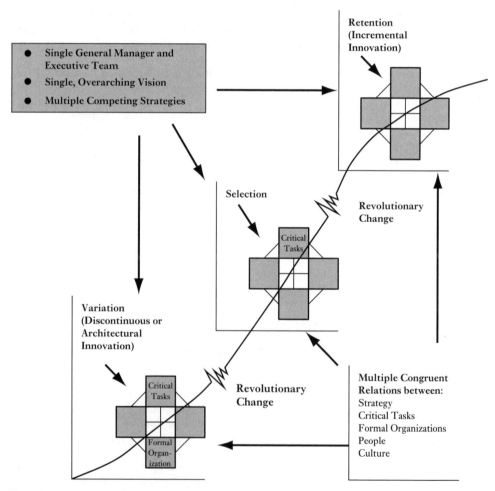

Figure 2   Managing Ambidextrously: Multiple Organizational Architectures and Innovation Streams

managed innovation concept to discuss how innovation requires teamwork, communication, problem solving, and implementation as integral parts of the successful innovation. The role of the leader/entrepreneur is particularly evident in the "anatomy of innovation." Adapted from Nolan (1989: 8), the model of this phenomenon (see figure 3) shows how the innovation process may exist in a typical firm. The figure shows the highs and lows, the questioning of strategic fit and successes that the innovation process creates. The break in the final curve indicates the limits of incremental innovation and the potential rewards of disruptive or game-changing innovations.

As innovation becomes increasingly managerial in focus, the embedded nature of innovation needs to be considered. A 2003 Boston Consulting Group Survey (Andrews and King, 2003) reported the growing importance of innovation to executives and identified practices that lead to accelerated growth through innovation. The results showed that ideas are plentiful, but firms do not adequately screen for success and do not know what is really going on throughout the organization. Andrews and King proposed a four-step plan to improve the flow of innovation:

1 Development of a data-driven diagnostic to set goals.
2 Providing a review process that is "central, senior, periodic, and decisive" and applied impartially.
3 Projects evaluated in light of strategic goals.
4 Redeploying resources to create value and momentum while avoiding a cost-cutting mentality.

These four steps offer an approach that can help organizations develop a mix in their innovation streams that sustains and promotes desired growth. Using any of the terminologies of innovation typologies with such an approach will help reach strategic goals. Hattori and Wycoff (2003: 26) provide a clear look at how innovation has changed from a managerial point of view by focusing on an "innovation shift," and which includes the following:

Old	New
Physical centers	Resources for all units
Focus on ideation	Focus on creating value
Employee orientation	Customer orientation
Passionate change agents	Teams create new culture

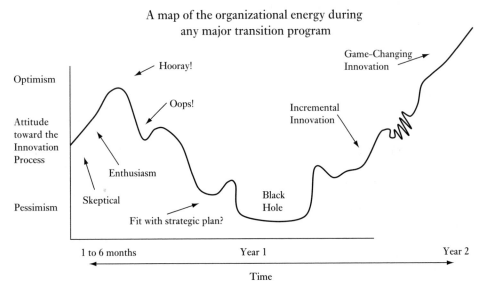

A map of the organizational energy during any major transition program

Figure 3   The Anatomy of Innovation
Source: adapted from Nolan (1989)

Training and facilitation	Coaching/project teams
Individual rewards	Team recognition
Individual/small group tools	Scalable tools for entire organization
Passive support from top	Active support

This kind of shift can be seen in Thomas Edison's work. McCormick (2001) argues that Edison's innovation work highlights the need for accepting failure, seeking the best talent, attracting resources, and considering customer needs as essential elements of innovation. In addition, Edison's lessons point to a need to focus on weaknesses to create competitive advantages as a way to overcome the incremental inertia discussed previously. Lack of resources can drive entrepreneurs to facilitate their innovation efforts. Edison also demonstrates how "play is to innovation what rules are to bureaucracy," showing he understood the need to make innovation a sustainable part of the culture.

Innovation has evolved from a concern with invention and ideas to a view that sustainable models, tools, and processes can be developed to increase the return and value-adding role of innovation. The embedding of these tools in developing the innovation stream concept in the organization appears to be an essential element of survival and growth. Tushman and O'Reilly (1997: 218) provide a way to help summarize this discussion by looking at their "lessons for winning through innovation," which are based on research reported in their book. A synthesis of key ideas includes the following:

1   Competitive vision, strategy, and objectives are the bedrock of managing innovation.
2   Innovation is a result of creative ideas successfully implemented.
3   Identifying performance gaps in the firm is essential to overcoming inertia that kills.
4   Ambidextrous organizations can manage multiple innovation streams to create success.
5   Innovation demands people, competencies, and processes to deal with conflicting demands.

These approaches all suggest the necessity of managing innovation and developing people who are innovative.

WHERE ARE THE PEOPLE IN THESE INNOVATION APPROACHES?

A recent interdisciplinary "boot camp" held at a northeastern university asked non-business faculty to describe "innovators." This group was not well acquainted with the processes discussed here and yet its ideas were consistent with the generally understood characteristics of innovators. The group's list included:

1   Action oriented
2   Agile
3   Commercial
4   Despises boredom and repetition
5   Flexible
6   Free thinker
7   Highly motivated
8   Inspired by obstacles
9   Intuitive
10   Networkers
11   Opportunistic
12   Risk tolerance
13   Status quo is unacceptable
14   Visionary

These terms describe the types of people that need to be developed to create an innovative organization.

A second key area included in all the approaches discussed here is the use of a team or group environment. Thompson (1992) suggested an "innovation team" consists of multiple roles that must be filled and which include idea generators, idea promoters, idea designers, idea implementers, and idea evaluators (for a full list of the tasks for each role, see Thompson, 1992: 193). These roles require actions similar to the orientation expressed in the list generated by the boot camp participants: innovators are opportunistic in focus, but they must think of commercialization and implementation. This individual–group–organizational innovation shift clearly places innovation at the heart of the organization.

CONCLUSION

To meet the demands of the next 50 years, firms will have to incorporate a model of innovation that makes use of the concepts discussed herein. Entrepreneurs and leaders hoping to emulate the innovation of early entrepreneurs need to incorporate a new vocabulary that includes the innovation streams, disruptive innovation, game-changing innovation, and other ideas presented here. Christensen (Wycoff 2004: 119) states: "There isn't anything more invigorating...than to hear an entrepreneur using the term "disruptive technology" that make no reference to me...When it's clear they got the idea and use it in everyday parlance, that's the ultimate triumph." It is this everyday usage and understanding of innovation processes that is the goal for innovation theorists, teachers, and practitioners.

To study innovation, several websites can be used. First, www.innovation.com network has tools, articles, and links that will make your search easier. Second, www.innovationtools .com provides a jumping-off point for the novice and the experienced person interested in innovation. Third, www.debonogroup.com is the ultimate guide to the work of Edward De Bono (1991), the father of lateral thinking and the innovation search process. These sources will facilitate efforts to understand innovation as a process and tool for organizational development.

Bibliography

Andrews, J. P. and King, K. (2003). *Boosting Innovative Productivity*. Boston, MA: Boston Consulting Group.

Avlonitis, G. J., Papastathopoulou, P. G., and Gounaris, S. P. (2001). An empirically-based typology of innovativeness for new financial services: Success and failure scenarios. *Journal of Product Innovation Management*, 18: 324–42.

De Bono, E. (1991). *Opportunities*. London: Penguin Books.

Hattori, R. A. and Wycoff, J. (2003). Innovation DNA. *Training and Development Magazine* (January): 25–50.

Heap, J. P. (1989). *The Management of Innovation and Design*. London: Cassel.

La Barre, P. (2003). The industrialized revolution. *Fast Company* (November): 115–20.

McCormick, B. (2001). *At Work with Thomas Edison: 10 Business Lessons from America's Greatest Innovator*. Canada: Entrepreneur Press.

Nolan, V. (1989). *The Innovator's Handbook*. London: Penguin Books.

Thompson, C. (1992). *What a Great Idea: The Key Steps Creative People Take*. New York: Harper Perennial.

Tushman, M. L. and O'Reilly, C. A., III (1997). *Winning Through Innovation: A Practical Guide to Leading Organizational Change and Renewal*. Boston, MA: Harvard Business School Press.

Udell, G. (1990). *Exploring the Innovation Process*. Springfield, MO: WIN Innovation Center.

Van de Ven, A. H. (1986) Central problems in the management of innovation. *Management Science*, 32: 590–607.

Wycoff, J. (2004). Enterprise innovation. Cited at *InnovationTools.com*.

R

radical innovations

Gautam Ahuja and PuayKhoon Toh

A radical innovation is one that represents a major breakthrough from the existing paradigm or way of doing things (Abernathy and Utterback, 1978). Such breakthroughs can be defined from two perspectives: the technological perspective or the user perspective. From the technological perspective, a radical innovation is one that departs from the existing technological trajectory to produce technological performance that is of an order of magnitude difference. If one views the development of each type of technology as progression along a path or trajectory, then a radical innovation represents a discontinuous "jump" in the trajectory, defining a new progression along which the technological development is to continue. Innovations with radical effects, when first introduced, tend to leave the technological arena in initial periods of flux. This is followed by a period of stabilization, when the new technology is understood and developed (Anderson and Tushman, 1990). A dominant design or industry standard then emerges from such radical change. The discontinuity created by a radical innovation tends to render the old trajectory obsolete. This implies a reduction in the value of competencies along the old technological trajectory, especially when such competencies are specific to the obsolete technology. For example, the introduction of compact disc technology drastically reduced the value of audiotapes and rendered the production competencies for audio tapes relatively irrelevant. Hence, radical innovations, by creating discontinuities in technological progression and changing industry standards, are often also competence destroying (Anderson and Tushman, 1990).

From the user's perspective, an innovation can be radical if it introduces a significant improvement in one or more user attributes of the product or introduces a new user attribute, hitherto not significantly associated with that product. For instance, the Airbus 380 increases significantly the load that an airline can transport through one aircraft. Thus, even if the underlying technologies do not represent significant novelty from a user perspective, the plane can still be considered a radical innovation. A radical innovation can sometimes generate new demand (as opposed to satisfying current consumer demand) by creating a new standard, and hence opening up a new market altogether. In Schumpeterian (1975) terms, radical innovations are the significant engines and drivers of the process of creative destruction, necessary for firm growth and societal progress.

An incremental innovation is the opposite of a radical innovation. An incremental innovation makes minor improvements over existing know-how, and enhances current technologies. It encourages progress along the existing technological trajectory without creating discontinuities and reinforces current paradigms. From a user perspective, incremental innovations make minor improvements in the existing set of user characteristics for a product (Saviotti, 1996).

Radical innovations are often associated with small firms, entrepreneurs, or new entrants to the industry. Although large firms tend to spend more on R&D, and thus on average tend to generate more innovations, radical innovations often build on novel and recent technologies that do not rely much on existing sets of other technologies. Entrepreneurs, who tend to operate in smaller firms, have the "advantage" of not having existing routines and standards that might constrain them. The lack of dogma or dominant paradigms makes it easier for them to employ new and novel knowledge in their creative activities. Large firms, on the other hand, have a tendency to fall into learning traps where they overlook distant times, distant places, and failures, due to their practiced process of simplification and specialization in solving problems (Levinthal and March, 1993).

While the key idea behind the definition of a radical innovation lies in the (great) extent of "newness" or novelty in the inherent invention, in empirical work the degree of "radicalness" of an innovation is often associated with the subsequent usage of the innovation or the pool of knowledge from which the innovation is generated. The greater the novelty of the innovation, the greater will be the difference between such technology and the existing ones, and therefore the greater will be the magnitude of the discontinuity that is created. When such radical innovation generates new and different demand and creates a new market, the subsequent usage of the innovation by others will be high. In the realm of technology, a radical innovation defines a new trajectory along which subsequent technological developments will be determined, and hence subsequent technologies will tend to draw heavily on the "newness" of this focal innovation that has defined the new trajectory. When new technological developments are measured by patent information, such usage of the focal innovation is reflected in the citations of the focal innovation by subsequent patents that are developed based on the novelty that this focal innovation encompasses. Because a more radical patented innovation (as opposed to an incremental one) is more likely to have created a new path of technological progress, it is more likely to be cited by subsequent patents. Therefore, the number of subsequent citations by other patents is often used as a measure of the degree of radicalness of an innovation (Trajtenberg, 1990; Ahuja and Lampert, 2001).

Another measure of radical innovation is related to the knowledge pool from which the innovation is generated. The more the focal innovation relies on prior or existing knowledge, the less likely is it that the innovation is going to be novel. This is because heavy use of existing knowledge suggests extensive reliance on existing paradigms. Innovations based purely on recombinations of existing knowledge components tend to be incremental. Novel inventions tend to be path-breaking and therefore typically do not follow existing paradigms, nor draw much on existing technologies. Hence, the extent of reliance on previous knowledge can also indicate the level of radicalness of the innovation. Again, patents are often used to measure radical innovations and in this context the radicalness of a patent is based upon the number of citations it makes to previous patents. While such measures of radical innovations are not perfect – as they are not *direct* measures of the radical nature of the innovation – the availability and reliability of the patent data and the lack of a better alternative make these measures the common ones used in the literature.

Bibliography

Abernathy, W. J. and Utterback, J. (1978). Patterns of industrial innovation. *Technology Review* (June–July): 40–7.

Ahuja, G. and Lampert, C. M. (2001). Entrepreneurship in the large corporation: A longitudinal study of how established firms create breakthrough inventions. *Strategic Management Journal*, 22: 521–43.

Anderson, P. and Tushman, M. L. (1990). Technological discontinuities and dominant designs: A cyclical model of technological change. *Administrative Science Quarterly*, 35: 604–33.

Dosi G. (1982). Technological paradigms and technological trajectories. *Research Policy*, 11: 147–62.

Levinthal, D. A. and March, J. G. (1993). The myopia of learning. *Strategic Management Journal* 14 (winter special issue): 95–112.

Saviotti, P. (1996). *Technological Evolution, Variety, and the Economy*. Brookfield, VT: Edward Elgar.

Schumpeter, J. A. (1975). *Capitalism, Socialism, and Democracy*. New York: Harper and Row.

Trajtenberg, M. (1990). A penny for your quotes: Patent citations and the value of information. *RAND Journal of Economics*, 21: 325–42.

real options

Rita Gunther McGrath

ORIGINS OF THE CONCEPT

Investment analysis in the field of finance fundamentally changed with ability to assess derivatives, also called financial options (Black and

Scholes, 1973). A financial option contract conveys the right, but not the obligation, to make an investment (usually termed "exercising" or "striking" the option) at some time in the future. A "put" option refers to the right to sell a stock (the underlying asset) at a specified price, while a "call" option conveys the right to purchase stock at a specified price. If the option is not exercised at the agreed time, it "expires" and becomes worthless. If the value of the underlying asset makes it worthwhile, the buyer sells or buys it and capitalizes on the difference between the option contract amount and the asset's actual value.

Three characteristics of value in financial options are worth noting. The first characteristic is the containment of loss. Because the exposure of an investor is limited to the price paid for the options contract, the loss such an investor might incur is limited, relative to the potential losses if the investment was made in the underlying asset rather than the option. The second characteristic is the expansion of upside potential. Because the benefit to an options investor is not limited, the potential upside to be gained is substantial. Third, investments in financial options are sequential: the decision to exercise an option or let it expire is made after the decision to invest. Investing in options under uncertainty allows an investor to limit losses by making commitment decisions only when uncertainty has been eliminated (because the actual price of the underlying asset is known at the time of exercise).

The theory of real options extends the logic underlying the investment in financial options to organizational resource investments. Originally explored with respect to capital budgeting (Myers, 1977), real options reasoning has been used to analyze many types of organizational resource commitments, including strategy evolution (Bowman and Hurry, 1993; Dixit and Pindyck, 1994), R&D (Mitchell and Hamilton, 1998; McGrath, 1997), joint ventures (Kogut, 1991), governance choices (Folta, 1998; Folta and Miller, 2002), and entrepreneurship (McGrath, 1999). The essential argument is that, under uncertainty, the value of an investment in a real asset will be greater when a similar approach is used to that used to invest in a financial option. Thus, an options oriented in-vestor would seek to minimize the downside exposure of his or her investment, to maximize the upside potential, and to sequence decisions so that major commitments are deferred until uncertainty has been reduced.

OPTIONS REASONING AS THE BASIS FOR INVESTMENT UNDER UNCERTAINTY

Options reasoning offers an alternative to (or at least a different perspective on) conventional rules for investment. Conventional wisdom relies on the net present value rule. Scholars interested in real options have proposed that in addition to present value, option value matters. The big risk of ignoring option value is a downward bias on return calculations (Myers and Turnbull, 1977: 332), leading to a systemic aversion to investments in uncertain projects, such as those involving entrepreneurship, innovation, R&D, or capability creation (Kester, 1984; Kogut and Kulatilaka, 2001).

A key source of option value has to do with creating flexibility through preserving future decision rights. As Merton (1998: 339) points out: "The common element for using option-pricing here is . . . the future is uncertain (if it were not, there would be no need to create options because we know now what we will do later) and in an uncertain environment, having the flexibility to decide what to do after some of that uncertainty is resolved definitely has value." Empirically, options reasoning has been found to be more consistent with the pattern of choices actually made by organizations than are other investment alternatives (most typically, discounted cash flow models). For instance, firms impose higher hurdle rates for investment than would be dictated by the NPV rule, and stick with investments that are underperforming longer than it might suggest (see Dixit, 1992, for a discussion of hysteresis effects).

For many scholars, the attraction of options reasoning lies in developing heuristics, or even decision rules, that would provide better insight into strategic resource allocation processes (Bettis and Hitt, 1995). Bowman and Hurry (1993: 760), for instance, suggest "the lens offers an economic logic for the behavioral process of incremental resource investment." One essential assumption is that strategic resources accumulate in a path-dependent manner, meaning that the future value of resources acquired today cannot be perfectly anticipated.

CURRENT DEBATES

As the real options research stream develops, scholars have begun to explore its limitations. Reuer and Leiblein (2000), for instance, found that contrary to what might be expected from options reasoning, there was no mitigation of downside risk in their pursuit of multinational ventures. Coff and Laverty (2001) question whether options analysis applies in cases of investments in knowledge assets because the nature of the underlying asset created is not clear. Adner and Levinthal (2004) argue that real options logic applies only to a narrow range of organizational investments, because as choice sets evolve over time, the structured investment, and particularly abandonment decisions that are central to the operation of the theory, cannot be distinguished from more generic behavioral processes that guide managers in making any sort of path-dependent decision.

Normatively, options reasoning has been partly blamed for the excessively optimistic valuations achieved during the Internet bubble of the late 1990s (Kogut and Kulatilaka, 2004). Over-valuation and over-investment are thus seen as consequences of excessively optimistic judgments of future potential. Another risk attributed to options reasoning is a potential for escalation of commitment due to (among other things) reluctance to terminate failing projects (Ross and Staw, 1986; see also Zardkoohi, 2004).

REAL OPTIONS REASONING IN ENTREPRENEURSHIP

Because investing in entrepreneurial ventures, independent start-ups, or ventures sponsored by established firms involves many of the same characteristics as making investments in options, some scholars have suggested that the options lens can help illuminate aspects of the entrepreneurship process that are poorly explained by using other approaches (McGrath, 1996, 1999). Investing under uncertainty has long been central to theories of the entrepreneurial venture (Knight, 1971) and to theories that attempt to explain the gains to entrepreneurial activity (Baumol, 1993; 2002; Rumelt, 1987). Entrepren-

eurial ventures further involve path-dependent investments in which later opportunities are only accessible because earlier investments were made (Ronstadt, 1988; Gregersen and Dyer, 2003).

The investment pattern relevant to options reasoning has long been advocated as appropriate for entrepreneurs, and often taught in the entrepreneurship classroom (Vesper, 1990). Professors have often advised their entrepreneurship students to keep investment limited until key uncertainties are resolved; to be prepared to aggressively pursue the upside; to stage, sequence, and monitor their investments; and to be prepared to abandon an idea when the upside no longer merits investment.

Options reasoning may also fruitfully be used to understand entrepreneurial investment and motivation, two key issues that have concerned both entrepreneurship scholars and other constituencies (such as public policy advocates). Scholars have found, for instance, that important decisions in entrepreneurship have not been made on the basis of objective exogenous criteria (such as earning less than the cost of capital). Rather, such decisions are often made on the basis of subjective criteria, such as the attractiveness of continued investment in a small business relative to other opportunities offered the entrepreneur, an implicit judgment of option value (Gimeno et al., 1997). Similarly, Bhide (2000) observed that the most significant decision point for entrepreneurs with respect to risk is not starting up, but rather the more substantial follow-on investment required to develop their fledgling businesses. This pattern echoes the sequential "option-followed-by-exercise" pattern options reasoning seeks to explain. Options reasoning also provides an economic logic for why individuals might invest in new ventures, despite considerable evidence that failure is highly likely (McGrath, 1999). For entrepreneurship scholars, options theory contributes to the range of perspectives on which they may draw to understand entrepreneurial behavior under conditions of uncertainty.

Bibliography

Adner, R. and Levinthal, D. (2004). What is not a real option? *Academy of Management Review*, 29: 74–85.

Baumol, W. J. (1993). *Entrepreneurship, Management, and the Structure of Payoffs*. Cambridge, MA: MIT Press.

Baumol, W. J. (2002). *The Free-Market Innovation Machine: Analyzing the Growth Miracle of Capitalism*. Princeton, NJ: Princeton University Press.

Bettis, R. A. and Hitt, M.A. (1995). The new competitive landscape. *Strategic Management Journal*, 16 (special issue): 7–19.

Bhide, A. (2000). *The Origin and Evolution of New Businesses*. New York: Oxford University Press.

Black, F. and Scholes, M. (1973). The pricing of options and corporate liabilities. *Journal of Political Economy*, 81: 637–54.

Bowman, E. H. and Hurry, D. (1993). Strategy through the option lens: An integrated view of resource investments and the incremental-choice process. *Academy of Management Review*, 18: 760–82.

Coff, R. and Laverty, K. (2001). Real options of knowledge assets: Panacea or Pandora's box? *Business Horizons*, 44: 73–9.

Dixit, A. (1992). Investment and hysteresis. *Journal of Economic Perspectives*, 6: 107–32.

Dixit, A. K. and Pindyck, R. S. (1994). *Investment Under Uncertainty*. Princeton, NJ: Princeton University Press.

Folta, T. B. (1998). Governance and uncertainty: The trade-off between administrative control and commitment. *Strategic Management Journal*, 19: 1007–28.

Folta, T. B. and Miller, K. D. (2002). Real options in equity partnerships. *Strategic Management Journal*, 23: 77–88.

Gimeno, J., Folta, T. B., Cooper, A. C., and Woo, C. Y. (1997). Survival of the fittest? Entrepreneurial human capital and the persistence of underperforming firms. *Administrative Science Quarterly*, 42: 750–83.

Gregersen, H. B. and Dyer, J. H. (2003). Generating strategic insight through catalytic questions. Symposium presented at the Academy of Management Annual Conference, Seattle, Washington.

Kester, W. C. (1984). Today's options for tomorrow's growth. *Harvard Business Review*, 62: 153–60.

Knight, F. H. (1971). *Risk, Uncertainty, and Profit*. Midway reprint. Chicago: University of Chicago Press.

Kogut, B. (1991). Joint ventures and the option to expand and acquire. *Management Science*, 37: 19–33.

Kogut, B. and Kulatilaka, N. (2001). Capabilities as real options. *Organization Science*, 12: 744–58.

Kogut, B. and Kulatilaka, N. (2004). Real options pricing and organizations: The contingent risks of extended theoretical domains. *Academy of Management Review*, 29: 102–10.

McGrath, R. G. (1996). Options and the entrepreneur: Towards a strategic theory of entrepreneurial wealth creation. *Best Papers Proceedings*, Academy of Management Annual meetings, Cincinnati, OH, 101–5.

McGrath, R. G. (1997). A real options logic for initiating technology positioning investments. *Academy of Management Review*, 22: 974–96.

McGrath, R. G. (1999). Falling forward: Real options reasoning and entrepreneurial failure. *Academy of Management Review*, 24: 13–30.

Merton, R. C. (1998). Applications of option-pricing theory: Twenty-five years later. *American Economic Review*, 88: 323–49.

Mitchell, G. R. and Hamilton, W. F. (1988). Managing R&D as a strategic option. *Research-Technology Management*, 27: 15–22.

Myers, S. C. (1977). Determinants of corporate borrowing. *Journal of Financial Economics*, 5: 147–76.

Myers, S. C. and Turnbull, S. M. (1977). Capital budgeting and the capital asset pricing model: Good news and bad news. *Journal of Finance*, 32: 321–33.

Reuer, J. J. and Leiblein, M. J. (2000). Downside risk implications of multinationality and international joint ventures. *Academy of Management Journal*, 43: 203–14.

Ronstadt, R. (1988). The corridor principle. *Journal of Business Venturing*, 3: 31–40.

Ross, J. and Staw, B. M. (1986). Expo 86: An escalation prototype. *Administrative Science Quarterly*, 31: 274–97.

Rumelt, R. P. (1987). Theory, strategy, and entrepreneurship. In D. J. Teece (ed.), *The Competitive Challenge: Strategies for Industrial Innovation and Renewal*. New York: Harper and Row, 137–58.

Vesper, K. H. (1990). *New Venture Strategies*. Englewood Cliffs, NJ: Prentice-Hall.

Zardkoohi, A. (2004). Do real options lead to escalation of commitment? *Academy of Management Review*, 29: 111–19.

risk management in corporate ventures

Stephen A. Allen

Visualizing, gauging, and managing venture risk are critical functions of entrepreneurship. Successful risk management reduces downside prospects, while preserving or not proportionately reducing upside possibilities.

Corporate ventures are defined here as material investments – of money and scarce talent – which have prospects for changing a firm's (or business unit's) competitive position, opportunity set, or financial footprint. They generally involve new business development, but may extend to new ways of doing business with current customers or other members of a company's value chain (Schumpeter, 1934). While risk management is treated in the context of large, established companies, underlying concepts are applicable to smaller firms and start-ups.

Visualizing Risk

Venture champions know that substantial risks come with the territory, yet their mental models of risk are often under-specified and subject to denial (Kahneman and Lovallo, 1993; March and Shapira, 1987). Bernstein (1996) observes that increasing acceptance that risks could be measured and actively managed dates only from early in the last century.

Mental models which recognize multiple dimensions of risks can provide a powerful foundation for deciding how and when they can be most effectively managed. First, contrary to common usage, the notion of risk should not be limited to prospects for downside outcomes. It also resides in failure to fully capture upside prospects of a venture. For example, a biotechnology firm recently launched a superior treatment for rheumatoid arthritis, but with production capacity which turned out to be substantially lower than market demand. While company executives had viewed this lower capacity investment as prudent risk management, it carried costs of forgone revenues of as much as $450 million and provision of a two-year window for competitors to enter the market. Aggressive investment to maximize potential first-mover returns is not always merited (Cottrell and Sick, 2001); however, managers need to estimate costs of decisions which place a ceiling on the upside of venture.

Further insight into venture risk can be gained by decomposing it into three interacting components, as suggested by the classic treatment of Knight (1921):

risk = (exposure)(uncertainty of benefits)(time)

Exposure results from decisions about size and timing of outlays to launch and sustain a venture. Uncertainty can relate to exposure along with onset, ramp, stability, and duration of cash inflows. The impacts of exposure and uncertainty of benefits on overall venture risk are time dependent: risk is not time invariant. Venture development involves learning (McGrath and MacMillan, 1995) and management of cash burn rates in order to attain key milestones and resolve uncertainties (e.g., technical feasibility, market acceptance, timing and vigor of competitor reactions). The staged investment common to venture capitalists recognizes the value and cost of uncertainty reduction, with start-ups being revalued (or abandoned) across multiple funding rounds (Sahlman, 1988). While similar approaches have been advocated for large company ventures (Hodder and Riggs, 1985), they remain uncommon in practice. Many large firms have adopted stage-gate systems, which link support levels to attainment of operational milestones (Cooper, 1990).

Linking Risk Analysis to Venture Decisions

Most large US and European companies require discounted cash flow analyses at stages in a venture's development which involve significant investment. While these formal justification procedures are designed to avoid investments with unattractive return prospects, they are generally applied late in the venture development process, after a project team has made most of the decisions which will influence their venture's risk-return profile (Allen, 2002). Viewed from the perspectives of venture champions in the middle of organizations, corporate investment justification practices provide signals on risk-return profiles unlikely to receive approval, but provide little help in developing and actively managing winners.

Allen (2002) advocates arming venture teams with capabilities for developing simple cash flow scenarios, which permit gauging risk-return trade-offs underlying key decisions about how their ventures should be configured. These analyses can inform decisions at two important stages in venture development. The first stage – lying between opportunity identification and a detailed go-to-market plan – is the time-frame within which several decisions will determine a venture's initial risk-return profile. These decisions include which capabilities to develop internally versus which to outsource, which early customer segments to target, channel selection, and initial scale of production and service capacities for going to market. Subsequent reversal of these decisions is generally expensive and time consuming. The second stage is after a first win (or lack thereof) in the market. This involves the next round of decisions regarding venture scale and scope.

Decisions at these two critical stages are often made in a piecemeal and iterative fashion, as market and technical knowledge accumulates. Parallel gauging of risk-return effects of alternatives for these decisions can yield several benefits: a more tightly integrated overall strategy; avoidance of lazy (underutilized) investments and inflexible cost structures; clarity regarding overall level of risk being incrementally built into the venture; and a stronger basis for developing formal appropriation requests. Case evidence reported by McKinsey and Company suggests that active use of simple risk-return analyses can have substantial effects on venture economics. In five consulting assignments involving capital intensive projects in chemical, mining, building materials, and mobile telephone businesses, use of these approaches helped venture teams increase expected net present value of their projects by 35–45 percent over initial plans. These improvements were based on capital savings of 15–45 percent and revenue improvements/cost reductions equal to 20–35 percent of the capital expenditure base (Carter, van Dijk, and Gibson 1996).

RISK MANAGEMENT STRATEGIES

Within broad technological and market constraints of their particular industries, venture champions have many possibilities for how to scope and actively manage their projects. The same venture can be structured to target quite different combinations of risk and return potential. Decisions on size, scope, timing, and course corrections for a venture reflect a combination of several generic strategies for bearing, sharing, and managing risk:

- *Bear substantial risk.* These are typically big bet situations in which the venture and its parent firm are unwilling to share returns or may be unable to find suitable partners. Examples include development of new commercial aircraft bodies, blockbuster pharmaceutical candidates, and contests for establishing technology standards. There is often a presumption of substantial and durable first-mover advantages.

- *Risk sharing can take many forms:* outsourcing parts of the value chain; joint ventures; contractual arrangements with customers and suppliers with lock-ins or options regarding price, volume, and duration (Billington, Johnson, and Triantis, 2003). Insurance and government investment incentives are also risk sharing mechanisms. Sharing risks involves sharing prospective returns; however, the sharing formula need not be proportional. Different parties have different capacities to bear and manage different risks, which can reduce total costs for bearing venture risk (Brealey, Cooper, and Habib 1996; Stulz, 1996).

- *Spread risks over time.* Sequential expansion of production capacity and sales and service infrastructure can limit exposure as uncertainties are progressively resolved. Merits of this strategy should be weighted against the countervailing risk of successfully developing a market and not being able to fully satisfy demand.

- *Input/output flexibility.* Flexible production technologies can be used to mitigate revenue or cost risks. The value of these approaches in adapting to changes in markets for end products or supplies should be weighed against potentially higher investment requirements and penalties to economies of scale.

- *Truncate losses or marginal performance.* Moves can range from downsizing parts of a venture to abandonment. These decisions tend to be more effective if abandonment criteria have been set before the fact, though venture champions often find such discipline difficult to apply when their immediate concern is growth.

Corporate entrepreneurs who tailor combinations of these risk management approaches to the particular challenges posed by their ventures can reduce downside prospects without unnecessarily sacrificing upside potential.

Bibliography

Allen, S. (2002). Corporate ventures and risk management: For best results, turn upside down. *Babson Entrepreneurial Review* (October): 17–30.

Bernstein, P. (1996). *Against the Gods: The Remarkable Story of Risk*. New York: John Wiley.

Billington, C., Johnson, B., and Triantis, A. (2003). A real options perspective on supply chain management in high technology. *Journal of Applied Corporate Finance*, 15 (2): 32–43.

Brealey, R., Cooper, I., and Habib, M. (1996). Using project finance to fund infrastructure projects. *Journal of Applied Corporate Finance*, 9 (3): 25–38.

Carter, J., van Dijk, M., and Gibson, K. (1996). Capital investment: How not to build the Titanic. *McKinsey Quarterly*, 4: 147–59.

Cooper, R. (1990). Stage-gate systems: A new tool for managing new products. *Business Horizons* (May–June): 44–54.

Cottrell, T. and Sick, G. (2001). First mover (dis)advantage and real options. *Journal of Applied Corporate Finance*, 14 (2): 41–51.

Hodder, J. and Riggs, H. (1985). Pitfalls in evaluating risky projects. *Harvard Business Review*, 63 (1): 128–36.

Kahneman, D. and Lovallo, D. (1993). Timid choices and bold forecasts: A cognitive perspective on risk taking. *Management Science*, 39 (1): 17–31.

Knight, F. (1921). *Risk, Uncertainty, and Profit*. Boston, MA: Century Press.

McGrath, R. and MacMillan, I. (1995). Discovery-driven planning. *Harvard Business Review*, 73 (4): 44–53.

March, J. and Shapira, Z. (1987). Managerial perspectives on risk and risk taking. *Management Science*, 33 (11): 1404–18.

Sahlman, W. (1988). Aspects of financial contracting in venture capital. *Journal of Applied Corporate Finance*, 1 (2): 23–36.

Schumpeter, J. (1934). *The Theory of Economic Development*. Cambridge, MA: Harvard University Press.

Stulz, R. (1996). Rethinking risk management. *Journal of Applied Corporate Finance*, 9 (3): 8–24.

S

sensemaking and entrepreneurship

C. Chet Miller

Sensemaking is an elusive concept. On the one hand, sensemaking implies a straightforward, unbiased process through which individuals and social collectives perceive, interpret, and draw conclusions about the objective world around them. This simple definition has intuitive appeal, and seems to capture the essence of what making sense of the world is all about. On the other hand, sensemaking implies a much more complex process, where developing an understanding of one's situation is still the key, but where perceptions are driven by preexisting personal and organizational identities, where interpretation of an existing world is placed in partnership with ongoing enactment of that world, and where conclusions are driven by plausibility rather than accuracy (see Weick, 1995). It is this complex definition that has proven useful in recent strategy, entrepreneurship, and organizational behavior research (e.g., Anand and Peterson, 2000; Orton, 2000; Vaara, 2003), and it is this definition that provides the basis for the discussion that follows.

SENSEMAKING BY THE ENTREPRENEUR

Entrepreneurs concern themselves with creativity and innovation as they attempt to exploit previously unexploited opportunities (Ireland et al., 2001). In the words of Drucker (1985), they "create something new, something different; they change or transmute values." Importantly, as they go about their creative endeavors, entrepreneurs often face a great deal of equivocality.

Equivocality is, within a single person or entity, the existence of multiple interpretations of an event, outcome, or set of experiences. In some situations, the meaning of an event is clear, or can be made clear with simple information gathering. The cause–effect relationships that generated the event are clear or easily determined, and what the event means for the future is clear or readily knowable. In other situations, particularly novel ones such as those encountered by entrepreneurs, multiple interpretations by a given individual are more likely, and choosing among the multiple interpretations is difficult given the novel and non-routine nature of the situation. It is this equivocality that forces sensemaking.

Consider a simple example. Apple Computer introduced the Newton in the early 1990s. The company sold 140,000 of these personal digital assistants in the first two years of the product. Was this a success or a failure? If a success, what explains the success? If a failure, what explains the failure? And what did it all mean for Apple's future endeavors? A few facts may help in answering these questions. First, Apple Computer was built on the success of the Apple II. It, however, sold only 43,000 of these personal computers in the first two years of the product. Second, the Newton was positioned in a new barely emerging market, just as the Apple II had been in the late 1970s. In such a market, smaller volumes in the early years and some technological issues might be expected. Was the Newton a success or a failure? By most accounts, it was a tremendous failure. Why? Because it generated low volume and had some technological issues (Christensen, 1997). Other accounts, however, tell a different story. In these alternative accounts, the Newton is viewed positively as a trailblazing, market-creating product (Christensen, 1997). Which interpretation is correct? Both? Neither? For those within Apple who held both interpretations and could not choose between them, how could the equivocality have been resolved? Going forward, what should Apple have learned from the Newton experience? This is a key sensemaking question, but it is very difficult to answer in a definitive way.

The role of identity.   An entrepreneur may have several identities. They may have an identity grounded in successful risk taking and out-of-box thinking (an entrepreneurial self), but they may also have an identity grounded in the ability to effectively apply existing rules and standards (an engineering self) or an identity grounded in steadfast defense of egalitarian values (an equality self). Which identity is used in a given situation affects what is noticed and affects the choice of variables and data for ongoing attention. What is noticed and focused upon in turn affects decisions and actions. Further – and this is a key aspect of sensemaking – which identity is used is driven not just by objective features of the situation and the predisposition of the entrepreneur, but also by how people around them respond to their actions. This dynamic is captured by a simple question: "How can I know who I am until I see what they do?" (Weick, 1995). For example, a project manager involved with the Apple Newton project may have been positively reinforced for focusing on technical excellence, which probably caused the individual to use their engineering identity. But when corporate management, the business press, and the technology press began to question the Newton's technology, the individual may have moved subconsciously to an entrepreneurial identity, where self-esteem would have been protected ("I have been working on an entrepreneurial project with many unknowns; I have not been working on an engineering project where the path from X to Y could be optimized").

The role of enactment.   Enactment means that entrepreneurs are partially responsible for many of the events, outcomes, and experiences they must interpret. In other words, entrepreneurs take actions over time and this influences the course of events. They are simultaneously creators and discoverers of what is out there.

Enactment sometimes involves straightforward actions, outcomes, and interpretations, such as when an entrepreneur establishes a strong cost accounting unit in her small firm and then hears complaints from organizational members about the loss of an entrepreneurial environment. Enactment, however, extends to richer conceptual territory as well. For example, it encompasses instances where individuals experiment on the world in order to test tentative explanations of past events. These experiments may influence ongoing events in unforeseen ways, forcing interpretations of a new set of circumstances. Enactment also extends to self-fulfilling prophecies, and such prophecies lie at the heart of much enactment (Weick, 1979). A simple example illustrates this common phenomenon. An entrepreneur feels that an angel investor (*see* BUSINESS ANGEL NETWORK) is being overly aggressive in monitoring the new business. Lacking the time or inclination to handle this, the entrepreneur attempts to wall himself off from the investor. The investor, who had not actually been aggressive in monitoring, reacts by stepping up efforts to stay in contact with the entrepreneur. The entrepreneur concludes that he has a real problem on his hands. This problem, which has in fact become real, is self-induced. Being careful with assumptions and preconceived notions is one lesson from a sensemaking perspective.

The role of plausibility.   Sensemaking is not necessarily focused on discovering or developing an accurate view of the world. Instead, it is focused on creating a plausible view, a view that basically fits the data but perhaps not perfectly so. Why is this important, and perhaps useful? The key idea is to avoid inaction based on too much investigation and too much thinking. Weick (1995) put it this way: "I need to know enough about what I think to get on with my projects, but no more, which means sufficiency and plausibility take preference over accuracy." Borrowing from pop culture in early twenty-first century America, "Just do it" seems to capture the sensemaking perspective.

Entrepreneurs often face dynamic, shifting environments, and cannot afford to become mired in too much analysis. Sensemaking that has the limited goal of plausible viewpoints frees entrepreneurs to act and then learn from experience.

Conclusion

Sensemaking offers an alternative to traditional perspectives on entrepreneurial information gathering, decision-making, and planning (*see* ENTREPRENEURIAL DECISIONS). In more traditional perspectives, information is gathered until the marginal cost of doing so exceeds the marginal benefit in discovering truth about an objective world. Sensemaking emphasizes the role of identity, enactment, and plausibility in understanding a subjective world. It offers a different way to think about entrepreneurs and entrepreneurial organizations.

In this essay, a basic but meaningful interpretation of sensemaking has been offered. In more elaborate treatments, the intersubjective nature of sensemaking and perhaps its retrospective flavor might also be emphasized.

Bibliography

Anand, N. and Peterson, R. A. (2000). When market information constitutes fields: Sensemaking of markets in the commercial music industry. *Organization Science*, 11: 270–84.

Christensen, C. M. (1997). *The Innovator's Dilemma: When New Technologies Cause Great Firms to Fail*. Boston, MA: Harvard Business School Press.

Drucker, P. F. (1985). *Innovation and Entrepreneurship: Practices and Principles*. New York: Harper and Row.

Ireland, R. D., Hitt, M. A., Camp, S. M., and Sexton, D. L. (2001). Integrating entrepreneurship and strategic management actions to create firm wealth. *Academy of Management Executive*, 15 (1): 49–63.

Orton, J. D. (2000). Enactment, sensemaking, and decision-making: Redesign processes in the 1976 reorganization of the US intelligence community. *Journal of Management Studies*, 37: 213–34.

Varra, E. (2003). Post-acquisition integration as sensemaking: Glimpses of ambiguity, confusion, hypocrisy, and politicization. *Journal of Management Studies*, 40: 859–94.

Weick, K. E. (1979). *Social Psychology of Organizing*, 2nd edn. Reading, MA: Addison-Wesley.

Weick, K. E. (1995). *Sensemaking in Organizations*. Thousand Oaks, CA: Sage.

social capital

Robert A. Baron

The field of entrepreneurship investigates a wide range of intriguing questions, but among these, two have long been recognized as especially important: (1) Why do some persons but not others choose to become entrepreneurs? (2) Why are some individuals much more successful in this role than others? Many factors play a role with respect to each of these issues, but one that appears to be relevant to both is the concept of *social capital*. In extant literature on entrepreneurship, this term is generally defined as referring either to (1) the ability of individuals to extract benefits from their social structures, networks, and memberships, or (2) these benefits themselves – the advantages individuals gain from their relationships with others (Nahapiet and Ghoshal, 1998; Portes, 1998).

Both definitions agree that social capital refers to positive outcomes accruing to individuals from their social ties with others – from being known to them, having a good reputation, and from being in established, continuing relationships with them. These ties provide them with access to a wide range of both tangible and intangible resources. Included among the tangible benefits individuals can derive from social ties are financial resources and enhanced access to potentially valuable information. Included among less tangible benefits are support, advice, and encouragement from others, as well as increased cooperation and trust from them. While the benefits provided by these latter resources are less readily measured in economic terms, they are still often highly valuable to the persons who obtain them. Thus, social capital is definitely worth possessing: it is an asset that often yields highly beneficial outcomes to the persons who possess it.

The social ties on which social capital rests are often divided into two major categories: *close or strong ties* – the strong, intimate bonds that exist between members of a nuclear family or very close friends – and *loose or weak ties* – social linkages of the type that occur outside families or intimate friendships; for example, links between persons who happen to work together or who do business on a fairly regular basis (e.g., Adler and Kwon, 2002; Putnam, 2000). Social ties can occur at either the individual level, between specific persons, or at a group or organizational level. In both cases, they often serve as the basis for *trust* – confidence by one or more persons in the motives and predictability of one or more others.

Close (strong) ties are often viewed as leading to, or at least being associated with, *bonding social capital* – they generate relationships between individuals that are based on mutual trust. Examples would be found in extremely high levels of mutual trust and concern between founding partners of a new venture or between founders and their children, if the latter are employed in the venture and are being groomed for succession. Loose or weak ties, in contrast, lead to (or are associated with) *bridging social capital* – they are useful in providing individuals with information that would otherwise be difficult or costly for them to obtain. (The term "bridging" refers to the fact that in such instances social capital serves as a bridge or connection between external networks, thus facilitating the flow of information between them.) An example would be the information individuals or organizations acquire from membership in business networks or trade associations. Over time, loose ties can sometimes develop into strong ones, in which case they would lead to relationships based on mutual trust.

Social capital should be distinguished from *human capital*, which refers primarily to the knowledge individuals possess – especially knowledge that can contribute to more productive and efficient entrepreneurial activity. This includes formal education, past experience in a given field, and specific training that is not part of formal degree programs. In short, human capital is focused more on what individuals *know* – the skills and knowledge they have acquired and bring to any work settings – while human capital refers more directly to *who they know*, and the depth, intensity, and positive nature of these relationships.

Social capital should also be differentiated from *social competence* – an array of skills that assist individuals in interacting effectively with others (e.g., Baron and Markman, 2003). Social competence includes such skills as the ability to perceive others accurately, to express one's own emotions and reactions clearly, to be persuasive, and to make a good first impression on others. It has been suggested that for entrepreneurs, social capital is a *necessary* condition: it helps them to "get through the door" so that they can meet, and interact with, potential investors, customers, and employees. However, once access to others has been gained through social networks, repu-

tation, and related aspects of social capital, it is the entrepreneurs' social competence which then determines the nature of their developing relationships with these persons – and, ultimately, their success (e.g., Baron and Markman, 2000).

Whatever its precise source and regardless of the specific form it takes, social capital has been found to play an important role in the entrepreneurial process. For instance, recent findings (e.g., Davidsson and Honig, 2003) indicate that factors contributing to the development of *bonding social capital* (e.g., having parents or close friends or neighbors in business; receiving encouragement from friends and family) are strongly associated with discovering or recognizing opportunities for new ventures and also with taking initial steps to start such ventures. Similarly, factors that contribute to the development of *bridging social capital* (e.g., membership in trade organizations) are related to performing the activities essential to converting recognized opportunities into viable new ventures, and to measures of important outcomes such as first sales or profit.

In sum, the concept of social capital calls attention to the fact that entrepreneurs definitely do *not* operate in a social vacuum. On the contrary, they depend on the support, advice, information, and financial resources provided by others. The broader and richer the social networks to which they belong – the higher their social capital – the greater their chances of obtaining such benefits and hence, the greater the chances that they will succeed in converting their ideas and dreams into profitable new businesses. Where entrepreneurship is concerned, then, there appears to be a substantial grain of truth in the biblical statement: "A good name is better than precious ointment" (Ecclesiastes 7:1).

Bibliography

Adler, P. and Kwon, S. (2002). Social capital: Prospects for a new concept. *Academy of Management Review*, 27: 17–40.

Baron, R. A. and Markman, G. D. (2000). Beyond social capital: The role of social skills in entrepreneurs' success. *Academy of Management Executive*, 14: 1–15.

Baron, R. A. and Markman, G. D. (2003). Beyond social capital: The role of entrepreneurs' social competence in their financial success. *Journal of Business Venturing*, 18: 41–60.

Davidsson, P. and Honig, B. (2003). The role of social and human capital among nascent entrepreneurs. *Journal of Business Venturing*, 18: 301–31.

Nahapiet, J. and Ghoshal, S. (1998). Social capital, intellectual capital, and the organizational advantage. *Academy of Management Review*, 23: 242–66.

Portes, A. (1998). Social capital. *Annual Review of Sociology*, 23: 1–24.

Putnam, F. (2000). *Bowling Alone: The Collapse and Revival of American Community*. New York: Simon and Schuster.

spin-offs

Matthew Semadeni

A spin-off is formally defined as the "divestment of a business division to shareholders through a distribution of the subsidiary's common stock in the form of a dividend" (Miles and Woolridge, 1999: 1). While a notable body of research exists on corporate spin-offs, very little has examined the spin-off event from the spin-off's perspective. To date, much of the extant research on corporate spin-offs has focused on either the parent firm or the market value created by the spin-off, with little attention given to the spin-off's performance, whether market or otherwise (see Woo, Willard, and Daellenbach, 1992, for a notable exception).

RATIONALES AND MOTIVES FOR SPIN-OFF

Tax implication is the overarching criterion governing the distribution of shares to shareholders through corporate spin-offs (the tax regulations governing spin-offs are found in Section 355 of the Internal Revenue Code). The distribution will be deemed tax free to both the parent firm and its shareholders if the spin-off meets certain conditions. For example, for the distribution to be considered tax free, the parent must divest 80 percent or more of the subsidiary, the parent and subsidiary must be engaged in active business for at least five years before the distribution date, and the transaction must have a legitimate business purpose (e.g., addressing anti-trust issues, increased focus on core businesses by the parent, enhanced capital market access, etc.). It is curious to note that "increasing shareholder value" does *not* constitute a legitimate business purpose per the In-

ternal Revenue Code guidelines (Miles and Woolridge, 1999).

Several motivations for spin-offs exist. First, the spin-off could be required to comply with regulatory rulings, including regulations surrounding a merger or acquisition or to address antitrust charges. Second, the spin-off could be motivated by a renewed focus on the parent's core businesses. Third, spin-offs could be motivated by a CEO succession event, where the organizational attachment to a particular division is low. Fourth, spin-offs may occur to remove excessive volatility from the corporation's performance. Fifth, conflict may arise between the corporation and the subsidiary or between the subsidiary and a key customer of the corporation. Sixth, a spin-off may be pursued if the parent believes that the combined value of the parent and child (under the corporate structure) is less than that which could be obtained if the two operated as independent entities.

While the motivations for undertaking a spin-off are varied and diverse, it is important to note that the motivations do not always favor the spin-off, but rather are generally done in line with the parent firm's best interests. This is not surprising, given that corporate managers control the fate of the subsidiary and will generally make decisions based on what is best for the corporation rather than the subsidiary. This point is noteworthy because the conditions under which the spin-off event occurs may not be optimal for the business that is spun-off, possibly placing it in a precarious position from the outset of its existence as an independent, publicly traded firm.

RESEARCH PERSPECTIVES ON SPIN-OFFS

The transformation from corporate subsidiary to independent, publicly traded firm generates interesting conditions from several theoretical perspectives, namely agency theory, transactions cost economics, and most recently upper echelons theory. Some cross-theoretical perspectives have also emerged. Each of these are treated separately below.

Agency theory. Two points are worth noting regarding the relationship between agency theory and spin-offs. First, spin-off affects the information asymmetry between shareholders and managers by changing information disclosure requirements and managerial monitoring (Krishnaswami and Subramaniam, 1999). (It is important to note that size does become a factor in determining whether or not analysts would follow a given spin-off, with larger spin-offs more likely to receive coverage than smaller spin-offs.) Second, spin-off allows for better managerial incentive arrangements, given that as an independent market entity, the board of directors can draft market-performance contingent contracts that will better align the interests of owners and top managers (Seward and Walsh, 1996). This is noteworthy because subsidiary managers often have incentives to manipulate accounting performance to their best advantage (see Aron, 1991). Hence, from an agency theory perspective, the spin-off event, taken by itself, should lead to positive market performance.

Transactions cost economics. Three points are worth noting regarding the relationship between transactions cost economics and spin-offs. First, transactions cost logic is a dominant rationale for diversification (Jones and Hill, 1988) and applying it to spin-offs suggests that there will be severance effects when a spin-off separates itself from its corporate parent. This logic suggests that these severance effects (i.e., the loss of financial economies, economies of scope, or economies of integration) will vary according to the spin-off's diversification relationship to its corporate parent, with more closely related spin-offs suffering the most severe effects. Second, spin-off eliminates any corporate cross-subsidies that the spin-off may have been paying to or receiving from other divisions of the firm (Powers, 1999). Third, the spin-off has the opportunity to negotiate its own contracts, which has been identified by researchers as beneficial in some instances (Hite and Owners, 1983). Contract negotiation autonomy presents an opportunity to the spin-off if it was required to use a sub-optimal contract negotiated at the corporate level by its former parent; however, it is important to note that in general the spun-off firm's bargaining position is usually weakened post-spin-off, given its smaller size and independent status separate from its corporate parent. Overall, from a transactions cost perspective the

performance implications for the spin-off are somewhat equivocal.

Upper echelons theory. Three points are worth noting regarding the relationship between upper echelons theory and spin-offs. First, top management characteristics will have a significant impact on the perspective taken by top management, with top management vision often being colored or constrained by characteristics and past experiences and existing mindsets and dominant logics (Prahalad and Bettis, 1986; Bettis and Prahalad, 1995) having an important framing effect on actions taken post-spin off. Second, in addition to their perspectives, the combination of human capital talent held by top management is important in determining future returns given that as a separate, independent entity, the spin-off will face a new set of challenges in addition to (or sometimes in the place of) those it faced as a division of a corporation (Hambrick and Stucker, 1999; Wruck and Wruck, 2002). Third, the spin-off event creates a significant change in organizational discretion (Hambrick and Finkelstein, 1987), providing spin-off managers far greater latitude of organizational action. In sum, upper echelons theory argues that the composition of top management will affect spin-off performance.

Cross-theoretical perspectives. Two cross-theoretical perspectives are particularly noteworthy. First, using both agency theory and transactions cost perspectives, Woo, Willard, and Daellenbach (1992) found that although spin-off announcements are generally met with a significant positive reaction (to both the parent firm and the spin-off), the expected performance gains for the spin-off are not always realized. Second, using upper echelons and agency theory, Seward and Walsh (1996) found that spin-offs facilitate the implementation of efficient internal governance and control practices, but that other factors must influence the value created by the spin-off announcement. These cross-theoretical perspectives provide interesting insights not available through the application of a single theoretical approach, but also revealed the need for further cross-theoretical work, with both sets of researchers noting their inability to go beyond their initial findings, calling for a

228   strategic entrepreneurship

deeper examination of many of the issues that they broach.

Most recently, Semadeni (2003) has integrated agency, transactions cost, and upper echelon perspectives on spin-off to generate a model of spin-off actions and performance. Using a seven-year window (two years prior to and up to five years post-spin-off) of managerial, accounting, and market data, Semadeni examined the spin-off as an entrepreneurial opportunity and proposed that certain strategic, financial, or institutional actions would occur post-spin-off due to the designation of new management, new monitoring/incentive arrangements, and severance effects from leaving the corporate parent. He found, however, that in large measure the strategic, financial, and institutional actions that would be expected according to upper echelons, agency, and transactions cost theories did not occur. In other words, although the spin-off-event should motivate the firm to act in a more entrepreneurial fashion, the actions expected from being freed from corporate oversight did not occur. Moreover, there was little connection between the expected strategic, financial, and institutional actions and performance post-spin-off. All this suggests that these traditional theoretical perspectives may not be appropriate in dealing with the dynamics of firm spin-offs. Thus, Semadeni's (2003) findings are important not only for what they found, but for what they did not. Although the three perspectives have been applied to spin-offs individually or partially together in the past, they had never been brought together in one set of empirical tests, and when they were, the results were equivocal. This suggests that none of the three perspectives provides clear insight into what affects firm performance post-spin off, implying that new theory needs to be developed to understand this significant organizational event.

Bibliography

Aron, D. J. (1991). Using the capital market as a monitor: Corporate spin-offs in an agency framework. *RAND Journal of Economics*, 22: 505–18.

Bettis, R. A. and Prahalad, C. K. (1995). The dominant logic: Retrospective and extension. *Strategic Management Journal*, 16: 5–14.

Hambrick, D. C. and Finkelstein, S. (1987). Managerial discretion: A bridge between polar views of organiza-tional outcomes. In L. L. Cummings and B. M. Staw (eds.), *Research in Organizational Behavior*, Vol. 9. Greenwich, CT: JAI Press, 369–406.

Hambrick, D. C. and Stucker, K. (1999). Breaking away: Executive leadership of corporate spin-offs. In J. A. Conger, G. M. Spreitzer, and E. E. Lawler, III (eds.), *The Leader's Change Handbook*. San Francisco, CA: Jossey-Bass.

Hite, G. and Owners, J. (1983). Security price reactions around corporate spin-off announcements. *Journal of Financial Economics*, 12: 409–37.

Jones, G. R. and Hill, C. W. L. (1988). Transaction cost analysis of strategy-structure choice. *Strategic Management Journal*, 9: 159–72.

Krishnaswami, S. and Subramaniam, V. (1999). Information asymmetry, valuation, and the corporate spin-off decision. *Journal of Financial Economics*, 53: 73–112.

Miles, J. A. and Woolridge, J. R. (1999). *Spin-Offs and Equity Carve-Outs: Achieving Faster Growth and Better Performance*. Morristown, NJ: Financial Executives Research Foundation.

Powers, E. A. (1999). Corporate restructuring: An analysis of spin-offs, sell-offs, and equity carve-outs. Unpublished dissertation, Sloan School of Management, MIT, Cambridge, MA.

Prahalad, C. K. and Bettis, R. A. (1986). The dominant logic: A new linkage between diversity and performance. *Strategic Management Journal*, 7: 485–501.

Semadeni, M. B. (2003). Leaving the corporate fold: Examining spin-off actions and performance. Unpublished dissertation, Mays Business School, Texas A&M University, College Station, TX.

Seward, J. K. and Walsh, J. P. (1996). The governance and control of voluntary corporate spin-offs. *Strategic Management Journal*, 17: 25–39.

Woo, C. Y., Willard, G. E., and Daellenbach, U. S. (1992). Spin-off performance: A case of overstated expectations? *Strategic Management Journal*, 13: 433–47.

Wruck, E. G. and Wruck, K. H. (2002). Restructuring top management: Evidence from corporate spin-offs. *Journal of Labor Economics*, 20: S176–S218.

strategic entrepreneurship

Michael A. Hitt and R. Duane Ireland

Entrepreneurship involves identifying opportunities and exploiting them (Venkataraman and Sarasvathy, 2001), whereas strategic management involves creating and sustaining a competitive advantage (Hitt, Ireland, and Hoskisson, 2005; De Carolis, 2003). Both are concerned about growth, creating value for consumers, and subsequently creating wealth for owners

(Amit and Zott, 2001; Ireland, Hitt, and Sirmon, 2003). While entrepreneurship focuses on new products, processes, and markets, strategic management emphasizes using them to gain an advantage over competitors (Barney, 1991; Lumpkin and Dess, 1996; Sharma and Chrisman, 1999). With their different yet complementary foci, both entrepreneurship and strategic management are integral to firm success.

Venkataraman and Sarasvathy (2001) suggest strategic management and entrepreneurship should be integrated. They use the metaphor of Romeo and Juliet. They suggest that entrepreneurship alone is like having Romeo with no balcony. Strategic management alone is similar to having the balcony but no Romeo. Both are needed to create firm success over the long term. Therefore, the integration of entrepreneurship and strategic management is referred to as strategic entrepreneurship. Strategic entrepreneurship involves identifying and exploiting opportunities while simultaneously creating and sustaining a competitive advantage (Ireland, Hitt, and Sirmon, 2003). Strategic entrepreneurship is important for both small and new firms and for large established firms as well. Established firms must be entrepreneurial, while entrepreneurial firms must also be strategic (Hitt et al., 2001, 2002; Ireland et al., 2001).

Strategic entrepreneurship has several dimensions to include developing an entrepreneurial mindset and culture, managing resources strategically, applying creativity and developing innovation, and leveraging the innovation through strategy to create a competitive advantage and thereby creating value for the end consumer. When value is created for the end consumer and done so efficiently, it then creates wealth for owners (the entrepreneur) (Ireland et al., 2003; Sirmon, Hitt, and Ireland, 2003). An entrepreneurial mindset is both an individual and an organizational phenomenon. Individuals can be entrepreneurial, but so too can organizations. To do so, they must have a mindset that makes them alert to entrepreneurial opportunities as well as to the rent-generating potential created by uncertainty (McGrath and MacMillan, 2000) (*see* NAVIGATING UNCERTAINTY). An entrepreneurial mindset also involves the use of real options logic in which opportunities may

be identified and acquired for future use (McGrath, 1999).

An entrepreneurial culture is one in which new ideas and creativity are expected, risk taking is encouraged, failure is tolerated, learning is promoted, innovations are championed, and continuous change is viewed as an opportunity (Ireland, Hitt, and Sirmon, 2003). An entrepreneurial culture requires that leaders nourish entrepreneurial capabilities within the firm (Alvarez and Barney, 2002). It also requires leaders to protect innovations that may threaten the current business model and even encourages questions about the firm's dominant logic.

Opportunities, once identified, must be exploited. To do so requires that the resources of the firm be managed strategically. Sirmon and Hitt (2003) suggest that this requires structuring the resource portfolio, bundling resources into productive capabilities, and leveraging the capabilities to create value for consumers and wealth for shareholders. Structuring the resource portfolio involves acquiring resources as needed, developing those resources more fully, and then when necessary, divesting resources that lose their value to the firm. Resources must also be bundled to create the capabilities to take actions. For example, financial capital, human capital, and even physical assets may be integrated to create capabilities in R&D, marketing, and production (Sirmon, Hitt, and Ireland, 2003). Leveraging those capabilities involves developing a strategy that will help create value for customers. When the value created for customers is superior to that value created by competitors, the firm gains a competitive advantage. If the firm is able to sustain that competitive advantage, it can create wealth for the owners.

However, in order to create value for the customer, the firm must use its capabilities to create innovation (Smith and Di Gregorio, 2002). Thus, firms creating innovations that have value for customers and are able to distribute them to consumers at a reasonable price for that value gain the advantage and create wealth for their owners. Essentially, firms must continuously innovate to effectively compete in the complex, global business environment. The requirement for constant and successful innovation is satisfied when organizations rely on their entrepreneurial talents and capabilities to act strategically and compete in the marketplace.

There are a number of interesting research questions for scholars to explore regarding strategic entrepreneurship. As a new area of inquiry, a critical question is defining the field's boundary. Because strategic entrepreneurship is an intersection of two fields of study, it is important for research to specify the attributes of each field that are required to form strategic entrepreneurship. Defining the boundaries of the independent fields remains challenging (Greve, 2003), meaning that specifying the boundaries of their intersection requires careful study and analysis. An extension of the field's boundary is the determination of theories with the greatest potential to inform our understanding of the phenomenon. Can strategic entrepreneurship best be specified and understood through a resource-based view lens, for example? Do transaction cost economics theory and institutional theory inform strategic entrepreneurship research and yield testable hypotheses? Another research question concerns isolating the variance (if any) in effective strategic entrepreneurship practices across various strata of firms (e.g., large versus small, new versus old, domestic versus international, and so forth). Finally, assessing the performance implications of strategic entrepreneurship is a vital topic warranting study. In this regard, does strategic entrepreneurship positively affect firm performance? If so, how strong is that effect and does the effect vary by type of performance measure? Examining these research questions as along with others will increase our understanding of strategic entrepreneurship.

Bibliography

Alvarez, S. A. and Barney, J. B. (2002). Resource-based theory and the entrepreneurial firm. In M. A. Hitt, R. D. Ireland, S. M. Camp, and D. L. Sexton (eds.), *Strategic Entrepreneurship: Creating a New Mindset.* Oxford: Blackwell, 89–105.

Amit, R. and Zott, C. (2001). Value creation in e-business. *Strategic Management Journal*, 22 (special issue): 493–520.

Barney, J. B. (1991). Firm resources and sustained competitive advantage. *Journal of Management*, 17: 99–120.

De Carolis, D. M. (2003). Competencies and imitability in the pharmaceutical industry: An analysis of their relationship with firm performance. *Journal of Management*, 29: 27–50.

Greve, H. (2003). Review of *Strategic entrepreneurship: Creating a new mindset. Administrative Science Quarterly*, 48: 348–51.

Hitt, M. A., Ireland, R. D., and Hoskisson, R. E. (2005). *Strategic Management: Competitiveness and Globalization.* Cincinnati, OH: South-Western Publishing.

Hitt, M. A., Ireland, R. D., Camp, S. M., and Sexton, D. L. (2001). Strategic entrepreneurship: Entrepreneurial strategies for wealth creation. *Strategic Management Journal*, 22 (special issue): 479–91.

Hitt, M. A., Ireland, R. D., Camp, S. M., and Sexton, D. L. (2002). Strategic entrepreneurship: Integrating entrepreneurial and strategic management perspectives. In M. A. Hitt, R. D. Ireland, S. M. Camp, and D. L. Sexton (eds.), *Strategic Entrepreneurship: Creating a New Mindset.* Oxford: Blackwell, 1–16.

Ireland, R. D., Hitt, M. A., Camp, S. M., and Sexton, D. L. (2001). Integrating entrepreneurship and strategic management action to create firm wealth. *Academy of Management Executive*, 15 (1): 49–63.

Ireland, R. D., Hitt, M. A., and Sirmon, D. G. (2003). A model of strategic entrepreneurship: The construct and its dimensions. *Journal of Management*, 29: 963–89.

Lumpkin, G. T. and Dess, G. G. (1996). Clarifying the entrepreneurial orientation construct and linking it to performance. *Academy of Management Review*, 21: 135–71.

McGrath, R. M. (1999). Falling forward: Real options reasoning and entrepreneurial failure. *Academy of Management Review*, 24: 13–30.

McGrath, R. M. and MacMillan, I. C. (2000). *The Entrepreneurial Mindset.* Boston, MA: Harvard Business School Press.

Sharma, P. and Chrisman, J. J. (1999). Toward a reconciliation of the definitional issues in the field of corporate entrepreneurship. *Entrepreneurship: Theory and Practice*, 23 (3): 11–27.

Sirmon, D. G. and Hitt, M. A. (2003). Managing resources: Linking unique resources, management and wealth creation in family firms. *Entrepreneurship: Theory and Practice*, 27: 339–58.

Sirmon, D. G., Hitt, M. A., and Ireland, R. D. (2003). Managing the firm's resources in order to achieve and maintain a competitive advantage. Paper presented at the annual Academy of Management meeting, Seattle.

Smith, K. G. and Di Gregorio, D. (2002). Bisociation, discovery, and the role of entrepreneurial action. In M. A. Hitt, R. D. Ireland, S. M. Camp, and D. L. Sexton (eds.), *Strategic Entrepreneurship: Creating a New Mindset.* Oxford: Blackwell, 129–50.

Venkataraman, S. and Sarasvathy, S. D. (2001). Strategy and entrepreneurship: Outlines of an untold story. In

M. A. Hitt, R. E. Freeman, and J. S. Harrison (eds.), *Handbook of Strategic Management.* Oxford: Blackwell, 650–68.

succession planning

Pramodita Sharma, Jess H. Chua, and James J. Chrisman

Succession planning refers to the deliberate and formal processes, decisions, and actions that facilitate the organizational transfer of management control from one individual to another (Sharma, Chrisman, and Chua, 2003a). As a topic of study, executive succession has received the most attention because of the centrality of CEOs in determining the strategic direction of a firm. Our focus herein is on succession planning in family firms where management control is to be passed from one family member to another (*see* FAMILY BUSINESS). Kesner and Sebora (1994) and Yeung (1998) provide overviews of succession in large, mature non-family firms. (For information on succession in young, entrepreneurial firms, *see* EXECUTIVE SUCCESSION IN ENTREPRENEURIAL BUSINESS.)

The antecedents and processes of succession planning in family and non-family firms are in most respects similar (Bagby, 2004). However, there are several important differences that should be kept in mind. First, in family firms, a leader's tenure is longer because succession cannot occur until potential successors from the next generation reach professional maturity. Thus, the event occurs less frequently than in non-family firms, and the process can span a greater length of time. Second, succession is rarely planned in family firms because to do so forces incumbents to confront their own mortality. This natural reluctance of family firm leaders to "let go" is exacerbated by the fact that they are usually in command of the succession process through their control of the dominant coalition. Third, the ready-made shortlist of successors in family firms makes it less likely that selection criteria, candidate evaluation, and even candidate preparation will be formalized. Fourth, family business succession is further complicated by the age and experience gaps between incumbents and successors. In the typical

North American family, the parent–child age gap is more than two decades. This is much wider than what would be typical between incumbents and successors in non-family firms. Experience gaps will, consequently, also usually be wider in family firms than in non-family firms.

The succession planning process in family firms may be directed by the incumbent leader alone, the incumbent leader and members of the owning family, including next-generation family members, or a task force or committee of insiders and outside advisors. Each option has its strengths and limitations; therefore, the alternative chosen will depend on the characteristics of the family, society, business, and industry (Le Breton-Miller, Miller, and Steier, 2004).

Similar to succession planning in non-family firms, the process in family firms is iterative rather than strictly linear and may require rethinking and recalibration at different stages (Le Breton et al., 2004). It is recommended that succession planning be preceded by a careful examination of the key stakeholders' shared vision. This entails consideration of both how the family can continue to add value to the business and how the business can do likewise for the family. This exercise should determine the firm's desired strategic direction and the family's role as a collective unit in its ownership, management, and governance. After such determination is made, the following steps are suggested to increase the odds of an effective leadership succession in family firms (Chrisman, Chua, and Sharma, 1998b).

DEVELOP SELECTION CRITERIA

A firm's shared vision and strategic direction should guide its development of selection criteria. In addition, cultural factors may have a bearing. For example, family structure and prevailing societal norms may stipulate a predetermined heir (as in primogeniture), a short list of possible successors (all male children or all interested family members), or a broader list (a combination of family and non-family members).

Research by Chrisman, Chua, and Sharma (1998a) indicates that integrity and commitment are the most important successor attributes sought by family firms. Competence ranks lower because competence without integrity and commitment is unlikely to help most families realize their visions for the business and the family. In fact, without a potential family successor committed to take over, succession planning will simply not start (Sharma, Chrisman, and Chua, 2003a).

In terms of competence and business related background, significant variations in selection criteria should be expected. For example, while family firms in stable industries may consider within-firm experience to be critical, those in emerging or changing industries may prefer entrepreneurial orientation and abilities (see ENTREPRENEURIAL LEADERSHIP).

EVALUATE THE POTENTIAL OF AVAILABLE CANDIDATES

Mechanisms must be developed for evaluating family members who are being considered as potential successors. These can include such disparate processes as hiring external parties to perform psychological and attitudinal tests, to informal multi-stakeholder assessments of the leadership potential of available candidates. In cases where the shared vision suggests an already available shortlist of family members, this step involves evaluating their current readiness for leadership positions and determining training and developmental needs. Where there is a significant mismatch between the needs of a the family firm and the readiness of available candidates, innovative solutions, such as installing bridge-managers to fill in until a family successor is ready, may become necessary (Le Breton-Miller, Miller, and Steier, 2004). Due to altruism and self-control problems, families may have special difficulties with this step in the succession planning process because of an inability to evaluate family members objectively (Schulze, Lubatkin, and Dino, 2003).

PREPARE THE POTENTIAL SUCCESSORS

Appropriate methods of training and development will vary depending on the abilities and interests of potential successors and a family firm's needs. A clear path of apprenticeship in terms of both the type and timing of training for family members should be established. A milestone approach is useful to evaluate the effectiveness of the training program, as well as the progress of potential successors in completing the program.

Aside from education and general management experience, development programs for potential successors should also focus on cultivating tacit knowledge and social capital, as these can provide a family firm with a basis for sustainable competitive advantage (Sirmon and Hitt, 2003). Tacit knowledge is knowledge that is difficult to codify and can be gained only through direct exposure and experience. This argues for the early involvement of potential successors in the business to develop deeper levels of firm-specific tacit knowledge. Its success requires a harmonious and positive relationship between a family firm's incumbent leader and potential successors in the family (Cabrera-Suárez, De Saá-Pérez, and Garcia-Almeida, 2001).

Social capital in the form of network ties, shared language and narratives, trust, norms, and obligations allows a family business leader to build more effective relationships with employees, suppliers, customers, and financial institutions and to garner resources through these relationships (Sirmon and Hitt, 2003). This may explain why family business leaders rated "respect from employees" as the third most important successor attribute (Chrisman, Chua, and Sharma, 1998a). Similar to tacit knowledge, social capital is developed through direct exposure to, and positive interactions with, the social network within which a family business functions.

SELECT AND INSTALL THE SUCCESSOR

This step involves deciding who will be the next CEO of a firm. In a family firm the best time to install a leader is when the designated successor is ready experientially to take over, and the exiting leader is ready emotionally to let go of the job. The timing is analogous to passing the baton between two runners: either too early or too late can result in disaster (Dyck et al., 2002). The decision should also be communicated to all stakeholders once it is made in order to smooth the transition.

CLARIFY THE POST-SUCCESSION ROLES

An important, yet often neglected step in the family firm succession planning process is determining the post-succession roles of the predecessor and the family members not selected. The most important difference in this respect between family and non-family firms is that in family firms the predecessor and the other candidates will continue to be at least indirectly involved as family members for the rest of their lives and frequently directly as co-owners and managers. The predecessor who is a parent will continue to have a very significant legitimate influence on the family and the firm, and the other candidates can form powerful family coalitions. This is quite different from the situation in non-family firms where a predecessor's continued involvement will either end or be of a much more limited duration (e.g., serving a term as chairman of the board). Likewise, the other candidates in non-family firms must either accept the implications of the decision for their positions or leave. This is because none of them will normally have significant ownership stakes in the firm.

DEVELOP PERFORMANCE EVALUATION AND FEEDBACK MECHANISMS

A final step in the succession planning process is to develop clear mechanisms to regularly evaluate successor performance and provide constructive feedback. Because of the gap between the time a succession decision is made and the performance outcomes of that decision, it is useful to set strategic as well as financial performance goals.

As noted above, research shows that most family firms do not plan for succession (Leon-Guerrero, McCann, and Haley, 1998). Researchers have also found that succession planning appears to contribute more to the family's satisfaction with the succession process (Sharma, Chrisman, and Chua, 2003b) than to firm performance (Morris et al., 1997).

Bibliography

Bagby, D. R. (2004). Enhancing succession research in the family firm. *Entrepreneurship: Theory and Practice* (forthcoming).

Cabrera-Suárez, K., De Saá-Pérez, P., and García-Almeida, D. (2001). The succession process from a resource- and knowledge-based view of the family firm. *Family Business Review*, 14: 37–46.

Chrisman, J. J., Chua, J. H., and Sharma, P. (1998a). Important attributes of successors in family businesses. *Family Business Review*, 11: 19–34.

Chrisman, J. J., Chua, J. H., and Sharma, P. (1998b). Managing succession in family firms. *Financial Post*, April 8. Part 6 of the Special Series on Mastering Enterprise.

Dyck, B., Maws, M., Starke, F. A., and Miske, G. A. (2002). Passing the baton: The importance of sequence, timing, technique, and communication in executive succession. *Journal of Business Venturing*, 17: 143–62.

Kesner, I. F. and Sebora, T. C. (1994). Executive succession: Past, present, and future. *Journal of Management*, 20: 327–72.

Le Breton-Miller, I., Miller, D., and Steier, L. (2004). Toward an integrative model of effective FOB succession. *Entrepreneurship: Theory and Practice* (forthcoming).

Leon-Guerrero, A. Y., McCann, J. E., III, and Haley, J. D., Jr., (1998). A study of practice utilization in family businesses. *Family Business Review*, 11: 107–20.

Morris, M. H., Williams, R. O., Allen, J. A., and Avila, R. A. (1997). Correlates of success in family business transitions. *Journal of Business Venturing*, 12: 385–401.

Schulze, W. S., Lubatkin, M. H., and Dino, R. N. (2003). Toward a theory of agency and altruism in family firms. *Journal of Business Venturing*, 18: 473–90.

Sharma, P., Chrisman, J. J., and Chua, J. H. (2003a). Succession planning as planned behavior: Some empirical results. *Family Business Review*, 16: 1–15.

Sharma, P., Chrisman, J. J., and Chua, J. H. (2003b). Predictors of satisfaction with the succession process in family firms. *Journal of Business Venturing*, 18: 667–87.

Sirmon, D. G. and Hitt, M. A. (2003). Managing resources: Linking unique resources, management, and wealth creation in family firms. *Entrepreneurship: Theory and Practice*, 27: 339–58.

Yeung, A. K. (1998). Succession planning. In C. L. Cooper and C. Argyris (eds.), *The Concise Blackwell Encyclopedia of Management*. Oxford: Blackwell, 645–6.

T

technology transfer

Allan Afuah

Technology can be described as the body of knowledge that underpins a product's design, manufacturing, marketing, sales, and delivery to customers – or simply as the body of knowledge that goes into making and selling products (the concepts and tools discussed apply to services as well). Thus, technology transfer is about transferring a body of knowledge. When the R&D unit of a chip maker transfers a new chip design to the fabrication area, it is transferring technology – the body of knowledge that underpins the new design – from one unit to the other. When an entrepreneur takes the knowledge and practices from his or her old company to found a new company, he or she is transferring technology to his or her start-up. When a car assembly plant is built in a developing country, technology is being transferred to the country. Most of the activities performed by the different units of a firm during new product development are technology transfer activities. Effectively, the success of many entrepreneurial ventures and of major firms whose revenues and profits come from new products/services depends on successful technology transfer.

Whether technology transfer is taking place within an organization or between organizations, there are certain factors that determine the effectiveness and efficiency of the transfer. Let us consider the inter-organizational factors first.

INTER-ORGANIZATIONAL TECHNOLOGY TRANSFER

Effective and efficient inter-organizational technology transfer depends on five factors: the characteristics of the organization that is receiving the transfer, the attributes of the organization from which the technology is being transferred, the nature of the technology being transferred, the transfer environment, and how well the transfer process is managed.

CHARACTERISTICS OF THE RECEIVER

Four characteristics of an organization determine the extent to which it can effectively and efficiently receive the technology being transferred, thereby facilitating the transfer: its absorptive capacity, its culture, its people, systems and structure, and the firm's strategic incentive for receiving the technology.

Absorptive capacity and complementary assets. To evaluate, assimilate, and transform new knowledge into say, new products/services, a firm needs to have some level of related knowledge. In other words, it takes related knowledge to absorb knowledge (Cohen and Levinthal, 1990). For example, one cannot expect medical doctors to be able to absorb the latest microchip technology and use it to design a "cutting edge" microchip – they do not have the related knowledge to absorb the new chip knowledge. The stock of related knowledge that a firm uses to evaluate, assimilate, and transform new knowledge is called its absorptive capacity (Zahra and George, 2002). A firm with the right absorptive capacity has an easier time diffusing technology into its divisional organizations and other units than one that does not. In addition to having related knowledge, a firm often needs complementary technologies and assets. For example, a bank that buys computers for its activities must also acquire the appropriate software and interconnectivity for the computer to be useful for bank transactions.

Culture. A firm's culture plays a very strong role in its ability to facilitate inter-organizational technology transfer. Many definitions of culture exist but I refer here to Uttal and Fierman's (1983) definition of culture as "a system of shared values (what is important) and beliefs (how things work) that interact with the organization's people, organizational structures, and systems to produce behavioral norms (the way we do things around here)." If the new technology conflicts in any way with a firm's shared values, its beliefs or norms, it will have a difficult time convincing the people who must perform the transfer activities. For example, an organization that suffers from a not-invented-here-syndrome (NIHS) is not likely to be very successful at bringing in new technologies from outside because its internal culture is likely to conflict with it. More importantly, if there are differences between the cultures of the transmitting and receiving organizations, the two organizations are likely to spend more time fighting than cooperating on transfer activities. This does not facilitate technology transfer.

People roles, systems and structure. Because people transfer technology, the roles that such people play can be critical. A technology transfer project with a champion who can articulate a vision of what the technology means to the organization and its value to participants in the transfer is more likely to succeed than one that does not have a champion. An organization with good gatekeepers – to translate questions from the organization's internal culture to what the outside world can understand, and vice versa – has a better chance of succeeding than one that does not. An organization's systems also matter. That is, the way the firm measures and rewards performance or punishes failure during technology transfer also matters. Structure is another important factor. A functional organizational structure, for example, favors technology transfer in which very deep knowledge in specific functional areas is needed, while a networked structure favors technology transfer in which the organization depends on other organizations for different technologies that can be integrated into its products.

Strategic incentives. The effectiveness and efficiency of a firm in evaluating and absorbing a new technology depends on where the technology fits in the organization's overall strategy. If a technology is critical to a firm's success, the firm will allocate more resources to the transfer process, supporting the technology with the necessary attention and investments. Such resources help build or augment the relevant absorptive capacity and build the appropriate culture and systems for transfer. For example, information technology is more critical to banking than to pharmaceuticals, and therefore information technology transfer is more critical to the former than the latter. Thus, banks invest more heavily in information technology than do pharmaceutical firms. Rather, pharmaceutical companies invest more in R&D and drug development.

CHARACTERISTICS OF THE TRANSMITTER

The organization from which a technology is being transferred also plays a major role in the success of the transfer process. In a way, the characteristics of the transferring firm that are important to the transfer process are analogous to those of the receiver.

Strategic incentives. The strategic incentives for a transferring firm are critical. One reason is because technology transfer is not always appropriate – a firm may not want its technology transferred to other companies when it wants to keep it proprietary. If a firm does not want its technology transferred to other firms, it can be protected through intellectual property rights or other blocking strategies. Although there usually are ways around blocking strategies, they nonetheless can reduce transfer effectiveness and efficiency. The organizations that block or limit the transfer of their technology usually need the technology to produce goods or services that provide an advantage in the markets in which they compete. For example, Intel fervently protected its microprocessor technology from being copied from the mid-1980s on.

If an organization wants to transfer its technology, it will invest in the transfer process. Organizations that want to transfer their technologies usually make their money from the transfer process, normally through licensing or product sales. In fact, even firms that do not want the technology embodied in their products to be copied still promote the use of their products. Product use also involves technology transfer.

NATURE OF THE BODY OF KNOWLEDGE

Technology transfer also depends on the nature of the technology: (1) whether the knowledge is explicit or tacit and (2) whether the knowledge is complex or simple.

Explicit versus tacit. The body of knowledge on which a product is based has two components: explicit and tacit. Explicit knowledge is easy to describe in words or encode in some form that can be understood by others. The material that is found in textbooks, including information on how to design products, manufacture, or deliver them, is explicit knowledge. The knowledge in design schematics, computer programs, or what a firm obtains when it reverse engineers a product is explicit knowledge. Because it can be encoded, explicit knowledge can be easily transferred over different media. Tacit knowledge, on the other hand, is difficult to express in words or encode in a form that can be understood by others. A great tennis player's knowledge of the game is largely tacit. When she plays the game she just does it. It is difficult for her to describe the exact force on the ball when it is being tossed up for the serve, how high the ball has to go before dropping back for the racket, how far back to take the racket, the rate at which the racket turns as it is approaching the ball, the torque on the racket, the speed at which she moves, and so on. Technology has important tacit components similar to tennis. Explicit knowledge has been described as *knowing about* and tacit knowledge as *knowing how*. In any case, explicit knowledge is easier to transfer because it can be encoded and communicated over media such as books, the Internet, products, etc. Tacit knowledge is more difficult to transfer and, as discussed below, it usually entails movement of people. Most technologies have both tacit and explicit components.

Complexity. The complexity of the technology to be transferred also matters. Transferring toaster technology is easier than transferring airplane technology. Complexity here refers to both the depth and breadth of total knowledge required. One measure of complexity is the number of components and linkages among them, and the depth and breadth of knowledge that underpins each component and linkage.

Thus, transferring a complex technology means conveying the deep and far-reaching knowledge that underpins each of the many components and the linkages among them. Human beings and organizations have cognitive limitations. These limitations make the transfer of complex and tacit knowledge very difficult.

TRANSFER ENVIRONMENT

The receivers and transmitters of a technology do not undertake transfer activities in a vacuum. The external environment in which transfer takes place also plays an important role. A firm's co-opetitors – the suppliers, customers, and complementary and related institutions with which a firm must cooperate and compete – also are important. This is because a receiver of a technology usually wants to use it to create value for its customers. But offering value using a technology usually requires the participation of co-opetitors and the use of complementary technologies. Thus, we can expect the transfer of semiconductor technology to be easier in Silicon Valley than in Detroit, while the transfer of car technology will be easier in the latter than in the former. (One reason is because most people in the environment have the necessary absorptive capacity.) The macro environment also matters. Quite simply, the country within which technology transfer takes place plays a critical role. A country's infrastructure, legal system, and physical and monetary policies, plus the existence of related industries and an educational system – all are important. For example, the transfer of a complex technology is easier in a country with an educated workforce than in one without such a workforce.

MANAGING TRANSFER

Managing technology transfer requires understanding the principles of effective and efficient transfer outlined above and using them to make the decisions that transfer the technology via the right media using the right mechanisms.

TRANSFER MEDIUMS

The body of knowledge and practices that compose a technology is usually transferred via three media: people, electronic means, and product and organizational routines. The best medium for transferring tacit knowledge is the individuals who hold the knowledge. One reason is because it is difficult for an individual to describe his tacit knowledge of what he does. Thus, the best way to transfer that knowledge to someone else is to observe the person in action and then learn from those actions by experiencing and practicing them (Nonaka, 1994). That is one reason why it is important to move around people with core knowledge or skills, allowing them to work with different units within an organization. Sometimes tacit knowledge is embodied in the actions of an organization. In that case, the best way to transfer the knowledge is to have the receivers of the knowledge come to the transmitting organization and learn by interacting, experiencing, and working with employees of the transmitting organization. The Internet, telephone, and other electronic media are best for explicit knowledge because they require encoding for transmission. The final transfer medium is a product. Products often embody much information for a potential imitator with the appropriate absorptive capacity. Thus, firms can learn a lot about the technology that underpins a product by trying to replicate its components and linkages.

TRANSFER MANAGEMENT MECHANISMS

Separate firms pursue technology transfer in different ways. Some hire key individuals from other firms and develop the technology internally around those people (Roberts and Berry, 1985). Some form strategic alliances, while others acquire companies. Finally, some acquire equity positions in start-ups that have the relevant knowledge. An important question for a manager is when each of these mechanisms is most appropriate. One model for exploring when to pursue each technology transfer mechanism is shown in figure 1. The vertical axis measures the extent to which the body of knowledge and practices that constitute the technology are tacit and complex, while the horizontal axis measures how much absorptive capacity the firm in question has. In Quadrant I, the firm has very little or no absorptive capacity and the knowledge to be transferred is simple and explicit. One way to bring in the technology is to hire individuals with the knowledge and build the necessary absorptive capacity around them. This is sometimes referred to as internal development. A firm in this quadrant can acquire an equity stake in another firm that has the technology, so that it can be gradually exposed to the knowledge and learn from it as time goes on. Very often the new technology resides in a new venture. In that case, one can offer venture capital to gain access to the new technology. In Quadrant II, the firm has the absorptive capacity and because the knowledge is simple and explicit, the firm can buy it from the market. This is sometimes referred to as an arm's-length market transaction. For example, buying a product from a firm and legally reverse engineering it represents transferring a technology by arm's-length market transaction.

In Quadrant III, the knowledge to be transferred is tacit and complex. Because the firm has the absorptive capacity, it can evaluate and assimilate the relevant knowledge. Therefore, it is in a good position to evaluate, acquire, and assimilate a firm that has the relevant technology. It can also form a joint venture or strategic alliance with a firm that has the technology. In a joint venture, two or more firms integrate their resources to form a separate legal entity in which they each own equity. A firm has an opportunity to learn in such an arrangement. In Quadrant IV, the firm has very little absorptive capacity, but needs to transfer complex and tacit knowledge. A firm could hire people with the relevant knowledge and build absorptive capacity around them. Joint ventures with patient partners can also help one build the absorptive capacity and assimilate the relevant knowledge.

INTRA-ORGANIZATIONAL TRANSFER

While we have explored technology transfer between organizations, some of the most important technology transfer takes place within organizations (Allen, 1984). For example, the transfer of a design from R&D to manufacturing represents technology transfer. Many of the ideas we have discussed for inter-organizational technology transfer apply to intra-organizational transfer. For example, incentives can be used to encourage an R&D group to have the designer of the product move on with the new design to manufacturing and help with the establishment of the manufacturing process for the new product, instead of "throwing the design over the wall" to manufacturing.

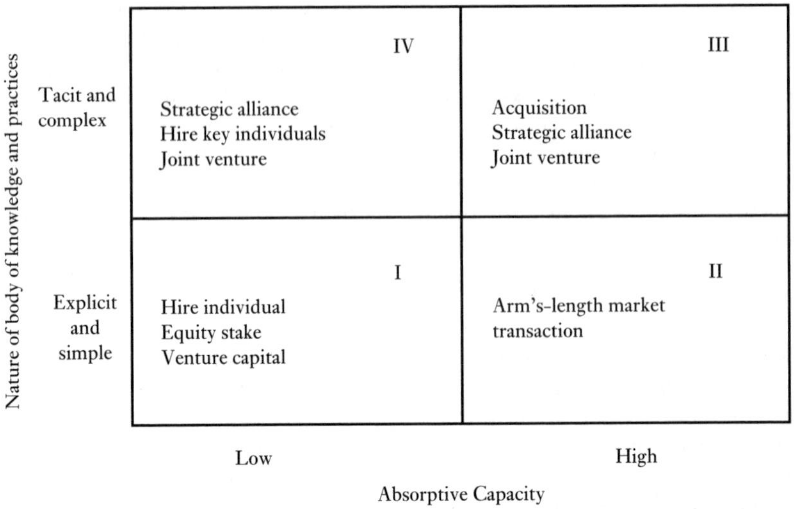

Figure 1

CONCLUSION

Most firms, sooner or later, have to deal with technology transfer. Because technology is the body of knowledge or practice that goes into making and selling products or services, technology transfer deals with knowledge transfer – moving knowledge from person to person, unit to unit, organization to organization, country to country, person to organization, and so on. This transfer depends on the nature of the technology, the characteristics of both receiver and transmitter, and the environment in which the transfer is taking place. Technology involving largely tacit and complex knowledge is much more difficult to transfer than one composed of largely explicit and simple knowledge. A firm with the relevant absorptive capacity, culture, systems, and strategic incentives is more likely to be effective at technology transfer than one that does not have these characteristics. The most effective medium to transfer a technology – people, electronic, organization, and products – depends on the type of technology. The mechanism used also depends on the type of technol-ogy. A firm that has no absorptive capacity for a complex and tacit technology must seek outside help via a joint venture, venture capital, or equity stakes, otherwise it faces a difficult time alone.

Bibliography

This article draws largely from Allan Afuah (2003), *Innovation Management: Strategies, Implementation and Profits.* Oxford: Oxford University Press.

Allen, T. (1984). *Managing the Flow of Technology.* Cambridge, MA: MIT Press.

Cohen, W. and Levinthal, D. (1990). Absorptive capacity: A new perspective on learning and innovation. *Administrative Science Quarterly*, 35: 128–52.

Nonaka, I. (1994). A dynamic theory of organizational knowledge creation. *Organization Science*, 5: 477–501.

Roberts, E. B. and Berry E. (1985). Entering new businesses: Selecting strategies for success. *Sloan Management Review*, 26 (3): 3–17.

Uttal, B. and Fierman, J. (1983). The corporate culture vultures. *Fortunes*, October 17.

Zahra, S. A. and George, G. (2002). Absorptive capacity: A review, reconceptualization, and extension. *Academy of Management Review*, 27: 185–201.

undercapitalization

Vance H. Fried

Undercapitalization occurs when a firm either fails to invest in the optimal mix of real assets because it cannot properly finance its investments, or experiences financial distress or bankruptcy because it has too much leverage in its capital structure. Undercapitalization is a readily observable, but scantily researched, phenomenon in entrepreneurial finance. It has been the subject of extensive interest in mainstream finance, but the supporting empirical work focuses on large firms.

UNDERINVESTMENT

Underinvestment, the finance literature's term for the first form of undercapitalization, occurs when a firm invests less than it should in real assets (assets, both tangible and intangible, used to carry on business) because it is costly or impossible to secure external financing. External equity financing is more costly than internal equity or debt financing, so when internal cash flow is available, firms invest freely. But when internal cash flows are inadequate to fund investment, the firm may be reluctant to invest because it does not want to seek more expensive external financing. Fortunately, the extra costs of external capital are generally not substantial; so, underinvestment occurs only on the margin and its negative effect on the firm is rarely severe. Hedging is proposed as the solution to this problem (Froot, Scharfstein, and Stein, 1993).

However, a more extreme form of underinvestment occurs under conditions of hard capital rationing. Hard capital rationing means that the firm's access to external capital is so limited that it is forced to decline projects with

substantial positive net present values. As a result, the long-term performance of the firm can be significantly harmed (Brealey and Meyers, 2003).

CAPITAL STRUCTURE

The significance of capital structure is a subject of great interest in finance. Firms prefer to finance first with either internal equity or debt. In the United States, debt is beneficial because of the tax shield. However, greater use of debt increases the risk of bankruptcy or financial distress. A firm is undercapitalized if it runs too high a risk of bankruptcy or financial distress. Because of information asymmetries, external equity is the worst source of capital and is only used to the extent internal equity and debt are insufficient (Newton, 1997).

Thus, the finance literature views undercapitalization as a potential problem for any firm. Based on personal observation, conversations with numerous entrepreneurs and financiers, and the literature, it appears that undercapitalization is a much larger problem for the entrepreneurial firm. There are three primary reasons for this: the nature of the entrepreneurial firm, the nature of the entrepreneur as financial manager, and the nature of entrepreneurial financial markets.

NATURE OF FIRM

Business risk is higher in entrepreneurial firms. Further, much of the risk is company specific and cannot be hedged. As a result, cash flows for the entrepreneurial firm are often highly unpredictable, thus increasing the chances of underinvestment, bankruptcy, and financial distress.

In addition to cash flow being unpredictable, the entrepreneurial firm often faces a growth situation where the amount of investment in needed real assets is much greater than concurrent cash flow. This increased gap between cash flow and necessary investment raises the risk of underinvestment.

Further, the costs of bankruptcy and financial distress are greater for entrepreneurial firms. There are significant economies of scale in bankruptcy proceedings, both for the firm and other parties involved. Short of bankruptcy, financial distress can significantly damage important relationships with the firm's stakeholders (e.g., customers, suppliers, and employees). This is a particular problem for entrepreneurial firms because their stakeholder relationships are often relatively new and fragile.

From a financial theory standpoint, much of the value of an entrepreneurial firm is in the real options the firm owns (Myers, 1977). The ability to exercise these options at the appropriate time is vital. If it becomes apparent that the firm cannot exercise its real options, then the value of the firm will decline precipitously.

NATURE OF DECISION-MAKER

Finance theory starts with the assumption that the decision-maker makes decisions in a totally rational manner, with the only motive being that of maximizing the total value of the firm (as opposed to any one class of securities, such as the existing stockholders). However, several important exceptions to the assumption are recognized.

A major agency problem exists when the manager is also the owner of highly leveraged equity. This may lead to situations where the manager causes the firm to pursue "projects which promise very high payoffs if successful even if they have a very low probability of success" (Jensen and Meckling, 1976). Ownership of highly leveraged equity is common in entrepreneurial firms. This is particularly true in venture capital financed firms. While these firms generally have little if any debt, their equity is often tiered with the manager owning common stock and the venture capitalist owning convertible preferred. As a result, the manager may bear little downside risk with the potential for large upside benefit. This can result in the manager making decisions that increase the likelihood of underinvestment, bankruptcy, and/or financial distress.

In addition to being an owner of leveraged equity, the manager is often the owner of controlling interest in the entrepreneurial firm. Corporate control is valuable to the manager, but potentially magnifies agency problems for the firm (Jensen and Ruback, 1983). Besides guaranteeing a job, control allows the owner/manager to set the firm's course. This is particularly important to entrepreneurial firms because enterprise control and autonomy are major nonfinancial rewards for many entrepreneurs. As a result, the entrepreneur/manager is reluctant to seek external financing, particularly external equity, with the outcome being an increase in the likelihood of underinvestment, bankruptcy, and/or financial distress.

Other psychological factors may increase the likelihood of undercapitalization in entrepreneurial firms. If the entrepreneur/manager is risk seeking, then the firm will accept a higher level of risk of underinvestment, bankruptcy, and financial distress than a firm with a risk-neutral or risk-averse manager. If the entrepreneur is overly optimistic, then the entrepreneur may see the amount of business risk as lower than it actually is, thus increasing the risk of the firm being undercapitalized.

NATURE OF CAPITAL MARKETS

Finance theory generally assumes that markets are efficient. However, this is often not the case for entrepreneurial firms. Most have equity needs that are not great enough to achieve minimum efficient scale in the public equity market because of that market's high information and contracting costs. The private equity market provides some relief but brings a higher cost of capital and often loss of control. This significantly reduces the attractiveness of external capital. Further, there are also scale economies in the private equity market that foreclose firms needing small amounts of equity from access to that market. Even if available, there is usually a significant time delay in acquiring private equity (Fried and Hirsrich, 1994).

Because entrepreneurial firms have significantly less access to external equity than large mature firms, they are more likely to operate under hard capital rationing. Further, financial distress often quickly leads to bankruptcy because the entrepreneurial firm may not be able to raise external equity when it is experiencing financial difficulties.

Taken together, these three reasons accentuate the risk of bankruptcy and financial distress in entrepreneurial firms. The entrepreneurial firm can generally avoid problems with bankruptcy and financial distress by being financially more conservative than a larger, more mature firm. However, at times, such conservatism leads to underinvestment.

Underinvestment is a major problem for many entrepreneurial firms. At times, the effects of underinvestment are hard to directly verify because the firm remains profitable. But, in many cases, underinvestment means the entrepreneurial firm is unable to attain or sustain operations on a positive cash flow basis. Overall, undercapitalization is a significant issue for entrepreneurial firms. Its negative effects are often dramatic and draconian.

Bibliography

Brealey, R. A. and Myers, S. C. (2003). *Principles of Corporate Finance*, 7th edn. New York: McGraw-Hill/Irwin.

Fried, V. H. and Hirsrich, R. D. (1994). Toward a model of venture capital investment decision-making. *Financial Management*, 23 (3): 28–37.

Froot, K. A., Scharfstein, D. S., and Stein, J. C. (1993). Risk management: Coordinating corporate investment and financing policies. *Journal of Finance*, 48: 1629–58.

Jensen, M. C. and Meckling, W. H. (1976). Theory of the firm: Managerial behavior, agency costs, and ownership structure. *Journal of Financial Economics*, 3: 305–60.

Jensen, M. C. and Rubak, R. S. (1983). The market for corporate control: The scientific evidence. *Journal of Financial Economics*, 11: 5–50.

Myers, S. C. (1977). Determinants of corporate borrowing. *Journal of Financial Economics*, 5: 147–75.

Newton, D. P. (1997). Capital structure. In D. Paxson and W. Wood (eds.), *The Blackwell Encyclopedic Dictionary of Finance*. Oxford: Blackwell.

university spin-outs

Andy Lockett, Donald Siegel, and Mike Wright

INTRODUCTION

In recent years, there has been a substantial rise in the number of university spin-outs (USOs) in many nations (Wright et al., 2002). This stylized fact is consistent with qualitative evidence presented in Siegel, Waldman, and Link (2003), which suggests that universities are increasingly likely to view equity ownership in a USO as an attractive alternative to licensing technologies in embryonic industries. Bray and Lee (2000) report that an equity position in a USO yields a higher average long-run return than that associated with the average license. As a result, there has been a concomitant rise in incubators and science parks at universities (Phan, Siegel, and Wright, 2004), which (in theory) nurture university-based spin-outs at various stages of development.

A potential problem for USOs is that universities typically lack substantial experience and expertise in managing such enterprises. This raises important issues regarding the relationship between a university's resources and capabilities and the establishment of successful USOs, beyond those faced by new high-tech ventures in general. Before outlining these issues, we provide a more precise definition of USOs.

DEFINING USOS

USOs are businesses that are dependent upon licensing or assignment of the institution's technology for initiation. This definition excludes companies established by graduates or university researchers that are not *directly* related to intellectual assets resulting from university research.

USOs can be disaggregated into those that are externally financed and those that do not receive such financial support. The willingness of external financiers (e.g., venture capitalists, business angels, industrial partners) to provide risk capital for a USO is a market signal of potential value. This distinction provides an important indicator of potential performance, since the simple creation of a USO does not mean that technology has been transferred successfully from the university to the private sector.

STAGE-BASED MODELS OF USO DEVELOPMENT

Researchers have sought to understand the processes involved in spinning out companies from historically non-commercial university environments. Studies have sought to model the spin-out process in terms of stages. Vohora, Wright, and Lockett (2004) employ a stage-based and resource-based framework. They find that the key stages that USOs must pass through if they are to develop are as follows: (1) the research phase; (2) the opportunity phase; (3) the pre-organization phase; (4) the reorientation phase; (5) the sustainability phase. Moving among these phases creates critical junctures, which are the key challenges that a USO faces in its development. Critical junctures arise because the new venture needs to acquire additional resources and capabilities if it is to progress to the next phase of development. Four key critical junctures have been identified in the development of spin-out companies: (1) opportunity recognition; (2) entrepreneurial commitment by a venture champion; (3) attaining credibility in the business environment; (4) achieving sustainable returns within their respective markets.

THE COMPOSITION OF THE USO TEAM

The composition of the USO team is a key resource in determining the success of the venture. The USO team may comprise a range of different parties, such as the academic who discovered the technology, a surrogate entrepreneur from industry, an industrial partner, a financier, and a university administrator. Formal team membership may be narrowly defined in terms of the actor having both ownership and an active role in management of the USO. However, more loosely connected team members may have important inputs into the team but do not satisfy these conditions for core membership. A key issue for the development of the USO is how to manage the complexity of the team over time. In particular, the size and complexity of the USO team likely will increase as the USO develops. This creates the issue of how to manage the process of team member entry. However, the contribution of some team members may only be important at certain stages of the USO development. Hence, team member exit may also be a feature of the development of USOs.

Traditionally, the academic in the USO has been viewed as both an inventor and entrepreneur, what Radosevich (1995) terms the inventor–entrepreneur approach. An alternative mode involves the introduction of a surrogate entrepreneur to work alongside the academic inventor. The surrogate entrepreneur provides commercial skills that the academic lacks, while

allowing the academic to continue with their research, which may provide future discoveries that help develop the USO. Franklin, Wright, and Lockett (2001) found that universities that generate the most start-ups have more favorable attitudes towards surrogate entrepreneurs.

Universities play a key role in facilitating the development of the USO through having clear policies regarding the spinning out of companies, appropriate systems of incentives and rewards, and access to external networks. Within this overall approach, the university's technology transfer officers (TTOs) may play a more hands-on role in nurturing the initial development of the USO.

Venture capital firms and business angels may help the USO access resources, putting governance systems in place, etc. However, there may be concerns as to whether venture capital firms possess the necessary skills to add value in addition to supplying risk capital for very early-stage ventures in specialist sectors, especially outside the US.

Alternatively, industrial partners may make an important contribution as part of the USO team in terms of financial and non-financial resources. While many academics have collaborated with industry on research projects, the commercialization of the scientific discoveries from this research through joint ventures with the industrial partners has been neglected in the literature. An exception is the work of Wright, Vohora, and Lockett (2004), which provides case-based evidence that joint ventures between the university and the industrial partner may help a USO overcome the critical junctures it faces.

THE ROLE OF THE UNIVERSITY IN THE SPIN-OUT PROCESS

Universities have been found to adopt different generic approaches to spinning out companies. Clarysse et al. (2004) examine the relationship between a university's resources, its strategy, and its ability to spin-out companies. They identified three distinct incubation models for managing the spin-out process, which they termed "Low selective," "Supportive," and "Incubator." These different models of managing the spin-out process have big resource implications for universities if they are to achieve their objectives. In particular, Clarysse et al. identified

W

winner's curse

Julio De Castro

The notion of a winner's curse has been developed for the examination of situations that occur in the context of auctions, particularly auctions in which bidders have common values. However, the concept can be applied to entrepreneurial behavior and can be a great hazard in the decision-making process of over-eager entrepreneurs. First, the concept and history of winner's curse is examined. Second, applications of the concept to the entrepreneurial context are explored. Third, examples of situations in which the winner's curse has been operative are presented.

THE CONCEPT OF WINNER'S CURSE

The concept of a winner's curse was introduced to discussions in economics research by Richard Thaler (1988). He explained that in an auction with common values – that is, an auction where the item has the same intrinsic value to all bidders, yet no bidder knows the exact value – it was likely that the winning bidder would bid an amount exceeding that item's intrinsic value. The main reason for this phenomenon is that the winning bid is likely to be based on the most optimistic estimate of the value of the item: ergo, the winner's curse.

The winner's curse phenomenon is particularly interesting regarding the assumptions about the rationality of individuals. If all individuals are rational, the winner's curse should not occur. But acting rationally in auctions, especially common value auctions, requires distinguishing between the expected value of the object, based only on the prior information available, and the expected value if the auction is won.

Furthermore, the seriousness of the winner's curse problem is affected by the number of bidders in an auction. When there are more bidders, a person has to bid more aggressively to win the auction. However, bidding more aggressively increases the probability of overbidding for the item. Thus, the individual overestimates the value of the object. Evidence from field studies suggests that even though learning can help decrease the problem, "learning is neither easy nor fast" (Thaler, 1988: 194). Evidence of the prevalence of the winner's curse is presented in both the finance and economics literatures (Kagel and Levin, 1986; Bazerman and Samuelson, 1983; Samuelson and Bazerman, 1985) and in real life. Examples of winner's curse include the bidding for free agent baseball players (Cassing and Douglas, 1980) and the market for corporate takeovers (Roll, 1986), as well as numerous anecdotal cases, such as the bidding for book publishing rights and for television interviews, and the auction of UMTS third generation phone licenses in Europe.

THE WINNER'S CURSE AND THE ENTREPRENEUR

The problems highlighted by the winner's curse can be particularly troublesome for entrepreneurs. In situations in which the individual is eager to enter the business and/or the opportunity, the likelihood of a winner's curse is high. Thus an entrepreneur that is highly interested in landing a particular opportunity could overbid for the business and the likelihood of earning a profit from a subsequent transaction is lessened.

Avoiding the winner's curse is a crucial concern for the entrepreneur. Given the nature of the entrepreneurial process, it is likely that eagerness to land new business or a new client will drive many entrepreneurs to incur the winner's curse. Furthermore, it is unlikely that a first-time entrepreneur will have the slack resources necessary to carry the extra costs from an overpriced acquisition. Incurring the winner's curse could lead to failure for new entrepreneurs. However, research shows that experience can be a moderating factor, in that more experienced bidders are less likely to incur the winner's curse. A new entrepreneur might not have the experience necessary to avoid the trap.

Kagel and Levin (1986) found that the winner's curse is more pronounced in larger groups. The worst scenario is the situation in which multiple new entrepreneurs bid for a new technology with uncertain payoffs. The results of the UMTS spectrum auctions in most Western European countries represent such a situation, although in this case most bidders, except firms such as Vodaphone and Orange, were former state telecom monopolies. The new technology and uncertainty of the outcomes, coupled with a system that was designed to generate the most revenue for governments, resulted in a situation in which there was a low probability bidders could recoup their investment. Additionally, most firms are struggling to implement the structural changes necessary for the system, and with no dates for implementation in the near future.

Finally, the eagerness of new entrepreneurs to land new businesses and to make the opportunity successful compounds the problems of winner's curse with the possibility of escalation of commitment. Escalation of commitment is the tendency to become entrenched in a failing course of action (Staw and Hoang, 1995; Staw, 1976). Entrepreneurs who have committed themselves to a particular course of action and have paid more for a product/service than its intrinsic value, might commit additional resources without favorable results in order to justify the original commitment. Even though Zardkoohi (2004) has argued that organizations in a competitive environment escalate commitment toward successful strategies and against failed strategies, it is not clear that entrepreneurial organizations are likely to overcome the problems created by the winner's curse.

Bibliography

Bazerman, M. (1984). The relevance of Kahneman and Tversky's concept of framing to organizational behavior. *Journal of Management*, 10: 333–43.

Bazerman, M. and Samuelson, W. (1983). I won the auction but I don't want the prize. *Journal of Conflict Resolution*, 27: 618–34.

Cassing, J. and Douglas, R. (1980). Implications of the auction mechanism in baseball's free agent draft. *Southern Economic Journal*, 47: 110–21.

Kagel, J. and Levin, D. (1986). The winner's curse and public information in common value auctions. *American Economic Review*, 76: 894–920.

Roll, R. (1986). The hubris hypothesis of corporate takeovers. *Journal of Business*, 59: 197–216.

Samuelson, W. and Bazerman, M. (1985). The winner's curse in bilateral negotiations. *Research in Experimental Economics*, 3: 105–37.

Staw, B. (1976). Knee-deep in the big muddy: A study of escalation of commitment to a chosen course of action. *Organizational Behavior and Human Performance*, 16: 27–44.

Staw, B. and Hoang, H. (1995). Sunk costs in the NBA: Why draft order affects playing time and survival in professional basketball. *Administrative Sciences Quarterly*, 40: 474–94.

Thaler, R. (1988). Anomalies: The winner's curse. *Journal of Economic Perspectives*, 2: 191–202.

Zardkoohi, A. (2004). Do real options lead to escalation of commitment? *Academy of Management Review*, 29: 111–19.

women's entrepreneurship

Patricia G. Greene and Candida G. Brush

Women's entrepreneurship is a growing phenomenon around the world. Despite the legal and social restrictions that limited their ownership of property and active participation in the marketplace, women have a long history of contributions to the household economy, often through small businesses that were sometimes unrecorded in numbers and impact (Wertheimer, 1977). Post-World War II, legislative enactments (e.g., Equal Credit Opportunity Act of 1974, etc.) and societal changes in the US catalyzed a dramatic increase in women's venture creation. Today, women entrepreneurs are a potent economic force as employers, customers, suppliers, and competitors in the world marketplace.

Definition and Statistics

The US government defines a woman-owned business as one that is at least 51 percent owned by a woman, who is also involved in the day-to-day operation of the business. Approximately 5.4 million or 28 percent of all US businesses meet this definition. In addition, women jointly own (50/50) an additional 3.6 million (18 percent) of businesses with men. By contrast, men own 11.4 million businesses (54 percent) (US Census Bureau, 2001). This reflects a rapid increase from the reported 1.5 million women-owned businesses in 1976. During this period, revenues and number of employees in women-owned businesses also grew significantly. Employment by women-owned businesses rose 28 percent between 1992 and 1997, compared to an 8 percent increase for all firms – more than three times the rate for all US firms of similar size (NFWBO, 2001). Earlier statistics show that women-owned businesses employ more than 18.5 million people (NFWBO, 1998). The US Economic Census of 1997 is also useful in reporting the most common types of businesses owned by women: services (55 percent), retail trade (17 percent), and FIRE, a category including combined fire, insurance, and real estate business ownership activities (9 percent).

Gender Differences

The literature offers two primary explanations for differences between men and women entrepreneurs. First, historically, the research base focused almost entirely on men. One study shows that less than 10 percent of all studies included or focused on women entrepreneurs (Baker, Aldrich, and Liou, 1997; Gatewood et al., 2002). While women may indeed share many characteristics and behaviors with their male counterparts, we cannot assume they are the same if we have not studied them either separately or together with men. This also means that what we know about entrepreneurship is based almost entirely on populations of men, and therefore the descriptions and prescriptions for success are male biased (Bird and Brush, 2002). Second, aside from obvious biological differences, we know that women are subject to dif-

ferent start-up circumstances by virtue of the regulatory, family, societal, and economic circumstances with which they must deal in starting new ventures. More specifically, work experience (role, type, and level) and educational background, family roles and expectations, and social relationships directly affect the starting point of business creation in terms of what is or is not possible.

Research shows differences between men and women in demographic characteristics, experience, and education, while similarities are found in motives and reasons for becoming an entrepreneur (see Brush, 1992; Gatewood et al., 2002). In studies about businesses, women-owned businesses are often smaller in size and revenues, in part due to their prevalence in service and retailing sectors (Brush, 1997).

Resource Differences

Entrepreneurs start with different bundles of capabilities and resources; specifically, human capital (education and experience), social capital (networks and contacts), and financial capital. These beginning resources are used to build a fledgling firm. Women entrepreneurs have relatively high stocks of human capital, generally described as either being college educated or having more education than her wage and salary counterpart. However, men and women are similar in level of education, but women are more likely to have a liberal arts background, while men more often have education in business or engineering (Brush, 1992; Carter, Williams, and Reynolds, 1997). The recent rise of women in business school programs (BS and MBA), law, and medicine is creating more similarities between men and women with regard to education. While both young men and women rate entrepreneurial knowledge as important, young women more often report being more aware of gaps in their entrepreneurial knowledge (Kourilsky and Walstad, 1998).

Another aspect of human capital is work experience. Occupational segregation and underrepresentation of women at upper management levels continue to persist. Women hold approximately 16 percent of the corporate officer positions in large US companies (Catalyst, 2002). Without managerial experience, women have less opportunity to enhance their endowments for business ownership. The extremely small number of women at the board and CEO levels may decrease the leadership decision-making experience that women need to start or acquire companies. In addition, occupational segregation may qualify women for service and retailing entrepreneurial endeavors but prevent them from gaining experience in non-traditional areas.

Also influencing women's human capital are the expectations about their family roles, which may restrict women in terms of time and acceptance as business owners. While the perspective that women's primary responsibility is at home has changed somewhat over past years, the view still has wide acceptance. This not only restricts women's time and acceptance as a business owner, but also leads to lowered expectations about financing needs, growth goals, and the "seriousness of the business" in the eyes of others (Brush, 1997; Gatewood et al., 2002).

Social capital is a second resource, and it can be considered in two ways. The individual networks of the founder or founding team serve as conduits for various types of capital to launch the business. Business founder(s) networks are the basis for the development of subsequent organizational networks crucial to venture start-up. While there are few significant gender differences in networking behavior (Aldrich et al., 1989; Katz and Williams, 1997), there are differences by sex in the composition of networks, with women's networks being smaller and more predominantly female, which may influence survival and performance.

Financial capital is the third crucial start-up resource. Entrepreneurial funds come from many sources, including personal savings, family, friends, banks, government programs, venture capital funds, and business angels. Often, the source of capital can be a prime determinant of the type of business selected. Women with greater sources of personal capital, possibly through a working spouse, have more opportunities for choice in regards to the initial resource base. This stands in contrast to women with very low levels of household income or personal savings, who have fewer resource options.

Research about access to debt capital shows that women and men have similar access to fin-

ancial capital from banks; however, the terms of loans, payback time, and interest rates are less favorable for women (Riding and Swift 1990; Buttner and Rosen; 1988). With regard to growth capital, women receive an extremely small percentage of the billions invested. While less than 3 percent of all new businesses receive venture capital at any time in their existence, women receive less than 5 percent of the total (Greene et al., 2001). Because equity funded ventures grow more rapidly, become larger, and create more wealth for owners and investors, this remains a challenge for women.

The performance of businesses started by women entrepreneurs has increased dramatically. In 1997, women-owned firms averaged $1.8 million in sales. By 2000, the average had grown to $2.4 million, but despite this growth, women-owned firms still lagged behind the national average of $12.3 million (Center for Women's Business Research, 2001). By 2000, nearly 60 percent of women-owned firms had less than $500,000 in revenues, compared to 44 percent of all firms with revenues at that level. At the mid-range sales level, the percentage of women-owned firms was similar to that of all other firms. In 2000, women, on average, employed almost 6 employees per firm compared to a little over 9 employees for all firms.

IMPLICATIONS

Research on women entrepreneurs focuses on the factors affecting the supply of women business owners, their entrepreneurial activities, and the societal and economic impact through wealth creation and increased innovation. Much of the research suffers from a lack of control for confounding factors such as class, race, and ethnicity. The domain of entrepreneurship has historically been a male preserve, but this is changing rapidly and opening many doors for future research.

Bibliography

Aldrich, H., Reese, P. R., Dubinin, P., Rosen, B., and Woodward, B. (1989). Women on the verge of a breakthrough?: Networking among entrepreneurs in the United States and Italy. In R. H. Borckhaus, Sr. et al. (eds.), *Frontiers of Entrepreneurial Research*, 560–74. Boston, MA: Babson College.

Baker, T., Aldrich, H., and Liou, N. (1997). Invisible entrepreneurs: The neglect of women business owners by mass media and scholarly journals in the USA. *Entrepreneurship and Regional Development*, 9: 221–38.

Bird, B. J. and Brush, C. G. (2002). A gendered perspective on organizational creation. *Entrepreneurship Theory and Practice*, 16 (4): 5–30.

Brush, C. G. (1992). Research on women business owners: Past trends, a new perspective, and future directions. *Entrepreneurship: Theory and Practice*, 16: 5–30.

Brush, C. G. (1997). Women owned businesses: Obstacles and opportunities. *Journal of Developmental Entrepreneurship*, 2: 1–25.

Buttner, E. H. and Rosen, B. (1988). Bank loan officers' perceptions of the characteristics of men, women, and successful entrepreneurs. *Journal of Business Venturing*, 3: 249–58.

Carter, N., Williams, M., and Reynolds, P. D. (1997). Discontinuance among new firms in retail: The influence of initial resources, strategy, and gender. *Journal of Business Venturing*, 12 (2): 125–45.

Catalyst (2002). Catalyst census of women corporate officers and top earners, http://www.catalystwomen.org/press_room/factsheets/COTE%20Factsheet%202002.pdf

Center for Women's Business Research (2001). *Removing the Boundaries*. Washington, DC: Center for Women's Business Research.

Center for Women's Business Research (2002). *Key Facts About Women Owned Businesses*. Washington, DC: Center for Women's Business Research.

Gatewood, E., Carter, N., Brush, C., Greene, P., and Hart, M. (2002). *Women Entrepreneurs, Their Ventures, and the Venture Capital Industry: An Annotated Bibliography*. Stockholm: ESBRI.

Greene, P. G., Brush, C. G., Hart, M., and Saparito, P. (2001). Patterns of venture capital funding: Is gender a factor? *Venture Capital International Journal*, 3 (1): 63–83.

Katz, J. A. and Williams, P. M. (1997). Gender, self-employment, and weak-tie networking through formal organizations: A secondary analysis approach. *Entrepreneurship and Regional Development*, 9 (3): 183–97.

Kourilsky, M. L. and Walstad, W. B. (1998). Entrepreneurship and female youth: Knowledge, attitudes, gender differences, and educational practices. *Journal of Business Venturing*, 13 (3): 77–88.

National Foundation for Women Business Owners (1998). *Research Findings*. Silver Springs, MD: NFWBO.

National Foundation for Women Business Owners (2001). *Facts and NFWBO Fact of the Week*. April 23. Silver Springs, MD: NFWBO.

Riding, A. L. and Swift, C. S. (1990). Women business owners and terms of credit: Some empirical findings of the Canadian experience. *Journal of Business Venturing*, 5: 327–40.

US Census Bureau (2001). *Survey of Women-Owned Business Enterprises, 1997*. Washington, DC: US Department of Commerce.

Wertheimer, B. M. (1977). *We Were There: The Story of Working Women in America*. New York: Pantheon Books.

Index

Ndorfer, H.   52
Neck, H. M.   75
negative net worth   8
Nelson, R.   45
nepotism   125–6
Nerkar, A.   243
Netscape   5
networks
  advantages of local   136
  and bankruptcy avoidance
    10
  and board directors   14, 17
  business angel   17–20
  cheerleaders   89
  in China   31
  coaches   89
  and development of
    entrepreneurial identity
    89–90
  entrepreneurial   98–100
  extended   197
  internal   6
  and knowledge creation
    166
  knowledge spillovers   136,
    175, 176–7
  networked incubators   150
  role models   89
  venture capitalists'
    contacts   246
  see also social capital
Neubaum, Donald O.   149–51
new ventures *see* ventures,
  new
Nike   200
Nohria, N.   150
Nolan, V.   210, 211
Nonaka, I.   45, 163–4, 164–5
Nortel Networks   158
Nucor Steel   6
Nurick, A. J.   205

O'Brien, J. P.   113
Oi, Walter   83
Oldham, G. R.   54
opportunity *see* entrepreneurial
  opportunity
options
  financial   215–16
  real   215–18
Oregon State University   129
O'Reilly, C. A., III   209–10,
  212
organizational capital   147
organizational isomorphism
  200

organizational structure and
  relationships
  boards   13–17
  business units   4–7, 44
  configuration approach to
    analysis   66–9
  and entrepreneurial
    intensity   93
  establishing in new
    ventures   171–5
  and technology transfer
    235
organizations
  **entrepreneurial service
    organizations   114–17**
  innovator   126
  reproducer   126
  see also ventures; ventures,
    new
orientation, entrepreneurial *see*
  entrepreneurial orientation
outsourcing   196–9
  core   199
  **in entrepreneurial
    ventures   199–201**
  peripheral   199
overconfidence   34–5
Oviatt, Benjamin M.   159–62
Owen, A. L.   82

Palich, L. E.   33
Panel Study of Entrepreneurial
  Dynamics (PSED)
  185–6, 187–8
Panera Bread   116–17
Partch, M. M.   155
**patent protection   156–7,
  202–4**
pay *see* reward schemes
Peng, M. W.   31
Pennsylvania, University of
  129
Penrose, E. T.   146
people processing services
  115
Pepsi Cola   151
performance
  and buy-outs   181
  and entrepreneurial
    expertise   78
  and entrepreneurial
    intensity   93
  and environment   105
  and EO   105
  and experience   168
  and human capital   82–4

and international
  expansion   160–1
IPO firms   153–4
and knowledge   105
and location   175–8
and outsourcing   200–1
and social networks   99–100
and spin-offs   228
and types of
  entrepreneur   140
women-owned
  businesses   250
see also competitive
  advantage; entrepreneurial
  growth
performance oversupply   56
peripheral outsourcing   199
Perry-Smith, J. E.   54
Petkova, Antoaneta   107–11
Petty, J. William   141–4
Pfarrer, Michael D.   50–3
pharmaceuticals industry   152,
  235
photography industry   203
Pinchott, G.   158
Pine, B. J.   115
Pittsburgh Paint Glass   204
planning fallacy   34–5
plant patents   202
Polanyi, M.   163
Polaroid Corporation   203
Porter, M. E.   5, 66
possession processing
  services   115
post-decision bolstering   34
Prahalad, C. K.   73–4
Prasad, D.   50
price, and market equilibrium
  49
Price-Babson College Fellows
  program   145
proactiveness
  and entrepreneurship   91–2
  and EO   104
process innovation *see*
  innovation
Procter & Gamble   5
product innovation *see*
  innovation
professional services   115
profits, and market
  conditions   182, 183
prominence   108
prospect theory   113
protocol analysis   76
Prowse, S.   18